MONETARY UNIONS AND HARD PEGS

Monetary Unions and Hard Pegs

EFFECTS ON TRADE, FINANCIAL DEVELOPMENT, AND STABILITY

Edited by

VOLBERT ALEXANDER

JACQUES MÉLITZ

and

GEORGE M. VON FURSTENBERG

OXFORD

UNIVERSITY PRESS

OXFORD
UNIVERSITY PRESS

Great Clarendon Street, Oxford OX2 6DP

Oxford University Press is a department of the University of Oxford.
It furthers the University's objective of excellence in research, scholarship,
and education by publishing worldwide in

Oxford New York

Auckland Bangkok Buenos Aires Cape Town Chennai
Dar es Salaam Delhi Hong Kong Istanbul Karachi Kolkata
Kuala Lumpur Madrid Melbourne Mexico City Mumbai Nairobi
São Paulo Shanghai Taipei Tokyo Toronto

Oxford is a registered trade mark of Oxford University Press
in the UK and in certain other countries

Published in the United States
by Oxford University Press Inc., New York

© CEPR 2004

The moral rights of the author have been asserted
Database right Oxford University Press (maker)

First published 2004

British Library Cataloguing in Publication Data
Data available

Library of Congress Cataloging in Publication Data
Data available

ISBN 0-19-927140-2

1 3 5 7 9 10 8 6 4 2

Typeset by Newgen Imaging Systems (P) Ltd., Chennai, India
Printed in Great Britain
on acid-free paper by
Biddles Ltd., King's Lynn, Norfolk

Foreword

In his 1969 book, *Money International*, Fred Hirsch, financial editor of *The Economist* in the 1960s, presented a diagram entitled "The Exchange Rate Pendulum," depicting swings in attitudes toward exchange rates over the two generations since the First World War. The swings go from fixity under the gold standard to flexibility in the immediate post-war period, to fixity with the return to normalcy in the 1920s, followed by flexibility with strains on the gold standard, deflation and competitive devaluations in the early 1930s. The pendulum then swung back to fixity after the Tripartite Agreement in 1936 and this period lasted through the Bretton Woods conference in 1944 and the early post-war period. Flexibility returned after the British devaluation in 1967 and the crisis developing in the international monetary system.

We could carry Hirsch's Pendulum forward another three decades, and find rising sentiment for flexibility with the breakdown of the Bretton Woods arrangements in 1971 and the move toward fluctuating exchange rates in 1973. But rising inflation and a falling dollar shifted the pendulum back toward fixity and stability, reflected in the formation of the European Monetary System in 1978, and Chairman Paul Volcker's shift to disinflation policies during the first Reagan term. The pendulum then swung back toward flexibility with the Plaza Accord in 1985 and the ERM crisis in 1992, only to swing once again toward fixity with the advent of the euro.

The euro may represent one of the turning points in the international monetary system, although such turning points are often seen only in hindsight. We can recognize 1873 as one turning point, when the breakdown of the bimetallic system led to the creation of the gold standard. Another was the creation in 1913 of the Federal Reserve System, an event of global significance because the United States was the emerging superpower. During the First World War the dollar replaced sterling as the pre-eminent currency, and in the next two decades, the dollar displaced gold at the center of the international monetary system. Looked at in this way, the breakdown of the system in 1971 was just another episode in the history of the dollar. Before and after that breakdown the dollar was the dominant currency.

A case can be made that the advent of the euro is a genuine turning point. For the first time since the dollar replaced the pound as the dominant currency, there has been a change in the power configuration of the system. Upon its creation, the euro became the second most important currency in the world. With its successful move through the transition and its expected expansion it can become an alternative to and even rival of the dollar. Instead of a world characterized by flexible exchange rates, we have a new world of currency areas, led by the dollar, euro, and yen.

The path to the euro was by no means straightforward. Demand for a European currency ebbed and flowed with the dollar cycle. We can think of a parallel to Hirsch's Pendulum in a "Eurofever" Pendulum reflecting swings of pro-Europe and anti-Europe sentiment. When the dollar was weak, Eurofever gained momentum, and when it was strong, it abated. Just think of the weakness of the dollar in the late 1960s and the Hague Summit; the weakness of the dollar in the late 1970s and the European Monetary System; and the weakness of the dollar in the late 1980s and the Delors Report and the Maastricht Treaty.

Of course, politics was a partner in the swings. Several events after, the Delors Report recommending a single European currency set the course of monetary union on almost automatic pilot. The end of the Cold War and the unification of Germany transformed the Delors Plan from a prophetic gamble into a political necessity. The plan was hustled through Dublin and Maastricht and even the ERM crisis in 1992 could not prevent the inception of the euro as a banking money in 1999 and as a full-fledged currency in 2002.

The euro was one of the most remarkable events in monetary history. Never before had important nations voluntarily agreed to scrap that symbol of sovereignty, the national currency. The economic advantages were there for all to see: Each inhabitant would get a world-class currency; each firm would get a continental capital market; each country would get a better monetary and fiscal policy; interest rates in most countries would become much lower; budget deficits would decline because of lower interest payments on the public debt; transparency of pricing would help to perfect arbitrage; wage insurgency would be curbed by the removal of devaluation; and everyone would benefit from lower transactions costs. But they could not be attained without a distinct political step pooling monetary sovereignty. Europe took the plunge but could other areas follow?

That there has been a marked demonstration effect there can be no doubt. The question now being asked all over the world is the following: Is an international monetary system based on national currencies fluctuating against one another optimal, or are different arrangements likely to be better? New currency groupings are being talked about in Asia, Latin America, and Africa.

The range of possibilities is enormous: Dollarization (or euroization), currency board systems, multilateral or unilateral monetary unions, single-currency versus multiple-currency monetary unions, and so forth. We need more studies of the experiences of countries experimenting with these alternatives.

There is also a larger question. Could the European example—or some variant of it—be transplanted to the world economy? The time may be ripe for a new generation to reject the nationalist solution of flexible exchange rates and work toward rebuilding an international monetary system. What would be the best way of going about establishing consensus on a new international monetary system?

This book, *Monetary Unions and Hard Pegs: Effects on Trade, Financial Development, and Stability*, could not have come at a more opportune time. It is right on the mark. It addresses exactly what its title promises: The reasons, modalities, and consequences of the various forms of monetary union, fully capturing the current state of the debate and some of its historical origins. Its subject connects with the swing of the Hirsch Pendulum away from fluctuating exchange rates and unstable currencies toward large currency areas and monetary unions, and could be a landmark in the literature on improvements in the international monetary system. The editors have done a superb job in arranging, introducing, and commenting on the material. It is a book that contains extraordinary insights and should be a must-read for officials in charge of monetary policies, for authorities on international monetary economics, and for students and teachers in the classroom.

Robert A. Mundell

—

Contents

List of Figures

List of Tables

Acknowledgments

Financial support and gifts in kind by donors and distinguished participants made possible the research presented in this volume. Base funding was provided by a three-year (2000–02) joint grant to Professors Volbert Alexander and George von Furstenberg under the TRANSCOOP program administered by the Alexander von Humboldt Foundation. Additional funding was provided by Fordham University and Justus-Liebig Universität Giessen, the Leon Lowenstein Foundation, Hypovereinsbank–HVB America, the German Information Center–New York, and Landeszentralbank Niedersachsen. Charles Wyplosz, as Co-Director of CEPR's International Macroeconomics Programme, provided valuable guidance and in-kind support.

Professors Sven W. Arndt, Claremont Graduate School and McKenna College; Thomas J. Courchene, Queen's University; and Harris Dellas, University of Bern and CEPR were members of the program committee. Three other members, Volbert Alexander, Justus-Liebig Universität Giessen; Jacques Mélitz, University of Strathclyde and CEPR; and George von Furstenberg, Fordham University, now Indiana University, also constituted the editorial committee. Most of the research studies accepted were first presented at a conference on "*Euro and Dollarization: Forms of Monetary Union in Integrating Regions*" held on April 5 through 6, 2002 at the Lincoln Center Campus of Fordham University's Graduate School of Business in New York City.[1] Three outstanding papers analyzing the 2001–02 disintegration of the currency-board regime in Argentina were added later.

The conference and publication program benefited from the views expressed in the distinguished experts' panel session on "Currency Consolidation in the Western Hemisphere and Beyond Euroland-12: Summing up the Prospects." The participants were Ignazio Angeloni, then Deputy Director General, Research, European Central Bank; Guillermo Calvo, Manager and Chief Economist, IDB, and Professor at the University of Maryland; Ricardo Hausmann, Professor of the Practice of Economic Development, John F. Kennedy School of Government, Harvard University; John P. Lipsky, Chief Economist and Global Head of Economics and Policy Research, JPMorgan Chase, and Robert A. Mundell, Nobel Laureate Professor of Economics, Columbia University. Thomas J. Courchene chaired this panel session.

Kurt Schuler, Senior Economist at the Joint Economic Committee of the U.S. Congress, gave a luncheon address on "Dollarization: At the Intersection of Economics and Politics." He was introduced by Father Joseph A. O'Hare, S. J., then President of Fordham University. The conference coordinator, von Furstenberg,

---

[1] Some of the other papers presented at this conference, such as von Furstenberg (2003) and Willett (2003), already have been published elsewhere.

chaired the program and editorial committees and saw to the preparation of the manuscript with the able editorial assistance of JoEllen Sehn. The support of Dean Sharon P. Smith, Communications Director Maureen Lynch, and Budget Administrator Inelly Lichtmann of the Fordham University Schools of Business is also gratefully acknowledged.

REFERENCES

von Furstenberg, G. M. (2003). "Price Insurance Aspects of Monetary Union." *Journal of Common Market Studies*, 41 (June): 519–39.

Willett, T. D. (2003). "Fear of Floating Needn't Imply Fixed Rates: An OCA Approach to the Operation of Stable Intermediate Currency Regimes." *Open Economies Review*, 14 (January): 71–91.

Notes on Contributors

Volbert Alexander is Professor of Money and Banking at the Economics Department of the University of Giessen (Germany). Prior to his appointment in 1986, he was Professor of Economics at the Universities of Trier and Siegen (Germany). From 1997 to 1999 he served as a Chief Economist and Director of Research at Hypobank in Munich. He is co-founder of a "priority" program, Monetary Macroeconomics, financed by the German Research Foundation. His main fields of interest and his current research are focused on European financial integration, monetary policy issues, and problems of short-term reactions in financial markets.

Ignazio Angeloni is Deputy Director General for Research in the European Central Bank. Before this, he was Director of Monetary and Financial Research at the Banca d'Italia. He holds an undergraduate degree from Bocconi and a Ph.D. from the University of Pennsylvania. He has worked at the IMF and taught at Bocconi and LUISS. He published mainly in the fields of monetary policy, banking, and financial markets. His recent research is in the following areas: Monetary policy strategies and rules; monetary policy transmission; the political economy of international unions. He is a member of the Eurosystem Monetary Policy Committee.

Guillermo A. Calvo is the Chief Economist of the Inter-American Development Bank, Director of the Center for International Economics and Distinguished University Professor at the University of Maryland, Research Associate at the NBER, and President of the International Economic Association. His main field of expertise is macroeconomics of emerging-market and transition economies. His recent work has dealt with capital flows and balance-of-payments crises in emerging-market economies. He has published several books and more than 100 articles in leading economics journals. Honors include a Simon Guggenheim Foundation Fellowship for 1980–81 and the King Juan Carlos Prize in Economics in 2002.

Benjamin J. Cohen is the Louis G. Lancaster Professor of International Political Economy at the University of California, Santa Barbara. At UCSB, where he has been a member of the faculty since 1991, Cohen teaches undergraduate and graduate courses on international political economy. He has previously taught at Princeton University and at the Fletcher School of Law and Diplomacy, Tufts University. His research interests mainly involve issues of international monetary and financial relations, and he has written about matters ranging from exchange rates and monetary integration to financial markets and international debt. His most recent books are *The Geography of Money* (1998) and *The Future of Money* (2004).

Cláudia Costa Storti is an Economist at the Banco de Portugal. She obtained degrees in economics from the Universidade Nova de Lisboa and from the University of Leuven, Belgium (Master of Science in economics). Her research interests include monetary integration, exchange rates and trade, institutional aspects of monetary policy, and the payments system.

James W. Dean has been a Professor of Economics at Simon Fraser University in Vancouver, Canada since he completed his Ph.D. at Harvard in 1973. He has also held visiting positions at twenty-two research institutes and universities world-wide, including Columbia, NYU and Kyiv-Mohyla in Kiev, where he has been a consultant to the National Bank of Ukraine. Having published widely on debt and currency crises, his particular passion is prognosis and prescription for pathological economies. Most recently he co-edited a book on dollarization for Oxford University Press that appeared in 2003.

Paul De Grauwe is Professor of International Economics at the University of Leuven, Belgium, and member of the Belgian parliament. He obtained his Ph.D. from the Johns Hopkins University. His research interests are international monetary relations, monetary integration, theory and empirical analysis of the foreign-exchange markets, and open-economy macroeconomics.

Augusto P. de la Torre is Senior Regional Financial Sector Advisor for Latin America and the Caribbean at the World Bank. He provides leadership to World Bank financial sector operations and research in the Region and is actively involved in the joint IMF–World Bank Financial Sector Assessment Program. He also works closely with the Office of the Chief Economist for Latin America and the Caribbean Region, focusing on macroeconomic and financial sector linkages and issues. He headed the Central Bank of Ecuador during 1993–96. In November 1996, he was chosen by Euromoney Magazine as the year's "Best Latin Central Banker." He is a member of the Carnegie Network of Economic Reformers.

Gerald P. Dwyer Jr. is a Vice-President at the Federal Reserve Bank of Atlanta, where he is in charge of the finance group in the Research Department. Since receiving his Ph.D. at the University of Chicago, he has been a faculty member at Texas A & M University, Emory University, the University of Houston and Clemson University. Mr. Dwyer also has been associated with the Federal Reserve Banks of St. Louis and Chicago. His research has been published in economics and finance journals, the Federal Reserve Banks of Atlanta and St. Louis Reviews, books and conference volumes. His research interests are financial markets and banking.

Edgar L. Feige is Professor of Economics Emeritus at the University of Wisconsin-Madison, Visiting Research Scholar at the Croatian National Bank and consultant to the International Monetary Fund. A graduate of Columbia University (BA 1958) and the University of Chicago (Ph.D. 1963) he has also taught at Yale University, the University of Essex, and Erasmus University, and held the Cleveringa Chair at the University of Leyden. He has served as a consultant to the United States Treasury Department, Bureau of Engraving and Printing; the Financial Crimes Enforcement Network; the Supreme Soviet of the Russian Federation; the Los Alamos National Laboratory; the Agency for International Development; the Board of Governors of the Federal Reserve System; and the National Research Council Task Force on Economies in Transition. His books and scholarly journal publications include works on underground economies, monetary theory and policy, dollarization, tax reform, and transition economies.

Eduardo Fernández-Arias is the Chief Economist of the Regional Operations Department I of the Inter-American Development Bank (Argentina, Bolivia, Brazil, Chile, Paraguay, and Uruguay). Prior to that, he was Lead Economist of the Research Department at the same institution, Research Economist of the International Economics Department of the World Bank, and Associate Professor of Economics at the University of the Republic of Uruguay. Mr. Fernández-Arias received a Ph.D. in Economics, as well as an MA in Statistics, from the University of California at Berkeley. His publications cover a range of analytical and empirical work on a variety of topics, including financial integration and capital flows, financial crises, and economic reform.

Hans Genberg is Professor of International Economics at the Graduate Institute of International Studies in Geneva, Switzerland. Since January 1999 has also been Head of Executive Education at the international center FAME (Financial Asset Management and Engineering) in Geneva. A Swedish national, Mr. Genberg holds a Ph.D. degree in Economics from the University of Chicago. He has been a visiting professor at the Graduate School of Business of the University of Chicago, and at the Ecole des HEC at the University of Lausanne, and he has held visiting appointments at the International Monetary Fund and the World Bank. His teaching and research deals primarily with international finance, monetary economics, and macroeconomics.

Alberto Isgut is Assistant Professor of Economics at Wesleyan University. He is a graduate from the University of Buenos Aires and holds a Ph.D. from the University of Toronto. He has consulted with USAID, the Canadian International Development Agency, and the Inter-American Development Bank, and he has been a visitor at the Research Department of the International Monetary Fund. His research has addressed the impact of international capital flows on developing countries, manufacturing investment and productivity in Colombia, non-farm income in rural Honduras, and the effect of common currencies on price dispersion across cities. His most recent work has been published in the *Review of Economics and Statistics, Journal of Development Studies, International Journal of Finance and Economics*, and *Economic Letters*.

Alejandro Izquierdo is Senior Research Economist at the Inter-American Development Bank. He was previously an economist in the Department of Economic Policy of the World Bank. He holds a Ph.D. from the University of Maryland, and has taught courses in macroeconomics and international finance at several Latin American universities. His current research interests include international finance issues in emerging markets, such as the amplification effects of collateral constraints under external shocks, identification and determinants of sudden stops in capital flows, and fiscal sustainability under the impact of financial crises. Together with P. R. Agenor, he is leading a World Bank project on the effects of external shocks and public expenditure allocation on poverty reduction, using computerized general equilibrium models.

Charles M. Kahn is the Bailey Professor of Finance and Professor of Economics at the University of Illinois. His research focuses on the effect of incentives and information asymmetry on economic institutions. He has been a National Fellow at the Hoover Institution at Stanford University, a Visiting Fellow at the Australian National University, an Overseas Fellow at Churchill College of Cambridge University. He has served as a consultant to the Bank for International Settlements on inter-authority coordination of bank regulation and as a visiting scholar at Federal Reserve Banks, including the Federal Reserve Bank of Atlanta, where he has researched incentive effects of payment and settlement systems.

Eduardo Levy Yeyati holds a Ph.D. in Economics from the University of Pennsylvania and is a Professor at the Business School of Universidad Torcuato Di Tella in Buenos Aires. He is a former Chief Economist of the Central Bank of Argentina, having previously worked at the International Monetary Fund and as an international consultant in the areas of banking and international and corporate finance. His recent articles have appeared in the *American Economic Review*, the *Journal of International Economics*, and the *European Economic Review*, and he is co-editor (with Federico Sturzenegger) of *Dollarization: Debates and Policy Alternatives* (MIT Press 2003).

James R. Lothian is Distinguished Professor of Finance in the Schools of Business of Fordham University and Editor of the *Journal of International Money and Finance*. He holds a doctorate in economics from the University of Chicago. He is a co-author of *The International Transmission of Inflation*, and has published extensively on domestic and foreign economic and financial topics in both scholarly journals and the financial press. His current research interests lie in the areas of international finance and money-macro. His past positions include Vice-President in charge of Financial Research for Citibank, N. A., and Visiting Professor of Economics, Stern School of Business, New York University. He has been a Research Associate of the National Bureau of Economic Research, and Visiting Scholar at the International Monetary Fund.

Jacques Mélitz is currently Professor of Economics at the University of Strathclyde. Previously, he worked for many years at the Centre de Recherche en Économie et Statistique (CREST), with which he is still affiliated, and was Professor of Economics at the Institut d'Études Politiques in Paris. Since 1983, he has held visiting positions at Harvard and Princeton Universities, has consulted for the OECD, the European Commission, the Federal Reserve, the International

Monetary Fund, the Bank of Italy and the Swedish Commission of Monetary Union. He has also been a research fellow of the CEPR since 1986. For the last couple of decades, his research has centered on international macroeconomics, most particularly European issues connected with the European Monetary System and European Monetary Union.

Robert A. Mundell The Royal Swedish Academy of Sciences awarded the 1999 Nobel Prize in Economic Sciences to Professor Mundell of Columbia University. It noted in the opening lines of its homage that he has established the foundation for theory which dominates practical policy considerations of monetary and fiscal policy in open economies. His work on monetary dynamics and optimum currency areas has inspired generations of researchers.

Volker Nitsch has been a Jr. Professor of Economic Policy at the Free University Berlin since 2003. Before that he was a Senior Economist at Bankgesellschaft Berlin, where he covered the European economy and capital markets and was widely quoted in the international press. In addition to providing policy-oriented advice, he does research on international trade, international finance, and economic geography. His current research focuses on issues related to trade and monetary integration. He holds a doctoral degree in economics from Humboldt University in Berlin.

Ugo Panizza is an Economist in the Research Department of the Inter-American Development Bank (IDB). He has also held positions at the University of Turin, the American University of Beirut, and worked as consultant for the World Bank. His research interests include Political Economy, International Finance, and the Public Sector Labor Market, and he has published papers in the *Journal of Development Economics, Journal of Public Economics, Journal of Economic Growth, Economics and Politics* and several other journals. Ugo Panizza holds a Laurea from the University of Turin and a Ph.D. in economics from Johns Hopkins University.

Guillermo Perry is Chief Economist of the Latin American and Caribbean Region at the World Bank. Prior to joining the World Bank, he served in senior government positions in Colombia, including those of Minister of Finance and Minister of Energy. He has also been director of two of Colombia's leading economic think tanks and has consulted for international organizations and numerous governments. His publications include several books and numerous articles on a range of subjects covering macroeconomics, fiscal and financial policy, international finance, and energy issues. Mr. Perry undertook doctoral studies in Economics and Operational Research at MIT.

Andrew K. Rose is B. T. Rocca Jr. Professor of International Business, Economic Analysis and Policy Group, Haas School of Business at the University of California, Berkeley, NBER Research Associate, and CEPR Research Fellow. He has consulted for a number of international and domestic institutions, including the IMF, the World Bank, the Federal Reserve, the U.S. Treasury, and the U.K.

Notes on Contributors

Treasury. His current research is in international trade and finance, and he was educated at MIT and the Universities of Toronto and Oxford.

Dominick Salvatore is Distinguished Professor of Economics at Fordham University in New York. He is a Fellow of the New York Academy of Sciences and Chairperson of its Economics Section. He was President of the International Trade and Finance Association in 1994–95 and is a Research Fellow at the Institute for European Affairs at the Vienna University of Economics and Business. He has also taught at the Universities "La Sapienza" and "Tor Vergata" of Rome, Triest, Krems, and Vienna. He published extensively in the field of international trade and finance. He is the editor of the Economics Handbook Series for the Greenwood Press and co-editor of the *Journal of Policy Modeling* and *Open Economies Review.*

João A. C. Santos is a Senior Economist in the Banking Studies Group of the Federal Reserve Bank of New York. His research interests include financial systems design, contract theory, banking, banking regulation, and corporate finance. His articles have been published in the *Journal of Financial Intermediation, Journal of Banking and Finance, Journal of Financial Services Research, Journal of Corporate Finance, Financial Markets, Institutions and Instruments,* and in various Federal Reserve publications. Dr. Santos joined the Bank in May 2000. From 1992 to 1994, he was a lecturer in the Department of Economics at Boston University. From 1994 to 1997 he was an economist at the Research Department of the Federal Reserve Bank of Cleveland, and from 1997 to 2000 he was an economist at the Research Group of the Bank for International Settlements. Dr. Santos received his licenciatura degree from the Department of Economics of the Universidade Nova de Lisboa in 1986, and his master's and doctoral degrees in economics from Boston University in 1995.

Sergio L. Schmukler is a Senior Economist in the Macroeconomics and Growth team, Development Research Group, of the World Bank and an associate editor of the *Journal of Development Economics.* He also works at the Office of Chief Economist for Latin America and is a visiting professor at the Center for International Economics at the University of Maryland. His Ph.D. is from UC Berkeley (1997). He previously worked at the Federal Reserve Board, the Inter-American Development Bank, and the Argentine Central Bank. His research is on international finance and international financial markets and institutions, and he has published in leading journals in these areas.

Luis Servén manages the regional research program of the World Bank's Latin American and Caribbean Region. Prior to joining the World Bank he worked at Spain's leading economics think tanks. He has taught at MIT, the Universidad Complutense and CEMFI in Madrid. He has published several books and numerous articles in academic journals on macroeconomics and international finance. His current research interests include exchange rate regimes, international portfolio diversification and intertemporal open-economy macroeconomic models. Mr. Servén holds a Ph.D. in Economics from MIT.

Ernesto Stein has been Senior Economist in the Research Department of the Inter-American Development Bank since 1994. He holds a Licentiatura degree in Economics from the University of Buenos Aires, and a Ph.D. in Economics from the University of California at Berkeley. His areas of expertise include international trade and integration, exchange rate regimes, decentralization and fiscal institutions. He has published several journal articles and book chapters on the economics of trading blocs, the political economy of inflation stabilization, and the effects of fiscal and political institutions on fiscal performance. His current research interests include issues related to regional integration, foreign direct investment, and exchange rate policy.

Ernesto Talvi, a University of Chicago Ph.D., is Executive Director of CERES (Center for Economic and Social Policy Research), a highly respected public-policy research institution in Uruguay, and permanent advisor to the Chief Economist of the Inter-American Development Bank (IDB), Guillermo Calvo. He is a founding member of the Executive Committee of the Latin American and the Caribbean Economic Association (LACEA). He teaches Dynamic Macroeconomic Theory at the Universidad ORT in Montevideo. A prolific writer, his areas of expertise include the macroeconomics of emerging markets, stabilization programs, fiscal policy, capital flows, and financial crises. Previously, he was Senior Research Economist at the IDB, Chief Economic Advisor of the economic team of Uruguay, and Head of Research of its Central Bank.

George M. von Furstenberg, a titled Professor of Economics at Indiana University, was the inaugural holder of the Robert Bendheim Chair in Economic and Financial Policy at Fordham University in 2000–2003. Work at the IMF (Division Chief in the Research Department, 1978–83) and at U.S. government agencies such as the President's Council of Economic Advisers (Senior Economist, 1973–76) and the Department of State (1989–90), alternated with his academic pursuits. His latest book projects have dealt with *Regulation and Supervision of Financial Institutions in the NAFTA Countries* and *Learning from the World's Best Central Bankers*. He joined the G8 Research Group in 1999 and in 2000 was President of the North American Economics and Finance Association focusing on integration processes in the Western Hemisphere.

1

Editorial Introduction to the Volume and Detailed Introductions to Each of its Four Parts

1.1 Introduction to the Volume

Much is happening in the real-world laboratories of monetary union, and this volume provides an effort to evaluate the results to date and to consider alternatives. With European Monetary Union (EMU) and its currency now an accepted reality, and with a growing list of countries formally dollarizing, interest in the subject of currency consolidation has ceased to be just academic. Even for countries that attempt to float independently with or without credible inflation targets it is getting ever harder to keep the dominant international currency denominations, U.S. dollar and euro, out of their economies, money supply, and all manner of contracts and balance sheets. Countries as diverse as Argentina and Poland, or even Ukraine, are struggling with the question of whether it is best to maintain or to dispense with a troublesome national currency that is giving them limited, costly, and erratic service as compared with the formal adoption of U.S. dollars or euros in business and finance. Smaller entities or countries, like Bosnia, Ecuador, El Salvador, Kosovo, and Montenegro, unable to maintain or introduce a credible independent national currency, have settled for unilateral dollarization or euroization already.

The choice of currency and exchange rate system by individual countries can affect the entire international financial system, and as such, has far-reaching consequences. Two basic objectives of international financial arrangements are

(1) To prevent financial crises, or in case they happen, to limit the damage; and
(2) To promote efficient financial intermediation and international capital flows.

This volume shows that currency consolidation, by shrinking the number of risky currencies and exchange rates in a region, may contribute importantly to both objectives, but that the form of monetary union affects the risks and benefits significantly too. In particular, political and economic equivocations such as hard pegs for national currencies may not prove hard enough to remain credible when the weather turns foul, as it did in Argentina after 1998.

1.1.1   Financial crisis prevention through currency consolidation

In emerging-market countries, financial collapse often involves the joint occurrence of banking, debt, and currency crises. The resulting economic problems tend to be severe. Bordo et al. (2001: 55–61), show, for instance, that in their sample of developed and developing countries, one or more of these crises occurred on average per country once every *eight* years in the 1973–97 period. In the case of joint banking and currency crises, it took almost four years on average before a country's rate of growth returned to its pre-crisis trend level. The cumulative loss of output amounted to 18.6 percent a year over the four years, more than twice the loss from recessions brought on by currency crises unattended by banking crises. Consequently, recent initiatives to strengthen the international financial architecture have aimed mainly to reduce the frequency, duration, and severity of joint banking and currency crises.

Currency consolidation can contribute significantly to that effort. In the aftermath of the 1997 Southeast Asian crisis, the international community shifted its support away from fixed but adjustable exchange rates toward the polar extremes of freely floating exchange rates on one side and hard fixes, like currency boards and currency unions, on the other. Since then it has become clear that freely floating exchange rates are a risk that countries with minor currencies rarely care to take. These countries have learned to regard any sharp exchange-rate movement as a threat to the stability of their financial, economic, and political systems. A report by an Emerging Markets Eminent Persons Group (EMEPG) aptly summarizes and explains the attitudes of developing countries:

Recent empirical studies suggest that exchange rates in emerging markets that do not have formal pegs have limited flexibility in practice because the central bank does not allow the exchange rate to float due to its own domestic inflation target and the constant speculative tendency towards overshooting. The monetary authorities appear in practice to tolerate a high volatility of reserves and interest rates in order to reduce the volatility of their exchange rates. Large economies whose external trade represents a relatively low proportion of activity, and where the domestic financial markets are sufficiently deep, can tolerate a floating exchange rate; most emerging markets—highly exposed to foreign trade with shallow capital markets—cannot do so. (EMEPG 2001: 24–5)

Argentina's experience in 2001–02 has also taught that currency boards may not be hard enough exchange-rate fixes unless they are seen to lead quickly to formal dollarization or monetary union. Even before the hard peg's soft underbelly was fully exposed in Argentina, a BIS Working Paper openly questioned whether a currency-board law is a commitment device at all, contrary to typical claims:

Occasional amendments to the relevant laws are not uncommon among modern currency board economies. In fact, there is often nothing substantial to rule out the possibility of changes, be they minor or major . . . Moreover, laws typically only outline how the currency board is to be organized and how it is to operate; the legal consequences of not playing by the rules are usually not explicitly stated anywhere. What legal action, if any at all, the public can take against the sovereign government in the event of a violation is also unclear. Thus the commitment effect of the law may not be so obvious after all. (Ho 2002: 20)

Since the extreme of free floating is not acceptable to emerging-market economies and currency board arrangements may not be sufficiently ironclad, some countries have pondered the merits of currency union, or the alternative of shedding their national currency entirely in favor of a foreign-issued currency or a new joint creation. Yet, national and international official bodies continue to downplay the contribution that currency consolidation can make to mitigating international financial crises. Thus, officials tout the sovereign prerogative of national money as a tool to be kept in reserve for providing emergency financing relief through inflation. There is even significant support for separate currencies as a way to maintain national regulatory barriers and to leave open the door to capital controls and other restrictions in case the discipline of international financial markets should be unduly harsh or capricious. The idea is that governments should not allow their currency and exchange arrangements to be decided by private preferences for different currency denominations. The following position on the choice of appropriate exchange-rate regime appears representative of educated opinion in developing countries:

The choice of exchange rate regime in order to avoid misalignment should be left to the government. This choice should not be constrained by international financial institutions to the 'corner' options of a permanently fixed parity or a free-float. An 'intermediate' exchange rate regime may well be preferable in practice for countries trading worldwide and subject to external financial shocks. This intermediate exchange rate regime may need to be supported by market-based intervention instruments or other appropriate regulations in order to contain speculative attacks. (EMEPG 2001: 26)

Several contributions in this volume take issue with this position. Intermediate regimes have been prone to financial crises in the past, and several authors point to regional monetary union as a means of strengthening the architecture of the international financial system. Because of currency substitution in emerging-market economies, flexible exchange rates pose a great risk. Exposure to banking, debt, as well as currency crises might be reduced in emerging markets if countries entered into regional monetary and economic unions with others who already possessed a widely held international currency. Furthermore, as the studies in Part II show, monetary union itself deepens economic union while assuring internal exchange-rate stability. The claim, further supported below, is that monetary union would mitigate exposure to each of the three types of financial crises.

Banking crises   With monetary union, problems of currency mismatch between assets and liabilities diminish for banks in emerging-market countries. Reduced vulnerability of the banking sector to currency crises helps to make such crises less likely. In addition, central bank action, initiatives taken by member governments as a group, and market pressures coming from an efficient part of finance within the union can improve the efficiency and soundness of local banking. Thereby, frequency, duration, and severity of banking crises may all be reduced.

Debt crises   Even though monetary union may facilitate borrowing in private markets, it largely decouples union-wide monetary policy from the national fiscal policy of members, and thereby precludes monetization of individual budget deficits. Thus, on the whole, monetary union hardens the government budget constraint. Of course, sovereign debt crises still can happen. Monetary union provides no assurance that a profligate government will not become so heavily indebted as to encounter a funding crisis that leaves it unable to borrow or to roll over external debt. But if a small enough country joins a large enough monetary union there will be little risk that the country's difficulties in financing its public debt will rock the exchange rate of the entire monetary union. Furthermore, a downgrade of any country's government debt inside a monetary union need not depress the creditworthiness of borrowers under that government's jurisdiction because they may have independent access to borrowing in the common currency. Any resulting crises, thus, will be contained. Accordingly, there will be a lesser need for international financial rescue packages organized by the IMF, bankruptcy courts, and international actions binding creditors. The principle of subsidiarity—letting issues be dealt with at the level at which they arise—will be more widely applicable when problems stemming from a country's fiscal misbehavior and overborrowing are largely confined to its own jurisdiction.

Currency crises   Use of a common currency in a large and economically integrated region tends to attenuate the impact of shocks, such as money-demand or portfolio-composition shocks, arising in any of its parts. "The larger the currency area, the greater is the resistance of the exchange rate to any given economic disturbance" (Mundell 1973: 150). In addition, after regional monetary union, member countries are less sensitive to exchange-rate shocks in so far as intra-union business accounts for a large part of their international trade and finance.

1.1.2   Unilateral versus multilateral monetary union

Having stressed the significance of monetary union for crisis prevention, there remains the question of the relative merits of different types of monetary union. As detailed in Part I of this volume, two basic types exist: Multilateral monetary union of the sort pioneered in Europe, and unilateral currency union, such as formal dollarization. It is a central fact that different countries do not face the same opportunities to adopt the two forms. Several Central and Eastern European countries reasonably can contemplate euroization or no euroization prior to entry into EMU, or euroization without subsequent entry. All three choices are meaningful. However, no country anywhere on the globe can reasonably contemplate multilateral monetary union with the United States—not for the foreseeable future. The United States is not open to the suggestion. Witness Chairman Greenspan's famous "three no's": No seignorage sharing, no inclusion in the U.S. regulatory and supervisory network except for consolidated home-country supervision of U.S. multilateral financial institutions, and no seat at the (FOMC) council where U.S. monetary policy is determined. Of course, the U.S. attitude could evolve as financial integration progresses in the Americas, and multilateral features, including seignorage sharing, eventually could be grafted onto a currency union with the United States. But, independently, the differences between multilateral and unilateral monetary union bear careful examination.

Accordingly, Parts III and IV focus on the politics and the public choices surrounding both forms of monetary union, and the tensions that may arise for lack of a monetary union (of either form) in an economic union. These parts also focus on dollarization and euroization in specific countries. In particular, Part III contains several distinguished studies of the origin and propagation of the 2000–03 Argentinean crisis and the lessons it holds for other countries seeking to avoid similar jeopardy. Part IV deals mainly with the infrastructure of the EMU and the division of responsibilities within the European Union between agencies of the Eurosystem (the European System of Central Banks) and member governments.

There is no question that multilateral monetary union is much more integrative than mere currency union. If we judge from the experience of EMU, multilateral monetary union follows regional economic union. The multilateral form of union takes years of advance preparation, rests on international treaties, and gives rise to multilateral decision making extending far beyond monetary policy. Deep institutional, regulatory, and legal transformations are a prerequisite for EMU, and these transformations imply substantial integration of capital markets, payment systems, interbank networks, and financial instruments and services. As a result, the benefits of multilateral monetary union go much further than those of the unilateral form. These benefits include the following:

An integrated financial system that provides all members with about the same level of interest rates for given credit risk   This level can be low if the monetary union harbors a country with a currency that was internationally prominent before unification. Indeed, the most direct contribution of a monetary union to productive investment and economic growth lies in the integration of capital markets and the resulting reduction in the level and prospective variability of capital costs toward the level that had prevailed beforehand in the financially most advanced country of the region. Through multilateral monetary union, differentially greater currency risk is eliminated for the other member countries.

A level playing field for all financial institutions in the monetary union in providing monetary services   To all evidence, competitive neutrality does not obtain when a country makes a unilateral decision to adopt a foreign currency such as the U.S. dollar. U.S.-based financial institutions have a formidable advantage in providing dollar-denominated financial services. Thus, they tend to take over much of the financial business in countries that choose to dollarize. By contrast, a Belgian bank is not at a particular disadvantage relative to a German or French bank in the provision of euro-denominated banking services.

Sharing of central bank profits from currency issue and central-bank intermediation according to a formula which rests on mutually agreed principles of equity   In the case of the Eurosystem, the distribution key is based on member countries' population and GDP. Therefore, it provides for a continuing flow of seignorage to all members, regardless of prior euroization. However, countries that have euroized partially or completely prior to acceding to EMU, indeed, have suffered a one-time loss of seignorage that is not made up (without special provisions) when they join since there will be less national currency to trade in for euro. Even so, future entrants into the EMU will get a much better deal than countries that decide to dollarize.

The greater ability of countries to enter a multilateral than a unilateral monetary union at an exchange rate lying in the vicinity of equilibrium   Under multilateral union, there are arguments for and against overvaluation that are, at least, fairly evenly balanced. On the one hand, multilateral union makes overvaluation of the expiring national currency politically attractive by enabling an entering country to get a large stock of the common money in return for retiring its national currency at the start. On the other hand, overvaluation is discouraged by its adverse effects on economic growth and employment. In addition, at least as regards EMU, the required maintenance of a stable exchange rate for two years prior to entry provides some assurance that the terms of irrevocable fixing are not disruptive. Under unilateral monetary union, political incentives are not similarly balanced. Rather, undervaluation may be encouraged by several factors. By choosing a low initial conversion rate, the unilateral entrant can preserve its international reserves, keep down the value of domestic-currency debt upon conversion to dollars, and become more competitive at the start. But trading partners may be injured and extra inflation may well ensue in the country that formally dollarizes at an undervalued rate.

Three other advantages to candidates for entry into EMU should be cited.

Sense of direction   The accession countries will obtain a clear road map and reform agenda to follow because of the well-defined procedures for entry into EMU. Evidently, countries that choose to dollarize unilaterally will need to draw up their own map, sometimes in an atmosphere of crisis and against strong internal opposition. In countries that have formally dollarized in recent years, such as Ecuador, the initial phase of the process was far more traumatic than it was, for instance, for Greece in joining EMU.

Credibility and permanence   Since formal dollarization is adopted unilaterally and without international treaty, it can be undone more readily than multilateral monetary union. Reversal is essentially a domestic matter. Consequently, the credibility of dollarization is smaller and the elimination of currency risk less complete. Any threat to undo dollarization and to resurrect a national currency or to introduce a multilateral issue, if taken to heart by international capital markets, could destabilize the U.S. dollar once formal dollarization has spread over a wide enough area.

Joint objective function The management of a multilateral monetary union serves the welfare of the entire membership while the management of a unilateral monetary union serves the welfare of the currency issuer. This issuer is likely to pursue its national political and economic objectives and may be able to exert various forms of "currency coercion" (see Kirshner 1995) which membership in multilateral monetary unions would preclude. In such a union, cooperative management by all the members promotes joint welfare maximization.

1.1.3 Concluding comments

There are many factors driving toward monetary union in the world today, and the research presented in this volume has much to say about their causes and consequences. The forces of currency consolidation now are far ahead of the political forces needed to bring them into appropriate institutional form. The pressures that lead to monetary union stem partly from market opportunities arising from the revolution in information and communications technology and from the development of global supply and marketing networks that impinge on financial markets. These pressures derive as well from recurring financial crises. They cannot be dissociated from the fact that there are about 200 different national currencies changing hands on the world monetary scene.

The political classes and central banks in most countries have been reluctant to admit the forces of currency consolidation, much less yield to them. The international financial institutions too are still in the habit of proffering advice to countries about national monetary and exchange rate policies on the assumption that getting rid of both is not even an option. As Rodrik (2003) has argued, emerging-market countries may have to choose between retaining what independent monetary means they still have to deal with currency and financial crises, or else, tying their hands through hard pegs and thereby lowering the chance of such crises at the price of bearing more devastating consequences if they, nevertheless, happen. In the deliberations over this choice, this volume tends to show that monetary union deserves a much more sympathetic hearing from home and international officials alike.

1.2 Introduction to Part I: Current and Past Concepts of Monetary Union

Decades ago, McKinnon (1973) considered the consequences for Europe of moving away from a world monetary system founded on the U.S. dollar and toward a dual system in which a European currency would share an equal role. He saw the change as posing questions going beyond the international distribution of seignorage to cover matters relating to the national ownership of industry and finance and the national control over monetary and fiscal policy. At around the same time the demise of the Bretton Woods system of exchange rates pegged to the dollar reduced the dependence of other advanced countries on U.S. policy in some respects.

Yet, the questions that McKinnon raised remain of central importance today in any assessment of U.S. dollar dominance. The overarching welfare question is still whether national fiat monies should be recognized or even promoted as natural regional or global monopolies. What degree of currency competition in the broad est sense of the term—remains viable and desirable?

McKinnon (1973: 88) identified four issues bearing on a possible European advantage in a European currency displacing the U.S. dollar-based monetary system. Paraphrased, they are

1. *The seignorage losses associated with using dollars as money* However, with a competitive banking structure as in the Eurodollar market, these losses are probably very small while the advantages of having a single international currency are very great.
2. *The reduction in the ownership and control of European industry* The current system implies some channeling of the European savings-investment process through dollar-based financial institutions.
3. *The European advantage of greater independence in monetary and fiscal policies* Since much economic instability in the post-war period has arisen out of unfortunate governmental policies, it is not clear (in McKinnon's eyes) how much this independence is worth.
4. *The instability of monetary policy within the United States* In the absence of full political integration, should the rest of the world be completely dependent on what the American Federal Reserve does? One might feel somewhat safer if there existed at least one other major competitive currency.

Some observers favor laissez-faire dollarization (see Schuler 2002). This would mean telling the government to get out of the business of determining what money people use in its jurisdiction and how, with whom, and where they choose to conduct their financial and banking business. The only proviso would be that the financial institutions issuing dollars provide accurate accounting information. Otherwise, "the market" could not properly discipline these institutions.

However, given the fact that the smooth functioning of financial intermediation is critical to the success of national economies, most governments like to keep a firm hand on the monetary and financial process. Further, as Angeloni notes in Part I, the governments may regret the atrophy of local expertise in supervision of the banking and financial system that U.S. dollarization may imply. There may be other adverse long-term consequences. If the advice to dollarize rests on a region's poor policy record, and there is no regard for potential for reform and financial development (as excessive concern with McKinnon's (1973) point 3 may imply), accepting such advice may simply foreclose opportunities for improvements.

With dollarization, U.S. financial institutions gain decisive, perhaps exclusive, operational and policy influence throughout the dollarized world. These institutions' assured access to the Federal Reserve and to other U.S. government agencies, and their basic advantages in getting private funding in dollar markets has this effect. In addition, dollarizing countries expose themselves significantly to U.S. public decisions. They become largely subject to U.S. government mandates addressed to U.S. financial institutions in extraterritorial activities. Furthermore, following dollarization, some major unresolved issues arise. Who bears the costs of bailouts or bankruptcy of any financial organization operating in foreign countries and which oversight agency is charged with guarding against insolvency and managing its consequences?

Dwyer and Lothian (Part I) consider the question of a common money circulating over a wide region in earlier centuries, extending roughly from Imperial Rome to Late Renaissance and beyond. Since the monies they study are full-bodied coins, they are able to abstract from the national limitations of central bank money. The importance of the market in determining the range of circulation is indeed a major part of their theme. They emphasize that the great coinages of the past achieved their position and acceptability by decentralized human action rather than collectivist design, that is, by free choice rather than government intervention or monopoly. Three characteristics gave certain gold and silver coins wide circulation in Europe and the Middle East for centuries: Trust, solid reputation, and convenience in use.

Trust is earned through quality control of weight and fineness. The trust lowers transaction costs through standardization in making frequent checking (assaying) unnecessary. Thereby it increases the extensive as well as the intensive margin in the use of the coin in trade and rudimentary finance. The reputation of an issuer for a firm and steady grip on power, a thriving empire or state, and a decent regard for long-term consequences, all foster trust in the fidelity of the issuer's coinage far into the future. With greater steadiness of weight and fineness comes more stable purchasing power over goods and services. Reputation, in turn, qualifies a particular coinage for use in denominating bills of exchange that can circulate over a wide area as bearer certificates.

Historically, certain physical characteristics of commodity money also helped give monies wide (to avoid the anachronistic term "international") usage. For instance, because a single high-valued coin is more compact and easier to transport than stacks of low-valued coins of the same fineness and total weight, large-value coins traveled farthest and circulated over the widest area. Some of the characteristics that allowed gold coins like the *solidus* (later known as *bezant*) to be accepted from end to end of the known world remain relevant today in analyzing the potential for international adoption of different brands of money. The comparative riskiness and ease of conversion of different monies is critical in the comparison. Both of these characteristics depend on the size and security of the issuing country's trading network. As a basic difference, though, the quality of a fiat money depends less on physical characteristics today. The quality of such money can only be ascertained by monitoring the foreign issuer's monetary policy objectives and the domestic political support behind those objectives. Compared with the commodity ideal of "stateless money," monies thus inevitably have become more political.

In case of monetary union, a single government may still maintain monetary control, depending on unilateral or multilateral monetary union. Angeloni (Part I) contrasts these two forms. Unilateral monetary union (often dollarization) means the adoption by a country of the money of another, without any implication of common consent. By contrast, multilateral monetary union results from agreement. The agreement can mean the adoption of a common currency differing from any of the existing ones, but regardless, it must cover the manner of setting up the necessary monetary institutions, and the way that monetary policy decisions will be made. As Angeloni explains further, in a unilateral monetary union, monetary policy must be supposed to be geared essentially to smooth the shocks hitting the anchor economy. By opposition, in a multilateral monetary union, each member participates in deciding the joint monetary policy, although each one's individual stabilization needs may not be closely met by the single monetary policy that is set for the euro area as a whole.

Both Angeloni and Salvatore (Part I) explore salient differences between the two types of monetary union in other respects as well. Of course, even in the multilateral case, there may still be large imbalances among the participants in terms of size and political influence. As Angeloni emphasizes, in the example of EMU, admission to the system entitles each country to one equal vote on the Governing Council of the European Central Bank (ECB), and therefore smallness can lead to disproportionately large representation. However, the right way to handle this problem is not to bar small countries from membership permanently, and thereby to leave them with no option to get the euro as their national currency except unilateral adoption. Rather, the problem should be handled in the future by changing the vote distribution to correspond more closely to differences in demographic and economic dimensions of country size. Using paid-up shares in the ECB's capital to decide the distribution is one way to do the trick.

Similarly, the ECB's attempt to treat formal unilateral euroization as a permanent obstacle to accession to EMU, even in the case of microstates such as Andorra, Monaco, and San Marino, is objectionable. There seems to be no basis for this attempt except the inherent impossibility of applying one or more of the Maastricht criteria to such countries. Salvatore points to another dilemma emanating from the Maastricht criteria: The candidate countries for admission with high rates of productivity growth in tradable goods will be unable to reconcile the required condition of stability of exchange rates with the required condition of stability of the price level (because of Balassa–Samuelson). Nonetheless, according to Nauschnigg (2002), the European Union and the Eurosystem have made it clear that there will be no derogation from the Maastricht criteria for the accession countries. Furthermore, unilateral adoption of the euro, or euroization, is not an acceptable step toward EMU either. These official positions, taken in combination, will need to be reconsidered if the European Union is to preserve the dynamism of the type of multilateral monetary union that is Europe's gift to the world.

Fixed exchange rates require sacrifice of an independent monetary policy in normal times. But, under a fixed exchange rate, no monetary policy may be able to foil a determined speculative attack. On the other hand, floating (often, sinking) exchange rates can be very destabilizing to the domestic economy of emerging-market countries and to their inflation and growth performance. Whatever the exchange-rate regime, the effectiveness of an independent monetary policy in the emerging economies is quite limited in a world of large capital flows and integrated capital markets. Both Argentina, on a fixed exchange rate, and Brazil, on a floating one, experienced the same lack of politically acceptable policy choices in different ways at various times during 1999–2002. Even if inflation targeting seems possible to such countries under floating exchange rates, the appearance may be largely illusory. Allowing the exchange rate to move down significantly will mean missing the inflation target, while allowing it to appreciate greatly can lay the ground for an external debt problem.

In the face of these tribulations, the unilateral adoption of a monetary union need not mean more surrender of autonomy than the decision to float. Regardless of floating or fixing, unilateral monetary union with a low-inflation currency may do more to stabilize those capital flows that are sensitive to exchange-rate expectations. So long as the monetary union holds up, exposure to exchange-rate volatility will go down to around the level witnessed between the leading currencies, essentially, the U.S. dollar and the euro, and less of a country's trade will be affected since less of it is conducted across currency boundaries. A good inflation performance would be all but guaranteed. Hence, monetary union, even if unilateral, emerges from the overview chapters in Part I as a superior choice for many emerging-market countries.

1.3 Introduction to Part II: Trade and Price Effects of Monetary Union

In the effort to quantify the gains from EMU, the European Commission (1990) came up with figures of 0.1–0.4 of 1 percent of GDP. These numbers result mostly from the elimination of bank charges for converting currencies and for contracts protecting against exchange risk. But the Commission strongly emphasized the possibility of wider gains stemming from the increased integration of goods and capital markets. For these other gains they offered no numbers. Those gains are also elusive. Still, a recent study by Rose indicates that the numbers could be large—much larger than ever anticipated before. In a test of a gravity model covering a worldwide sample of countries, Rose (2000) reported that monetary union more than triples bilateral trade. Some have expressed doubts about his results as resting on a small subsample of observations consisting mostly of tiny countries. Yet, the tests include controls for the size of the trading partners, as measured in a number of ways: By GDP, population, and land area. They also control for distances, common borders, common language, political union, free trade agreement, and past colonial relationships. Consequently, many researchers have taken Rose's results to heart, and have tried to refine and explain his findings.

The first three chapters in Part II, by Mélitz, Rose, and Nitsch, all contribute to this re-examination. The closing chapter, by Isgut, pertains to a closely related issue. It deals with the impact of monetary union on the integration of markets via prices of goods and services. The chapter shows that monetary union promotes the law of one price, and as such, supports Rose's conclusion that monetary union enhances trade and competition.

Every contribution to this Part relies on the gravity model of trade. A fundamental aspect of that model is that greater distance between two countries reduces the bilateral trade between them. Mélitz begins by pointing out that this feature is curious in one respect: The Ricardian model of trade could suggest that increased distance in some dimension will promote trade. So far as countries are further from one another along the North–South axis, there will be differences in climate and, plant and animal life between them. There could also be differences in required insulation, cooling, and heating. Those differences will then promote trade based on comparative advantage, and the relevant promotion of trade may go beyond agriculture and the extractive industries to cover construction, energy consumption, and optimal production technique. On this hypothesis, Mélitz introduces the absolute value of differences in latitude between countries. After controlling for distance in the usual sense, he finds that his index of differences from North to South consistently enters very significantly with the expected *positive* sign in the bilateral trade equations. Moreover, the presence of this additional variable does not detract from the negative influence of distance, as measured in the usual fashion.

Mélitz then tackles the central problem of the improbably large impact of distance on foreign trade in gravity models. With each percentage point increase in distance, usual estimates indicate around a percentage point or more decrease in trade. This is considerable. On account of the dramatic decline in transportation costs since the mid-nineteenth century, the impact of distance on foreign trade should have fallen. But this reduction in impact has not happened. Why? To help solve this puzzle, Mélitz proceeds by distinguishing between a substitution and a scale effect of distance. Specifically, he breaks down distance between two trading partners into the distance between them relative to all foreigners, and their distance from all foreigners. Greater relative distance between them should yield a substitution effect on their trade with one another relative to the rest: It should damage their trade with each other *in favor of trade with those foreigners who are closer.* But their distance from all foreigners (on average) should damage their foreign trade generally, including their trade with one another, *in favor of domestic trade.* On this view, it would not be strange at all if relative distance increasingly diminished trade over time as transportation costs fell. This would simply mean that as the distance barrier fell, distance became more important in deciding *how far* goods would travel abroad. Only distance from all foreigners—or "remoteness"—should bear a smaller negative impact on foreign trade over time.

It turns out that the distinction between relative distance and remoteness is significant in explaining the geography of trade in Mélitz's sample for 1970–95. The two factors enter separately with the expected negative sign. In addition, relative distance is decidedly the more important of the two influences. This finding helps to reconcile the earlier evidence concerning distance with the facts about transportation costs.

Finally, Mélitz deals with the effect of political influences on trade, including the influence of free trade association, former colonial ties, and currency union. At this juncture, his focus shifts to Rose's earlier spectacular results about monetary union. In Part II of this volume Rose counts nineteen studies that have dealt with his results thus far. The number of estimates of the effect of currency union on trade in these studies (383) is sufficiently large for meta-analysis. In other words, Rose (Part II) is now able to consider the estimates as a set of observations about the true parameter regarding the impact of currency union on trade. He can, thus, apply statistical analysis to the observation set. This analysis leads him to conclude in favor of a doubling rather than a tripling or more of trade. In addition, this new estimate does not depend on his own numerous contributions to the nineteen previous studies, and it is statistically highly significant.

Even before obtaining the results reported in this volume, Rose had already come to rely more on the estimate of a doubling of trade based on his joint work with Glick in Glick and Rose (2002). It may be interesting to show why this more recent estimate of his has greater merit than his earlier one in Rose (2000). Rose's original estimate of the effect of monetary union on trade is not only large, but larger than his corresponding estimate of the effect of other political ties, like free trade agreement or political union, on trade. It is hard enough to see how monetary union could triple trade. But it is perhaps even more difficult to understand how a single currency could foster greater trade than the elimination of tariff barriers or belonging to the same country. As a result, there had been an earlier suspicion that Rose's estimate of the impact of monetary union, as such, still contains some effects of free trade and political union. The countries that enter into monetary union with one another often have close political ties in other respects as well, even when they have not signed a free trade agreement and are not party to any other political pact.

In his subsequent work with Glick, Rose uses a much larger set of panel data than in his original paper, consisting of annual time series and going back as far as possible in time. That is, his new data set contains a true time series dimension as well as a cross-sectional one. This added dimension permits him to estimate separate "between" and "within" coefficients for the impact of monetary union. The "between" coefficient relates to the cross-sectional effect. In this regard, the Glick and Rose study does not differ from Rose's earlier one, and therefore the earlier suspicion still exists that the estimate concerns a joint effect of membership in monetary union and the closeness of other political ties. However, in the case of the "within" coefficient, Glick and Rose offer something new. This next coefficient captures the impact of entry and exit from monetary union. In line with these observations, as regards the "between" coefficient, Glick and Rose obtain approximately the same estimate as Rose had in his earlier

14   *Editorial Introduction*

work, whereas in the case of the "within" effect, they obtain a markedly lower estimate than Rose had before. This new coefficient, which accords with the results of Rose's present meta-analysis, is also statistically very significant. It implies a "mere" doubling of trade.

Yet, even a doubling of trade is considerable. Skeptics will, therefore, wish to dig further. They may even wish to question Rose's general statistical approach. One possibility is to insist on case studies, and therefore to examine, for example, the exit of Ireland from monetary union with the United Kingdom (Thom and Walsh 2002), or the decision of Luxembourg and Belgium to form a monetary union (Nitsch 2002). Another tack is to insist that there is a severe problem of heterogeneity in the data, and therefore to require matching techniques between individual country pairs (Persson 2001).

Nitsch (Part II) belongs somewhere between these two extremes. He tries to control for heterogeneity by studying only a single monetary union at a time and by compiling a balanced sample, consisting only of members and non-members that are in the same geographical region and of comparable economic size. This is his procedure in studying the East Caribbean currency union and the CFA franc zone. In both cases, he uses a gravity model. His estimates show a doubling of trade in the example of the CFA franc but no significant impact of the East Caribbean currency union. In both instances, adding country-fixed effects blunts many of the results, not only for currency union, but also for other basic variables. Nitsch also experiments with cross-effects between currency union and output and finds them significant. This finding is interesting, since the usual theoretical derivations of the gravity model with homothetic utility functions and constant returns to scale in production imply no cross-effects of output with anything else.

Closely related work has dealt with the effect of political borders on price dispersion. Paralleling the original findings by Rose (2000), this literature similarly obtains unbelievably large effects of political borders on price differences between regions (see McCallum 1995; Engel and Rogers 1996). In further parallel, this literature has already spawned at least one effort to show that those high estimates are exaggerated: That of Anderson and van Wincoop (2003, compare Feenstra 2002). One of the suspected reasons for the sizable impact of political borders on price deviations has always been a difference in currencies. Parsley and Wei (2001) confirm this hypothesis. Isgut (Part II) adds new variables and goes further than Parsley and Wei in showing that different currencies impede the law of one price. Closer adherence to the law of one price implies closer trade ties. Thus, the findings of Isgut and of Parsley and Wei support Rose's conclusion that monetary union increases competition and trade, and this on the basis of completely different data, concerning prices of individual goods and services in many cities in different parts of the world. Quite notably, Isgut finds not only that monetary union reduces price dispersion, but also that such union is "one order of magnitude more important than a mere reduction in exchange rate volatility."

1.4 Introduction to Part III: Monetary Integration in Latin America

Empirical experience with economic integration reveals three basic facts: First, economic integration can be a long and difficult process. Second, deep and durable economic integration is not possible without monetary integration. Lastly, in a globalized economy with liquid international capital, a greater degree of monetary integration than is currently present is unavoidable because small currencies are subject to currency substitution and are vulnerable to currency crises.

All chapters in this part reflect the importance of one or more of these basic facts in Latin America. First, Fernández-Arias, Panizza, and Stein (Part III) analyze the attempts of Mercosur to stimulate economic integration exclusively by trade agreements, while leaving exchange-rate policies in the hands of the individual countries. One central conclusion is that the successes of integration are very limited without accompanying exchange-rate agreements. Misalignments tend to foment protectionist policies between member countries, scale back or eliminate free trade arrangements, dislocate foreign direct investments and often lead to currency crises. Thus, trade agreements require a degree of support from exchange-rate coordination in order to safeguard and promote economic integration.

A free trade agreement should be designed at least to preclude such massive exchange-rate misalignments as can easily lead to currency crises and wholesale disruption of trade and finance among members. Argentina and Brazil, two members of Mercosur, provide a striking example of what can go wrong otherwise. Argentina chose to maintain a currency board with the U.S. dollar in 1991–2001, while Brazil went over to a free float beginning in January 1999. When the Brazilian *real* sharply depreciated over the year 1999, a real overvaluation of the Argentine Peso followed. By the middle of 2002, the situation had reversed as the Argentine peso had gone into a freefall after the collapse of its currency board. The *real* was then the overvalued currency in Mercosur, and exchange-rate pressure shifted to Brazil, thus further straining what was left of economic cooperation in the organization. In 2003, the debate resumed as to whether Mercosur should turn to a common external anchor, the U.S. dollar, or could credibly develop its own zone of exchange-rate stability and engage in a joint float against the dollar.

Fernández-Arias, Panizza, and Stein (Part III) elaborate the tensions existing between the requirements of trade and exchange arrangements within countries belonging to regional common markets like Mercosur. In Argentina, for example, financial considerations and investor preferences favor dollarization while trade and optimal currency area (OCA) criteria speak against it. Such tensions can lead to harsh policy dilemmas, as brought out by Perry and Servén as well later in Part III.

Although this is not their main theme, de la Torre, Levy Yeyati, and Schmukler (Part III) shed some light on the contrasting monetary experiment of Ecuador in

Latin America. The country introduced the dollar unilaterally in March 2000 in order to import stability after decades of fruitless efforts to implement the reforms necessary for stable economic development. But Ecuador's failure to prepare the way for unilateral entry into a monetary union meant that all the necessary adjustments had to take place after the introduction of the dollar as sole legal tender. As Ecuador's experience clearly displays, there is a sequencing problem requiring attention whenever a country decides to abandon a separate currency.

Preceding dollarization, Ecuador saw unstable monetary and fiscal policies, volatile exchange rates, currency substitution, and a large underground sector. To find the correct exchange rate at the start of dollarization under such circumstances is nearly impossible. But if the conversion rate to the U.S. dollar is set at the wrong level, the result may be severe economic dislocation. In case of an undervalued home currency, the initial dollar prices are too low, and this will lead to high inflation rates. However transitory the inflation may be, it will have a significant bearing on labor relations, public deficits, and country risk. One of the salient facts of the Ecuadorian experiment is that the country chose a marked undervaluation at the start. Accordingly, high inflation followed the introduction of the dollar. The monthly rates peaked at 108 percent (in annual terms) in September 2000.

We conclude that success in importing stability by introducing the dollar as the national currency is far from certain. Without the right preparation, formal dollarization may not be strong enough to rein in fiscal deficits to levels that are compatible with economic and political stability. If instability follows, all bets are off: A new crisis could lurk, and national money or its surrogates could make a return.

In a recent evaluation of monetary regime options for Latin America, Berg et al. (2002) conclude that dollarization is only desirable if three conditions are met: The credibility of the monetary authorities must be lost irreversibly, the country must have strong enough links to the U.S. economy, and the demand for dollar-denominated financial assets must be keen. Except for some small countries in Central America, no country in the Western Hemisphere meets all three conditions. Argentina only meets the last one. As regards the first two, though the country's monetary authorities have lost credibility, they have never done so irreversibly, but have lost it time and again. In addition, Argentina does not have strong economic links with the United States. However, it does have such links with Brazil, a country that succeeded in maintaining a nearly fixed exchange rate with the dollar (through a very slow crawl) for about four years ending in early 1999. This may suggest adding a consideration of the degree of dollarization or dollar-pegging of close trading partners to the proposed list of criteria for gauging a country's suitability for dollarization.

To analyze the crisis in Argentina and to provide any exchange-rate advice to the country is one of the severest challenges facing economics in recent years. Three teams of leading international specialists confront this challenge in Part III. All three groups of contributors recognize that fiscal unsustainability, debt, and banking problems lurked just below the surface prior to the crisis and were waiting to come out into the open at the first sign of a major depreciation of the real effective exchange.

For Calvo, Izquierdo, and Talvi (Part III), the likely trigger event was the Russian crisis of August 1998. This disturbance brought most capital imports to a sudden stop in the country. As the stop turned out to be unexpectedly persistent, the disturbance eventually induced emergency "reforms" and fiscal retrenchment. But these catch-up measures proved too little and too late, as they pushed the country against the limits of pain toleration. The difficulties were compounded by the fact that Argentina is a relatively closed (C) economy. Its low supply of tradable goods means that the needed change in the real exchange rate in order to achieve any given adjustment was high. Because of the wage and price rigidities in the country, the required change in the real exchange rate could not be attained under the currency board. Worsening the problem was de facto dollarization (D) of a large part of bank, business, and government liabilities and currency mismatches (M). These two extra factors rendered the required real exchange-rate change still more painful. The combination of CDM brought the whole system of financial intermediation into jeopardy at the mere hint of an exchange-rate crisis.

Elements of this CDM syndrome also appear in de la Torre, Levy Yeyati, and Schmukler's account (Part III) of the linkage between the solvency of the banking system and the solvency of the government. Every attempt to alleviate either problem in Argentina aggravated the other. For example, when the banks were forced to hold more government debt, they became even shakier than before. The special Argentinean brew of a hard peg and little flexibility in nominal wages, fiscal spending, or financial contracting turned into a Faustian bargain. It raised the exit costs from the currency board regime that had started so well to catastrophic levels without averting the catastrophe in the end. De la Torre, Levy Yeyati, and Schmukler advance one interesting suggestion for improving the final terms of this unenviable bargain: Respect the dollar obligations regarding stocks but impose pesofication at the margin. In other words, avoid outright confiscation of capital, try to amortize the previously dollarized currency-board obligations progressively over time, but allow new business to take place at a depreciated exchange rate in a national currency that could then be allowed to float.

Perry and Servén, in their capstone chapter to Part III, emphasize endogenous crisis propagation through Argentina's inappropriately cross-geared financial systems and the resulting tendency to amplify shocks—even small ones—to an unusual degree. While differing with Calvo et al. (Part III) in relying less on external shocks to explain the onset and depth of the crisis, they agree that the real appreciation of the peso had brought the currency about 50 percent above its equilibrium value by the time the country began to break its currency board commitments one by one. But because of the starting conditions, the fall in the peso up to and beyond the float formally adopted in February 2002 quickly led to a depreciation going so far as to be devastating in itself. Once liability dollarization extends to an entire economy, as in the Argentinean example, depreciation produces the opposite of debt dilution in the non-tradable goods and services sector. That sector has no dollar-receivables to counterbalance the increase in its real indebtedness, leaving it in even worse shape than the tradables sector. Hence, though changes in loan classification may be desired in the case of tradables too, tougher classification standards should be applied in the future to claims on the non-tradables sector in such countries. Furthermore, to reduce vulnerabilities, it will be imperative to delink the solvency of the financial system from problems of quality of sovereign debt by imposing strict mark-to-market and risk-weighted capital requirements on both public and private debt. Stress testing and risk analysis under pre-crisis conditions shows that banks and government in Argentina were much more vulnerable to exchange-rate movement than they were in a group of other Latin American countries. These countries in the comparison also weathered external shocks similar to those that affected Argentina rather easily. On this basis, Perry and Servén conclude that Argentina's collapse had more to do with internal defects of its financial system than external shocks. Taken together, this part focuses on dilemmas and policy conundrums facing countries in difficulties. Whether the tension is between trade agreements and exchange rate disagreements or between time-consuming reforms and the adoption of a foreign currency as home money ahead of reforms, the only choices are second or third best. As long as countries remain saddled with a legacy of bad government, inadequate institutions, and poor economic policy, nothing better may be available. And as de la Torre et al. (Part III) point out, the classical stress on the fix versus float dilemma is mistaken if there is a need to build institutions that provide for adequate flexibility and control in either case.

1.5   Introduction to Part IV: Common Monies, Political Interests, and Infrastructure

Parts I and III of this volume explore the rigors and possible advantages of monetary union for countries planning either unilateral adoption or accession to an existing monetary union. This part focuses instead on the optimal size and design of monetary union from the point of view of the countries supplying the money—that is, the producers, rather than the consumers, of currency consolidation services. It also discusses the financial infrastructure that the supplying countries should adopt, in light of their special position, and the level—national or supranational—at which different aspects of the performance of the enlarged monetary organizations should be supervised and regulated.

In the case of a unilateral adoption of a monetary union, the financial infrastructure of the adopting country is likely to be highly conditioned by the government and financial institutions of the anchor country. Hence, for the anchor country, as Cohen (Part IV) points out, monetary power becomes a dimension of state and business power. For the dollarized country, on the other side, such "institutions substitution" (see Mendoza 2002) carries both opportunities and risks. Foreign adoption of the U.S. dollar creates a currency dependence that can be, and at times has been, exploited by the United States to its political and economic advantage.

Why then does Cohen question the rational self-interest of the United States in actively promoting dollarization? One reason is the possibility that the choices of dollarizing countries could eventually limit U.S. freedom of movement as well. For instance, once dollarization has occurred on a large scale, a flight from the dollar accompanied by widespread de-dollarization could disrupt the U.S. economy and finances worldwide. Furthermore, despite the absence of formal obligations or insurance commitments, the United States may be under pressure to avoid financial crises in countries that choose to rely on the dollar and U.S. financial institutions. U.S. interests, as well as prestige and reputation for fair dealing, may be at stake. Hence, even if the Federal Reserve focuses solely on national economic welfare, this welfare may become more intertwined with that of other countries. It is difficult to see how the United States can avoid some effort to manage inevitable mutual risk exposure to events in other economies that become near-integral parts of U.S. business and finance. In this view, the country may be better off trying to keep dollarization from spreading very far.

Even without much wider formal adoption of the U.S. dollar as domestic currency, the country's international role in trade and finance appears secure. So far as market forces are allowed to hold sway over the allocation of international financial business and "denomination rents," the dollar is not likely to lose ground. In fact, there has been a resurgence of the dollar as the external anchor currency in much of continental East Asia, as the yen continues its decline as an international currency (McKinnon 2001). Consequently, even any future expansion of the euro will not necessarily mean a corresponding reduction of the role of the U.S. dollar in the world. Recently new factors have come into play. For instance, the U.S. government has begun actively to encroach on bank accounts under its jurisdiction through new laws and regulations since 2002. This behavior has probably already cost the dollar some loss of international good will relative to the euro. Similar encroachments on the legal rights of depositors in the euro area are unlikely because of the need to reach multilateral agreement in the EMU. Since the member countries of EMU need to compromise with one another, they are far less capable of exploiting the political advantages of their currency hegemony than the United States is able to do. One of the interesting differences between unilateral and multilateral monetary union may thus be that the latter produces a common money with less of a political hook.

What can we learn from West European monetary integration about the process of accession of Central European Countries? If we judge from the late-accession countries in the EMU that were formerly unstable, including Greece, one basic lesson appears. Countries with good prospects of full membership in EMU in the near term can implement the required reforms for entry without experiencing a serious recession if they adhere strictly and credibly to their stabilization strategy. Indeed, the situation is easier for Central European countries in one important respect than it was for unstable West European countries a dozen or more years ago: They can join an existing and stable monetary union rather than having to take part in building one. Still, in order to enter EMU, they must bring down inflation, restructure their labor and capital markets, and achieve sound fiscal positions.

There are some respects, though, in which the Central European countries are now at a disadvantage relative to their West European predecessors. Quite significantly, they are subject to massive currency substitution. Dollars and, increasingly, euros serve as cocirculating media of exchange and stores of value in these countries. The study by Feige and Dean (Part IV) analyzes the processes of currency substitution in all the major Central and East European economies and offers more comprehensive measures of the use of foreign currencies in trade and the denomination of contracts. The authors distinguish substitution of foreign for domestic currency from substitution in a broader range of financial assets that are quoted and settled in foreign rather than domestic currency. They analyze what is common and what is distinct about the factors that drive both forms of substitution. In this way, they refine the required data concepts to measure the degrees of currency and asset substitution, dollarization, and euroization, in East European countries. Because different methods of measurement yield very different estimates, further empirical investigation will clearly be needed to pin down the extent to which foreign currencies serve in transition countries and for what purposes. Network externalities enter into consideration in that regard.

In close connection, Costa Storti and De Grauwe (Part IV) offer a technological perspective on the optimal size of a currency union. They regard currencies as networks with separate payment and settlement systems and with a variety of other network-specific protocols that are partially incompatible with one another. The growing ease of electronic conversion can go a long way to reduce the transaction costs. Yet, only monetary union can merge the networks to the point of erasing problems of match-up and transfer between the systems entirely. The potential for network expansion, and hence the optimal domain of monetary union, could become very large indeed. Various factors, including network externalities on the demand side and economies of scale on the supply side, even suggest that just a single global money would eventually survive as the market solution.

Costa Storti and De Grauwe point to several technological factors that will prevent such an extreme outcome. First, network externalities may well cease to operate at the margin. At some high enough level of operation, the size externalities of absorbing yet another currency system on the outer fringe of a zone of economic activity may simply fail to offset the added costs of doing so. There will then be no willingness to pay for extra users. Second, the new Internet-based information technology (IT) could make it cheaper to maintain different monies. It could do so by strengthening the variety and depth of interconnections between the existing national monetary networks and reducing transaction costs between them. There are difficulties of organizing mergers of national monetary networks, as witnessed by the fact that the euro area itself still remains an incomplete merger. Therefore, the IT-driven reduction in the cost of interconnecting national systems may allow a number of networks to coexist. In that case, though, the new IT also may destabilize fixed exchange-rate systems by permitting (possibly facilitating?) speculative attack. The resulting increase in exchange risk will then tend to raise the costs of maintaining separate currencies. All in all, Costa Storti and De Grauwe conclude that the new IT will tend to increase the optimal size of monetary unions and reduce the number of currencies that remain viable in the world, though the number will stay greater than one. The basic value of their pioneering effort lies in carefully sorting out the underlying economic issues rather than conclusive results.

The remaining two chapters deal not with the optimal size of a monetary union but with accession conditions and the optimal distribution of functions at different political levels within the union. One interesting question arises in regard to the accession countries: Should they introduce the euro early or should they wait until they have successfully passed the whole Maastricht-type qualification period? Of course, financial markets will anticipate the answer. If the market expects the euro to become the official money of a country, contracts will not wait for that step. Indeed, there is a catch-22 situation shaping up for these countries: Their very effort to enter EMU will invite substantial euroization beforehand. According to Genberg (Part IV), the announcement of an upcoming official changeover to the euro could be the trigger causing many agents to switch to the new currency in a coordinated fashion. But this switch will make the Maastricht criteria more difficult to meet and can only reduce the benefits of accession. Euroization will clearly interfere with the required stability of the national exchange rate for two years prior to entering EMU. In addition, euroization will reduce the central bank's monetary liabilities. This will cost the country resources, since upon accession the country will only obtain euros for free in exchange for monetary base in the form of home currency.

Genberg argues that it would be unfair to new members in the EMU to let them lose real resources for euros (as they will in so far as they euroize beforehand) when the original members did not need to do so. One way to remedy this situation is for the central bank to receive euros equal to the money in circulation at the beginning of the transition period rather than at its end. But even this may not suffice for equal treatment of the newcomers, since in some cases, a substantial fraction of the money supply had already consisted of precursor currencies to the euro (especially the DM) for decades beforehand.

Kahn and Santos (Part IV) delve further into the optimal division of responsibilities for bank supervision and the function of lender-of-last-resort (LLR) between national agencies and the ECB. Angeloni (Part I) supported the existing distribution of these responsibilities in the EMU. Banking supervision, he argued, is best done nationally, partly because any costs of financial rescues will fall primarily on the national taxpayer. But if so, decentralized LLR is consistent.

Kahn and Santos consider and model the matter in depth by taking into account the incentives of regulators, that is, the bureaucrats in charge of administering the bank regulatory program(s). Regulators' objectives are some combination of the socially desirable and bureaucratic concerns. In the case of bank supervision, the bureaucratic concerns arise both because of the internal resources needed for prudential supervision and the effort of reputation-building by the regulatory agency. Bureaucratic concerns go further in the case of those supervisory agencies that bear the financial costs of bank closures and of other consequences of lax oversight or excessive forbearance themselves. Those agencies may internalize more of the moral hazard effects of bureaucratic practices than other supervisory agencies. Still, as a result of internal bureaucratic concerns, regulatory action will always tend to deviate from the social optimum. Regulatory theories of institutional design attempt to determine the optimal assignment of the regulatory function at the national or supranational level based on these kinds of hypotheses.

Using this approach, Kahn and Santos arrive at a different conclusion than Angeloni's: Regulatory systems should not be left at the national level. Doing so reduces the system's effectiveness when banking markets have already become integrated across the member countries through monetary union. However, if for political reasons, only one of the two regulatory functions may be centralized, the supervisory function should be the one and the LLR function should be left at the national level. The opposite choice—centralizing the LLR function while leaving the supervisory function at the national level—could eliminate the incentive of the supervisor to engage in monitoring. Thus, the integration of banking markets impinges on the best choice of centralization or decentralization of the supervisory and LLR functions. While Kahn and Santos rely entirely on theoretical models to reach their conclusion, Barth et al. (2002) provide much related empirical evidence on the impact of the structure, scope, and independence of bank supervision on the banking industry.

The overall impression that emerges is that unilateral monetary union must develop multilateral features if it is to spread very far. Further, multilateral monetary union must progressively free itself of too many unilateral elements. In addition, the current division of functions between national and supranational levels within the euro area may not be appropriate. Several features of EMU are also tailor-made for the founding members of the club, but are not fair, suitable, or hospitable to candidates for accession. While a clear spur to economic growth and convergence of peripheral countries, EMU has yet to yield salient growth or stability benefits for the core countries themselves. This may explain some of the reluctance of the core members, as gatekeepers of the system, to facilitate expansion of EMU on altered terms.

REFERENCES

Anderson, J. E. and van Wincoop, E. (2003). "Gravity with Gravitas: A Solution to the Border Puzzle." *American Economic Review*, 93 (March): 170–292.

Barth, J. R., Nolle, D. E., Phumiwasana, T., and Yago, G. (2002). "A Cross-Country Analysis of the Bank Supervisory Framework and Bank Performance." Paper presented at 77th Annual Conference of the Western Economic Association International, Seattle, June 29 to July 3.

Berg, A., Borensztein, E., and Mauro, O. (2002). "An Evaluation of Monetary Regime Options for Latin America." *North American Journal of Economics and Finance*, 13 (November): 213–35.

Bordo, M., Eichengreen, B., Klingebiel, D., and Martinez-Peria, M. S. (2001). "Is the Crisis Problem Growing More Severe?" *Economic Policy*, 32 (April): 53–82.

EMEPG Seoul Report (2001). *Rebuilding the International Financial Architecture*, October.

Engel, C. and Rogers, J. H. (1996). "How Wide is the Border?" *American Economic Review*, 86 (December): 1112–38.

European Commission (1990). "One Market, One Money." *European Economy*, 44 (October).

Feenstra, R. C. (2002). "Border Effects and the Gravity Equation: Consistent Methods for Estimation." *Scottish Journal of Political Economy*, 49 (December): 491–506.

Glick, R. and Rose, A. K. (2002). "Does a Currency Union Affect Trade? The Time Series Evidence." *European Economic Review*, 46 (June): 1125–51.

Ho, C. (2002). "A Survey of the Institutional and Operational Aspects of Modern-Day Currency Boards." *BIS Working Paper*, No. 110, Monetary and Economic Department, March.

Kirshner, J. (1995). *Currency and Coercion: The Political Economy of International Monetary Power*. Princeton University Press.

McCallum, J. (1995). "National Borders Matter: Canada–U.S. Regional Trade Patterns." *American Economic Review*, 85 (June): 615–23.

McKinnon, R. I. (1973). "The Dual Currency Regime Revisited." In H. G. Johnson and A. K. Swoboda (eds.), *The Economics of Common Currencies*. Cambridge, MA: Harvard University Press, pp. 85–90.

— (2001). "After the Crisis, the East Asian Dollar Standard Resurrected: An Interpretation of High-Frequency Exchange-Rate Pegging." In J. E. Stiglitz and S. Yusuf (eds.), *Rethinking the East Asian Miracle*. New York: Oxford University Press, pp. 197–246.

Mendoza, E. G. (2002). "Why Should Emerging Economies Give up National Currencies: A Case for 'Institutions Substitution'." *NBER Working Paper* No. 8950, May.

Mundell, R. A. (1973). "A Plan for a European Currency." In H. G. Johnson and A. K. Swoboda (eds.), *The Economics of Common Currencies*. Cambridge, MA: Harvard University Press, pp. 143–72.

Nauschnigg, F. (2002). The Euro and the Use of Foreign Currencies in Central and Eastern Europe, draft, Oesterreichische Nationalbank, May.

Nitsch, V. (2002). "The Non-Causality of the Common Currency Effect on Trade: Evidence From the Monetary Union Between Belgium and Luxembourg." Bankgesellschaft Berlin, unpublished.

Parsley, D. C. and Wei, S. J. (2001). "Limiting Currency Volatility to Stimulate Goods Market Integration: A Price-Based Approach." *NBER Working Paper* No. 8468, September.

Persson, T. (2001). "Currency Unions and Trade: How Large is the Treatment Effect." *Economic Policy*, 33 (October): 433–48.

Rodrik, D. (2003). "Argentina: A Case of Globalisation Gone too Far or not Far Enough?." In J. J. Teunissen and A. Akkerman (eds.), *The Crisis that Was Not Prevented: Lessons for Argentina, the IMF, and Globalisation.* The Hague, NL: Forum on Debt and Development, pp. 15–21.

Rose, A. K. (2000). "One Money, One Market: Estimating the Effect of Common Currencies on Trade." *Economic Policy*, 30 (April): 7–33.

Schuler, K. (2002). "Dollarization, At the Intersection of Economics and Politics." Draft, Joint Economic Committee, U.S. Congress, May, www.dollarization.org.

Thom, R. and Walsh, B. (2002). "The Effect of a Common Currency on Trade: Lessons from the Irish Experience." *European Economic Review*, 46 (June): 1111–23.

PART I

Current and Past Concepts of Monetary Union

2

Euroization, Dollarization, and the International Monetary System

DOMINICK SALVATORE

A great debate is taking place in many nations, especially small ones, in Central, Eastern, and Southern Europe, in the Baltic States, and in the Americas on the need and benefits of abandoning the national currency in favor of the euro or the dollar. This chapter examines the benefits and the costs of euroization or dollarization, it analyzes the ways in which the two processes are similar and different, and it examines the effect that the process of euroization and dollarization is likely to have on the functioning of the present and future international monetary system.

2.1 Introduction

The past decade has seen a revolution in financial markets around the world. The deregulation of domestic financial markets, the liberalization of international capital flows, the rapid financial innovation in the form of new instruments (derivatives), and the arrival of powerful computers and telecommunications have dramatically lowered the cost of information gathering, processing, and transmission. As a result, world financial markets have experienced explosive growth. Since 1980, the total stock of financial assets has increased two-and-a-half times faster than the growth of real GDP of industrial countries and the volume of daily trading in foreign exchange, bonds, and equities has increased more than ten times faster than GDP.

Financial liberalization has resulted in huge benefits to savers and borrowers as capital has tended to flow to its most productive uses around the world, but it has also led to fears that this has sharply reduced the effectiveness of monetary policy. Fears have been expressed that in a world of deregulated capital markets and huge international capital flows, central banks may have lost the power to set interest rates and that changes in interest rates may have much less effect on the economy than they did one or two decades ago. Forrest Capie and Geoffrey Wood (1994), Capie et al. (1996), and the International Monetary Fund (IMF 1994) have indicated that, while this is not true, for the most part, for financially and economically large areas and countries, such as the euro area (EA), the United States, and Japan, it is certainly true for financially and economically small and autonomous open economies—which represent most of the world's countries.

This, together with the potential benefits (examined later) of euroization or dollarization, has led many small open countries that are not already part of the EA or that have not already unilaterally adopted either the dollar or the euro to consider doing so in the near future.

The effectiveness of monetary policy also depends in a crucial way on the type of exchange rate arrangements that the nation chooses to have. We know from international financial theory that with perfect international capital mobility, monetary policy would be completely ineffective with a fixed exchange rate system. Under such a system, the nation must passively allow its money supply to change in such a way as to ensure external equilibrium in defense of the par value of the currency. Thus, the nation loses control over the money supply and cannot use monetary policy to correct a domestic imbalance such as inflation and/or recession. On the other hand, a flexible exchange rate system allows the central bank to have an independent monetary policy even with highly mobile financial capital internationally, but the central bank gives up control completely over its exchange rate, and large and frequent fluctuations in exchange rates can be very destabilizing for the domestic economy. Thus, neither alternative seems satisfactory for small open economies. This led many small open economies to explore the benefits of euroization or dollarization, even unilaterally (if belonging to a common currency area, such as the EA, is not open or possible).

Thus, a great debate is taking place in many nations, especially small ones, in Central, Eastern, and Southern Europe, in the Baltic States, and on the American Continent on the need and benefits of abandoning the national currency in favor of the euro or the dollar. This chapter examines first the benefits and the costs of euroization or dollarization, as well as the ways in which the two processes are similar and different. Then I turn to the effect that the process of euroization and dollarization is likely to have on the functioning of the present and future international monetary system.

2.2   Euroization in Central, Baltic, and Southeastern European Countries

There are two important questions that need to be answered with regard to the euroization of Central European countries, the Baltic States, and Southeastern European countries in line for admission into the European Union (EU) and the EA. The first is what is the best exchange rate arrangement in the years prior to admission into the EA? The second is what are the benefits and costs that these nations can expect from eventually belonging to the EA in view of their weaker economic and financial situation?

2.2.1   Exchange rate arrangements prior to admission into the euro area

Table 2.1 presents the current exchange rate arrangements of Transition Economies in Central Europe, the Baltic and Southeastern Europe, as well as of Cyprus, Malta,

Table 2.1. *Exchange rate arrangements and monetary policy framework of candidate countries in June 2001*

	Exchange rate arrangements	Monetary policy framework
Central Europe		
Czech Republic	Managed floating	Monitors various indicators
Hungary	Crawling peg	IMF-supported program
Poland	Independent floating	Independent floating
Slovak Republic	Managed floating	Monitors various indicators
Bosnia-Herzegovina	Currency board (euro)	IMF-supported program
Croatia	Managed floating	IMF-supported program
Slovenia	Managed floating	Monetary aggregate target
Yugoslavia FR	Managed floating	IMF-supported program
Baltic States		
Estonia	Currency board (euro)	IMF-supported program
Latvia	Fixed peg against SDR	IMF-supported program
Lithuania	Currency board (US dollar[a])	IMF-supported program
Southeastern Europe		
Albania	Independent floating	IMF-supported program
Bulgaria	Currency board (euro)	IMF-supported program
FYR Macedonia	Fixed peg against euro	Exchange rate anchor
Romania	Managed floating	IMF-supported program
Cyprus	Fixed peg against SDR	Exchange rate anchor
Malta	Fixed peg against composite	Exchange rate anchor
Turkey	Independent floating	IMF-supported program

[a] Switched to the euro in February 2002.

Source: IMF (March 2002).

and Turkey, which are in line for admission into the EU and the EA as of June 2001. To be noted is that a country could be part of the EU but not the EA (as it is now the case for the United Kingdom, Sweden, and Denmark), but a country cannot be part of the EA without belonging to the EU. A country, however, could adopt the euro as its currency unilaterally (as Panama and Ecuador have done with the dollar) without being part of either the EU or EA. This is the situation confronting the candidates for admission into the EU and EA prior to admission. Hungary, Poland, and the Czech Republic will probably be admitted to the EU and the EA in the next few years, but some other countries (such as Romania, Bulgaria, and Turkey) will probably have to wait for as a long as a decade (see Salvatore 2001).

From Table 2.1 we see that the candidate countries (CC) now have many different exchange arrangements, ranging from currency boards (or exchange rates rigidly fixed to a foreign currency, SDR, or composite) to independent floating, and different monetary policy frameworks, from IMF-supported programs to inflation targeting. The question then arises as to the best exchange rate system in preparation for admission into the EU and EA. Here, CC face the dilemma of achieving simultaneously stable exchange rates and stable prices, as required for admission into the EA. Specifically, with fixed exchange rates and high productivity growth, these countries will not be able to contain price increases to 2 percent but may instead face inflation in the range of 3–5 percent per year. Although these rates of inflation are not excessive, they violate the nominal inflation convergence criterion required for admission into the EA. And if CC were to allow their exchange rates to appreciate (as a reflection of their strong productivity growth—as postulated by the Balassa–Samuelson effect), they would violate the stability-of-exchange rate criterion for admission.

The Balassa–Samuelson effect refers to the pressure on non-tradable goods prices to rise when the price of tradable goods are not allowed to fall (as it occurs if the domestic currency is not allowed to appreciate) when the productivity in tradable goods rises rapidly (a feature of economies undergoing a productivity catch-up to advanced economy levels). Since the Balassa–Samuelson price increases are not symptoms of macroeconomic imbalance and are required to preserve microeconomic equilibrium, however, there would be justification for the EU to relax either the price or exchange rate convergence criterion for admission into the EA for the CC that face this dilemma.

More generally, a fixed exchange rate system appears to be a natural anchor for small open economies that are converging rapidly with a major currency bloc. However, exchange rate pegs are open to the criticism that they heighten market pressures in a world of liberalized international capital flows and can be viewed by the markets as a safe one-way bet and can be attacked—exactly as it happened in the financial crisis in Southeast-Asia emerging market crisis of mid-1997. In fact, concerns about the vulnerability of pegs have led to the adoption of a currency board in Bosnia-Herzogovina, Estonia, Lithuania, and Bulgaria, and led to interest in early "euroization" in some CC. These regimes (currency boards or unilateral euroization), however, have drawbacks for economies in rapid transformation because they allow limited room for banking support, and eliminate a key safety valve in case of financial shocks.

An alternative to currency boards or unilateral euroization is inflation targeting, as now followed by Poland. One fundamental issue is whether inflation targeting, on the road to EU and EA accession, will prove less vulnerable than pegs to speculative pressures. Although many observers believe pegs are exceptionally demanding on policy makers, they also recognize that inflation-targeting regimes present the serious dilemma at times of large potential capital inflows, of either having to abandon the inflation target or having to allow a real appreciation of the nation's currency, and either of these could quickly lead to an unsustainable current account deterioration.

Given these uncertainties, some economists have advocated hybrid regimes of crawling pegs and inflation targeting in the range of 3–5 percent for CC.

But these violate both the stable exchange rate and the inflation criteria for participating in the euro. Here, however, it is important to keep in mind that the requirements for joining the EU (the Copenhagen criteria) are different from the Maastricht and Stability Pact criteria for joining the EA. The Copenhagen criteria include, among others, the existence of a functioning market economy able to meet EU competitive pressures and able to sustain the obligations of membership. This means that the most advanced CC may satisfy the Copenhagen criteria for admission into the EU before being able to meet the more stringent Maastricht and Stability Pact criteria for participating in the EA. That would leave the problem of reconciling exchange rate and price stability in the CC even after entering the EU.

2.2.2 Benefits and costs of belonging to the euro area for candidate countries

The effects resulting from the introduction of the euro have been amply examined both in Europe and in the United States, and most economists on both sides of the Atlantic generally agree with the analysis and with the benefits and costs that are likely to result from its introduction. The benefits that CC can be expected to receive upon joining the EA are the same—only quantitatively larger. The benefits are

(1) The elimination of the need to exchange their currencies for euros;
(2) the elimination of excessive volatility of their currencies (Salvatore 2002*a,b*);
(3) more rapid economic and financial integration with the EU members;
(4) greater economic discipline;
(5) sharing the seignorage from issuing more euros in the future with other EA members;
(6) elimination of the currency and country risk and, thus, a lower cost of borrowing in international financial markets;
(7) greater economic and political importance.

The most serious problem facing CC upon admission into the EU and EA is how to respond to a major asymmetric demand and supply shock. It is practically inevitable that a large and diverse single-currency area like the EA will face periodic asymmetric shocks that will affect various member nations differently and drive their economies out of alignment. With a less developed economy and financial sector, less flexibility, and lower international competitiveness, the new entrants into the EA are likely to face an even greater problem of how to deal with asymmetric shocks than established EA members. In such a case, there is little that a CC can do. The nation cannot use contractionary monetary policy or allow its currency to appreciate to combat excessive growth and inflation because of the common currency. The only thing that the nation could do to contain inflationary pressures would be to pursue a restrictive fiscal policy, but that is not easy to do and could severely cut national growth (Salvatore 1997).

Supporters of the single currency reply that the requirements for the establishment of single currency will necessarily increase labor market flexibility in CC and, by promoting greater intra-EU trade, a single currency will also dampen nationally differentiated business cycles. Furthermore, it is pointed out that highly integrated EU capital markets can make up for low labor market flexibility and provide an adequate automatic response to asymmetric shocks. These automatic responses may not be sufficient, however. It is also true that meeting the Maastricht criteria will increase labor market flexibility, but this is, at best, a slow process, especially for the new CC entrants. Furthermore, "excessive" capital flows may work perversely by reducing the incentive for the introduction of fundamental labor market liberalizing measures and, by pushing up the euro exchange rate, they may even produce supply shocks of their own in EA members.

In the final analysis, a major asymmetric shock may result in unbearable pressure in the CC because of limited labor mobility and other internal rigidities. In short, CC may face the same problem (but in a magnified form) that Ireland faced during 1999 and 2000 when it experienced very high growth and inflation rates, thus requiring a tighter monetary policy than the European Central Bank (ECB) pursued because Germany, Italy, and most other EA countries were stagnating. In such a case, the need to pursue a strongly contractionary fiscal policy to contain inflationary pressures will slow down the growth and convergence of CC to the standard of living of the rest of the EU and EA.

2.3   Dollarization in the Americas

In the Americas, there is no plan for the joint establishment of a common currency, as in the case of Europe—at least for the foreseeable future. Therefore, the only choice open to Latin American countries wanting a common currency is unilateral dollarization. This would bring major benefits, but also some significant costs to the countries adopting the dollar as their currency, and it also presents some major differences from CC becoming part of the EA.

2.3.1   The benefits of dollarization

Besides the Commonwealth of Puerto Rico and the U.S. Virgin Islands in the Americas, Panama has had full or official dollarization since 1904. Ecuador fully dollarized in 2000 and El Salvador in 2001. Since 2001, Guatemala has been nearly fully dollarized. Several other Latin American countries are also strongly considering full dollarization. Many business people in Mexico, Canada, and even Brazil are advocating full dollarization of the entire American continent. Argentina, on the other hand, had a currency board (or nearly one) from 1991 until the end of 2001, when it collapsed in the face of a deep economic crisis. Under a currency board, the national currency circulated alongside the dollar, but the national central bank relinquished control over the nation's money supply and its ability to conduct an independent monetary policy. By retaining its own currency alongside the dollar, however, the currency board still left Argentina vulnerable to exchange rate and financial crises arising out of fear of devaluation of the national currency *vis-à-vis* the dollar. The currency risk forced the nation to pay a significant interest-rate premium on its international borrowing. This was the reason that Argentina began to consider full or official dollarization in early 1999 when it came under heavy pressure from Brazil's (its major economic partner in and dominant economic power in Mercosur) sharp devaluation. With the financial crisis actually deteriorating in fall 2001, Argentina again faced the choice of either devaluing the peso or full dollarization. In January 2002, Argentina devalued and then let the peso float more or less freely against the dollar. By April 2002, the peso has depreciated to more than 3.0 pesos per dollar.

The benefits and costs that a country faces by dollarizing are similar to those of euroization (Salvatore 2003). (*a*) The nation avoids the cost of exchanging the domestic currency for dollars and the need to hedge foreign exchange risks. (*b*) The nation will face a rate of inflation similar to that of the United States as a result of commodity arbitrage, and interest rates tend to fall to the U.S. level, except for any remaining country risk (i.e. political factors that affect security and property rights in the nation). That is, dollarization removes the currency but not the country risk, but this can still be very beneficial to the nation and may even lead to a reduction in the country risk. For example, fully dollarized Panama had a much lower interest rate than Argentina (which had a currency board) and still lower than Brazil (the least dollarized of the three countries). (*c*) By eliminating foreign exchange crises, dollarization reduces or eliminates the need for foreign exchange and trade controls, fosters budgetary discipline, and encourages more rapid and full international financial integration. It has been estimated that Argentina's growth during the past decade would have been 2 percentage points higher with dollarization than without it (Joint Economic Committee of the U.S. Senate 2000). Furthermore, since the collapse of the Bretton Woods System, only Panama (a fully dollarized country) among all developing countries did not have a single year with inflation exceeding 20 percent, and only Panama never imposed any restriction on the purchase or sale of dollars in the nation.

Dollarization also imposes some costs on the country. These are

1. The dollarizing country will have to sustain the cost of replacing the domestic currency with the dollar, which has been estimated to be about 4–5 percent of GDP for the average Latin American country. Alternatively, the (flow) cost of dollarization is the loss of interest on the central bank's holdings of foreign bonds or other interest-earning assets, which has been estimated to range between 0.5 percent of GDP per year for Argentina to 1.3 percent of GDP per year for Brazil (Joint Economic Committee of the U.S. Senate 2000).

2. A dollarized country loses independence of monetary and exchange rate policies. The country will face the same monetary policy of the United States, regardless of its cyclical situation. A dollarized country, however, is likely to be closely integrated with the United States and become more synchronized with the U.S. business cycle over time (and thus have less need for an independent monetary and exchange rate policy). In a world of large capital flows and integrated capital markets, the effectiveness of an independent monetary policy by a small open economy is, in any event, very limited—unless the nation restricts international capital flows, which could seriously dampen its growth. Similarly, a dollarized nation loses the ability to correct a balance of trade deficit or deal with an oil shock by devaluing or allowing its currency to depreciate because of the high inflation that usually results from devaluation nullifies its effectiveness. Thus, the real cost of giving up an independent monetary or exchange rate policy on the part of a dollarizing country is, for the most part, rather small. Bluntly, a "real" economic shock usually requires real economic adjustment and pain, which an exchange rate change can only temporarily soften rather than eliminate.

3. Finally, by dollarizing, a country loses its central bank as a lender of last resort to bail out domestic banks and other financial institutions in a crisis. However, the lender-of-last-resort capability of an emerging-market central bank is largely illusory without inordinately large international reserves, which are beyond the reach of most emerging market economies. Furthermore, nothing prevents a dollarizing country from setting aside liquid funds to lend to domestic banks in a crisis and/or arranging lines of credit with foreign banks (as Argentina did in the late 1990s), or for foreign banks to provide credit to domestic banks (as they did in Panama). A system-wide banking problem is also less likely to occur in a fully dollarized country that is moving toward international financial integration. Of course, dollarization cannot solve the problem of a country living beyond its means and facing an unsustainable budget deficit or debt burden. A good example of this was Argentina in fall 2001. Dollarization does, however, expose the problem sooner and impose a discipline that a non-dollarized country does not face.

2.3.2   Good candidates for dollarization in Latin America

Good candidates for dollarization are small open economies for which the United States is the dominant economic partner and which have a history of poor monetary performance, and hence very little economic-policy credibility (see Gaetano Antinolfi and Todd Keister 2001; and Guillermo Calvo 2001). Most of the small countries of Latin America, especially those in Central America as well as the Caribbean nations fit this description very well. In fact, Panama, Ecuador, El Salvador, and Guatemala are now more or less fully dollarized. Honduras, Nicaragua, and Costa Rica are seriously considering it. Once we move from small to large countries, however, it becomes more difficult to come up with clear-cut answers.

Argentina has had a currency board since 1991 and this operated reasonably well until 1999 when Brazil was forced first to devalue the real and then allowed it to sharply depreciate. With the peso rigidly tied to the dollar, Argentina suffered a huge loss of international competitiveness *vis-à-vis* Brazil (its largest trade partner) and plunged into recession. Besides having had a grossly overvalued currency, Argentina also had an out-of-control budget deficit and these conditions resulted in a serious economic and financial crisis in fall 2001. Tightening up its public finances in order to encourage foreign investments only deepened the recession and led to riots in the streets without succeeding in attracting many more foreign investors because of their fear that Argentina would abandon its currency board and devalue the peso. This left Argentina only two choices: Devaluing the peso or fully dollarizing. Abandoning its currency board and devaluing the peso, however, could return Argentina to the hyperinflation of the late 1980s and so Argentina was very reluctant to take that road. Dollarization was not without risks either. Specifically, while it would eliminate the foreign exchange risk and very likely attract more foreign investment inflows, dollarization would not eliminate Argentina's international competitiveness problem, especially with respect to Brazil, nor would it solve Argentina's budget problems. As it was, Argentina was forced to essentially abandon its currency board and, first, to devalue the peso and then letting it float.

The ideal situation for Argentina would have been if Brazil also dollarized, but this, for a country such as Brazil that considers itself to be the leader of South America, seems to be entirely out of the question in the near future. It is inconceivable that Brazil would give up its central bank and its currency without having a strong say in the conduct of the dollar-area monetary policy—something that the United States is clearly not about to grant. And a monetary policy à la EU is not even being considered in the Americas. In any event, it makes little economic sense for Brazil to dollarize in view of its very different economic structure with respect to the United States.

One way to resolve its international competitiveness problem would be for Argentina to tie the peso to the Brazilian real. Adopting Brazil's currency, however, would expose Argentina to many of the serious monetary and financial problems that Brazil faces. The best decision for Argentina, therefore, seems to be full dollarization. The elimination of the foreign exchange risk (that financial markets believed to exist because of the possibility that Argentina would abandon its currency board) would lead to lower interest rates and could attract enough foreign capital to overcome the recession, improve Argentina's international competitiveness and stimulate its growth. The United States, for its part, could have facilitated the official dollarization of Argentina by sharing its seignorage with Argentina (as it is done in the EA) from the use of the dollar in Argentina. Of course, Argentina would also want access for its banks to the discount window at the Federal Reserve System in time of crisis, cooperation on banking supervision, and possibly a seat at the Federal Reserve Board—things that the United States (as indicated above) was not going to provide.

The optimal or first best situation, of course, would be if Argentina were able to manage its own economy efficiently and with discipline. Short of this, however, full dollarization seems to be the only way out of the difficult predicament in which the nation has found itself since the fall of 2001. It is true that dollarization would not solve Argentina's debt and budget problems, but it would force it to deal with those problems quickly and forcefully—no matter how painful.

Ecuador dollarized unilaterally in January 2001 in the midst of a political and economic crisis precipitated by Brazil's devaluation of the real, and without any assistance from the United States—not even seignorage sharing, and so did El Salvador at the beginning of 2001 (from a non-crisis situation). El Salvador, however, with the support of the U.S. Treasury and the World Bank will probably be able to negotiate with the IMF a stand-by agreement to provide it funds in case of a crisis, thus essentially replacing its central bank as a lender of last resort.

More sensible and feasible than in Brazil would also be the dollarization of Mexico, which is more integrated with the U.S. economy and faces less (but by no means insignificant) political problems in dollarizing than Brazil. With its economy much more integrated with the U.S. economy than Mexico's, Canada would seem to be an even better candidate for dollarization than Mexico. But Canada is doing very well economically and it does not seem interested in switching to the U.S. dollar.

2.3.3   Differences between joining the euro area and dollarization

There are some basic differences between joining the EA as the CC are eagerly waiting to do and unilateral dollarization in the Americas (the only choice now open in the Americas for countries that would like to have a common currency). Although the topic is being discussed, Canada regards dollarization as neither necessary nor desirable. Pursuing this matter further, we then need to ask why is Canada doing so well economically without dollarization? The answer is clear. It is because Canada is highly integrated both financially and economically in the global economy and pursues sound economic policies. If Mexico could become as highly integrated in the world economy and if it were able to follow as sound economic policies as Canada, then dollarization would make much less sense for Mexico also. In general, dollarization would make sense for Mexico if it would (a) speed up Mexico's integration into the world economy, (b) encourage Mexico to follow better economic policies, and (c) if, in the final analysis, it would significantly stimulate economic growth. But clearly, these are questions, not answers.

When the question is then asked as to why North America or all of the Americas should not have a common currency (the dollar) if Europe does, the answer is that Europe created ECB and all participating nations, no matter how small, have a voice in the making of the common monetary policy. The members of the EA share a common currency; they do not adopt some other country's currency (which would be the case in unilateral dollarization). Members of the EA share in the seignorage from the euro and their aims are full monetary, economic, and political integration. None of these things is true for the Americas or even for North America. Thus, aside from the small open economies of Central America, the case for dollarization from North America or for all of the Americas can only be justified with traditional optimum currency area analysis, as supplemented or superseded by other financial sector developmental issues (Richard Harris 2002; George von Furstenberg 2002), or from the economic discipline that it would impose on a country that is unable to effectively and efficiently manage its economy.

Since the United States is not ready to open its borders (particularly its southern border) to migrants and establish a common central bank, the American continent is not ready for a common currency, not even North America. Besides, the Constitution of the United States (Article I, Section 8) assigns the power to coin money and to regulate the value of money to the U.S. Congress, and so it would be unconstitutional for any other nation to share the power to issue dollars and regulate its value with the U.S. Congress. To be sure, the "Ryan" Bill HR2617 introduced by Representative Ryan in the U.S. House of Representatives on July 24, 2001 to promote international monetary stability calls for the sharing of seignorage with officially dollarizing countries. In any event, monetary union and a common currency are not even being considered for NAFTA at this point in time (see Michael Chriszt 2000). Thus, Canada, Mexico, Argentina, and other countries in the American continent must individually decide whether full unilateral dollarization makes economic and political sense for them. For Argentina and Mexico it may, for Canada and Brazil it may not.

2.4 Euroization, Dollarization, and the International Monetary System

With most trade and financial relations conducted within, rather than among, the three major trading blocks (the EU, NAFTA, and Asia centered on Japan), there will normally be less concern about the euro/dollar and euro/yen exchange rates. Hence it has been expected (Willem Buiter 2000) that these exchange rates would be very volatile, especially when the three blocks face different cyclical conditions and shifting market perceptions about economic and financial prospects. In fact, however, neither of these exchange rates has been particularly volatile during 1999–2001 relative to the prior record for the exchange value of the ECU with the dollar and the yen. Large exchange rate volatility, by adding to transaction costs, would affect the volume and pattern of international trade. These costs, however, are usually not very large and firms engaged in international trade and finance can easily and cheaply cover them. Potentially more damaging to the smooth functioning of the international monetary system are the wide and persistent exchange rate misalignments that can arise among the world's three leading currencies. An overvalued currency has the effect of an export tax and an import subsidy on the nation and, as such, it reduces the international competitiveness of the nation or trading block and distorts the pattern of specialization, trade, and payments. A significant exchange rate misalignment that persists for years cannot possibly be hedged away and can impose significant real costs on the economy in the form of unemployment, idle capacity, and bankruptcy, and these may lead to serious protectionism and trade disputes. This is exactly what happened when the U.S. dollar became grossly overvalued in the first half of the 1980s.

The only way to limit excessive exchange rate misalignment among the euro, the dollar and the yen is by greater macroeconomic policy coordination among the three major trading blocks than has hereto been possible. Successful international policy coordination did prevent the financial crises in emerging markets (Mexico in 1994–95, East Asia 1997–99, Russia in summer 1998, Brazil in early 1999, and Argentina and Turkey in 2000–01) from spreading or having a lasting damaging effect on other emerging markets and on advanced market economies. But policy coordination among the United States, the euro area and Japan has only been limited and sporadic rather than extensive and continuous in the past, and it is unlikely that it will be much greater in the near future.

To be sure, by reducing the number of key currencies, the euro simplifies international cooperation among the major economic areas and makes the process of exchanging information and views more efficient. This will be even more so if and when the British pound becomes part of the euro. The creation of the euro also limits the ability of the United States to impose its will in international financial matters. This will ultimately benefit the United States by forcing it to keep its house in order and be more disciplined.

2.5   Conclusions

The deregulation of domestic financial markets and the liberalization and huge increases in international capital flows during the past decade has sharply reduced the effectiveness of monetary policy, especially in small open economies. This, together with the potential benefits of euroization or dollarization, has led many small countries in Europe to seek admission into the EU and the EA, and many Latin American countries to dollarize or to consider dollarization unilaterally (since there are no prospects of establishing a common currency in the Americas other than adopting the dollar). There are many major benefits that a country would receive from joining the EA, but there are also some significant costs, the most important of which is how to deal with asymmetrical shocks, which these countries will surely face upon joining. There is also disagreement as to the best exchange rates arrangements for these nations prior to admission.

Unilateral dollarization is expected to confer to Latin American countries benefits similar to those received by European countries joining the EA, with one major difference—the dollarizing countries do not share a common currency but adopt another nation's currency, have no say in the conduct of monetary policy, and do not share in seignorage. Good candidates for dollarization are small open economies for which the United States is the dominant economic partner and which have a history of poor monetary performance and hence very little economic-policy credibility. For other countries, such as Canada and Brazil, dollarization may not make much economic sense. For Mexico, dollarization makes sense if it would lead to more rapid integration into the world economy and much faster economic growth. For Argentina, dollarization is a second-best solution if the nation is unable (as it now seems) to put its economic, fiscal, and monetary house in order.

REFERENCES

Antinolfi, G. and Keister, T. (2001). "Dollarization as a Monetary Arrangement for Emerging Markets." *Federal Reserve Bank of St. Louis Review*, 83 (November/ December): 29–40.

Bank for International Settlements (cited as BIS) (1994). *Macroeconomic and Monetary Policy Issues Raised by the Growth of Derivatives Markets.* Basle: BIS.

Buiter, W. H. (2000). "Optimal Currency Areas: Why does the Exchange Rate Regime Matter?" *CEPR Discussion Paper* No. 2366, January.

Calvo, G. A. (2001). "Capital Markets and the Exchange Rate, with Special Reference to the Dollarization Debate in Latin America." *Journal of Money, Credit, and Banking*, 23 (May): 312–34.

Capie, F. and Wood, G. E. (eds.) (1994). *Monetary Economics in the 1990s.* New York: St Martin.

— Goodhart, C., and Fisher, S. (1996). *The Future of Central Banking.* Cambridge: Cambridge University Press.

Chriszt, M. (2000). "Perspectives on a Potential North American Monetary Union." *Federal Reserve of Atlanta Economic Review*, 85 (November/December): 29–38.

Harris, R. D. (2002). "Foreign Direct Investment and Optimal Currency Areas." Draft, Simon Fraser University, March.

International Monetary Fund (cited as IMF) (1994). "Exchange Rate Regimes in an Increasingly Integrated World Economy." *Occasional Paper 195*, ch. 4.

— (2002). *International Financial Statistics.* Washington, DC, March.

Joint Economic Committee of the U.S. Senate (2000). "Basics of Dollarization." Washington, DC: U.S. Senate.

Salvatore, D. (1997). "The Unresolved Problem with the EMS and EMU." *American Economic Review*, 87 (May): 224–6.

— (2001). "The Problems of Transition, EU Enlargement, and Globalization." *Empirica*, 15 (July): 1–21.

— (2002a). "The Euro: Expectations and Performance." *Eastern Economic Journal*, 28 (Winter): 121–36.

— (2002b). "The Euro, the European Central Bank, and the International Monetary System." *The Annals of the American Academy of Political and Social Science*, 579 (January): 153–67.

Salvatore, D. (2003). "Which Countries in the Americas should Dollarize?" In D. Salvatore, J. Dean, and T. Willett (eds.), *The Dollarization Debate.* New York: Oxford University Press, pp. 196–205.

von Furstenberg, G. M. (2002). "One Region, One Money: Implications of Regional Currency Consolidation for Financial Services." *The Geneva Papers on Risk & Insurance,* 27 (January): 5–28.

3

Unilateral and Multilateral Currency Unions: Thoughts from an EMU Perspective

IGNAZIO ANGELONI

I discuss the distinction between unilateral and multilateral currency unions taking the experience of European Monetary Union (EMU) as a basis. Unilateral currency union is the adoption by a country of the money of another, without consent or agreement. Multilateral union happens when two or more countries decide to adopt a new common currency, setting up the necessary institutions jointly. Six aspects are considered: Macroeconomic stability, seignorage distribution, last-resort lending, fiscal implications, central bank structures, and resilience to stress. From all these viewpoints, multilateral unions are shown to have important advantages. I conclude that, when feasible, multilateral unions are worth their extra institutional complexity.

3.1 Introduction

For those in Europe, like myself, interested in monetary arrangements and in monetary policymaking, the last few years have been very exciting. The long road leading to the single European currency has just been concluded: With the introduction of euro notes and coins, twelve European countries have made their long-standing project of monetary unification a full reality. But this is not the end of the process. The future accession of new countries in the European Union, and at a later stage in the euro area, calls for further consolidation and reform of EMU's monetary arrangements. And quite aside from this, the process of building and maintaining the European Central Bank's (ECB's) reputation, based on good performance, never ends. No doubt, many challenges are ahead of us.

This text has much benefited from the contribution of Carsten Detken. I also received useful comments from V. Gaspar, P. van der Haegen, G. Pineau, and F. Mazzaferro. The views expressed here are my own, and do not involve the European Central Bank.

3.2 Unilateral and Multilateral Currency Unions: Elements for a Comparison

The post-war history was a rich laboratory in monetary institution making. In the 1990s the political transformations following the end of the cold war accelerated the pace of monetary innovation. Partly conflicting trends have emerged. At first, the number of sovereign countries in the world has increased, and with it the number of distinct currencies. More recently, an opposite tendency may have emerged with the number of moneys beginning to fall again. The fact is that the historical link between sovereign power and the printing press is weakening, not only because of central bank independence, but also because many countries decide, for one reason or another, to forgo their right to create and use a currency of their own. Recent research has provided very interesting explanations for this phenomenon (see Alesina and Barro 2001). My aim here is more limited: It is not to discuss *why* countries decide to adopt a currency different from the national one, but *how* such adoption takes place. More precisely, my focus is on the distinctions between "unilateral" and "multilateral" types of monetary unions (U-CU and M-CU). The EMU experience is crucial in this respect, since EMU is the most prominent example of M-CU, both in history and today.[1]

I start with some definitions. By U-CU, I mean simply the adoption by a country of the money of another, without this implying any common consent or agreement on the adoption, or the modalities by which it occurs. U-CU can be "official," if it results from government policy, or "de facto," if it happens spontaneously. Unilateral unions are often referred to as "dollarizations," but in fact the existing experiences involve the US dollar only in half of the cases. There are today in the world thirty-two countries that have implemented a U-CU (this is about 15 percent of the number of sovereign nations) of which sixteen have adopted the U.S. dollar. The total population of the thirty-two countries amounts to little over 50 million, less than 1 percent of the world population. These numbers suggest that U-CU is an option chosen, on average, by very small countries.[2]

By multilateral currency union (M-CU) I mean instead the situation arising when two or more countries decide together to adopt a common currency, different from any of the existing ones, to set up the necessary monetary institutions and make monetary policy decisions by way of a common and consensual agreement. As I mentioned, EMU is the main example, though there are other instances.[3]

---

[1] Historical monetary unions include the monetary union of colonial New England, the Latin Monetary Union, the Scandinavian Monetary Union and the East African Currency Area. See, for example, Buiter and Grafe (2002).

[2] I am grateful to F. Mazzaferro, C. Nerlich, C. Thimann, and A. Winkler for providing this data.

[3] The Eastern Caribbean Currency Union and the West African Currency Union also possess certain multilateral features. Their currencies maintain fixed exchange rates, respectively with the U.S. dollar and the euro. EMU is the only case where the common central bank conducts a fully autonomous monetary policy.

Among the many angles from which the benefits and disadvantages of U-CU and M-CU can be compared, I will focus on six:

1. *Macroeconomic stability* Macroeconomic stability (e.g. of price level and output) is a key purpose of monetary management. In our context the key question is: How do U-CU and M-CU fare in terms of allowing (or impeding) macro-stabilization, for all countries that participate in the union?
2. *Distribution of seignorage* How do the two forms of union compare in this respect?
3. *Provision of lending of last resort (LLR)* Do the two forms of union leave space for this key central banking function, and how?
4. *Fiscal implications* In principle, the adoption of a particular form of CU should have little or no implications for fiscal behavior (except for the extent of monetary financing). In practice this is not the case, as we shall see. What are the fiscal implications of the two forms of union?
5. *Preservation of the central bank operational functions* The importance of this aspect is rarely recognized by academic research. The central bank's contact with the financial markets is a "public good" with potential positive spillovers in various areas of policymaking. The contact with banks and financial institutions provides a wealth of information relevant to monitor economic developments and financial stability. How do U-CU and M-CU compare in this respect?
6. *Resilience to stress* This is the key consideration that to some extent overlaps with all the others. How do U-CU and M-CU compare as to their ability to withstand tensions and fend off centrifugal forces?

3.3 The Architecture of EMU

I now wish to briefly describe how EMU functions as a M-CU. I shall do so by briefly explaining how EMU faces the six challenges I have just enumerated.

Macro-stability From the viewpoint of its decision-making procedures and monetary policy strategy, EMU is completely symmetric. Monetary policy decisions are taken by the Governing Council, made up of six Executive Board members and twelve National Central Bank (NCB) governors.[4] Each Council member has one vote, votes in a personal capacity and is bound by the Treaty to an aggregate, area-wide monetary policy objective. National governors do not represent their own country when they sit in the Council.

The primary objective of the ECB is to maintain price stability in the euro area. The Council itself has chosen, at the start, to define price stability as an *increase*

---

[4] The modality of appointment of Council members differs: The six Executive Board members are appointed through a European procedure, while the NCB governors are national appointees.

(i.e. *positive* change) in the (cross-country harmonized, area-wide) index of consumer prices of below 2 percent. This goal is to be achieved over the medium term, which means that temporary and limited deviations from this benchmark are tolerated.[5] The relevant consumer price index is calculated as a consumption-weighted average of national indices. Hence, in this way—and not by giving unequal voting weights in the Council and asking its members to represent their countries—the different sizes of national economies *are actually* reflected in the ECB policy. The presence of national governors in the ECB's decision-making body ensures that the necessary expertise and information are available when decisions are made.

The symmetry in the ECB's monetary policy strategy is strengthened in a number of other ways. All analyses and indicators provided to Council members focus on the euro area as a whole, except when national, regional, or sectoral information is indirectly relevant for area-wide developments. A notable example is given by the money supply (quantified mainly by a broad aggregate of monetary assets, M3) which plays a prominent role in the ECB strategy. M3 is defined in area-wide terms. The "reference value" for its annual expansion (i.e. the benchmark rate of growth, any deviations against which are regarded as prima facie indication of potential inflationary or deflationary pressures) is also area-wide, as are the models used to calculate it.

In short EMU's symmetric decision-making implies a corresponding symmetry in the way in which monetary policy reacts to stress and performs its stabilizing function. Each EMU member can count on a "quantum" of monetary stabilization that corresponds to its weight in the euro area economy.

Seignorage distribution   Seignorage income in EMU is pooled and allocated to the participating NCBs in accordance with their respective paid-up shares in the ECB's capital. The allocation ensures that the relative income positions of NCBs are not affected in the future by shifts in banknote circulation. In a transitional period, up to 2007, the initial differences in national seignorage revenues with respect to the ECB's capital key (due mainly to different shares of currency in circulation, both inside and outside the euro area) will be phased out. Hence, the arrangement concerning seignorage reflects the symmetry and the multilateral nature of the underlying agreements, and ultimately of the EU Treaty.

Emergency liquidity assistance   EMU has been criticized for lacking a lender of last resort function, or more broadly a financial stability framework. This criticism is unfounded. The LLR function in EMU rests with the national central banks, acting under well-established and agreed guidelines. Decentralized LLR is consistent, from an incentive viewpoint, with the fact that banking supervision is provided nationally. In turn, this reflects the fact that any costs of financial

---

[5] The medium-term orientation acknowledges that short-term volatility in prices cannot (and should not, lest imparting undue volatility to key economic variables) be controlled by the central bank (Issing et al. 2001).

rescues, which are ultimately fiscal, fall onto the national taxpayer, not the European one.

Decentralization of LLR does not imply lack of coordination, let alone confusion of roles. A number of aspects deserve mention. Procedures have been agreed both to secure the necessary flow of information within the system, and to prevent that liquidity autonomously provided by NCBs in the context of their LLR function interferes with the desired monetary policy stance. The flow of information among national supervisory authorities and with the ECB takes place mainly via the European System of Central Banks (ESCBs) Banking Supervision Committee, which includes both central banks and non-central-bank supervisors.

The current decentralized setting of prudential supervision and last-resort assistance within EMU must be assessed against the fact that, up to now, the large majority of European banks still rely on their domestic, national customer basis, so that cross-border externalities are limited (though obviously not absent, given the interbank linkages). In 1999, about 90 percent of deposits and loans to the non-bank private sector were domestic (although growth rates of cross-border loans have recently been more than twice as large as for domestic loans). With European financial integration proceeding, different solutions might become necessary in the future.

The fiscal angle   From the start, the fiscal framework has been recognized as a key component of the EMU architecture, necessary to support the viability of the single currency. Fiscal criteria were adopted as precondition for all countries adopting the euro. After that, the Stability and Growth Pact (SGP) is the instrument providing the minimum necessary coordination for fiscal and budget policies that otherwise remain a fully national responsibility. The SGP[6] requires member states not to exceed a general government deficit to GDP ratio of 3 percent and to keep the public debt below 60 percent of GDP. Exceptions to the 3 percent ceiling can be granted in severe recession, while violations are subject to sanctions. Budgetary positions must remain close to balance or in surplus in the medium run. The aim of these provisions is to leave room for automatic stabilizers to operate during economic downturns, while at the same time preserving longer-term fiscal sustainability. National governments submit to common scrutiny of their annual stability or convergence programs, specifying the planned future fiscal policy. The European Commission has the responsibility to administer this surveillance process and to initiate, when necessary, its procedures for scrutiny and sanction.

Is this system working? If one looks at the conditions in which public finances were in many European countries only a few years back, and those in which they are now, the unavoidable conclusion is that it is. Obviously, all multilateral

---

[6] SGP is intended to include here both the fiscal provisions in the Treaty and the successive clarifications and regulations in the same area provided by the European Council and by the Council of Ministers.

agreements constraining individual behavior are subject to occasional tensions or imperfections, and the SGP is no exception. But even in the recent (and much discussed) circumstances where the ECOFIN council has decided not to bring forward the procedure against certain countries, the peer pressure built into the EMU fiscal framework has worked. The countries concerned have made commitments and taken actions that they probably would not have otherwise.

Retaining the operational functions of central banks   Within the ESCB, NCBs keep on playing an important operational role, under ECB coordination. NCBs provide supporting and back-office functions for all open market operations, and maintain their contact with the financial markets. NCBs not only participate in the conduct of monetary policy but are also part of the monitoring and information gathering process that gravitates around the meetings of the Governing Council. Last and not least, NCBs run the national components of the area-wide payment system—the so-called TARGET—which has been especially developed to support interbank transactions in euro.

Resilience to stress   The short history of EMU, the evolutionary nature of some of its institutions and the imponderability of future events—the next stress is always different from the previous ones—strongly discourages making overly strong predictions. I can make three observations. First, EMU brings together a group of relatively homogeneous and well-diversified economies, with broadly similar monetary transmission mechanisms,[7] commercially and financially integrated, for which the occurrence of strong and asymmetric economic stress, on the demand or the supply side, should not be regarded as likely. Second, all these economies have reached monetary unification after a long process of convergence and preparation, during which regulatory institutions, market structures, and public opinion have had time to adapt and prepare. Disruptive "political" stress, though not impossible, is likewise unlikely. Third, the symmetric nature of decision making in EMU, where each participant forgoes part of its national sovereignty in exchange for a corresponding portion of area-wide sovereignty, with clearly established consensual rules of constitutional form, should provide an element of resilience in coping with stress, economic and political. Against any potential centrifugal forces that one can conceive today, the built-in incentives should induce each of the participants to remain in the game and play by the rules of the game, lest it lose much of its acquired "capital" of participation and influence. I add that, in my view, cohesion is likely to increase over time, alongside with experience in working with the new institutions and as a consequence of their success. This has been the case so far during the last three years.

3.4   Unilateral and Multilateral Unions: What are the Differences?

On this subject, I will offer only a few selected remarks that start directly from my reading of the EMU experience.

---

[7] Angeloni et al. (2002).

The stabilizing role of monetary policy A central difference between U- and M-CU consists in the scope for monetary stabilization policy. In a unilateral union, monetary policy is automatically geared to smooth only the stress hitting the anchor economy. The "anchored" (or "dollarized") economy is a passive partner. On the contrary, in EMU the stabilization role may be limited, but can still be provided to an extent proportional to the weight of the domestic economy in the union. The stabilization role of monetary policy may well be overrated, as argued by Calvo and Reinhart in a recent paper.[8] But if it has some value, in some circumstances, the "anchored" country is likely to be better off in a M- as opposed to a U-CU. Even if such a role is restricted mainly to providing a stable medium-term nominal framework (as is the case of the ECB strategy), it should help each participating country if the characteristics of such a framework reflect features and preferences of all participants in the union rather than only one of them. This points to a weakness, economic and political, of U-CU relative to M-CU.

Seignorage In a unilateral union, seignorage exclusively accrues to the anchor country, except when explicit agreements provide for some redistribution (in which case the U-CU would not be entirely unilateral).[9] The loss of seignorage for the "anchored" country's taxpayer can be substantial.[10] In EMU seignorage revenues are pooled and shared, as already noted, though their importance tends to be negligible in quantitative terms.[11] The difference between the two systems gains importance in countries where the tax system is relatively inefficient, so that seignorage constitutes a significant source of government revenue.

Lender of last resort function In a unilateral union, the ability of the central bank to provide emergency liquidity assistance is restricted to its availability of foreign exchange reserves.[12] Since in most cases the "anchored" country would not choose to keep a large amount of reserves, this would amount to a diminished ability to perform LLR. The loss of the LLR function in unilateral unions can create problems particularly in cases where the process is accompanied by large

---

[8] However, as long as the monetary policy authority can avoid the inflation-bias problem by commitment, the loss of domestic monetary policy remains a true loss; Alesina and Barro (2001).

[9] The only existing example where seignorage is actually shared in a unilateral union is between Lesotho, Namibia, and South Africa. In mid-2000 a bill was discussed in the U.S. Senate envisaging such cooperation with dollarized countries, triggered by the prospect that Argentina would dollarize.

[10] Such costs include both an initial one-off cost arising from replacing the national currency in circulation with foreign bank notes and coins, and the recurring loss due to the lack of future earnings derived from issuing new money. Estimates (probably on the high side) for some Latin American countries during the first half of the 1990s averaged 4.5 percent of GDP for the former and 2.3 percent of GDP for the latter cost. See Bogetic (1999).

[11] This is due both to the low level of inflation and monetary base, and to the fact that a large part of the latter (bank reserves) are remunerated at market rates.

[12] As argued by Guillermo Calvo, official borrowing could substitute for official reserves for LLR purpose. I think substitution could never be perfect, however. Borrowing conditions could worsen in times of stress, and borrowing itself could in such circumstances convey negative signals to the market. See also Calvo and Reinhart (2002).

capital inflows and monetary relaxation, which would lead to excessive lending by the domestic banking system.

Fiscal incentives   When moving from a currency peg or currency board to a monetary union, the constraint on fiscal policy is likely, in the short run, to be alleviated. This might generate incentives to use fiscal discretion more actively.[13] At first sight, this incentive should work similarly in a unilateral and a multilateral monetary union. In practice though, recognizing the existence of externalities, a multilateral union is more likely to establish an institutional framework guarding against this risk, as the EMU experience shows. In unilateral unions, developing such framework may be politically more difficult.

Central bank functions   In a unilateral monetary union, there is little incentive for the "anchored" country to maintain, or establish, a well functioning central banking operational capability. A central bank stripped of its basic functions and responsibilities might lose (or never develop) the necessary know-how of how to interact with markets. This may be detrimental for the functioning of domestic financial markets,[14] and create an unequal playing field for the domestic banks. There may also be a loss of policy-relevant information. In EMU, where all NCBs continue to operate (under coordination by the ECB), these risks are reduced.

Resilience to stress   All these elements combined suggest, in my view, that U-CUs should be inherently more fragile relative to well-designed M-CUs. Their asymmetric nature exposes them to the risk of loss of political support. The costs of re-introducing a domestic currency in a formerly dollarized country, perhaps by a nationalistic-oriented political leadership, do not seem insurmountable.[15] As I have argued, cohesion should naturally be larger in a multilateral union, where the costs and benefits from participation are more symmetric and balanced.

3.5   Conclusions

Multilateral currency unions, such as EMU, undoubtedly entail a large degree of institutional complexity and require international political consensus. In exchange for that, they provide a number of safeguards that are likely to result in more cohesion and better monetary and fiscal management.

By contrast, a country entering a U-CU abandons the stabilization role of monetary policy, receives no seignorage, essentially forgoes its lender of last resort function, is less protected against wrong fiscal incentives, and risks losing its central bank know-how. Hence, it is likely to be more exposed to a variety of stress, first of all an erosion of political support.

[13] Fiscal policy may even become more effective when the threat of monetizing government debt is alleviated; see Detken (1999).

[14] This is the reason why some countries adopting currency boards (such as Hong Kong and Argentina) have tried to preserve certain central bank operational functions; see Mihalke (1997).

[15] This argument is made convincingly by Buiter and Grafe (2002).

I am obviously not concluding that multilateral solutions can fit or are possible in all circumstances. In many real world cases, the conditions for such solution simply do not exist—normally when there is a large imbalance among the participants, either in terms of size, credibility, or political influence. But *when they do exist*, the extra institutional effort is likely to pay for itself.

REFERENCES

Alesina, A. and Barro, R. (2001). "Dollarization." *American Economic Review*, 91 (May): 381–5.

Angeloni, I., Kashyap, A., Mojon, B., and Terlizzese, D. (2002). "Monetary Transmission in the Euro Area: Where do We Stand?" *ECB Working Paper* No. 114.

Bogetic, Z. (1999). "Official or Full Dollarization: Current Experiences and Issues." draft.

Buiter, W. and Grafe, C. (2002). "Anchor, Float, or Abandon Ship: Exchange Rate Regimes for the Accession Countries." *Banca Nazionale del Lavoro Quarterly Review*, 55 (June) 111–42.

Calvo, G. and Reinhart, C. (2002). "Fear of Floating." *Quarterly Journal of Economics*, 117(2): 379–408.

Detken, C. (1999). "Fiscal Policy Effectiveness and Neutrality Results in a Non-Ricardian World." *ECB Working Paper* No. 3.

European Central Bank (2001). "Decisions on the Issue of Euro Banknotes and on the Allocation of Monetary Income." Press release.

Issing, O., Gaspar, V., Angeloni, I., and Tristani, O. (2001). *Monetary Policy in the Euro-Area, Strategy and Decision-Making at the European Central Bank*. Cambridge: Cambridge University Press.

Mihalke, D. (1997). "Currency Board Arrangements: Issues and Experiences." *Occasional Paper 151*, Washington, DC: International Monetary Fund.

4

International Money and Common Currencies in Historical Perspective

GERALD P. DWYER, JR. AND JAMES R. LOTHIAN

We review the history of international monies and the theory related to their adoption and use. There are four key characteristics of these currencies: High unitary value, relatively low inflation rates for long periods, issuance by major economic and trading powers, and spontaneous, as opposed to planned, adoption internationally. The economic theory of the demand for money provides support for the importance of these characteristics. The value of a unit is arbitrary for a fiat money, but the other characteristics are likely to be important for determining any fiat money that will be the international money in the future. If the euro continues to exist for the next half-century or so and has a relatively stable value, we conclude that the euro is likely to be serious competition for the dollar as the international money.

4.1 Introduction

Is the euro likely to supplant the dollar as an international money? Such a question might seem premature, especially since the euro has been physically in existence only for a few years. We are inclined to think that it is not too early to start to think about this issue seriously since the implications are large for the world's monetary landscape.

The move to a circulating euro on January 1, 2002 has been followed by little or no difficulty in the twelve countries involved. By most prognostications, moreover, the future for the new currency looks very good. That was not the case at all a decade ago, as devaluations and widened currency bands shook the Exchange Rate Mechanism (ERM). Skepticism with regard to the future of a single currency abounded among both economists and financial professionals.

A major reason for this shift in opinion has, doubtless, been the change in the underlying economic environment in the countries involved, in particular the greater convergence in monetary policies that took place during the intervening period.

The purpose of this chapter is to review the historical evidence on the question of international monies. In contrast to other studies, we adopt a very broad temporal perspective, beginning with a discussion of the Byzantine gold solidus or bezant that was introduced by the Emperor Constantine and that served as a world currency for the next seven centuries. We continue with a review of medieval monetary history and the international currencies of the Italian city states.[1] We then turn to a discussion of the various international monies that have existed from the early modern period to the present.

Using this review of the historical evidence as a background, we go on to discuss the theory surrounding this issue. The underlying questions of interest are with the factors affecting the establishment of common currencies and, more important, their longevity. Here, we return to the earlier analyses of Carl Menger (1892) and a century later Friedrich A. Hayek (1978a). In both analyses, the key distinction using some terminology borrowed from Hayek (1978b [1967]) is between monetary institutions that are the result of human action but not human design and institutions that are planned and orchestrated from on high.

4.2   Historical Overview

4.2.1   The early Middle Ages

International monies, monies that circulate for use in transactions across national boundaries, begin with the silver drachma first coined in ancient Athens in the fifth century BC (Chown 1994). Judged on the basis of the hoards that have been uncovered, not just within the Mediterranean region but throughout Europe and well into Asia, the coinage of Rome—first the gold *aureus* and the silver *denarius* after the currency reforms of Augustus—became the drachma's successor.[2] Beginning with Nero (AD 54–68) and continuing into the early fourth century, currency debasement and inflation became the rule. An unsurprising effect of this continual depreciation was a decline in the acceptability of the Roman coinage outside the narrower confines of the Roman empire. The *denarius*, which had its specie content reduced entirely, ceased to function as money internationally. The *aureus* kept its fineness in terms of specie but was issued as a lighter coin and became more commodity than money, being valued by weight rather than by its face value.

After earlier attempts at reform failed, the Emperor Constantine introduced a new currency, the *solidus*. Called the *nomisma* by the Greeks and the *bezant* by Western Europeans, the *solidus* continued to be minted in Byzantium until that city fell to the crusaders in 1203, and for a while thereafter was still minted in Nicea, the new seat of the then much diminished Byzantine Empire.

The *solidus* was a relatively heavy, full-bodied gold coin meant for use in large transactions. It soon became an international currency. The Greek monk

---

[1] On these issues see Cipolla (1967) and Lothian (2002).

[2] This discussion of Roman currency draws on Einzig's (1970) monograph on exchange-rate history. As Cohen (1998) points out, there was a substantial overlap period after Rome's ascendancy in which the silver drachma continued to circulate along with the Roman coinage.

Cosmas Indicopleustes, a contemporary observer—writing during the reign of the Emperor Justinian I (AD 527–65)—reports that the *solidus* was "accepted everywhere from end to end of the earth."[3] He goes on to say that it is "admired by all men and in all kingdoms, because no kingdom has a currency that can be compared to it." The economic historian and medievalist R. S. Lopez (1951) in reviewing the *solidus'* history uses the term "Dollar of the Middle Ages" to describe it. Based on the hoards of coins that subsequent research has uncovered, he traces its sphere of influence from England to India, an area in which he claims (1951: 211) it was accepted "as an instrument of payment as good as gold itself."

The *solidus* contained the equivalent of 4.5 g of pure gold. The British gold sovereign and the ten-dollar gold U.S. Eagle by way of comparison contained roughly 8.0 and 8.8 g, respectively. Valued at current market prices the gold in the *solidus* would be worth roughly $42 and the gold in the eagle and the sovereign $73 and $68, respectively. Numismatic evidence suggests, moreover, that the *solidus'* gold content varied little from the fourth century through the mid-tenth century.

The result was an international money with an historically unparalleled life span. The *solidus* did not, however, enjoy a monopoly over this full period. From the end of the seventh century, it shared its position with the *dinar*, an almost identical coin minted in various parts of the Moslem world. Introduced in the last decade of the seventh century by Abd el Malek, the fifth caliph (AD 685–705) of the Syrian Umayyad dynasty, the *dinar* like the *solidus* kept a stable metallic content for centuries.

The fall from grace of the *solidus* and the *dinar* began at roughly the same time and for very much the same reasons. Fiscal strains led to increased money creation which for commodity monies means debasement in one or both of two forms: (*a*) a decrease in the weight of the coins and (*b*) an alteration of their relative specie content, their fineness. From the standpoint of the usefulness of the currency in trade and hence confidence in it, the first is the less harmful of the two. Coins can be valued by weight. Even without debasement, coins often become worn through use and were weighed to determine their value.

For the *solidus*, debasement by reducing the weight started in the late tenth century under the Emperors Nicephorus Phocas (963–69) and John Tzimiskes (969–76) and continued into the eleventh century. As so often has been the case, financing high levels of government expenditures was the impetus for debasing the money.[4] The death knell for the *solidus'* status as an international currency was sounded in the late eleventh century when the fineness was

---

[3] The phrase "dollar of the middle ages" is that of R. S. Lopez (1951). Both Lopez (1951: 209) and Cipolla (1967: 15–16) cite the statement by Indicopleustes. Cipolla goes on to discuss corroborative evidence reported by earlier historians of the subject.

[4] Sussman (1993) presents a sound analysis of later debasements, which illustrates the general principles and raises the right questions. Rolnick et al. (1996) present some stylized observations about debasements and Velde et al. (1999) present a simple analysis that highlights the general asymmetric information that can rationalize the profitability of debasements.

reduced. Nevertheless, a *solidus* of close to the old weight was still minted (along with inferior coins) in the early thirteenth century in Nicea following the fall of Constantinople to the Crusaders in 1203. Debasement of the *dinar* also began in the late tenth century. The explanation again appears to be largely fiscal.

4.2.2   The thirteenth-century commercial revolution and the European return to gold

Although the reach of the *solidus* extended well into Northern Europe, it was used most extensively in the Mediterranean region. Northern Europe as well as Western Europe had no counterpart to the *solidus* and was otherwise less of a money economy than either the Byzantine Empire or the Moslem nations.

That situation changed in the thirteenth century. The thirteenth century was extraordinary in a number of ways. It was a time of great learning and considerable scholarly interchange by all accounts.[5] It was the start of a European commercial revolution, the chief manifestation of which was substantially increased trade not only within Europe itself, but also between Europe and the rest of the world. It also was a time of considerable financial innovation including the return to gold coinage in Western Europe.

International trade was centered around the fairs that were held regularly throughout Europe, the fairs of Champagne being the most important. These fairs also were foreign-exchange centers. Initially the moneychangers at the fairs, who also were merchants and gave rise to the term "merchant banker," confined their activities to manual exchange, the changing of one type of coin for another. Then as bills of exchange increasingly came into use, the moneychangers increased their roles and became intermediaries in this market.

The reintroduction of a Western European gold coinage took place in 1252 with the striking of two full-bodied gold coins in Northern Italy—the *genoin* of Genoa and then a few months later the *fiorino* (or *florin*) of Florence. These two coins, but particularly the florin, were the world currencies. In the fifteenth century, however, their place was taken by the *ducato* of Venice. All three coins circulated side by side with coins of two other sorts—token coins used in small transactions and silver coins used in somewhat larger transactions.

Gresham's Law did not come into play for any of these three coins because exchange rates among the various coinages remained flexible. The data that exist for this period suggest that there was a surprisingly active market in foreign exchange. Exchange-rate data, in fact, indicate why the two coins, the *florin* and the *genoin*, were attractive and became international currencies. We can see this in Table 4.1, which lists exchange rates relative to the *florin* at fifty-year intervals for a variety of currencies.

---

[5] See Spufford (1984) on the commercial revolution and the financial developments that accompanied it. On broader cultural issues—philosophical and economic thought and university life—see Gilson (1991) and Schumpeter (1954).

Table **4.1**. *Indices of exchange rates relative to the Florentine* florin

	1252	1300	1350	1400	1450	1500
Austria	90	100	141	225	333	495
Castile		100	431	1,137.9	2,586.2	6,465.5
Cologne	37.5	100	336.3	630	915	1,680
England	80	100	100	96	121.3	146.7
Flanders		100	128.3	255.2	373.3	609.5
France	80	100	250	220	312.5	387.5
Rome	58.8	100	138.2	214.7	290.2	382.4
Venice	75	100	100	145.3	181.3	193.8

Source: Lothian (2002), based on data from Spufford (1988).

What stands out is the depreciation of all currencies relative to the *florin*, shown by the upward trend in the exchange rates. A major cause of these movements was the series of debasements that took place in all of the European countries throughout this era. A second influence was the discovery and subsequent mining of silver in several European countries during the fifteenth century. These data are not consistent with the modern notion that a metallic money necessarily is a stable money.

A second point to notice in Table 4.1 is the difference in the pace at which the exchange-rate depreciation occurred. The English pound sterling, for example, showed relatively little movement, a drop in value of 0.2 percent per year over these two and a half centuries. The Castilian *marivedi*, in contrast, registered a decline of 2.0 percent per year over the 200 years for which data on it are available.

The debasement of these currencies does not seem to have been matched by increases in the various countries' price levels. The likely reason is that increases in money supplies were themselves matched at least to some degree by increases in real output and in desired quantities of money demanded.

These currencies, therefore, also served as units of account for bills of exchange, credit instruments which began in the thirteenth century to evolve into the principal form of international settlement.[6] The primary purpose of these bills of exchange was to eliminate shipment of specie when goods were bought and sold. The mechanism was simple and evidently also quite effective, since the bill of exchange remained the major instrument used in foreign transactions until the end of the nineteenth century. Discountable bills still survive in modified form today, with payment now commonly being ensured by letters of credit.

[6] De Roover (1974: 210–12) traces the development of bills of exchange to the letters of exchange and cambium contracts used a century or so before. See McCusker (1978: 19–23) and Neal (1990: 6–9) for discussions of the mechanics of the transaction involved in the use of bills of exchange, and Einzig (1962) for a broader historical treatment.

A standard scenario involving the use of bills of exchange was something of the following sort: An English merchant wants to buy cloth from an Italian exporter. To pay for this transaction and to avoid having to ship specie, the English merchant purchases a bill of exchange from a London merchant banker The bill of exchange is then sent as payment to the Italian exporter who ships the cloth and remits the bill to a merchant banker in Florence. The Florentine banker in turn pays the Italian exporter in *florins* and then settles with the London banker. This settlement could be simply a bookkeeping transaction, the Florentine banker canceling offsetting obligations to the London banker, or settlement could involve a shipment of specie at some future time at which the two have agreed to reconcile their books. The use of bills of exchange became increasingly widespread from the thirteenth century on.

4.2.3   Common characteristics of early international monies

Cipolla (1967) reviews monetary developments in both the early and later medieval period and points to three common characteristics of the various international monies. The first is high unitary value. We have already discussed this in connection with the solidus. It was also true of the dinar and the three Italian coins. The dinar contained approximately 4.25 g and the three Italian coins contained approximately 3.5 g of gold. Valuing these at today's price of gold of roughly $290 per troy ounce, this works out to prices of roughly $40 and $32, respectively. In the United States today, by way of comparison, most cash transactions are still carried out using twenty-dollar bills.

The second characteristic that the medieval monies shared during their respective heydays was intrinsic stability. They all kept the same weight and fineness during these periods though their values in terms of goods and services did change over time. Correspondingly, in each instance after debasement set in, the currency eventually ceased to serve as an international money.

The third characteristic is that the various currencies were all issued by strong economic powers that were active in international trade. Since we will go on to consider international monies in today's context of fiat monies, it is useful to consider how well these characteristics apply to fiat monies.

Intrinsic stability, the second of these requisite characteristics, would seem to be the most relevant for the success of fiat monies as well as metallic monies. In current terminology, it provided a nominal anchor. It applies with at least equal force to fiat monies as to commodity monies since the real value of fiat money can be easily affected by the issuer, something not as directly manipulable by issuers of commodity monies.

A large economy with a substantial presence in world trade, the third observed characteristic, is somewhat harder to pin down. Recently developed search-theoretic models of money, which we review below suggest, however, that such scale effects do indeed matter. An alternative view is that a strong trade-oriented economy is simply an indicator of brand-name capital. Like sterling during the period in which Britain was the world's major power and the dollar today, such currencies could be viewed as subject to less risk of political upheaval. In either case, this generalization again applies with equal or greater force to fiat monies.

High unitary value, the first characteristic, is another matter entirely. The value of a unit of money is certainly not much of a restriction on fiat monies, because fiat monies weigh relatively little and it is cheap to change the units to whatever value makes them useful in international transactions. Cipolla, however, suggests that it might in fact be a mark of prestige. Lopez (1951) in his discussion of early medieval monies makes a similar observation. He says (1951: 214–15):

Clearly, then, the bezant was more than a lump of gold. It was a symbol and a faith, the messenger of the divine emperor to his people and the ambassador of the chosen people to the other nations of the world. We cannot make fair appraisal of the monetary policies of the empire in strict economic terms since moral and psychological values also were involved and since these values by affecting the internal stability and international prestige of the state had, in their turn, a bearing on economic conditions.

It is perhaps more obvious now than when Cipolla wrote that there is a fourth characteristic of these various world currencies: All of them were simply adopted. None of these international monies arose due to anyone's intention to create a new international money. Rather, their roles as international monies evolved due to their becoming generally acceptable to others over time. They, thus, achieved their status without any laws being passed, without any official monetary conferences being held, and without any foreign ministers issuing joint communiqués. They became world monies, to use Hayek's (1978*b*) terminology in his article of that name, as "the result of human action and not of human design."

4.3 International Monies from the Seventeenth Century to the Present

4.3.1 Later international monies

International monies have continued to be used in more recent times. As the sixteenth century wore on, the center of international trade shifted from the Mediterranean region and the Italian city states to the northwest corner of Europe, first to Antwerp and then rather abruptly near the close of the sixteenth century to the Dutch Republic. In the century that followed, the Dutch economy experienced rapid growth. The United Provinces as a result became the world leader in shipping and in trade as well as in international finance. The Dutch currency also became the key currency in international transfers. It remained so, moreover, for most of the seventeenth and eighteenth centuries (see Dehing and 't Hart 1997). Its strong suit, in addition to the preeminent Dutch economic and financial position, was its intrinsic stability.

The rise of the guilder was an evolutionary process. At the end of the sixteenth century, close to 800 different foreign coins were accepted in the Dutch

Republic as money, and by 1810 the number had increased to nearly 1000 (Dehing and 't Hart 1997). Out of this bewildering array, the guilder emerged as the unit of account and the primary transactions currency. These two functions were, however, split between two versions of the currency. The guilder banco, the deposit entries on the books of the Bank of Amsterdam, became the unit of account. The circulating silver guilder was the medium of exchange. The two guilders—banco and coin—were closely but not rigidly linked. In 1638 the Amsterdam magistrates set a par value for the bank money in terms of the circulating medium, with the guilder banco at a slight premium. This premium, the *agio*, remained generally small and quite stable. From 1638 to 1775, the agio was 4.1 percent, implying an average internal rate of exchange between the two of 104.1 in guilder coinage per 100 guilder banco. The standard deviation of the agio over this period was only 1.1 percent.[7] The debasements that had been characteristic of the guilder until roughly 1630 was a thing of the past. As John McCusker (1978: 42) summarizes the situation, "The unchanging metallic content . . . during the seventeenth and eighteenth centuries made Dutch money—with sterling—one of the soundest, most stable currencies in the world."

During the course of the seventeenth century, Dutch economic growth slowed appreciably and English growth began to accelerate (Israel 1995). Near the end of that century, England started to develop into a financial power. The initial event here was the chartering of the Bank of England in 1694. Rapid development of English commercial banking followed. In the latter half of the eighteenth century, the number of London banks increased close to threefold and the number of banks outside London—the country banks—grew even faster, from a dozen or so in 1750 to 334 in 1797 to double that number in 1810 (Ashton 1955: 179–83). During this period, the London Stock Exchange also was formed and an active market in foreign exchange developed.

By the last quarter of the eighteenth-century England had replaced the Dutch Republic as the world's leading trading nation and London had replaced Amsterdam as its chief financial center (Jonker 1997). Throughout, sterling remained a relatively stable currency and, although this stability was temporarily interrupted in the decade or two surrounding the Napoleonic Wars, it was reestablished soon afterwards and maintained until the start of the First World War. Sterling as a result, became the new international currency, benefiting not only from its inherent stability but also, and we think more importantly, from the new British primacy in international trade and finance.[8]

The United States became the world's largest economy in the late nineteenth century, with U.S. real Gross Domestic Product (GDP) surpassing U.K. real GDP in the last third of that century. British financial and monetary dominance, however, continued until the start of the First World War. The outbreak of war was

---

[7] These data are taken from McCusker (1978: 46–51, table 2.6).

[8] See Benjamin J. Cohen (1998: 31–2) for a discussion of the links between Britain's increasing importance in international finance after 1815 and the rise of sterling as an international currency.

associated with substantial gold flows to the United States from Europe including the United Kingdom. New York, which had already become a major financial center, benefited and London lost. After the Armistice in November of 1918, the world tried to get back to normal. Many of the belligerent countries returned to gold in the early 1920s. The United Kingdom only did so in 1925, after first experiencing half a decade of wrenching deflation. Sterling retained some of its status as an international money and reserve currency for a time but the position of the U.S. dollar in both regards strengthened. Then the Great Depression and the Second World War intervened and financial and trade links between countries, as much else, were disrupted.

The U.S. dollar was designated the official reserve currency of the fixed exchange-rate system designed at the Bretton Woods Conference in 1944. After the war ended, the dollar not only took on this role but became a widely used international money as well as a currency used in domestic transactions in various countries. A good idea of what went on during this period and its resemblance to times past is indicated by Cipolla's discussion (1967: 13) in his monograph on medieval monies in which he, like Lopez (1951), compares the solidus to the dollar:

These pieces of paper (i.e. dollars), I knew, were more generally acceptable than any European currency. In any part of Europe there could be no difficulty in finding people who would take them as money. I could spend them everywhere, asking for everything. They were, they are, the international currency *par excellence.*

Fixed exchange rates among the world's currencies broke down in 1971 under the pressures unleashed by inflationary U.S. monetary policy (Darby et al. 1983; Bordo 1993). Many believed at the time that the subsequent move to floating exchange rates would reduce the dollar's role. This was wrong on several counts. Official holdings of dollars as reserve assets remained high and greatly increased. Private demands for dollars increased, particularly once the United States got inflation under control and as other countries' inflation worsened. One indication of the extensiveness of this phenomenon is provided by the considerable number of papers in this volume that discuss dollarization.

4.3.2 Further empirical generalizations

This later experience is consistent with earlier experience: Stability of value as well as country size and prominence in trade clearly matter. What appears important also, however, is financial development. All three of the later international currencies—the guilder, sterling, and the dollar—were issued by countries with dominant positions in international finance and relatively unfettered markets. Cohen (1971, 1998) discusses this last characteristic under the headings of "exchange convenience" and "capital certainty." George S. Tavlas (1998) makes a similar point. He states that "the issuing country should possess financial markets that are substantially free of controls, broad (i.e. containing a wide variety of financial instruments), and deep (that is, having well-developed secondary markets)." Tavlas also argues that the issuing country must be politically stable and militarily powerful. This was certainly true of the three countries issuing these later international monies. It was also the case for the issuers of the earlier monies.

4.4   Theoretical Considerations

On one level, it is trivial to say that international fiat monies have arisen due to their being generally acceptable. A domestic fiat money arises due to its being generally acceptable in transactions and for no other reason. Why should an international fiat money be any different? Possibly the level of indeterminacy is more obvious for international fiat money. Perhaps it seems obvious that Argentine people would prefer to use the Argentine government's fiat money if other things are the same. It is much less obvious whether an Argentine will pick American, Brazilian, British, or Swiss money when using non-Argentine money.

If legal restrictions are ignored, there is no particular reason to expect people in Argentina to bear substantial costs to use money issued by the Argentine government rather than by some other government. While people may be willing to bear some costs to use domestically produced money due to national pride or other nonpecuniary considerations, there is no reason to think that they will bear substantial costs. Programs to encourage people to buy domestically seldom, if ever, succeed. People buy the clothing that has the highest value to them personally, even if it is produced by foreigners. There is an important difference, though, between money and other domestic goods such as clothes.

The money that is useful depends on what money is used by others, whereas a pair of shoes will be equally useful whether everyone else wears domestic or foreign shoes. This implies that there is a coordination problem that must be solved for choosing money, a problem that is largely irrelevant for clothes. It would be easy, though, to overemphasize the greater importance of coordination for money compared to other goods. Driving a foreign car is more useful if some other people drive one too because repair facilities will be nonexistent otherwise. The producer of the good, whether a car or a money, has an incentive to assist users.

The choice of a fiat money is a radical indeterminacy. Why did people in the United States in the 1790s use United States dollars rather than pounds sterling or French francs? It might seem that legal-tender laws resolve the question to some extent. Legal tender laws require that a money be acceptable in payment. Everything else the same, if one money is legal tender and the other is not, the one that is legal tender seems likely to be the money used. This observation has not, however, been demonstrated in a well-articulated theory. In any case, alternative monies rarely are perfect substitutes.

4.4.1   More stable money

One reason that alternative monies are not perfect substitutes is that likely inflation rates for different monies can differ substantially. Expected inflation and variable unexpected inflation impose costs on holders of the money, and both expected inflation and variable unexpected inflation can generate revenue for an issuer of money. Expected inflation is costly to a holder of money because the real value of the money depreciates while it is being held. More variable unexpected inflation can generate costs because the environment is less predictable and the risk of engaging in various activities is higher. Expected inflation generates revenue directly to the issuer because printing more money creates higher inflation. More variable unexpected inflation can generate more revenue because the unexpected higher inflation can be supplied by printing more money, and the unexpected lower inflation raises the real quantity of cash balances demanded, which can be met by printing more money (Auernheimer 1974). The literature on time consistency and related issues, starting with Barro and Gordon (1983), shows that alternating periods of high inflation fueled by printing money and low inflation with money printed to provide the increased demand for money are difficult to sustain as an equilibrium. Even so, the incentive to produce such an outcome means that it can affect even a rational expectations equilibrium. Moreover, this incentive can affect the transition to a rational expectations equilibrium when agents are learning the preferences of the money issuer.

In models with learning, governments can acquire a reputation for producing low, predictable inflation, but they also can acquire reputations for producing high inflation (Sargent 1999). Even if the choice of local currency is affected by legal tender laws, the choice of an international money is not affected directly by such laws. Hence, a money's reputation is all the more important for determining which money will be used as international money. As a result, it is not surprising that Cipolla (1967) places substantial weight on the stability of the money for determining what will be used as international money. It surely is important.

4.4.2 International trade

Why might it also matter how much international trade is done by a country, as Cipolla (1967) suggests? At first glance, it is not obvious why this should matter at all. Even though Switzerland is a small country, people might well find Swiss francs to be the most useful currency and the emphasis above on inflation would suggest that as a real possibility. Even if a high-inflation country engages in a lot of trade, why would anyone want to use its money as an international medium of exchange?

Reflection on the functions of money, though, suggests that the quantity of trade will matter, and recent theoretical research provides support for this notion. The functions of money directly related to trade include its being a unit of account and a medium of exchange. Considering costs of changing prices—menu costs—suggests that reputation for low inflation is likely to be the important attribute for what currency is used as a unit of account because it affects the frequency of price changes. On the other hand, if the money used for a trade is different from the money used for posting the price, there is little obvious gain from posting the price in a stable currency since the actual transaction price in the unstable money has to be computed from the posted price in the stable money and the current exchange rate between the stable money and the unstable money. Menu costs interpreted narrowly would have to be very important in order to justify posting prices in a money different from the one used in the transaction. In domestic economies, prices commonly are posted in currencies other than the one used in trades only in the case of extraordinary inflations. Hence, it seems likely that the money used as an international unit of account will tend to be the dominant international medium of exchange.

Search-theoretic models of money show why the amount of international trade will matter for the choice of the money used as a medium of exchange. The indeterminacy of the choice of a particular fiat money as an international medium of exchange is very clear in the context of the search theories of money introduced by Kiyotaki and Wright (1989) and elaborated in a series of papers culminating in Trejos and Wright (1995). These search-theoretic models are particularly well suited to examining the general issue of international money because they do not impose the use of any particular money, or of money at all. Cash-in-advance models presuppose that a money must be used, and models with money in the utility function presuppose that a money is useful. Search theories of money allow for the endogenous choice of a money to solve the general problem of finding a double coincidence of wants.

The generality of allowing for an endogenous choice of money is bought at the price of the theoretical analysis being highly stylized. The choice of a particular international money is examined in Matsuyama et al. (1993) and Trejos and Wright (1996). In these search-theoretic models of international money, countries are defined effectively by the probability that people will meet, and people can trade when they meet. People within a country have a probability of meeting another person from their country and a separate probability of meeting a foreigner. The probability of meeting a person within the country is assumed to be higher than the probability of meeting a foreigner. Trade is effected by an exchange of a money for a good when both sides find such a trade advantageous. This trade can be an exchange for domestic or foreign money.[9] Matsuyama et al. (1993) show that the likelihood of using a foreign money is higher in equilibrium if the other country is larger and if the probability of meeting a foreigner is higher.

In short, a country that is larger and engages in more international trade is more likely to have its money used as an international money. This conclusion is derived holding constant other characteristics of the money, including the stability of the money.

---

[9] Barter will not occur because demand and production are structured to rule out a double coincidence of wants.

These models have multiple steady-state equilibria for any sizes of economies and degrees of integration, even holding constant the reputation of the money for stability. While it is possible at this level of generality just to say that there are multiple equilibria and leave it at that, it is neither desirable nor necessary to do so. Additional factors will determine the actual equilibrium observed. As Menger (1892: 250) summarizes the point, even the use of money domestically is "the spontaneous outcome, the unpremeditated resultant, of particular, individual efforts of the members of a society, who have little by little worked their way (to a particular solution)." Actions that, in themselves, do not have any obvious implications for what money or monies will be international money can affect the actual money used.

Even if there are many possible equilibria, it is plausible that the likely inflation rates generated by a currency are of central importance among the variables affecting the actual equilibrium.

Other factors may matter too. On one level, there are curious things about the euro coins and notes.[10] The euro coins differ by country of issue, with different backs on each. The notes are the same in all countries. These notes depict arches and other monuments, but the monuments are not real. The supposition apparently is that Germans would not be impressed by their currency having pictures of the Arc de Triomphe, and similarly the French would not be impressed by their currency having pictures of the Brandenburg Gate. Perhaps this will not matter; then again, it may turn out to matter.

4.5 Conclusions

A useful set of stylized facts emerges from our historical review of international monies spanning the fourth to the twentieth century. A sequence of international monies has existed historically, each occupying center stage sometimes for several centuries and eventually being replaced by the next. The only exception is the dollar, which is the current international money and, therefore, has not been replaced. These currencies have four key characteristics: They had high unitary value, they had relatively low inflation rates for long time periods, they were issued by major economic and trading powers, and they became international monies by human action rather than by design.

Economic theory explains the roles of these factors. The size of a country matters because it affects the likelihood that someone in another country will trade with someone from that country and therefore the usefulness of a common money in trading. On the other hand, there is no necessary reason that people from two different countries will pick any particular money—especially a particular fiat money. Historically, this coordination problem was solved partly by the relative values of metals, and therefore the usefulness of their denominations,

---

[10] The euro was introduced with a substantial period to overcome some of the issues raised by Selgin (1994).

and partly by the historical evolution of the choice of money. With fiat monies, the historical evolution of the use of any particular money assumes prime importance because the size of a monetary unit is relatively easier to change. Relative inflation rates affect the cost of holding different monies, and therefore will affect the actual money used.

In recent centuries, international monies have been issued by countries with important financial markets to which foreigners have relatively free access. The relative importance of this factor is an important question for future research.

What does this analysis suggest for the euro? The euro area is large enough in terms of trade to be a serious competitor to the dollar as an international money. Indeed, some European countries that are not part of the European System of Central Banks (ESCB) have adopted the euro. Whether the euro will replace the dollar in other geographic areas depends on two factors. The cost of holding euros relative to the dollar–largely determined by the relative inflation rate of the euro relative to the dollar–will be very important.

A more important factor for the euro than for other international monies, though, is the permanence of the European Central Bank (ECB) and ESCB itself. The European Common Market is an international organization and, while the single new money–the euro–has been created in ways that raise the cost of leaving the ESCB, it is not impossible for a country to quit the system. The ESCB is more nearly analogous to a currency union than to an international money in some respects, and currency unions' history has been one of formation and disintegration (Bordo and Jonung 2000). If the European area evolves more nearly into a common government, then such disintegration becomes impossible short of civil war. Otherwise, it is an issue to be decided by participants in an individual country. In sum, the future of the euro itself is in doubt.

Conditional on the euro persisting for, say, fifty or a hundred years and the European Common Market not evolving into a single government, the euro may well supplant the dollar as international money if the euro's inflation rate is low relative to the dollar's inflation rate. If it does, then the euro will be the first international money that arose from planning rather than evolution.

REFERENCES

Ashton, T. S. (1955). *An Economic History of England: The 18th Century.* New York: Barnes and Noble.

Auernheimer, L. (1974). "The Honest Government's Guide to the Revenue from Money Creation." *Journal of Political Economy,* 82 (May–June): 598–606.

Barro, R. J. and Gordon, D. B. (1983). "A Positive Theory of Monetary Policy in a Natural Rate Model." *Journal of Political Economy,* 91 (August): 589–610.

Bordo, M. D. (1993). "The Bretton Woods International Monetary System: A Historical Overview." In Michael D. Bordo and Barry Eichengreen (eds.), *A Retrospective on the Bretton Woods System.* University of Chicago Press for the NBER, pp. 3–104.

— and Jonung, L. (2000). *Lessons for EMU from the History of Monetary Unions*. London: Institute of Economic Affairs.

Chown, J. F. (1994). *The History of Money from AD 800*. London: Routledge.

Cipolla, C. M. (1967). *Money, Prices, and Civilization in the Mediterranean World, Fifth to Seventeenth Century*. New York: Gordian Press.

Cohen, B. J. (1971). *The Future of Sterling as an International Currency*. London: Macmillan; New York: St. Martin's Press.

— (1998). *The Geography of Money*. Ithaca, NY: Cornell University Press.

Darby, M., Lothian, J. R., and Gandolfi, A. E., Stockman, A. C., Schwartz, A. J. (1983). *The International Transmission of Inflation*. University of Chicago Press for the NBER.

Dehing, Pit and 't Hart, M. (1997). "Linking the Fortunes: Currency and Banking, 1550-1800." In Marjolein 't Hart, Joost Jonker, and Jan Luiten van Zanden (eds.), *A Financial History of the Netherlands*. Cambridge and New York: Cambridge University Press, pp. 37-63.

De Roover, R. (1974). "Business, Banking, and Economic Thought in Late Medieval and Early Modern Europe." University of Chicago Press, 1974 (collected papers edited by J. Kirshner).

Einzig, P. (1970). *The History of Foreign Exchange*, 2nd edn. London: Macmillan.

Gilson, E. (1991). *The Spirit of Medieval Philosophy*. University of Notre Dame Press.

Hayek, F. A. (1978*a*). *The Denationalization of Money: An Analysis of the Theory and Practice of Current Currencies*. London: Institute of Economic Affairs.

— (1978*b*). "The Result of Human Action not of Human Design." In F. A. Hayek (ed.), *Studies in Philosophy, Politics, Economics, and the History of Ideas*. University of Chicago Press.

— (1995). *The Dutch Republic: Its Rise, Greatness and Fall, 1477-1806*. Oxford: Clarendon Press.

Jonker, J. (1997). "The Alternative Road to Modernity: Banking and Currency, 1814-1914." In Marjolein 't Hart, Joost Jonker, and Jan Luiten van Zanden (eds.), *A Financial History of the Netherlands*. Cambridge and New York: Cambridge University Press, pp. 94-123.

Kiyotaki, N. and Wright, R. (1989). "On Money as a Medium of Exchange." *Journal of Political Economy*, 97 (August): 927-54.

Lopez, R. S. (1951). "The Dollar of the Middle Ages." *Journal of Economic History*, 11 (Summer): 209-34.

Lothian, J. R. (2002). "Exchange Rates." *Oxford Encyclopedia of Economic History*. New York: Oxford University Press.

Matsuyama, K., Kiyotaki, N., and Matsui, A. (1993). "Toward a Theory of International Currency." *Review of Economic Studies*, 60 (April): 283-307.

McCusker, J. J. (1978). *Money and Exchange in Europe and America, 1600-1775. A Handbook*. Chapel Hill, NC: University of North Carolina Press for the Institute of Early American History and Culture.

Menger, C. (1892). "On the Origins of Money." *Economic Journal*, 2 (June): 239-55.

Neal, L. (1990). *The Rise of Financial Capitalism*. Cambridge: Cambridge University Press.

Rolnick, A. J., Velde, F. R., and Weber, W. E. (1996). "The Debasement Puzzle: An Essay in Medieval Monetary History." *Journal of Economic History*, 56 (December): 789-808.

Sargent, T. J. (1999). *The Conquest of American Inflation*. Princeton University Press.

Schumpeter, J. A. (1954). *History of Economic Analysis*. New York: Oxford University Press.

Selgin, G. (1994). "On Ensuring the Acceptability of a New Fiat Money." *Journal of Money, Credit and Banking*, 26 (November): 808–26.

Spufford, P. (1984). "Le rôle de la monnaie dans le révolution commericiale du xiiie siècle." In J. Day (ed.) *Etudes d'histoire monétaire*. Lille: Presses universitaires de Lille.

— (1988). *Money and its Use in Medieval Europe*. Cambridge and New York: Cambridge University Press.

Sussman, N. (1993). "Debasements, Royal Revenues, and Inflation in France During the Hundred Years' War 1415–1422." *Journal of Economic History*, 53 (March): 44–70.

Tavlas, G. S. (1998). "The International Use of Currencies: The U.S. Dollar and the Euro." *Finance & Development*, 35 (June): 46–9.

Trejos, A. and Wright, R. (1995). "Search, Bargaining, Money, and Prices." *Journal of Political Economy*, 103 (February): 118–41.

— and — (1996). "Search-Theoretic Models of International Currency." *Federal Reserve Bank of St. Louis Review*, 78 (May/June): 117–32.

Velde, F. R., Weber, W. E., and Wright, R. (1999). "A Model of Commodity Money, with Applications to Gresham's Law and the Debasement Puzzle." *Review of Economic Dynamics*, 2 (January): 291–323.

PART II

Trade and Price Effects of Monetary Union

5

Geography, Trade, and Currency Union

JACQUES MÉLITZ

This chapter reports on four basic results of tests of the standard gravity equation. First, geography can serve to reflect comparative advantage as well as transportation costs. Second, the effect of distance on bilateral trade is mostly a substitution effect between closer and more distant trade partners rather than a scale effect on total foreign trade. Third, special political relationships, such as free trade agreements and currency union, do not produce any trade diversion in the aggregate, but increase trade with outsiders as well as among the parties to the relationship. Fourth, Rose's surprisingly high estimate of the impact of currency union on trade stems partly from a selection bias, but even following a correction for this bias, the estimate remains high.

5.1 Introduction

The gravity model is now a workhorse in empirical study of trade and serves to deal with such varied questions as the importance of political borders (McCallum 1995), free trade agreements (Frankel 1997) and currency unions (Rose 2000). The proper specification of the model has, therefore, become a matter of general concern. In this chapter, I report on tests dealing with three questions about the model. The first one relates to the possibility that geography may serve to reflect comparative advantage and not only transportation costs. The second concerns the distinction between substitution and scale effects in the model. To what extent does distance reduce trade with more distant countries in favor of trade with closer ones rather than damage foreign trade in general? Likewise, to what extent do special political relationships, such as free trade agreements and currency unions, increase trade within the group at the expense of trade with outsiders instead of increasing foreign trade in general? The third and last series of tests pertains to Rose's surprisingly high estimate of the impact of currency union on trade, which asserts that such union will more than quadruple trade among the members. A brief opening word may be said about the motivation for each of these separate tests and the results.

I would like to thank Ronald MacDonald, Mathilde Maurel, and Andrew Rose for valuable comments.

5.2 Motivation and Results

Great-circle distances in gravity models serve to reflect transportation costs. But there are other measures of distance that could reflect comparative advantage instead. So far as comparative advantage depends on differences in climate and seasons, this factor could be reflected simply in differences in latitude between countries. The latitude of a country affects the length of its days, its sunlight, its temperatures, and seasons and alters not only its plant and animal life and the yield of its land and waters, but its required insulation, energy, and equipment and its optimal production techniques. Diamond's (1997) fascinating history of mankind strongly suggests that production opportunities can often be reproduced through selective planting, breeding, tooling, and exertion at any given latitude on earth, but that similar efforts to do so become increasingly futile as we move North or South. If so, as long as we control for great-circle distances (and therefore transportation costs), greater distance along the North–South axis should increase, not diminish, trade. As I shall show, that is exactly what happens. When great-circle distances are taken into account, the larger the absolute difference in latitudes between two countries North and South of the equator, the greater their bilateral trade. This effect of geography shows up consistently with *t* values of the order of ten without disturbing the rest of the gravity equations. Furthermore, the effect retains this order of significance in all of the extensions below.

As regards the substitution or scale effects of the various influences on trade in the gravity model, some preliminary discussion is required. Attempts over the last twenty years to provide theoretical underpinnings for the model assume that aggregate output in each country (or region) is given and the output must be sold either at home or abroad. Accordingly, any reduction in the bilateral trade of a country with another means an equal increase in its trade with third countries or at home. Without knowing the sign and the size of the associated change in trade with third countries, nothing can be said about the change in domestic trade. Notwithstanding, changes in bilateral trade are sometimes merely aggregated to obtain effects on total foreign trade in applications of gravity equations (e.g. Frankel and Romer 1999; Frankel and Rose 2002). In general, repercussions on third countries are frequently neglected.

These last remarks echo a recent complaint of Anderson and van Wincoop (2003) about the failure to pay adequate attention to the constraints on aggregate trade in estimating gravity equations for bilateral trade. In order to deal with the problem, they propose a non-linear method of estimating these equations that incorporates "multilateral trade resistance," or a term expressing the tariff-equivalent of all of the barriers to trade (both domestic and foreign), viewed as a whole. I propose instead—if only as a start—to introduce separate variables to reflect possible substitution or scale effects of bilateral trade on trade with third countries and to see whether these variables emerge as significant and which sign they bear. Of my relevant experiments, I will report only on those relating to distance and special political relationships.

As regards distance, my study uses relative distance to reflect possible substitution effects between different foreign countries, where relative distance refers to the absolute distance between a trading pair divided by their average distance to third countries (to be defined more precisely below). When relative distance enters in the tests side by side with average distance to all the rest, relative distance emerges as the larger and statistically more significant of the two. Thus, most of the impact of distance in the usual gravity equations of bilateral trade must be attributed to substitution effects between alternative trade partners.

This last result may help to understand some previous evidence. Even though transportation costs have fallen greatly over the last two centuries, applications of gravity equations to the second half of the nineteenth century (Flandreau 1995) and the interwar period (Eichengreen and Irwin 1995) show lower effects of distance on trade than more recent applications over the last thirty years. If the effects of distance on bilateral trade refer mostly to aggregate trade, there is a puzzle. In that case, distance should have declined in influence over the last couple of centuries. If, instead, the effects of distance refer mostly to substitution between alternative trade partners, there is no difficulty of interpretation. With the fall in transportation barriers over time, relative distances could simply count much more now in deciding *how far* goods will travel abroad than they did earlier.

On the issue of the scale or substitution effects of political associations, the study considers all five political variables that Rose (2000) and Frankel and Rose (2002) introduce into gravity equations: Namely, currency union, membership in a common country (as in the case of Greenland and Denmark or the Falklands and the U.K.), regional trade agreements, relations between former colony and colonizer and relations between former colonies of the same colonizer. The results show that all five variables increase trade among the parties to the relationships. In addition, the first three relationships–all of them except those concerning former colonial relations–also breed trade with outsiders, and therefore increase foreign trade in the aggregate. Similar tests by other researchers covering the same study period–1970–95–concur. Frankel experimented widely with the effect of free trade agreements on outsiders in studies with Stein and Wei, (e.g. Frankel et al. 1995, 1998; Frankel and Wei 1998) and in his pooled results (Frankel 1997: ch. 10), reports the same promotion of trade with outsiders. In addition, Rose and Frankel–Rose find similar trade-creating effects for currency unions. I simply display the generality of the finding: All privileged political relationships except those associated with past colonialism promote foreign trade between the principals and the rest.

If this be puzzling, it is perhaps less so in regard to currency union than free trade agreement (FTA) and political association. Consider free trade. Admittedly, a reduction in trade barriers between two countries without any similar lowering of barriers with the rest may be trade-diverting. Based on this logic, Frankel invokes special political hypotheses in order to explain his result that FTAs foster trade with outsiders. Drawing from the literature, he cites various possibilities: Competitive liberalization; the possible build up of a political constituency in favor of liberalization through the revelation of export-competitiveness after countries enter into a FTA; and so forth (Frankel 1997: ch. 10). But a currency union can be viewed with a different eye. If some countries form a currency union, there are fewer currencies and fewer units of account in the world and therefore lower trade barriers for everyone. Hence, currency union may not represent a discriminatory reduction of trade barriers at all. For example, since the euro started circulating as a currency in 2002, and therefore bank drafts could be written conveniently in euros in commodity trade, British and Swedish households have been able to store euros instead of twelve monies in commodity trade with euro members. The households have also been able to benefit from fewer units of account in this trade. Thus, they can now reap many of the same advantages of lower transaction costs, greater ease of calculation and greater transparency of prices that the members of the European Monetary Union (EMU) get. Furthermore, in so far as EMU broadly interferes with political controls on capital movements and instructions to fund managers to hold home-currency assets, the arrangement promotes capital-market integration worldwide. In theory, as Obstfeld and Rogoff (1996, 2001) demonstrate, this could mean more trade in goods in general.

As regards currency union, Rose has surprised everyone (including himself) with the size of the impact on trade that he found. He has also reported numerous tests of the robustness of his finding. The further experiments here concern the suspicion (occasionally voiced elsewhere)[1] that his sample of currency unions is biased and the unions always occur between countries with unusually low trade barriers between one another. If that were so, the impact of currency union in Rose's tests might largely reflect other factors besides a common currency. In fact, Rose's data permits testing this hypothesis. My tests exploit the presence of other political variables in the analysis (whose coefficients are therefore not to be considered "nuisance parameters," in opposition to Rose's designation). Interestingly, the tests confirm the suspected bias, but the correction for it only moderates Rose's result without upsetting the outcome. More precisely, the correction cuts down the estimate of the impact of currency union on the log of trade by half. As a consequence, therefore, currency union, as such, doubles instead of roughly quadrupling trade. On this basis, I conclude that the tests essentially support Rose's stand.

In more recent work with van Wincoop, Rose offers a different ground for reducing his earlier estimate of the influence of currency union on trade (Rose and van Wincoop 2001), or at least does so in the case of currency unions between countries that already traded a lot with one another beforehand (including the EMU). The argument is that, in these cases, currency union would not reduce the price of home goods nearly as much in trade within the union as it does for the existing currency unions in his sample, since bilateral trade with the partners would already be much higher as a percentage of total foreign trade in the first

---

[1] See the comment by Marco Pagano in the Economic Panel discussion of Rose's paper (Rose 2000: 39), and Persson (2001).

place. More generally, Rose and van Wincoop apply Anderson and van Wincoop's concept of multilateral trade resistance to lower Rose's estimate in the event of new currency unions between close trading partners. However, my argument is independent. According to it, Rose's coefficient of currency union mixes up effects of other political factors enhancing trade with the effects of a single currency.

A more recent paper still, by Glick and Rose (2002), offers evidence supporting both my criticism of Rose's earlier work and my reduction in his estimate of the impact of currency union on trade. In this joint study, the authors employ an enlarged data set, which contains many more time series observations for individual trading pairs. As a result, they are able to obtain an estimate of the impact of currency union for individual trading pairs over time, or "within" as well as "between" estimates. Their "between" estimate of this impact is as high as Rose's earlier ones, while their "within" estimate drops to the lower level in my study. Glick and Rose pose their lower "within" estimate as the right one, without commenting on the reason for their higher "between" one. I shall argue that the gap between the two stems from the fact that the lower estimate properly concerns the impact of currency union as such, whereas the higher one, in line with Rose's earlier results, does not do so but regards the combined impact of currency union and other influences on trade.[2]

The discussion will cover each of the tests in succession and will end with a few brief general remarks.

5.3 The Data and Initial Tests

All of the tests rest on the data in Frankel and Rose (2002), which is available on Rose's web site.[3] My indebtedness to Rose for making his data public and for including detailed instructions on how to use it, is enormous. I made two initial changes in the data set: One concerning distance, the other language. Whereas Rose locates countries at their geographical center (in conformity with the CIA), I place them wherever their most populous city stands (as found on the CD-ROM *encarta*). Subsequently, the arc-geometry formula for great-circle distances serves me for calculating the bilateral distances between trading partners. This method produces identical results to those found in the atlases and related web sites.[4] In the case of language, I kept Rose's series but made a few obvious corrections (most of which he subsequently incorporated). The difference in our measures of great-circle distances could matter in studying parts of the world with complicated political geographies, including Western Europe and Southeast

---

[2] Pakko and Wall (2001) report no impact of currency union at all on trade (nor membership in a free trade area) in a more radical challenge to Rose's stand. They do so by introducing separate fixed effects for all individual country pairs. But in this case, all the geographical variables disappear from the analysis, since those variables do not vary by country pair. Effectively, Pakko and Wall drop the gravity model altogether.   [3] www.haas.berkeley.edu/~arose.

[4] For details, consult Bob Chamberlain, "What is the best way to calculate the distance between two points?" at www.census.gov/cgi-bin/geo//gisfaq?Q5.1.

Table 5.1. *The basic gravity model and geography*

	Frankel–Rose	Same following data changes	Effect North–South	Effect of difference in absolute latitudes	Both effects
Log distance	−1.15	−1.11	−1.26	−1.16	−1.26
	(0.025)	(0.024)	(0.03)	(0.03)	(0.03)
Log product of real GDP	1.40	1.39	1.37	1.38	1.37
	(0.01)	(0.01)	(0.01)	(0.01)	(0.01)
Log product of population	−0.47	−0.46	−0.42	−0.44	−0.42
	(0.02)	(0.02)	(0.02)	(0.02)	(0.02)
Log product of land area	−0.16	−0.17	−0.18	−0.17	−0.18
	(0.01)	(0.01)	(0.01)	(0.01)	(0.01)
Common land border (0,1)	0.62	0.70	0.84	0.82	0.84
	(0.13)	(0.13)	(0.12)	(0.12)	(0.12)
Number of landlocked in pair (0, 1, 2)	−0.39	−0.36	−0.41	−0.39	−0.41
	(0.04)	(0.04)	(0.04)	(0.04)	(0.04)
Common language (0,1)	0.87	0.91	0.92	0.94	0.92
	(0.06)	(0.06)	(0.06)	(0.06)	(0.06)
Log North–South Difference			0.23		0.23
			(0.02)		(0.03)
Log Difference in Absolute Latitudes				0.15	0.003
				(0.02)	(0.03)
R^2	0.63	0.63	0.64	0.64	0.64
RMSE	2	2	1.99	1.99	1.99

Note: Regressand is log of bilateral trade in real American dollars. Number of Observations is 31,101 for the first column, 31,010 for the rest. Year-specific fixed effects are not reported. Robust standard errors recorded in parentheses.

Asia. For example, Rose's measure places East Germany closer to the United Kingdom than West Germany and France still further from the United Kingdom than West Germany, whereas mine does the opposite (with London–Paris setting the U.K.–France distance and London–Frankfurt the UK–West Germany one). But those changes turn out to be trivial over the entire world sample of observations of bilateral trade. (The correlation between our two measures of distance in the world sample of over 40,000 observations is 0.987.) Similarly, my changes in denoting common languages between countries have no impact on the estimates (though this might alter if we examined language in detail).[5]

The first two columns of Table 5.1 show the estimate of the basic gravity equation with Rose's data prior to my changes and following them. The dependent

[5] Nitsch (2002) does find some significant changes in estimates resulting from a more extensive modification of Rose's data than mine. Yet, for the moment, it is not possible to tell how much Nitsch's finding depends on a failure to pool the data for different years. As regards language, my modifications and Nitsch's are almost identical.

variable is bilateral trade and the first four independent variables are distance, the product of the country pairs' GDPs, the product of their populations and the product of their land areas. These variables are in logs. The next three variables on the list are dummies showing whether the countries have a common border, whether one or both or neither of them are landlocked, and whether they share a common language. This particular choice of variables is now common. The data covers approximately 98 percent of all world trade and is recorded every five years from 1970 through 1995. Dummies are included for the individual years but are not reported. Table 5.1 also shows robust standard errors. Since the observations for identical country pairs (one to six) are likely to be highly correlated, those standard errors are further corrected for clustering by country pair. The regressions rest on 31,010 observations rather than all the 40,000–some in the sample on account of missing values for some of the variables (predominantly GDP). The results in the first column hinge on the exact data in Frankel and Rose (2002) and those in the second column follow my modifications. The two sets are indistinguishable.

5.4 The Forces of Geography

The relevant gravity equation is known to be broadly consistent with the model of monopolistic competition in trade (subject to Anderson and van Wincoop's reservations). But recent research shows that it can also be obtained from models with homogeneous goods. Proceeding from homogeneous goods, Deardorff (1998) showed how to derive the equation from the factor proportions model. Proceeding similarly, Eaton and Kortum (1997) obtained the equation from random technological differences between countries. Nonetheless, efforts to introduce factor proportions directly into the equation have had little success thus far (see Frankel 1997: 134) and though Eaton and Kortum did get good results with technological knowledge, they did so only with respect to manufacturing in nineteen OECD countries.

Yet, geography alone could carry information about comparative advantage, and therefore could carry information about both factor proportions (Deardorff) and international differences in production functions (Eaton and Kortum). As mentioned above, so far as the comparative advantage of different countries is related to differences in climate and seasons, differences in latitude North–South should capture the variable. Such differences, by themselves, though, would treat Argentina as distant from Greece, whereas the two countries are at comparable latitudes in the two hemispheres and have similar climates. As a result, I experimented with differences in *absolute* latitudes, as well as differences North–South.[6] The differences in absolute latitudes would then relate specifically

---

[6] If we let lat1 and lat2 stand for the respective latitudes of country 1 and country 2 in a trading pair (with Northern latitudes positive and Southern ones negative), then the North–South Difference is $|lat1 - lat2|$ and the Difference in Latitudes is $||lat1| - |lat2||$.

to climate, whereas the differences North–South would also pertain to the opposition of the seasons in the two hemispheres and any factors of environment that are associated with the separate features of the Northern and Southern hemispheres (as, for example, the higher ratio of land to water in the North).

As shown in columns (3), (4), and (5) of the table, if used alone, either one of these two measures of latitudinal distance (respectively labeled North–South Difference and Difference in Absolute Latitudes) emerges as highly significant and with the expected positive sign. But when joined together, the North–South variable is dominant.[7] Indeed, the Difference in Absolute Latitudes becomes insignificant. For this reason, I will strictly keep the North–South Difference in the subsequent discussion. However, the correlation between the two measures of latitudinal distance (in logs) is high: 0.73. Therefore, the North–South Difference should perhaps be viewed as largely standing for both.

5.5 The Effects of Distance

Does the impact of distance on bilateral trade reflect switching between closer and more distant partners, or does distance affect aggregate foreign trade, or both? One simple way to get at this question is to introduce some measure of relative distance between countries, or to consider the distance between countries relative to the average distance between country pairs and all of the other countries in the world. To be specific, let the straight-line average of the (great-circle) distances of a country from all the other 185 in the sample be termed remoteness.[8] If we use d_{ij} to refer to the distance between countries i and j and R_i and R_j to refer to their respective remoteness, the relative distance between countries i and j can be defined as $d_{ij}^2/R_i R_j$. This relative distance variable is clearly intimately related to the concept by the same name that Deardorff (1998) introduced into the gravity model (compare Bergstrand 1998). The variable is also entirely in the spirit of Anderson and van Wincoop's measure of "multilateral trade resistance" (except that their term combines all of the barriers to trade in the gravity

---

[7] Another geographical variable that has frequently appeared in the discussion is distance from the Tropics. See, for example, Sachs and Warner (1997) and Rodriguez and Rodrik (2001). This next variable is supposed to reflect the low trade of countries near the Equator resulting from a poverty of endowment. (For a radically different interpretation of this variable, though, see Hall and Jones 1999.) Based on the same notation as in the preceding note, the distance from the Tropics is $|lat1| + |lat2|$. The variable is always insignificant in my tests.

[8] The most remote country in my data set is New Zealand; the least is Austria. Note that this use of the term "remoteness" differs from the literature. Remoteness is generally not conceived as a pure geographic variable at all, but as a reflection of the opposite pull of third countries on the trade of a country with a specific trade partner. In this last usage (where output weights enter for alternative trade partners), the "remoteness" of Australia in its trade with New Zealand, for example, is greater than its "remoteness" in its trade with the United States. See Helliwell (1998). I find my use of the term more intuitive. Note that in more recent work, Helliwell has started using ALT (for "alternative trading partners") instead of "remoteness." See Helliwell and Verdier (2001).

equation in a single term: Political borders, differences in language, differences in currency—everything).

There is a relative distance for each observation in the database. If we take the average of these relative distances, the value cannot be far from 1 (it is actually 1.03). Therefore, if expressed in logs, the variable will be centered on zero and will show negative values for relative distances below the mean and positive values for relative distances above the mean. But the log of the product of remoteness $R_i R_j$ will always be positive. Suppose then, that we run a regression that includes both relative distance and the product of remoteness in logs. (Evidently, this is equivalent to including distance since $\log(d_{ij}^2/R_iR_j)$ plus $\log R_i R_j$ equals $\log d_{ij}^2$.) If the bilateral distances d_{ij} induce no substitution effects at all in trades with alternative country pairs but always damage aggregate foreign trade, the coefficient of relative distance should be insignificant and close to zero while that of remoteness should be significantly negative. Suppose, instead, that trading distances below the mean really raise trade at the expense of trading distances above the mean while they do not affect aggregate foreign trade. Then the relative distance variable should be significantly negative while the impact of remoteness should be close to nil. Of course, even in this last instance, we would hesitate to conclude that distance does not affect aggregate trade, since if that were the case, then when entered alone, absolute distance d_{ij} would be insignificant, which we know to be false. However, distance could bear both a substitution and a scale effect on foreign trade. Therefore, relative distance and remoteness could both enter simultaneously with significant negative signs.

The first column in Table 5.2 repeats the earlier estimate in Table 5.1 with the Difference North–South but without the Difference in Absolute Latitudes. The second column in Table 5.2 next substitutes remoteness $(R_i R_j)$ for absolute distance and the third column includes both relative distance and remoteness together. The exact correlation between relative distance and remoteness in logs is low, only 0.23. From the second column, we see that if remoteness simply replaces bilateral distance (d_{ij}) as the measure of distance, the significance of distance falls, but remains very high. In addition, the coefficients and Student ts of border and language (especially border) notably rise and the coefficient of North–South Difference turns negative. This is not surprising, since these last three variables now largely reflect geographical proximity between trading pairs. But the third column is the fundamental one. When relative distance and remoteness are both present together, relative distance completely dominates remoteness, with a Student t about 15 times higher. In addition, the impact of North–South Difference returns to a positive value and this positive value is the same as before in column (1). To all evidence, therefore, distance exerts mostly a substitution effect rather than a scale effect on foreign trade.

As mentioned before, this last result helps to interpret some earlier evidence. Previous authors have commented on the improbably high magnitudes of the effects of distance on aggregate trade in gravity equations (e.g. Grossman 1998). But according to the last column of Table 5.2, a percentage fall in distance only

Table 5.2. *The effect of relative distance*

Log distance	−1.26		
	(0.03)		
Log relative distance			−0.68
			(0.02)
Log product of remoteness		−1.08	−0.18
		(0.08)	(0.07)
Log product of real GDP	1.37	1.38	1.38
	(0.01)	(0.02)	(0.01)
Log product of population	−0.42	−0.49	−0.42
	(0.02)	(0.02)	(0.02)
Log product of land area	−0.18	−0.18	−0.19
	(0.01)	(0.01)	(0.01)
Common land border (0,1)	0.84	2.44	0.73
	(0.12)	(0.13)	(0.13)
Number of landlocked in	−0.41	−0.35	−0.36
pair (0, 1, 2)	(0.04)	(0.05)	(0.04)
Common language (0,1)	0.92	1.3	0.84
	(0.06)	(0.07)	(0.06)
Log North–South Difference	0.23	−0.16	0.26
	(0.02)	(0.02)	(0.02)
R^2	0.64	0.58	0.64
RMSE	1.99	2.14	1.98

Note: Regressand is log of bilateral trade in real American dollars. Number of Observations is 31,010. Year-specific fixed effects are not reported. Robust standard errors recorded in parentheses.

raises *aggregate* trade by around one-third of one percent (2×0.18 or 0.36 since $R_i R_j$ relates to distance squared) rather than over one percent (1.26, if we judge from column 1). The rest of the impact of distance concerns the cross-country composition of trade. The result also helps to understand why distance has risen, not fallen, as an influence on *bilateral* trade with the drop in costs of transportation over time. While falls in transportation costs might have been expected to reduce the impact of remoteness (as indeed they seem to have),[9] they could well have increased the impact of distance on bilateral trade in deciding whether to ship near or far.[10]

5.6   The Effects of Political Associations

The next series of tests concern the five political variables in Rose and Frankel's tests: Currency Union, Political Union, Free Trade Area (FTA), Ex-Colonial Relationship and Ex-Common Colonizer. According to Rose's series, some

[9] Boisso and Ferrantino (1997) notably show that exports travel longer distances since 1960.

[10] Of course, if transportation costs should ever become tiny, further reductions in these costs would not continue to raise the influence of relative distance on bilateral trade.

countries (territories or departments in certain cases) in a political union also belong to a "free trade area" (to use the Rose 2000 term) whereas others do not, depending on whether there exists a separate free trade agreement between them. Instead, I adopt the principle that a political union always implies a free trade area, and therefore score country pairs as belonging to a FTA only if they are not part of a Political Union. This will clarify the subsequent interpretation of the results, as we will see. Following this further change in the data (in addition to the earlier ones in the preceding section), the estimate of the basic gravity equation is the one in the first column of Table 5.3. As we know already from Frankel and Rose (2002), all five political variables appear with positive and significant signs. The least significant of these signs, with a Student t of 2.4, regards Political Union. But this political variable is the one that possesses the least number of observations. There are only forty-seven cases of Political Union entering in the tests (because of no missing complementary data), while there are 284 such cases of Currency Union, 427 ones of Ex-Colonial Relationship, 764 ones of FTA and 2,630 ones of Ex-common Colonizer. These other four political variables all have Student ts over 6.

The next column admits effects on trade with outsiders. Specifically, the column adds dummy variables for country pairs consisting of one member of a political association and one non-member. Thus, the dummy Currency Union/Outsider concerns trade between one member of a currency union and one non-member, the dummy Political Union/Outsider between one member of a political union and one non-member, FTA/Outsider between one member of a free trade area and one non-member and Ex-colonized/Colonizer/Outsider between one ex-colonized or ex-colonizer and a country which is neither one. This last dummy does double duty for the effects of Ex-Colonial Relationship and Ex-Common-Colonizer on outsiders.[11] Identically constructed dummy variables have served in a similar way in other studies. Frankel (with and without coauthors) uses FTA/Outsider in order to test for substitution or scale effects of FTAs on outsiders,[12] and both Rose and Rose–Frankel use Currency Union/Outsider in such tests for currency unions. Furthermore, these earlier studies report the same results for the relevant dummies: That is, both FTAs and currency unions increase trade with outsiders. As indicated before, I largely exhibit the generality of the finding. Instead of merely testing for third-country effects of different political variables one at a time, I test for all of them together and show that monetary union, Political Union and FTAs all promote trade with

---

[11] Any effort to introduce separate dummies for the impact of Ex-Colonial Relationship and Ex-Common-Colonizer on outsiders would only lead to confusion. Both dummies would comprise cases of trade between an ex-colonized and an outsider, and the main differences between the two would concern instances of an Ex-Colonial Relationship or an Ex-Common Colonizer, and therefore would be reflected in these other two variables.

[12] Though he refers instead to a variable that he terms "openness," which combines FTA and FTA/Outsider (but when used together with FTA, essentially denotes FTA/Outsider).

Jacques Mélitz

Table 5.3. *The effects of political associations*

			Revised definitions of political variables[a]	Further revised definitions of political variables[b]
Log relative distance	−0.64	−0.65	−0.65	−0.65
	(0.02)	(0.02)	(0.02)	(0.02)
Log product of	−0.11	−0.18	−0.19	−0.18
remoteness	(0.07)	(0.07)	(0.07)	(0.07)
Log product of	1.40	1.35	1.36	1.36
real GDP	(0.01)	(0.02)	(0.02)	(0.02)
Log product of	−0.43	−0.37	−0.37	−0.37
population	(0.02)	(0.02)	(0.02)	(0.02)
Log product of	−0.17	−0.18	−0.18	−0.18
land area	(0.01)	(0.01)	(0.01)	(0.01)
Common land	0.75	0.80	0.80	0.79
border (0, 1)	(0.12)	(0.13)	(0.13)	(0.13)
Number of landlocked	−0.31	−0.29	−0.30	−0.30
in pair (0, 1, 2)	(0.04)	(0.04)	(0.04)	(0.04)
Common language	0.49	0.49	0.48	0.48
(0, 1)	(0.06)	(0.06)	(0.06)	(0.06)
Log North–South	0.26	0.25	0.25	0.25
Difference	(0.02)	(0.02)	(0.02)	(0.02)
Currency Union	1.45	1.59		
(0, 1)	(0.18)	(0.19)		
Strict Currency Union			1.89	2.10
(0, 1)			(0.24)	(0.49)
Combined Currency			2.18	2.43
Union (0, 1)			(0.22)	(0.18)
Political Union (0, 1)	1.01	1.35	0.98	0.98
	(0.42)	(0.43)	(0.64)	(0.64)
Free Trade Area (0, 1)	1.03	1.16	1.24	1.24
	(0.10)	(0.11)	(0.11)	(0.11)
Ex-Colonial	1.95	1.52	1.57	1.57
Relationship (0, 1)	(0.13)	(0.14)	(0.14)	(0.14)
Ex-Common-Colonizer	0.50	0.56	0.55	0.57
(0, 1)	(0.08)	(0.09)	(0.09)	(0.09)
Currency Union/		0.30	0.34	0.34
Outsider (0, 1)		(0.04)	(0.04)	(0.04)
Political Union/		0.25	0.29	0.29
Outsider (0, 1)		(0.05)	(0.06)	(0.06)
FTA/Outsider (0, 1)		0.29	0.29	0.29
		(0.05)	(0.05)	(0.05)

Table 5.3. (*Continued*)

		Revised definitions of political variables[a]		Further revised definitions of political variables[b]
Ex-Colony/Colonizer/		0.03	0.04	0.04
Outsider (0, 1)		(0.04)	(0.04)	(0.05)
R^2	0.65	0.65	0.65	0.65
RMSE	1.96	1.94	1.94	1.94

[a] All of the observations of joint membership in a Currency Union and a Political Union or a Free Trade Area are now classified under Combined Currency Union. These observations have also been removed from Political Union and Free Trade Area. The dummies Political Union/Outsider and FTA/Outsider have been redefined accordingly.
[b] All of the observations of joint members of a Currency Union who had the same colonizer in the past have now been added to Combined Currency Union. (There are no similar cases of a previous colony and colonizer who are in a currency union.) These observations have been removed from Common Ex-Colonizer, and the dummy Ex-Colony/Colonizer/Outsider has been redefined accordingly.

Notes: Regressand is log of bilateral trade in real American dollars. Number of Observations is 31,010. Year-specific fixed effects are not reported. Robust standard errors recorded in parentheses.

outsiders. Furthermore, in all three cases, the trade creation among the members of the political associations themselves is much higher than that with outsiders, but both effects are well marked. It may be noted as well that in the tests concerning influences on third parties, the number of observations relating to third-party effects is a multiple of the one relating to the associated effects on the principals themselves (by an order of four). Also, the new dummy variables do not detract from anything in the rest of the equation.

5.7 Currency Union

The final part of the discussion focuses on the hottest topic in connection with the political variables: The impact of Currency Union. This last political variable has a coefficient of around 1.5 with a Student t of 8 in columns (1) and (2). Taken at face value, the coefficient would say that entering into a currency union increases trade between the members by a factor of 3.5 (exp(1.5) $\simeq$ 4.5). But there is good reason to think that countries will only form a currency union if they already enjoy particularly close economic or political ties with one another. If so, much of the 1.5 coefficient of currency union may be attributable to features of the relationship having nothing to do with a common currency.

The first two columns of Table 5.3 are consistent with this interpretation, since the coefficient of Currency Union in these columns exceeds those for either Political Union or FTA. It is extremely difficult to see how removing the frictions of separate currencies could possibly promote trade more than removing protective trade barriers or entering into political union (which I interpret to mean removing trade barriers as well). Thus, those first two columns can be said nearly to invite the hypothesis that currency unions share many of the attributes of FTA and Political Union in the tests, whatever the political engagements may be. At least this hypothesis merits testing. In fact, a test is possible.

It so happens that the 284 usable observations of bilateral trade between members of a currency union (because of no missing complementary data) divide into 108 cases of country pairs that are also members of a political union or a FTA and 176 country pairs that are not. Of the 176 observations of pairs in a currency union belonging to neither a political union nor a FTA, most concern Africans with a shared colonial past. If we remove these next African examples from the previous 176 in order to isolate currency unions between pairs with no other relevant political affiliation whatever, we are down to only fifty-six observations. Those fifty-six essentially fall into three groups: Liberia, the Turk Caicos Islands, Panama, the Bahamas, the British Virgin Islands, Bermuda, and the United States, all of which use the U.S. dollar; African countries in a franc zone but without past colonial ties to France; and a heterogeneous lot consisting of the Australia–Kiribati–Nauru ensemble, Bhutan and India and Ireland and the United Kingdom prior to 1980. My proposed tests exploit these divisions in the sample.

Column (3) of Table 5.3 distinguishes between the currency unions consisting of country pairs that are not members of a political union or a FTA, labeled Strict and the rest, labeled Combined (in which there happen to be no cases of pairs composed on an earlier colonized and colonizer). Column (4) interprets Strict Currency Unions even more narrowly as even excluding country pairs with a past common colonizer (thus leaving only fifty-six examples). In both columns (3) and (4), the variables Political Union, Free Trade Area, Ex-Colonial Relationship, and Ex-Common Colonizer are redefined so as to exclude the cases of Combined Currency Union. As a result, all pairs belonging to a Combined Currency Union appear under no other political rubric. The four relevant dummies pertaining to trade with outsiders in columns (3) and (4) have been redefined accordingly as well (except that there has been no effort to construct separate dummies concerning the effects of Strict Currency Union and Combined Currency Union on outsiders and Currency Union/Outsider has been retained as such).[13]

The estimates in columns (3) and (4) confirm the hypothesis that currency unions imply exceptionally close trade ties, whether the countries in the relationship

---

[13] The reason for avoiding the fabrication of two such dummies is similar to the one for failing to provide separate dummies for the impact of colonized/colonizer and common colonizer on outsiders (footnote 11): any such attempt would simply raise problems of interpretation.

belong to a common country or have signed a free trade covenant. If Rose's interpretation of the coefficient of Currency Union is correct, the coefficient of Combined Currency Union in column (3) should be much higher than that of Strict Currency Union, since this coefficient should reflect the combined influence of currency union and either Political Union or FTA (a combined influence that is not reflected elsewhere in the equation). But this is not the case. The difference between the two coefficients is only about 0.3. Instead, it would need to be around 1.2 to reflect the impact of Political Union or FTA (predominantly FTA) according to the rest of the equation and the difference between 0.3 and 1.2 is statistically significant.[14] The same conclusion holds in column (4): The coefficient of Combined Currency Union is not nearly high enough above that of Strict Currency Union to admit the supplementary effect of nationhood or free trade agreement.[15]

However, the estimates in columns (3) and (4) are also impossible to reconcile with the view that currency union does not raise trade at all. To see this, consider the coefficient 2.18 of Combined Currency Union in column (3). According to the rest of this column, the part of this coefficient reflecting nationhood or FTA should be around 1.2. Another 0.25 may be added to reflect the fact that nearly one-half of the observations of Combined Currency Union relate to country pairs that not only belong to the same nation or a FTA, but also share a common earlier colonizer (0.5 applied to one half of the observations yields 0.25). This gives a total of 1.45. Therefore, currency union must account for the difference of 0.73, or 2.18 minus 1.45 and this difference is statistically significant.[16] The 0.73 estimate is also coherent. It would mean that of the 1.89 coefficient of Strict Currency Union, 1.16 of it—a reasonable amount in light of the rest of the estimate—should be attributed to combined effects of lower trade barriers and past colonial relations rather than a common currency, as such.

In the case of column (4), similar reasoning requires a higher estimate than 0.73 for the impact of a common currency, as such, since the previous attribution of 1.45 to other factors applies only to about two-thirds of the observations of Combined Currency Union and as regards the remaining third (relating strictly to country pairs with a shared colonial past), the right attribution is 0.5. This yields a weighted-average attribution to other factors of around 1.1. Consequently, currency union must account for 1.3 of the coefficient of 2.4 of Combined Currency Union. All in all, therefore, I come to an estimate of the impact of currency union on trade of about 0.7–1.3. The lower estimate, 0.7, is

---

[14] The presence of a shared colonial past does not affect this comparison, since cases of such a shared past are proportionally just as significant for Strict Currency Union and Combined Currency Union alike. In addition, the coefficient of Ex-Common Colonizer is only 0.5.

[15] The lower statistical significance of Political Union in columns (3) and (4) than (1) and (2) must be put down to the fact that there are only twenty-nine cases of political union without currency union, and therefore only twenty-nine relevant observations in columns (3) and (4) instead of the forty-seven relevant ones in columns (1) and (2).

[16] I abstract in this reasoning from the possibility of joint effects of common currency, an FTA or a political union, and a shared colonial past that differ from the sum of the three separate effects.

my preferred one, because of the paucity of instances of a Strict Currency Union in column (4), which makes that column more doubtful. Even so, the exponential of 0.7 is close to 2. Therefore, we are still talking about a doubling of trade, if no longer about a quadrupling or more.

This estimate of the downward adjustment of Rose's figure for the impact of currency union on trade is admittedly rough. Interestingly enough, though, the result is confirmed by more recent work by Rose together with Glick. My effort rests on a data set containing at most six observations per individual trading pair and therefore relates essentially to the cross-sectional evidence. By contrast, Glick and Rose (2002) use *annual* series starting as early as 1948 and going up to 1997 in a study covering over 230 countries (IMF country codes) and harboring over 200,000 data points. As they possess many more observations per individual country pair, Glick and Rose are able to employ panel data econometrics to estimate a separate coefficient for the impact of currency union on bilateral trade *over time*. More exactly, they are able to furnish a "within" as well as a "between" estimate for the impact of currency union. Their "within" estimate relates strictly to the impact of entry into, or exit from, currency union for individual country pairs, whereas their "between" estimate, with close bearing on all of Rose's previous work, concerns cross sections or different pairs. Their former estimate does not mix up effects of currency union with those of close trade and political ties, while their latter one continues to do so.

Glick and Rose's "within" estimate is 0.74 and their "between" estimate 1.57. Effectively, therefore, their "within" estimate matches exactly mine for the impact of a common currency on bilateral trade after the corrections, while their "between" one basically repeats Rose's own earlier estimates for the impact of currency union, alone or with Frankel and my uncorrected estimates in columns (1) and (2) of Table 5.3. There could hardly be closer correspondence. Admittedly, Glick and Rose's "within" estimate is statistically superior to mine as regards the impact of currency union as such. But my effort clarifies the gap between their "within" and "between" estimates, which they leave unexplained.

The 0.7 estimate of the impact of currency union on trade might be lowered still more in the instance of countries that already trade intensely with each other by following Rose and van Wincoop in the systematic adoption of the concept of "multilateral trade resistance" in the tests. Of course, the scope for doing so is narrowed in my case since some aspects of "multilateral trade resistance" are already present in the reasoning—specifically, respecting distance and countries belonging to any of the five relevant political associations. Still, since I do not control systematically for the adverse impact of political frontiers on foreign trade, there remains room for further application of Rose and van Wincoop's argument. However, I believe this to be even truer for Glick and Rose.

Once we take the position that all of the estimates of the influence of currency union on bilateral trade prior to Glick and Rose's pertain to cases of low trade barriers, whether formal trade or political agreements exist to that effect, it becomes difficult to assign a separate empirical interpretation to the estimates of

Currency Union/Outsider as distinct from those of Political Union/Outsider, FTA/Outsider and Ex-Colony/Colonizer/Outsider. Nonetheless, these estimates generally point to effects on (the log of) trade with outsiders of about one-third to one-sixth the size of those on (the log of) trade between the principals in the political relationships. Therefore, the best estimate of the impact of currency union, as such, on (the log of) trade with outsiders is one-third to one-sixth of 0.7. As mentioned earlier, theory offers little ground to dispute this effect on outsiders. But a systematic application of the concept of "multilateral trade resistance" could modify the estimate.[17]

5.8 Conclusion

Gravity equations yield remarkably good statistical fits. This study focuses broadly on the proper variables to include in these equations. Two of the results are satisfying from a general conceptual standpoint. The forces of geography can be marshaled to exhibit the impact of comparative advantage on trade in gravity equations. It is also rewarding to find some explicit evidence of substitution effects of distance on trade with different foreign partners. The rest of the results do not necessarily fit neatly into preconceived ideas. We have no fundamental cause to think that closer political associations between countries will open them up to trade with everyone, or at least such general reasons as we have are contestable. I have argued that those positive effects on trade with third countries can be most easily explained in the case of currency unions. But even as regards currency unions, the positive effects on trade with outsiders would not necessarily have been predicted beforehand. It may also be satisfying to obtain estimates

---

[17] What about the result of introducing country fixed-effects into the estimates? It is important to note that, in this case, all of the variables that are defined by country and that are time-invariant drop out. This includes remoteness, land area, and landlocked. In addition, since population (also defined by country) sticks to a trend, it can hardly be expected to enter significantly. However, all of the other variables—notably those whose values depend on the country's trade partner—should be unaffected. The results for the test corresponding to the one in Table 5.3, column (2) (and thus prior to any distinction between Strict and Combined currency union) follows. I omit the 185 fixed effects (twenty-five of which drop out because of insufficient observations).

Bilateral Trade = −0.7 Relative Distance + 1.06 Real GDP + 0.54 Border + 0.5 Common Language
          (0.015)   (0.038)   (0.13)   (0.06)
  + 0.19 North–South + 1.05 Currency Union + 1.3 Political Union + 0.6 FTA + 1.63 Ex-Colonial
  (0.02)   (0.22)   (0.41)   (0.14)   (0.13)
  + 0.7 Ex-Common-Colonizer + 0.086 Currency Union/Outsider + 0.17 Political Union/Outsider
  (0.09)   (0.077)   (0.11)
  + 0.144 FTA/Outsider − 0.048 Ex-Colony/Colonizer/Outsider
  (0.058)   (0.038)
$R^2 = 0.73$; Number of observations = 31,010; Number of clusters = 7,963.

As can be seen, the results are highly confirmatory. The only doubts of any note that arise concern the positive third-country effects of Currency Union and Political Union. Compare the discussion of Pakko and Wall (2001) in n. 2.

of the impact of currency union on trade which are far below Rose's, or which can be interpreted to be so. Still, those effects on trade are pretty high.

All the results of the study, whether satisfying or not, are complicating. No longer is it possible to say that distance merely reflects costs and frictions in trade. Rather, distance in some dimension also reflects opportunities for trade. In addition, based on the traditional great-circle measures, distance in bilateral trade must be seen as combining both substitution effects between alternative foreign trade partners and scale effects on aggregate foreign trade (where those aggregate effects may be substitution effects between foreign and domestic trade). Fitting together and sorting out all of these effects of distance would be an undertaking. Finally, attempts to fit gravity equations into a neat theoretical groove have often treated political unions and free trade associations as trade-diverting. But such attempts, as well as any putative future attempts to treat currency union the same way, go contrary to the facts. The gravity model thus may need to be specified in a way that allows for complementary effects on bilateral trade with third countries. There is no problem in theory. But in practical application, such specification will complicate the programming of the constraints on total trade in bilateral trade relations, or the construction of "multilateral trade resistance." For example, Rose and van Wincoop (2001) have simply excluded all complementary effects on third countries.

REFERENCES

Anderson, J. and van Wincoop, E. (2003). "Gravity with Gravitas: A Solution to the Border Puzzle." *American Economic Review*, 93 (March): 170–92.

Bergstrand, J. (1998). "'Comment' on Deardorff." In J. Frankel (ed.), *The Regionalization of the World Economy*. University of Chicago Press, pp. 23–8.

Boisso, D. and Ferrantino, M. (1997). "Economic Distance, Cultural Distance and Openness in International Trade: Empirical Puzzles." *Journal of Economic Integration*, 12 (December): 456–84.

Deardorff, A. (1998). "Determinants of Bilateral Trade: Does Gravity Work in a Neoclassical World?" In J. Frankel (ed.), *The Regionalization of the World Economy*. University of Chicago Press, 7–22.

Diamond, J. (1997). *Guns, Germs and Steel: A Short History of Everybody for the Last 13,000 years*. New York: Random House.

Eaton, J. and Kortum, S. (1997). "Technology and Bilateral Trade." *NBER Working Paper* no. 6253.

Eichengreen, B. and Irwin, D. (1995). "Trade Blocs, Currency Blocs and the Reorientation of Trade in the 1930s." *Journal of International Economics*, 38 (February): 1–24.

Flandreau, M. (1995). "Trade, Finance, and Currency Blocs in Nineteenth Century Europe: Was the Latin American Union a Franc-zone? 1860–1880." In J. Reis (ed.), *Historical Perspective on International Monetary Arrangements*. Basingstoke, U.K.: Macmillan, pp. 71–89.

Frankel, J. (1997). *Regional Trading Blocs in the World Economic System*, Institute for International Economics.

— and Romer, D. (1999). "Does Trade Cause Growth?" *American Economic Review*, 89 (June): 379–99.

— and Rose, A. K. (2002). "An Estimate of the Effect of Currency Unions on Trade and Output." *Quarterly Journal of Economics*, 117 (May): 437–66.

— Stein, E., and Wei, S.-J. (1995). "Trading Blocs and the Americas: The Natural, the Unnatural and the Super-natural." *Journal of Development Economics*, 47 (June): 61–95.

— — and — (1998). "Continental Trading Blocs: Are they Natural or Super-natural?" In J. Frankel (ed.), *The Regionalization of the World Economy*. The University of Chicago Press, pp. 91–120.

— and Wei, S.-J. (1998). "Regionalization of World Trade and Currencies: Economics and Politics." In J. Frankel (ed.), *The Regionalization of the World Economy*. The University of Chicago Press, pp. 189–226.

Glick, R. and Rose, A. (2002). "Does a Currency Union affect Trade? The Time Series Evidence." *European Economic Review*, 46 (June): 1125–51.

Grossman, G. (1998). " 'Comment' on Deardorff." In J. Frankel (ed.), *The Regionalization of the World Economy*. The University of Chicago Press, pp. 29–31.

Hall, R. and Jones, C. (1999). "Why do Some Countries Produce so Much More Output Per Worker than Others?" *Quarterly Journal of Economics*, 114 (February): 83–116.

Helliwell, J. (1998). *How Much Do National Borders Matter?* Washington, DC: Brookings Institution.

— and Verdier, G. (2001). "Measuring International Trade Distances: A New Method Applied to Estimate Provincial Border Effects in Canada." *Canadian Journal of Economics*, 34 (November): 1024–41.

McCallum, J. (1995). "National Borders Matter: Canada–US: National Trade Patterns." *American Economic Review*, 85 (June): 615–23.

Nitsch, V. (2002). "Honey, I Shrunk the Currency Union Effect on Trade." *The World Economy*, 25 (April): 457–74.

Obstfeld, M. and Rogoff, K. (1996). *Foundations of International Macro-economics*. Cambridge, MA: MIT Press.

— and — (2001). "The Six Major Puzzles in International Macroeconomics: Is there a Common Cause?" In B. S. Bernanke and K. Rogoff (eds.), *NBER Macroeconomics Annual 2000*, 15, pp. 339–89.

Pakko, M. and Wall, H. (2001). "Reconsidering the Trade-creating Effects of a Currency Union." *Federal Reserve Bank of St. Louis Review*, 83 (September/October): 37–45.

Persson, T. (2001). "Currency Unions and Trade: How Large is the Treatment Effect?" *Economic Policy*, 33 (October): 433–62.

Rodriguez, F. and Rodrik, D. (2001). "Trade Policy and Economic Growth: A Skeptic's Guide to Cross-National Evidence." In B. S. Bernanke and K. Rogoff (eds.), *NBER Macroeconomics Annual 2000*, 15, pp. 261–324.

Rose, A. (2000). "One Money, One Market: Estimating the Effect of Common Currencies on Trade." *Economic Policy*, 30: 7–45.

— and van Wincoop, E. (2001). "National Money as a Barrier to International Trade: The Real Case for Currency Union." *American Economic Review*, 91 (May): 386–90.

Sachs, J. and Warner, A. (1997). "Fundamental Sources of Long-run Growth." *American Economic Review*, 87 (May): 184–8.

6

Comparing Apples and Oranges: The Effect of Multilateral Currency Unions on Trade

VOLKER NITSCH

I explore whether the two existing multilateral currency unions–the CFA franc zone in West and Central Africa and the Eastern Caribbean Currency Union (ECCU)–have a measurable effect on intraregional trade. I find that membership in a currency union indeed tends to promote trade, but the pattern of intra-union trade deviates much less from otherwise similar non-union trade than previous estimates of a large trade-multiplying effect of common currencies suggest. I also explore whether the common currency effect differs across country pairings, and find that economically large countries benefit most strongly from sharing a common currency.

6.1 Introduction

Recent empirical findings suggest that the adoption of a common currency has a large positive effect on bilateral trade. Analyzing trade flows between 186 countries, Andrew K. Rose (2000) estimates that membership in a currency union triples trade; two countries that share a common currency trade about three times as much with each other than two otherwise similar countries using different currencies. In a similar fashion, Reuven Glick and Rose (2002) examine changes in exchange rate regimes and find that bilateral trade approximately doubles/halves as a pair of countries forms/dissolves a currency union.

These results, derived from large cross-sectional data sets, have been questioned for at least two reasons. First, the actual number of country pairs that share a common currency is very small, typically less than one percent of the data. In principle, this is no problem but if the small subset differs from the rest

Chapter prepared for the CEPR/Fordham conference "Euro and Dollarization: Forms of Monetary Union in Integrating Regions." I am grateful to Jacques Mélitz, and conference participants at Fordham University for valuable comments and suggestions. Opinions expressed in this chapter do not necessarily represent the views of Bankgesellschaft Berlin.

of the sample, nonlinearities might affect the results. Second, the common
currency group in these data sets covers a large number of very different
experiences. In fact, the currency unions can be broadly summarized in three
different groups: (*a*) small, poor, and distant dependencies (typically islands)
that use the currency of their former colonial power or current home country
(e.g. Guadeloupe, St. Helena); (*b*) countries that have (mainly one-sidedly) adopted
the currency of a larger neighboring country (e.g. Bhutan, The Bahamas); and
(*c*) multilateral currency unions among regional neighbors (e.g. the ECCU). Since
there is no reason to assume that the effect of monetary integration on trade is
identical across these three groups,[1] a direct application of the estimated coefficient to recently proposed integration schemes may be inappropriate.[2]

To deal with these issues, Rose and his collaborators provide extensive
robustness checks. In particular, they experiment with a large number of additional controls. They also present results for different subsets of their sample
by dropping observations, and show that their estimates are robust to these
modifications.[3] However, since other estimation techniques (Torsten Persson
2001) and case studies (Rodney Thom and Brendan Walsh 2002; Nitsch 2002*b*)
yield much smaller estimates, serious doubts remain.

In this chapter, I propose an alternative (cross-sectional) approach to estimate
the effect of monetary integration on trade. In particular, I focus on the two
existing multilateral currency unions, the CFA franc zone in West and Central
Africa and the ECCU, and estimate their effect on the pattern of *intraregional*
trade. This approach offers two main advantages. First, both currency unions
share several characteristics with other recent projects of multilateral monetary
integration such as the European Monetary Union (EMU) or the proposed monetary union among the Arab Gulf states. Most notably, the member countries
are a very homogeneous group of geographically proximate countries with
similar production structures, similar historical experiences and social customs,
and a substantial base of formal and informal cooperation. Second, the focus
on intraregional trade allows a *direct* comparison of a country's trade with a
currency union member and an "otherwise similar" country using a different
currency. Thus, instead of trying to control for a large and diverse set of
country characteristics, this approach seeks to avoid nonlinearities in the first
place.

---

[1] For instance, the currency unions come with very different legal and institutional arrangements.
Eduardo Levy Yeyati (2003) and Nitsch (2002*a*) estimate the trade effects of different currency unions
separately and find indeed considerable differences.

[2] It is even debatable whether the first group of currency unions distinguished above, in which the
use of a common currency is due solely to a historical accident and not the result of independent
choice, provides any useful insights for current moves towards monetary integration. At best, they
may form a good control group to disentangle the trade effects of monetary integration from other,
non-monetary forms of cooperation.

[3] In the next chapter, Rose makes another forceful contribution to support his point.

To preview the main results, I find that multilateral currency unions have on average a positive effect on intraregional trade. CFA franc countries trade about 55 percent more with each other than with a typical non-union country in West and Central Africa, while the estimate for the ECCU is smaller and statistically not significantly different from zero. In any case, the trade-enhancing effect of multilateral monetary unions is considerably below Rose's estimate of factor three, thereby confirming other estimates of a positive but moderate effect of common currencies on trade. Moreover, exploring the extent to which the currency union effect differs across country pairs, I find that especially economically large countries appear to benefit from a common currency.

The chapter is structured as follows. Section 6.2 provides some background about the multilateral currency unions on which the empirical analysis is based. Section 6.3 presents the methodology and data. Section 6.4 shows the results, and Section 6.5 concludes.

6.2   Background

Before EMU, there were already two multilateral currency unions; both largely maintaining earlier systems of monetary cooperation after former colonies had gained independence.

In Africa, the French colonial franc was followed by two distinct franc-based monetary unions, the West African Economic and Monetary Union (WAEMU), originally established in 1962, and the Central African Economic and Monetary Community (CAEMC), founded in 1964. These two regional groupings together form the CFA franc zone; although the CFA franc is issued separately by each subzone and stands for the Communauté financière africaine in West Africa and for the Coopération financière en Afrique in Central Africa, it is exchangeable one-for-one against each other and collectively pegged to the euro (and formerly the French franc). Current members of the CFA franc zone are Benin, Burkina Faso, Côte d'Ivoire, Guinea-Bissau, Mali, Niger, Senegal, and Togo in the WAEMU; and Cameroon, the Central African Republic, Chad, the Republic of Congo, Equatorial Guinea, and Gabon in the CAEMC. Combined, the fourteen members have a population of 102 million, and total GDP was an estimated 47 billion US dollars in 2000.[4]

In the Caribbean, eight small island territories form the (ECCU): Antigua and Barbuda, Dominica, Grenada, St. Kitts and Nevis, St. Lucia, St. Vincent and the Grenadines, and the two British dependencies Anguilla and Montserrat. Having shared most of their monetary history, British colonial territories in the Caribbean (then also including Barbados, British Guyana, and Trinidad and Tobago) agreed already in 1946 to establish a unified currency system based on

---

[4] For more details about the CFA franc zone, see, for example, Ernesto Hernández-Catá (1998) and Paul Masson and Catherine Pattillo (2001). Patrick Honohan and Philip R. Lane (2000) provide an excellent history of monetary integration in Africa.

the West Indian dollar, and the British Caribbean Currency Board was created in 1950. With the formation of the Eastern Caribbean Currency Authority in 1965, the West Indian dollar was replaced by the Eastern Caribbean dollar. The currency, initially still pegged to the British pound at the same exchange parity, was linked to the U.S. dollar in 1976. The combined population of the ECCU was 568,000 in 1998, with a total GDP of about 2.5 billion U.S. dollars.[5]

The most interesting feature for my purposes, however, is that in both monetary unions internal trade is relatively small. Since the member countries are mainly primary commodity producers, they trade little among themselves; most of their exports and imports are with industrial countries. Members of the CFA franc zone export coffee, cocoa, cotton, fish products, timber, and groundnuts (with some countries also being strongly dependent on a single commodity such as bauxite in Guinea, uranium in Niger, and oil in Nigeria) so that intra-WAEMU trade is only an estimated 12 percent of the countries' total trade (ignoring informal trade), while for CAEMC, the estimate is even lower at about 6 percent (Masson and Pattillo 2001). For ECCU members, traditionally producers of banana, sugar, and root crops (tourism is now the most important source of foreign exchange earnings), a rough estimate suggests that internal trade accounts for less than 10 percent of the countries' total trade.

The advantages of monetary integration for promoting trade within these regions may therefore appear to be limited. Even if intraregional trade is small, however, and thus most of the countries' trade is unaffected by the monetary arrangement, the common currency effect (i.e. the percentage change in intra-union trade relative to another regional neighbor country that uses a different currency) can still be important.

6.3   Methodology and Data

Following Rose (2000), I use an augmented gravity model to estimate the effects of currency unions on trade. The only notable difference is that I run separate regressions for intraregional trade in West and Central Africa and the Caribbean. Given this focus on two very homogeneous country groups, the number of controls is reduced. In fact, apart from the two standard gravity variables distance and output, I add only a few extra conditioning variables. In particular, I estimate an equation of the form:

$$\ln(T_{ijt}) = \alpha + \beta_1 \ln(Y_i Y_j)_t + \beta_2 \ln(Y_i Y_j / Pop_i Pop_j)_t + \beta_3 \ln D_{ij} + \beta_4 Lang_{ij} + \beta_5 Cont_{ij} + \beta_6 ComCol_{ij} + \gamma CU_t + \varepsilon_{ijt}, \tag{1}$$

where T_{ijt} denotes the real bilateral trade between countries i and j at time t, Y is real GDP, Pop is population, D is the distance between i and j, $Lang$ is

---

[5] Frits van Beek et al. (2000) and Masson and Pattillo (2001: appendix 3) provide a good overview about the ECCU.

a common language dummy, *Cont* is a common land border dummy, *ComCol* is a common colonizer dummy, *CU* is the common currency dummy, and ε is a stochastic error term.

The data is taken mainly from Jeffrey A. Frankel and Rose (2002).[6] This data set contains information on total bilateral trade (deflated by the U.S. GDP chain price index) for the period from 1970 to 1995 in five-year-intervals. All the other data are recalculated and cross-checked with their original sources. These are the *Penn World Table* (PWT) 5.6 for population and real GDP per capita data, merged with data from the World Bank's *World Development Indicators* where data from the PWT is missing, and the CIA *World Factbook* for information on geographic coordinates, languages, contiguity, and colonizers.[7]

Since I focus on intraregional trade flows, my samples include the following countries (in addition to the actual currency union members): Angola, the Democratic Republic of Congo, Gambia, Ghana, Guinea, Liberia, Mauritania, Nigeria, and Sierra Leone in West and Central Africa; and Aruba, the Dominican Republic, Guadeloupe, Haiti, Jamaica, Martinique, Netherlands Antilles, and Trinidad and Tobago, in the Caribbean.[8] The Caribbean sample does not include all countries and territories in the region. For ECCU member Anguilla I have no trade data so that this British dependency is dropped. The Bahamas, Barbados, Bermuda, British Virgin Islands, Turks and Caicos Islands, and the U.S. Virgin Islands are excluded because they either use the U.S. dollar directly as their national currency or operate a hard peg to the U.S. dollar; since the Eastern Caribbean dollar is also linked to the U.S. dollar with a fixed parity, an inclusion of these islands would bias the integration effects of the ECCU downward. The Cayman Islands and Cuba are excluded because I have no data on per capita income. Taken together, my samples consist of twenty-three countries in Africa and fourteen countries or territories in the Caribbean, yielding a total of 253 (=23(22)/2) and 91 (=14(13)/2) potential bilateral trade observations per year, respectively. Due to missing observations, however, the actual sample is often considerably smaller.

Table 6.1 presents some summary statistics of the key variables. At least four observations are noteworthy. First, the actual data sample covers in both cases only less than one-half of the potential universe of observations; the majority of the 1518 (=253(6) years) data points in Africa and the 546 (=91(6) years) data points in the Caribbean are missing. Second, the data are indeed, as intended, very homogeneous across the two subsets in the regions. Means and standard deviations are broadly similar for the currency union and the non-union samples.

---

[6] The data are kindly provided by Andrew Rose on his web site (http://faculty.haas.berkeley.edu/arose).

[7] There are some minor differences which do not affect the results. I have also experimented, for instance, with an alternative distance measure derived from the geographic location of the countries' largest cities (see Jacques Mélitz, this volume), but the results were basically identical.

[8] In a few cases, membership changes over time; these changes are considered in the currency union dummy.

Table 6.1. *Descriptive statistics*

	Total	Currency union	Non-currency union
CFA Franc			
Bilateral trade	7.86 (2.58)	8.26 (2.51)	7.67 (2.60)
Distance	7.24 (0.68)	7.28 (0.62)	7.22 (0.71)
Output	30.85 (1.61)	30.70 (1.08)	30.92 (1.80)
Output per capita	13.81 (0.70)	14.09 (0.79)	13.68 (0.62)
Language	0.60 (0.49)	1.00 (0.00)	0.42 (0.49)
Colonizer	0.49 (0.50)	0.96 (0.21)	0.28 (0.45)
No. of observations	432	134	298
Eastern Caribbean dollar			
Bilateral trade	8.13 (2.09)	7.52 (1.43)	8.44 (2.30)
Distance	6.27 (0.94)	5.50 (0.65)	6.66 (0.81)
Output	27.24 (2.71)	24.29 (1.34)	28.75 (1.86)
Output per capita	16.10 (1.00)	15.96 (0.98)	16.17 (1.00)
Language	0.61 (0.49)	1.00 (0.00)	0.42 (0.49)
Colonizer	0.60 (0.49)	1.00 (0.00)	0.40 (0.49)
No. of observations	243	82	161

Note: The table reports the means (standard deviations) for different data samples.

However, ECCU members are particularly tiny, a bit poorer, somewhat closer in distance, and have less bilateral trade than the other Caribbean islands in the sample. Third, all members of a currency union speak a common language. (Since Portuguese-speaking Guinea-Bissau entered the CFA franc zone only in 1997, it is consistently treated as a non-member in my data set.) Fourth, the ratio of currency union observations to non-currency union observations is now about 1 : 2 compared with 1 : 100 in Rose's large cross-country sample.

6.4   Results

6.4.1   Basic results

Table 6.2 shows the results of the gravity regressions. The first column presents the estimation results of pooled regressions for West African trade.[9] The coefficients on the standard controls are all statistically highly significant and economically reasonable; a one percent increase in the countries' GDP raises their bilateral trade by about 0.7 percent, while a one percent increase in the bilateral distance lowers trade by about 0.6 percent.

---

[9] I have also experimented with separate regressions for individual years, but due to the wildly varying number of observations, comprising for each year quite different combinations of country pairs, the coefficient estimates were very imprecise.

Table 6.2. *Does a common currency affect regional trade patterns?*

	West and Central Africa	Eastern Caribbean
Currency union	0.63*	−0.22
	(0.32)	(0.30)
Distance	−0.60**	−0.67**
	(0.19)	(0.11)
Output	0.71**	0.65**
	(0.07)	(0.07)
Output per capita	0.11	0.44**
	(0.17)	(0.14)
Language	0.14	0.02
	(0.34)	(0.26)
Border	1.60**	
	(0.29)	
Colonizer	0.81*	2.51**
	(0.37)	(0.29)
No. of observations	432	243
S.E.R.	2.10	1.33
R^2	0.34	0.59

* Denotes significance at the 5% level.
** Denotes significance at the 1% level.

Notes: OLS estimation. White heteroskedastic-consistent standard errors are in parentheses. Constant and year dummies not reported.

The main variable of interest, however, is the estimated coefficient on the currency union dummy. This coefficient is positive and statistically significant. The magnitude of 0.63 implies that the countries of the CFA franc zone trade on average about 1.9 times (exp[0.63] = 1.88) as much with each other than they do with other countries in West and Central Africa. This estimate confirms findings that a single currency enhances trade, but is considerably smaller than Rose's (2000) estimates of an average common currency effect of more than factor three.[10] There is another notable difference, however. While Rose finds that the currency union effect clearly exceeds the effects of sharing a common border or having the same colonizer, the results for West and Central Africa suggest that the effect of monetary integration on trade is slightly smaller than having the same colonizer, and much smaller than having a common land border. Instead of dominating other forms of integration, membership in a currency union rather yields "conventional" effects of reducing transaction costs

---

[10] Using price differences as measure of market integration, David Parsley and Shang-Jin Wei (2001) also find for the CFA franc zone a positive integration effect (i.e. lower price dispersion), but the estimated effect is smaller than that for the U.S. dollar, hard pegs (such as currency boards), and the euro.

(perhaps with one exception: The surprisingly insignificant effect of speaking the same language; this dummy, however, is highly collinear with the common colonizer dummy).[11]

The second column in Table 6.2 performs a similar analysis for the Caribbean sample. Again, the gravity framework works well in explaining bilateral trade flows, even between these tiny Caribbean islands; both higher GDP and shorter distances increase trade. Also, there is a very strong and statistically highly significant effect of having the same (ex-)colonizer. Most notably, however, trade between member countries of the ECCU does not deviate significantly from the pattern explained by these standard gravity variables; the coefficient on the currency union dummy is statistically indistinguishable from zero at conventional levels of significance. If anything, the negative γ coefficient suggests that trade between islands sharing a common currency may be less-than-proportional. This result generally confirms the findings for the CFA franc zone; monetary integration on a multilateral basis has a much smaller effect on trade than pooled estimates for a broad set of currency unions suggest, even if the exact size of the trade effect may vary across the different experiences of monetary integration.

6.4.2 Extensions

To check the robustness of the results, I provide two sorts of extensions. In a first exercise, I follow Rose and Eric van Wincoop (2001) and add country specific effects. As shown in the two left columns of Table 6.3, this specification tends to yield lower estimates of γ (similar to Rose and van Wincoop's findings). The estimated γ coefficient for the CFA franc zone falls to 0.35, meaning that the trade-enhancing effect of a common currency is reduced to only 42 percent (exp[0.35] = 1.42). With a t-statistic of 0.82, the coefficient is even no longer statistically different from zero. For the ECCU, the estimated common currency effect becomes positive (and thus correctly signed), but remains statistically insignificant. Without taking the result too literally, the estimate suggests that intra-ECCU trade exceeds trade between islands using different currencies by about 9 percent (exp[0.09] = 1.09).

A second extension deals with one of the major shortcomings of the previous analysis, the fact that the results are based on only a small fraction, less than one-half, of the potential universe of country pairings. Mostly due to missing trade data, many country pairings are excluded from the analysis. In the remaining two columns of Table 6.3, I present the results of a very crude approach to proxy for these missing trade observations.

In particular, I fill in missing trade observations with the average (real) trade values for the years for which I have data. This appears to be a more promising

---

[11] I have repeated the regression with Rose's original data and produced basically identical results.

Table 6.3. *Extensions*

	Country fixed effects		Proxying for missing trade observations	
	West and Central Africa	Eastern Caribbean	West and Central Africa	Eastern Caribbean
Currency union	0.35	0.09	0.46*	−0.02
	(0.43)	(0.34)	(0.19)	(0.29)
Distance	−0.58*	−0.75**	−0.52**	−0.68**
	(0.26)	(0.12)	(0.13)	(0.10)
Output	3.63*	1.20	0.68**	0.64**
	(1.82)	(0.97)	(0.05)	(0.06)
Output per capita	−2.93***	−0.78	0.17***	0.59**
	(1.75)	(0.84)	(0.10)	(0.12)
Language	0.24	0.26	−0.25	0.23
	(0.35)	(0.92)	(0.22)	(0.24)
Border	1.64**		1.63**	
	(0.33)		(0.18)	
Colonizer	1.05*	1.88	0.68**	2.25**
	(0.47)	(1.49)	(0.22)	(0.26)
Country fixed effects?	Yes	Yes	No	No
No. of observations	432	243	1,007	307
S.E.R.	1.92	1.15	2.08	1.42
R^2	0.45	0.70	0.33	0.56

* Denote significance at the 5% level.
** Denote significance at the 1% level.
*** Denote significance at the 10% level.

Notes: OLS estimation. White heteroskedastic-consistent standard errors are in parentheses. Constant, year dummies and, if applicable, country fixed effects not reported.

approach than simply substituting missing trade values by a hypothetically small figure.[12]

The results are interesting. In West and Central Africa, the estimated trade-expanding effect of the CFA franc zone falls again sizably relative to the base specification. The coefficient on the currency union dummy, while still significant, drops to 0.46, implying that members of the CFA franc zone trade about 58 percent (exp[0.46] = 1.58) more than West and Central African countries with different currencies. This result strongly confirms other estimates of a positive but relatively moderate currency union effect on trade (Mélitz, this volume; Persson 2001).

---

[12] Silvana Tenreyro (2001) proposes a similar approach.

In the Caribbean, the trade effect of a common currency remains statistically insignificant; the estimated γ coefficient becomes essentially zero when the number of observations is increased.

6.4.3   Does the Currency Union effect differ across country pairs?

Another interesting issue is to explore whether the trade effect of monetary integration differs across country pairings. The aim of this exercise is twofold: First, there is some interest in the fact itself; to find that monetary integration affects the intensity of trade relations within a currency union differently would provide additional evidence that the aggregate estimate of the common currency effect on trade masks considerable heterogeneity among individual experiences (Levy Yeyati 2003; Michael W. Klein 2002; Nitsch 2002b). Second, if the common currency effect varies within the union, one might then also ask under which conditions monetary integration is likely to add to the intensity of trade relations among members.

To test the extent to which the common currency effect varies across country pairs, I add a number of interaction terms, in which the currency union dummy is multiplied by bilateral distances, pairwise output and pairwise output per capita, respectively, measured as the difference from the mean for the currency union sample. Positive coefficients on these variables would then imply that the trade effect of monetary integration is particularly strong in country pairs with this specific characteristic, and vice versa, while the γ coefficient captures the trade effect for a country pair with sample-average incomes, per capita incomes and distance.

Table 6.4 shows the results.[13] Interestingly, a clear pattern emerges. While for both analyzed currency unions, bilateral distance between members has no measurable effect on their intensity of trade, the interaction term with pairwise output is positive and statistically significant. This implies that the trade effect of a common currency is particularly strong for economically large countries. A potential explanation for this finding is that larger countries are more likely to have a diversified production structure and, generally, may operate as regional suppliers so that they benefit most strongly from a single currency.

Another interesting observation is that the particularly low estimate of the integration effects of the Eastern Caribbean dollar appears to be mainly the result of disproportionately low trade between ECCU members with above-average per capita income. For the Caribbean as a whole, I find the standard gravity result; the higher the country pairing's GDP per capita, the larger their bilateral trade. Entering a (separate) control for differences in per capita income among currency union members, however, yields a negative coefficient, suggesting that trade between ECCU country pairings with a high per capita GDP is significantly less-than-proportional. If one controls for this effect, the γ coefficient is positive and statistically highly significant.

---

[13] Entering the interaction terms separately does not change the results.

Table 6.4. *Does the currency union effect differ across country pairs?*

	West and Central Africa	Eastern Caribbean
Currency union	0.43*	1.26**
	(0.20)	(0.37)
Currency union × Distance	−0.27	−0.15
	(0.19)	(0.20)
Currency union × Output	0.68**	0.50**
	(0.11)	(0.13)
Currency union × Output per capita	0.20	−0.92**
	(0.19)	(0.20)
Distance	−0.44**	−0.65**
	(0.14)	(0.12)
Output	0.59**	0.62**
	(0.05)	(0.06)
Output per capita	0.03	0.70**
	(0.13)	(0.14)
Language	−0.05	0.31
	(0.22)	(0.27)
Border	1.66**	
	(0.18)	
Colonizer	0.36	2.13**
	(0.24)	(0.29)
No. of observations	1,007	307
S.E.R.	2.04	1.40
R^2	0.36	0.57

* Denotes significance at 5% level.
** Denotes significance at 1% level.

Notes: OLS estimation. White heteroskedastic-consistent standard errors are in parentheses. Constant and year dummies not reported.

6.5 Conclusion

Recent findings suggest that the adoption of a common currency has a large positive effect on bilateral trade. The evidence, however, is based on a broad sample of very different experiences, covering overseas territories that use the currency of their colonial power, countries that declare unilaterally the adoption of a foreign currency (dollarization), and countries that decide multilaterally to share a common currency.

This chapter aims to disentangle the effect of monetary unions on trade. In particular, the aim is to explore whether the two existing multilateral currency unions—the CFA franc zone in West and Central Africa and the ECCU—have a measurable effect on *intraregional* trade.

I find that membership in a currency union has only little effect on bilateral trade; two countries sharing a common currency trade, at best, about 55 percent more with each other than with an otherwise similar non-union member in the region. This effect is considerably smaller than previous estimates of a trade-multiplying effect of common currencies of up to 300 percent.

I also explore whether the common currency effect differs across country pairings, and find that economically large countries benefit most strongly from sharing a common currency.

REFERENCES

Frankel, J. A. and Rose, A. K. (2002). "An Estimate of the Effect of Common Currencies on Trade and Income." *Quarterly Journal of Economics*, 117 (May): 437–66.

Glick, R. and Rose, A. K. (2002). "Does a Currency Union Affect Trade? The Time Series Evidence." *European Economic Review*, 46 (June): 1125–51.

Hernández-Catá, E. (1998). "The West African Economic and Monetary Union: Recent Developments and Policy Issues." *Occasional Paper* 170, Washington, DC: IMF.

Honohan, P. and Lane, P. R. (2000). "Will the Euro Trigger More Monetary Unions in Africa?" *UNU/WIDER Working Paper* No. 176, Helsinki: United Nations University (UNU)/WIDER, March.

Klein, M. W. (2002). "Dollarization and Trade." *NBER Working Paper* No. 8879, Cambridge, MA: NBER, April.

Levy Yeyati, E. (2003). "On the Impact of a Common Currency on Bilateral Trade." *Economics Letters*, 79 (April): 125–29.

Masson, P. and Pattillo, C. (2001). "Monetary Union in West Africa (ECOWAS): Is It Desirable and How Could It Be Achieved?" *Occasional Paper* 204, Washington, DC: IMF.

Nitsch, V. (2002a). "Honey, I Shrunk the Currency Union Effect on Trade." *The World Economy*, 25 (April): 457–74.

— (2002b). "The Non-Causality of the Common Currency Effect on Trade: Evidence from the Monetary Union Between Belgium and Luxembourg." Draft, Bankgesellschaft Berlin.

Parsley, D. and Wei, S.-J. (2001). "Limiting Currency Volatility to Stimulate Goods Market Integration: A Price-Based Approach." *IMF Working Paper* No. 01/197, Washington, DC: IMF, December.

Persson, T. (2001). "Currency Unions and Trade: How Large is the Trade Effect?" *Economic Policy*, 33 (October): 433–62.

Rose, A. K. (2000). "One Money, One Market: Estimating the Effect of Common Currencies on Trade." *Economic Policy*, 30 (April): 7–33.

— and van Wincoop, E. (2001). "National Money as a Barrier to International Trade: the Real Case for Currency Union." *American Economic Review*, 91 (May): 386–90.

Tenreyro, S. (2001). "On the Causes and Consequences of Currency Unions." Draft, Harvard University, November.

Thom, R. and Walsh, B. (2002). "The Effect of a Common Currency on Trade: Lessons from the Irish Experience." *European Economic Review*, 46 (June): 1111–23.

van Beek, F., Rosales, J. R., Zermeño, M., Randall, R., and Shepherd, J. (2000). "The Eastern Caribbean Currency Union: Institutions, Performance, and Policy Issues." *Occasional Paper* 195, Washington, DC: IMF.

7

The Effect of Common Currencies on International Trade: A Meta-Analysis

ANDREW K. ROSE

Nineteen recent studies have investigated the effect of currency union on trade, resulting in 383 point estimates of the effect. Here, I provide a quantitative attempt to summarize the current state of debate; meta-analysis is used to combine the disparate estimates. The chief findings are that (*a*) the hypothesis that there is no effect of currency union on trade can be rejected at standard significance levels, (*b*) the combined estimate implies that currency union approximately doubles trade, and (*c*) the estimates are heterogeneous and not consistently tied to features of the studies.

7.1 Introduction

In this short chapter, I briefly review the small recent literature that estimates the effect of common currencies on trade. I use meta-analysis to provide a quantitative summary of the literature.

The next section briefly reviews the literature qualitatively. Section 7.3 is the heart of the chapter; it provides the quantitative meta-analysis that studies the preferred point estimates of the nineteen different studies collectively. Section 7.4 reviews the (almost 400) different point estimates tabulated in the literature, and the chapter ends with a short conclusion.

7.2 A Short History of the Literature

In the summer of 1999, I began to circulate a paper that estimated the effect of currency union on trade; *Economic Policy* subsequently published this paper in 2000. I exploited a panel of cross-country data covering bilateral trade between 186 "countries" (really different trading partners) at five-year intervals between 1970 and 1990. The trade data was drawn from the *World Trade Data Bank* ("WTDB"), which contains data for a large number of country-pairs (thereby effectively

---

I thank Justin Wolpers for helpful comments, and conference attendants at Fordham University. The data set, sample output, and a current version of the paper are available at my website.

rendering the analysis cross-sectional), though with many missing observations. In this data set, only a small number of the observations are currency unions; further, countries in currency unions tend to be either small or poor (or both).

The surprising and interesting finding was that currency union seemed to have a strong and robust effect on trade. Using a linear "gravity" model of bilateral trade to account for most variation in trade patterns, my point estimate was that the coefficient for a currency union dummy variable (which is unity when a pair of countries share a common currency and zero otherwise) has a point estimate of around $\gamma = 1.21$. This implies that members of currency unions traded over three times as much as otherwise similar pairs of countries *ceteris paribus*, since $\exp(1.21) > 3$. While there was no benchmark from the literature, this estimate seemed implausibly large to me (and many others).[1] Almost all the subsequent research in this area has been motivated by the belief that currency union cannot reasonable be expected to triple trade.

There have been a number of different types of critique. Some are econometric. For instance, Thom and Walsh (2002) argue that broad panel studies are irrelevant to, for example, the European Monetary Union (EMU), since most pre-EMU currency unions involve countries that are either small or poor. They adopt a case study approach, focusing on the 1979 dissolution of Ireland's sterling link; Glick and Rose (2002) provide related evidence.

Others have stressed the importance of relying on time series rather than cross-sectional variation. The time series approach has the advantage of addressing the relevant policy issue ("What happens to trade when a currency union is created or dissolved?" rather than "Is trade between members of currency unions larger than trade between countries with sovereign currencies?"). This can be done most obviously by using country-pair specific "dyadic fixed effects" with panel data. This is difficult to do sensibly using the WTDB because there is such little time series variation in currency union membership after 1970 as recognized in my original paper and by for example, Persson (2001); nevertheless, see Pakko and Wall (2001). However, Glick and Rose (2002) exploit the almost 150 cases of currency union exit and entry they find when the panel analysis is extended back to 1948 using the IMF's *Direction of Trade* data set.

In my original paper, I stressed that only about 1 percent of the sample involves pairs of countries in currency unions. Persson (2001) argues that this makes standard regression techniques inappropriate since currency unions are not created randomly, and advocates the use of matching techniques; see also Rose (2001) and Tenreyro (2001).

Nitsch (2002) is concerned with aggregation bias, and argues that combining different currency unions masks heterogeneous results. Along the same lines, Levy Yeyati (2001) divides currency unions into multilateral and unilateral currency unions (as did Fatás and Rose 2001), while Mélitz (2001) splits currency

---

[1] Actually, make that many many others.

unions into those that are also members of either a political union or regional trade area, and others that are neither; see also Klein (2002).

Tenreyro (2001) argues that sampling the data every fifth year (as I did in my original paper) is dangerous, since trade between members of currency unions may not be large enough to be consistently positive. She advocates averaging trade data over time, and argues that this reduces the (otherwise biased) effect of currency union on trade. While this may be true with the WTDB data set employed by Tenreyro, it seems not to be true of the DoT data set, where no bias is apparent (see my website for details).

Rather than focusing on post-Second World War data, some have extended the data set back to the classical gold standard era. Flandreau and Maurel (2001) and López-Córdova and Meissner (2001) use data sets that include monetary unions from the pre-First World War period. Estevadeoral et al. (2002) estimate a lower bound on the currency union effect by using membership in the gold standard; the inclusion of their estimates imparts a slight downward bias to the meta-analysis below.

A number of researchers have followed my original paper in worrying about reverse causality, including Flandreau and Maurel (2001), López-Córdova and Meissner (2001), and Tenreyro (2001). It is possible to also take a more structural approach as I do in my work with van Wincoop (Rose and van Wincoop 2001), which also takes account of country-specific effects.

Finally, some research takes a big effect of currency union on trade as given, and seeks to determine the implications of this estimate, for example, output (Frankel and Rose 2002) or business cycle coordination (Flandreau and Maurel 2001). Other aspects of the behavior of currency union members are examined by Rose and Engel (2002) and Fatás and Rose (2001).

In all, a number of papers have provided estimates of the effect of currency union on international trade. Obviously many of these estimates are highly dependent; they sometimes rely on the same data set, techniques, or authors. Still, there seem to be enough studies to warrant at least a preliminary meta-analysis.

7.3   Meta-Analysis

Meta-analysis is a set of quantitative techniques for evaluating and combining empirical results from different studies. Essentially, one treats different point estimates of a given coefficient as individual observations. One can then use this vector of estimates to estimate the underlying coefficient of interest, test the hypothesis that the coefficient is zero, and link the estimates to features of the underlying studies. Since there are currently a number of studies that have provided estimates of γ, the effect of currency union on trade, meta-analysis seems an appropriate way to summarize the current state of the literature. Stanley (2001) provides a recent review and further references.

One begins meta-analysis by collecting as many estimates of a common effect as possible. To my knowledge, there are nineteen papers that provide estimates

Andrew K. Rose

Table 7.1. *Meta-analysis of currency union effect on trade (γ)*

	Pooled estimate of γ	Lower bound of 95% CI	Upper bound of 95% CI	p-value for test of no effect
Fixed	0.77	0.72	0.83	0.00
Random	0.73	0.58	0.88	0.00
Fixed without Rose	0.80	0.71	0.90	0.00
Random without Rose	0.57	0.32	0.83	0.00

of the effect of currency union on bilateral trade, which I denote γ. I tabulate these in Appendix 7.A1, along with the associated estimates of γ (and its standard error) that seems to be most preferred or representative (if a preferred estimate is not available). While I have strong views about the value of some of these estimates (or lack thereof), I weigh each estimate equally, simply because there is no easily defensible alternative weighting scheme.

The most basic piece of meta-analysis is a test of the null hypothesis $\gamma = 0$ when the nineteen point estimates (and their standard errors) are pooled across studies. This classic test is due originally to Fisher (1932) and uses the p-values from each of the (nineteen) underlying γ estimates. Under the null hypothesis that each of the p-values is independently and randomly drawn from a normal [0,1] distribution, minus twice the sum of the logs of the p-values is drawn from a chi-square. The hypothesis can be rejected at any standard significance level, since under the null hypothesis; the test-statistic of 577 is drawn from $\chi^2(38)$.[2] While there is manifestly considerable heterogeneity between the different estimates, the fixed and random effect estimators are quantitatively similar, as I show in Table 7.1. They are also economically substantial; both pooled estimates of γ indicate that currency union more than doubles trade (as $\ln(2) \simeq 0.69$). Also, none of these conclusions change if my six studies are dropped; the test-statistic rejects the hypothesis of no effect, as under the null of no effect, 203 is drawn from $\chi^2(26)$.

There is little indication that any single study is especially influential in driving these results. If the studies are omitted from the meta-analysis one by one, one finds the following point estimates for γ (tabulated in Table 7.2 along with a 95 percent confidence interval).

While I tried to choose the preferred/representative estimates to match the intentions of the authors, I did . . . choose them. An alternative way to proceed is to use a more mechanical procedure to choose the underlying estimates of γ for the meta-analysis. This is easy, since each of the underlying studies provides a number of individual γ estimates. Thus, an alternative I now deploy is to use

---

[2] Edgington's small sample correction leads to the same conclusion.

Table 7.2. *Sensitivity of meta-analysis of* γ *to individual studies (fixed effects)*

Study omitted	Coefficient	95% CI	95% CI
Rose	0.75	0.70	0.81
Engel–Rose	0.77	0.72	0.82
Frankel–Rose	0.76	0.70	0.81
Rose–van Wincoop	0.77	0.71	0.82
Glick–Rose	0.82	0.76	0.89
Persson	0.77	0.72	0.83
Rose	0.78	0.72	0.85
Honohan	0.77	0.72	0.82
Nitsch	0.77	0.72	0.82
Pakko–Wall	0.77	0.72	0.83
Walsh–Thom	0.78	0.73	0.84
Mélitz	0.77	0.72	0.83
López-Córdova and Meissner	0.77	0.72	0.83
Tenreyro	0.77	0.72	0.83
Levy Yeyati	0.77	0.72	0.83
Nitsch	0.78	0.72	0.83
Flandreau and Maurel	0.70	0.65	0.76
Klein	0.77	0.72	0.83
Estevadeoral, Frantz	0.79	0.73	0.84
Combined	0.77	0.72	0.82

the (nineteen) median estimates of γ from the nineteen underlying studies to construct an alternative set of γ estimates (and associated standard errors) suitable for meta-analysis. I also use the estimates at the 25th, 10th, and 5th percentiles.[3] Table 7.3 repeats the meta-analysis using these four alternative data sets. The default "preferred" estimates from Table 7.1 are tabulated at the top to facilitate comparison.

The pooled meta-estimate of γ falls as one moves away from the median estimate towards estimates that are lower within individual studies (by design). But it is interesting to note that even using the γ estimates taken from the 5th percentile of each underlying study, the hypothesis of no effect of currency union on trade can be rejected at conventional significance level. Further, all the effects are economically substantive. The lower bound for the lowest estimate is 0.15, implying an effect of currency union on trade of some 16 percent.

One might then ask which design features of the individual studies account for the differences across individual estimates of γ. It would be fun and interesting to

---

[3] Thus, my initial study contains fifty-two estimates of γ. The median of these is 1.285 (with standard error of 0.13). The 25th percentile estimate is 1.1 (0.14); the 10th percentile is 1.09 (0.26); and the 5th percentile estimate is 0.96 (0.15). If there is an even number of estimates in the underlying study, I choose the higher estimate when, for example, the median lies between two estimates.

Table 7.3. *Sensitivity of meta-analysis of γ to choice of "preferred" estimate*

		Pooled γ estimate	Lower bound, 95% CI	Upper bound, 95% CI	p-value for H₀: no effect
Preferred	Fixed	0.77	0.72	0.83	0.00
Preferred	Random	0.73	0.58	0.88	0.00
Median	Fixed	0.61	0.56	0.67	0.00
Median	Random	0.85	0.58	1.13	0.00
25th-Percentile	Fixed	0.30	0.26	0.35	0.00
25th-Percentile	Random	0.52	0.30	0.75	0.00
10th-Percentile	Fixed	0.21	0.17	0.25	0.00
10th-Percentile	Random	0.37	0.16	0.57	0.00
5th-Percentile	Fixed	0.15	0.12	0.18	0.00
5th-Percentile	Random	0.36	0.18	0.55	0.00

Table 7.4. *Meta-analysis: Bivariate determination of γ across studies*

Study characteristic	Slope coefficient (|z-statistic|)	Intercept (|z-statistic|)
Number of observations in study	0.00 (0.0)	0.72 (7.2)
Number of countries in study	0.00 (0.6)	0.64 (3.9)
Number of years in study	−0.00 (0.4)	0.78 (4.7)
Standard error of γ	−0.99 (1.2)	0.91 (5.2)
Dummy for post-Second World War study	−0.03 (0.1)	0.75 (3.8)
Dummy for cross section or panel study	0.24 (1.2)	0.54 (3.0)
Dummy for Rose as author	0.38 (2.3)	0.59 (5.8)

explain the variation in γ estimates across studies with a large number of study characteristics. Unfortunately, given the paucity of studies, it does not seem wise to use multivariate meta-regression techniques very intensively. Nevertheless, I report in Table 7.4 the results of a series of bivariate meta-regressions. Each row tabulates the intercept and slope coefficient from a different bivariate regression, where the regressand is the set of nineteen γ estimates, and the independent variable is listed at the left of the table.

There are two interesting positive results in Table 7.4, and one negative finding. First, there is not a positive relation between the number of observations and γ. The fact that there is no positive (let alone significant) relation between the sample size and the estimates of γ raises a seriously worrying question as to whether the underlying empirical phenomenon is authentic (Stanley 2001). Second, papers that I have coauthored have consistently higher point estimates of γ (though other papers still have an economically and statistically significant effect of currency union on trade). Finally, there do not seem to be any other strong relationships between other characteristics of the studies (e.g. the span or nature of the data set) and point estimates of γ.

To summarize, the meta-analysis indicates two strong findings and a weak one. First, the hypothesis that there is no effect of currency union on trade can be rejected at standard significance levels when the results from the individual studies are pooled. Second, the pooled effect is not just positive but economically significant, consistent with the hypothesis that currency union approximately doubles trade. Third, the preferred estimates of γ from individual studies are not closely linked to the characteristics of the studies.

7.4   Different Estimates of γ and its Significance

Each of the nineteen studies provides a number of different estimates of γ. For instance, my original paper provided over fifty estimates of γ as a result of sensitivity analysis. In all, there are currently 383 estimates of γ (and accordingly, 383 associated t-statistics for the hypothesis of an insignificant γ). Simply averaging across these 383 different estimates of γ produces a mean of 1.4; the average t-ratio is 5.7.

I provide histograms of the 383 γ estimates and their t-statistics in Figure 7.1. I personally estimated some 134 of them, and the meta-analysis of Table 7.4 shows that I typically find higher results than others. Accordingly, I split the data into two: Those I estimated, and those estimated by others.

The top left graphic in Figure 7.1 is a histogram of the 132 point estimates of γ I estimated that are less than six.[4] Immediately below on a comparably scaled graph are the 249 estimates produced by others. The two graphics to the right of the figure are analogues that portray the corresponding t-statistics.[5]

What does the graphic show? The vast majority of the point estimates of γ are positive; only thirty of the 383 (<8 percent) are negative. Most are also economically large; 63 percent exceed 0.7 in magnitude, a number that implies that currency union is associated with a doubling of trade. It is interesting to note in passing that one cannot reject the hypothesis of equal means across my estimates and those of others, at even the 10 percent level (the t-test for equality of means across the two sets of γ estimates is 1.56).

It is clear that many of the estimates are also statistically significant. The median t-statistic is four; over three-quarters (290/383) exceed two. My t-ratios tend to be larger than those of others, but over two-thirds of the t-statistics of others are at least two (the median is 2.8).

---

[4] That is, two large outliers are not graphed; I estimated both.
[5] This time, eleven t-statistics are dropped from the graph. All are larger than twenty, and I estimated none.

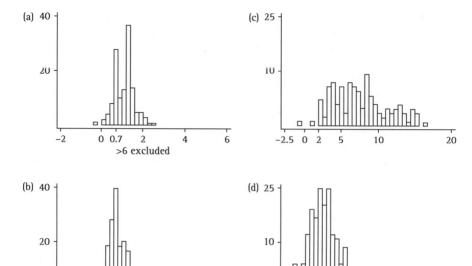

Figure 7.1. *The estimated effect of currency union on trade (a) and (b) Rose's and other point estimates and (c) and (d) Rose's and other t-ratios, respectively*

Finally, one can also combine the different estimates that exist within the nineteen studies, on a paper-by-paper basis. Table 7.5 provides nineteen rows (one for each study), which perform meta-analysis within the individual study to arrive at both fixed and random-effect estimates of γ. I also tabulate the z-statistics which test the null hypothesis $H_0: \gamma = 0$, and the associated p-values. The number of estimates provided by each study is also tabulated.

Table 7.5 clearly shows heterogeneity across γ estimates. While none are significantly negative and most are significantly positive, they vary considerably.

7.5   Conclusion

It is too early to claim much for a meta-analysis like this. Nineteen studies sounds like a lot. But one would prefer thirty observations before starting to appeal to the large of law numbers. Further, the extant studies are dependent and not all of equal interest, two features that I have ignored above. The different estimates of this effect are heterogeneous and cannot be linked to study features such as the sample size. Thus it would be unreasonable for anyone to have too much confidence in the meta-analytic estimate of the effect of currency union on trade.

Table 7.5. *Meta-analysis: Bivariate determination of γ across studies*

Study		Coefficients	Asymptotic z-statistics	p-values	No. of estimates
Rose	Fixed	1.29	50.6	0.00	52
	Random	1.31	32.9	0.00	
Engel–Rose	Fixed	1.35	7.4	0.00	5
	Random	1.35	7.4	0.00	
Frankel–Rose	Fixed	1.63	19.8	0.00	5
	Random	1.63	11.8	0.00	
Rose–van Wincoop	Fixed	0.23	13.8	0.00	18
	Random	0.65	7.7	0.00	
Glick–Rose	Fixed	0.70	59.3	0.00	37
	Random	0.77	27.8	0.00	
Persson	Fixed	0.65	7.7	0.00	6
	Random	0.59	4.8	0.00	
Rose	Fixed	0.82	43.5	0.00	17
	Random	1.06	8.9	0.00	
Honohan	Fixed	0.35	3.7	0.00	12
	Random	0.36	1.9	0.05	
Nitsch	Fixed	3.00	111.4	0.00	83
	Random	1.55	6.8	0.00	
Pakko–Wall	Fixed	0.87	8.5	0.00	6
	Random	0.33	0.9	0.35	
Walsh–Thom	Fixed	−0.01	−0.6	0.57	7
	Random	0.02	0.6	0.54	
Mélitz	Fixed	1.89	21.7	0.00	6
	Random	1.91	10.8	0.00	
López-Córdova and Meissner	Fixed	0.72	21.6	0.00	47
	Random	0.72	20.7	0.00	
Tenreyro	Fixed	0.80	9.5	0.00	4
	Random	0.71	4.2	0.00	
Levy Yeyati	Fixed	1.01	16.4	0.00	19
	Random	1.06	11.4	0.00	
Nitsch	Fixed	0.46	5.6	0.00	8
	Random	0.43	2.6	0.01	
Flandreau and Maurel	Fixed	0.94	35.9	0.00	8
	Random	0.90	7.3	0.00	
Klein	Fixed	0.09	2.5	0.01	25
	Random	0.37	2.0	0.05	
Estevadeoral, Frantz, and Taylor	Fixed	0.43	0.37	0.50	18
	Random	0.45	0.35	0.55	

That said, a quantitative survey of the literature shows substantial evidence that currency union has a positive effect on trade. When the estimates are examined collectively, this effect is large in terms of both economic and statistical significance, implying that currency union is associated with a doubling of trade.

REFERENCES

Fatás, A. and Rose, A. K. (2001). "Do Monetary Handcuffs Restrain Leviathan? Fiscal Policy in Extreme Exchange Rate Regimes." *IMF Staff Papers*, 47 (Special Issue): 40–61.

Estevadeoral, A., Frantz, B., and Taylor, A. M. (2002). "The Rise and Fall of World Trade, 1870–1939." Draft, UC Davis.

Fisher, R. A. (1932). *Statistical Methods for Research Workers*, 4th edn. London: Oliver and Boyd.

Flandreau, M. and Maurel, M. (2001). "Monetary Union, Trade Integration, and Business Cycles in 19th Century Europe: Just Do It." *CEPR Discussion Paper* No. 3087.

Frankel, J. A. and Rose, A. K. (2002). "An Estimate of the Effect of Currency Unions on Trade and Output." *Quarterly Journal of Economics*, 117 (May): 437–66.

Glick, R. and Rose, A. K. (2002). "Does a Currency Union Affect Trade? The Time Series Evidence." *European Economic Review*, 46 (June): 1125–51.

Honohan, P. (2001). "Discussion." *Economic Policy*, 33 (October): 457–61.

Klein, M. W. (2002). "Currency Unions and Trade: A Comment." Draft, Tufts University.

Levy Yeyati, E. (2001). "On the Impact of a Common Currency on Bilateral Trade, Universidad Torcuato Di Tella." Draft, available at www.utdt.edu/~ely/Commoncurrency.pdf.

López-Córdova, J. E. and Meissner, C. (2001). "Exchange-Rate Regimes and International Trade: Evidence from the Classical Gold Standard Era." UC Berkeley, avail. at www.haas.berkeley.edu/groups/iber/wps/cider/c00-118.pdf.

Mélitz, J. (2001). "Geography, Trade and Currency Union." *CEPR Discussion Paper* No. 2987.

Nitsch, V. (2002). "Honey, I Shrunk the Currency Union Effect On Trade." *The World Economy*, 25 (April): 457–74.

Pakko, M. R. and Wall, H. J. (2001). "Reconsidering the Trade-creating Effects of a Currency Union." *FRB St. Louis Review*, 83 (May): 37–45.

Persson, T. (2001). "Currency Unions and Trade: How Large is the Treatment Effect?" *Economic Policy*, 33 (October): 435–48.

Rose, A. K. (2000). "One Money, One Market: Estimating the Effect of Common Currencies on Trade." *Economic Policy*, 30 (April): 7–33.

—— (2001). "Currency Unions and Trade: The Effect is Large." *Economic Policy*, 33 (October): 449–61.

—— and Engel, C. (2002). "Currency Unions and International Integration." *Journal of Money, Credit, and Banking*, 34 (November): 1067–89.

—— and van Wincoop, E. (2001). "National Money as a Barrier to Trade: The Real Case for Monetary Union." *American Economic Review*, 91 (May): 386–90.

Stanley, T. D. (2001). "Wheat from Chaff: Meta-Analysis as Quantitative Literature Review." *Journal of Economic Perspectives*, 15 (3): 131–50.

Tenreyro, S. (2001). "On the Causes and Consequences of Currency Unions." Draft, Harvard University, November.

Thom, R. and Walsh, B. (2002). "The Effect of a Common Currency on Trade: Ireland Before and After the Sterling Link." *European Economic Review*, 46 (June): 1111–23.

Appendix 7.A1. *Estimates of the effect of currency union on trade*

Author	Year	γ	S.E. of γ
Rose	2000	1.21	0.14
Engel–Rose	2002	1.21	0.37
Frankel–Rose	2002	1.36	0.18
Rose–van Wincoop	2001	0.91	0.18
Glick–Rose	2002	0.65	0.05
Persson	2001	0.506	0.257
Rose	2001	0.74	0.05
Honohan	2001	0.921	0.4
Nitsch	2002	0.82	0.27
Pakko and Wall	2001	−0.378	0.529
Walsh and Thom	2002	0.098	0.2
Mélitz	2001	0.7	0.23
López-Córdova and Meissner	2001	0.716	0.186
Tenreyro	2001	0.471	0.316
Levy Yeyati	2001	0.5	0.25
Nitsch	[a]	0.62	0.17
Flandreau and Maurel	2001	1.16	0.07
Klein	2002	0.50	0.27
Estevadeoral, Frantz, and Taylor	2002	0.293	0.145

[a] This part.

Notes: Estimates of γ and standard error from ln (Trade) = γ Currency Union + controls + error.

8

Common Currencies and Market Integration Across Cities: How Strong is the Link?

ALBERTO E. ISGUT

Using two balanced panels of up to 124 goods and services prices and up to 116 international cities, this chapter studies the determinants of price dispersion across city pairs in 2001. Using controls for cities located in the same country, regional trading areas, common languages and historical links, price dispersion increases with geographical distance, nominal bilateral exchange rate volatility, and differences in economic development. Price dispersion is significantly lower across cities located in the euro area. It is also lower for cities that use the U.S. dollar or have currencies hard pegged to it, though the effect is less robust.

8.1 Introduction

The removal of trade barriers associated with the process of economic integration leads to an expansion of markets across countries. As national borders become less relevant in determining the origin of goods consumed in a country, two effects are likely to occur. First, international trade is likely to increase for goods whose domestic prices differed most visibly before the removal of trade barriers. Second, as there are more possibilities for arbitrage across countries, domestic prices should become more similar across economically integrated countries.

Despite the presumption that borders should matter less and less as economic integration progresses, the empirical literature has produced some surprising results. John McCallum (1995) measured for the first time how larger trade flows within a country are compared to trade flows across countries. He found that trade flows across Canadian provinces were more than twenty times larger than trade flows across Canadian provinces and U.S. states, after accounting for the

I thank George von Furstenberg, Jacques Mélitz, John Bonin, and seminar participants at Fordham Business School and Wesleyan University for helpful comments. I am responsible for any remaining errors.

effect of geographic distance and economic size.[1] The border effect has also been found to be relevant when looking at price variability across pairs of cities. In a regression framework similar to McCallum's (1995), Charles Engel and John H. Rogers (1996) found that consumer prices were significantly more variable for pairs of cities located across the U.S.–Canadian border than for pairs of cities located within the same country.

Among several possible explanations of why borders matter so much, even for pairs of countries with no trade barriers and extensive trade links such as United States and Canada under the free trade agreement (FTA), the exchange rate regime has received much attention lately. In particular, and motivated by the introduction of the euro, the hypothesis that currency unions lead to increases in trade among its member countries has been closely examined. Trade might increase partly because of the removal of transaction costs associated with exchange rate operations. More importantly, the use of the same currency eliminates the uncertainty associated with the actual or potential volatility in the nominal exchange rate. Although importers and exporters can protect themselves from such uncertainty, at least in the short run with the use of forward markets, long-term commercial plans involving imports or exports are subject to substantially more uncertainty than commercial plans that rely mainly on the domestic market. This extra uncertainty might be at the root of the border effects found in the data.

The evidence obtained thus far supports the hypothesis of a positive link between membership of currency unions and trade. Andrew K. Rose (2000; this part), Rose and van Wincoop (2001), and Glick and Rose (2002) have found that countries that belong to the same currency union trade with each other around twice as much as countries that use different currencies. Increased trade, however, is not the only possible effect of the greater economic integration associated with the use of a shared currency. As argued, for example, by Richard B. Freeman (1995), the mere threat of increased competition from foreign producers may cause domestic producers to lower their prices, even if imports do not increase much. Therefore, if the use of a common currency expands markets beyond national borders, we should expect to see less price dispersion across cities that belong to the same currency union.

In a recent study based on a large sample of ninety-five consumer prices across eighty-three cities around the globe, David C. Parsley and Shang-Jin Wei (2001) have found evidence that prices are more similar for pairs of cities located in countries that share the same currency. Their main regression was similar to the one by Engel and Rogers (1996) mentioned above, but because the latter was based on only two countries (U.S. and Canada) that did not share the same currency, it could only assess the existence of a border effect. By having a much

---

[1] While McCallum's (1995) data were for 1988, before the signing of the FTA, subsequent work by John F. Helliwell (1998) corroborated the importance of the border effect during the first half of the 1990s.

larger sample that includes countries that belong to currency unions, such as the euro or the CFA franc, or have a hard peg regime to the U.S. dollar, such as Panama and Hong Kong, Parsley and Wei were able to explore a much richer set of hypotheses.

This chapter follows the footsteps of Parsley and Wei (2001) in trying to probe the relationship between currency unions (and hard pegs) and price dispersion across cities. Although I use the same source of disaggregated price data as Parsley and Wei (2001), from the Economist Intelligence Unit (EIU), I focus on data for 2001, which was not available in their sample. In addition, I break up the data in different ways and add explanatory and control variables that were not previously explored in studies of price dispersion across cities. In so doing I attempt to probe how strong is the link between shared currencies and market integration for consumer goods and services across cities.

8.2   Data and Methodology

The main data source is the EIU's *City Data* database.[2] This database includes annual observations of domestic currency prices for over 160 goods and services for up to 123 cities during the period 1990–2001. In this chapter I use prices for the year 2001 only. Of all the goods and services available some were excluded from the analysis because they had too many missing observations; others were excluded because they did not add significant information. Many goods in the database have two prices, such as supermarkets and mid-price stores. In these cases the lower of the two prices was kept.[3] Two services, taxi rides and residential telephone service, were difficult to compare across cities because their pricing differs often substantially across cities (e.g. some cities have just a flat rate, while others have a fixed plus a variable rate). In these cases, I combined the information on fixed and variables rates in the database into a single price.[4] After these initial exclusions and adjustments, the number of goods was reduced to 140. Of all the cities, I needed to eliminate Lyon because of data problems, winding up with 122 cities.

An important problem of the data set is that many cities have incomplete price data. As a result, the two-way panel of cities and goods is unbalanced. This is problematic because the price data is used to construct measures of price

---

[2] The EIU markets this database mainly for marketing managers, business travelers, and human resources officers who need to design compensation packages for expatriate workers. The price data is collected twice a year by local researchers who physically visit outlets to record price levels. For more information, refer to the EIU data services web site www.eiu.com/data.

[3] I preferred to use the lower of the two prices rather than selecting supermarkets because in developing countries supermarkets are sometimes more expensive than small stores.

[4] For example, the database includes the initial meter charge for a taxi ride and the rate per additional kilometer. I combine both pieces of information as the price of a 5 km taxi ride. Similarly, I compute the price for residential telephone service on the basis of 300 min a month of local calls.

dispersion across pairs of cities, such as the standard deviation or the inter-quartile range (IQR)[5] of

$$q_{ij,k} = \log(p_{ik}/x_i) - \log(p_{jk}/x_j), \tag{1}$$

where i and j index cities, k indexes good, and p and x represent, respectively, the domestic currency price of k and the exchange rate (defined as units of local currency per U.S. dollar). Clearly, if the number of goods k available differs across city pairs, the standard deviation or IQR of $q_{ij,k}$ may vary arbitrarily, regardless of underlying economic causes.

Because of the potential problems of using an unbalanced panel, I work with two balanced subpanels, which I refer to as the diverse and the OECD panels. The diverse panel was obtained by maximizing the geographical coverage subject to the constraint of having a reasonably large basket of goods and services to compare. Dropping the six cities with most missing goods led to a panel of 116 cities and sixty-nine goods and services. This panel includes fifty-five cities from high-income OECD countries and sixty-one cities from developing countries. The OECD panel, in contrast, was obtained by maximizing the number of goods and services subject to the constraint of having a reasonable number of cities. Dropping the seventeen goods with most missing cities led to a panel of seventy-nine cities and 123 goods and services. This panel includes all the fifty-five cities from high-income OECD countries plus twenty-four cities from developing countries.

The main items compared across cities, in order of importance, include food and beverages, household supplies and personal care items, and clothing (75 percent of the diverse panel and 67 percent of the OECD panel). A variety of services, ranging from color film development to a routine checkup with a family doctor represent around 15 percent of the items in both panels. The availability of a rather complete basket of nineteen non-tradable services for the OECD panel allows me to run separate regressions for tradables and non-tradables. For comparison purposes I also run a regression for the unbalanced panel used by Parsley and Wei (2001), which includes eighty-three cities and between sixty and ninety-five goods per city. A detailed list of the cities and goods and services available in each of the three panels is available from the author upon request.

The dependent variable of the analysis, the standard deviation or the IQR of $q_{ij,k}$, is computed for all the possible pairs of cities included in each panel. For example, the diverse panel has $116 \times 115/2 = 6{,}670$ observations and the OECD panel has $79 \times 78/2 = 3{,}081$ observations. However, many of these observations may not convey useful information. Not all the countries are commercially integrated with each other. As a matter of fact some countries do not even trade with other countries or trade so little to be commercially irrelevant to each other.

---

[5] The IQR (defined as the distance between the third and the first quartile) is a simple measure of spread that gives the range covered by the middle half of the data. In contrast to the standard deviation, the IQR is robust to outliers.

In a robustness check I reduce the sample by eliminating all the pairs of countries with little or no trade.

The data on bilateral trade flows used to select pairs of countries with little or no trade was extracted mainly from the data set prepared by Glick and Rose (2002).[6] Because that data set did not include Taiwan, I complemented the information with the *World Trade Flows, 1980–97* database compiled by Robert C. Feenstra.[7] For each pair of countries in the sample I computed the following measure of trade importance for the year 1997:

$$t_{ij} = 0.5(((m_{ij} + x_{ij})/(M_i + X_i)) + ((m_{ji} + x_{ji})/(M_j + X_j))) \qquad (2)$$

where m_{ij} represents imports of country i from country j, x_{ij} exports of country i to country j, and M_i and X_i are, respectively, total imports and total exports of country i. The first term of the sum represents the importance of trade with country j from the perspective of country i, and the second term represents the importance of trade with country i from the perspective of country j. If the average is low, it means that the countries are unimportant to each other as trade partners. In some of the regressions I eliminate pairs of countries for which t_{ij} is less than 1 percent.

The regression model estimated is

$$s_{ij}(q_k) = \beta_0 + \beta_1 \log(d_{ij}) + \beta_2 (\log(d_{ij}))^2 + \beta_3 \log(\bar{y}_{ij})$$

$$+ \beta_4 \max\{y_i, y_j\}/\bar{y}_{ij} + \beta_5 s_{ij}(x_t) + \gamma_1 euro_{ij} + \gamma_2 CFA_{ij}$$

$$+ \gamma_3 dollar_{ij} + \delta_1' RTA_{ij} + \delta_2' country_{ij} + \delta_3 language_{ij}$$

$$+ \delta_4' history_{ij} + \varepsilon_{ij}.$$

The dependent variable $s_{ij}(q_k)$ represents the dispersion of goods and services prices between city i and city j. This dispersion is measured as either the standard deviation or the IQR of a basket of k goods and services. d_{ij} is the great circle distance between cities i and j.[8] $\bar{y}_{ij}$ is the mean per capita GDP of the countries where cities i and j are located. The GDP figures are for 1999 and are converted from local currencies to U.S. dollars using market rates.[9] The variable $\max\{y_i, y_j\}/\bar{y}_{ij}$ is the ratio between the maximum and the mean per capita GDP of the countries where cities i and j are located. This measure, which ranges

---

[6] This database is available in STATA format at Andrew Rose's web site www.haas.berkeley.edu/~arose/RecRes.htm (accessed January 2002).

[7] For further information on the World Trade Flows, 1980–97 database refer to www.iga.ucdavis.edu/wtf.html.

[8] The latitude and longitude of each city, which was necessary to compute the great circle distance formula, was obtained from the United Nations web site www.un.org/Depts/unsd/demog/ctry.htm (accessed January 2002).

[9] *Source*: United Nations web site www.un.org/Depts/unsd/social/inc-eco.htm (accessed March 2002). The figure for Taiwan was obtained from the publication, The Republic of China—Five Decades on Taiwan, consulted on-line at www.taipei.org/info/roc/decades.htm (accessed March 2002).

from 1 to 2, is introduced to capture income inequalities across the two cities. $s_{ij}(x_t)$ represents the volatility over time (t) of the bilateral exchange rate between the countries where cities i and j are located. It is computed as the standard deviation of monthly log differences in the nominal bilateral exchange rate between January 1999 and April 2001.[10]

The dummy variables $euro_{ij}$, CFA_{ij}, and $dollar_{ij}$ take a value of one when cities i and j are located in countries that belong to the same currency union or that have a hard peg arrangement with the same currency. For example, $CFA_{ij} = 1$ when i and j are located in either Cameroon, Cote d'Ivoire, Gabon, Senegal, or France, and $dollar_{ij} = 1$ when i and j are located in either Argentina, Ecuador, Hong Kong, Panama, or the United States.

The vectors of dummy variables RTA_{ij}, $country_{ij}$, $language_{ij}$, and $history_{ij}$ control for other characteristics that might reduce the volatility of prices across city pairs. RTA_{ij} takes a value of one when both cities are located in the same regional trading area. See the Appendix for the list of RTAs considered. $country_{ij}$ takes a value of one when both cities are located in the same country. The diverse and OECD panels contain, respectively, eighteen and twelve countries with multiple cities. These control variables are particularly important to differentiate between the use of the same currency from other unobservable institutional characteristics associated with being located in the same country. Finally, $language_{ij}$ and $history_{ij}$ take a value of one when the cities are located in countries that share, respectively, the same main language or a common historical link. Refer to Appendix 8.A1 for a definition of these dummy variables.

To provide some insight on the data set, Table 8.1 presents information on the goods and services which are least and most expensive, and least and most variable compared to the median U.S. prices. Not surprisingly, nine out of the twenty least expensive goods and services are non-tradable services. Five other goods are fresh fruits and vegetables, which, although potentially tradable, are probably cheaper when bought from local producers. In contrast, all but one of the most expensive goods are tradable, mostly nonperishable goods. As it can be inferred from the table, there is a high negative correlation $(r = -0.65)$ between median goods price and price dispersion (measured as the IQR): Goods or services with the lowest prices tend to have the highest dispersion across cities. Notice that nine of the twenty cheapest goods are among the twenty with the highest dispersion and six of the twenty most expensive are among the twenty with the lowest price dispersion.

Table 8.2 presents the cities whose prices are least and most expensive, and least and most variable compared to the median U.S. prices. As it would be expected, all the least expensive cities are located in developing countries. There is also a negative correlation between median city price and price dispersion

---

[10] *Source*: International Monetary Fund's International Financial Statistics database. The exchange rate for Taiwan was obtained from the U.S. Federal Reserve's FRED database at www.stls.frb.org/fred/data/exchange.html (accessed March 2002).

Table 8.1. *Price comparisons across goods, 2001*

Lowest prices		Highest prices	
Product	Median	Product	Median
One X-ray at doctor's office or hospital	−0.93	Paperback novel (at bookstore)	0.31
Routine checkup at family doctor	−0.90	Television color (66 cm)	0.28
		Ham: whole (1 kg)	0.27
Cigarettes local brand (pack of 20)	−0.83	Regular unleaded petrol (1 l)	0.24
Tomatoes (1 kg)	−0.80	International foreign daily newspaper	0.23
Gas monthly bill	−0.78	Laundry (one shirt)	0.16
Carrots (1 kg)		Facial tissues (box of 100)	0.16
Hire of tennis court for 1 hour	−0.68	Instant coffee (125 g)	0.13
Taxi rate for a 5 km ride	−0.66	Lamb: stewing (1 kg)	0.12
Onions (1 kg)	−0.63	Bacon (1 kg)	0.12
Lemons (1 kg)	−0.63	Gin Gilbey's or equivalent (700 ml)	0.12
Soap (100 g)	−0.63		
Visit to dentist (one X-ray and one filling)	−0.62	Electric toaster (for two slices)	0.12
White bread (1 kg)	−0.61	Peas canned (250 g)	0.09
Cigarettes Marlboro (pack of 20)	−0.61	Shampoo & conditioner in one (400 ml)	0.08
Beef: filet mignon (1 kg)	−0.57	Laundry detergent (3 l)	0.07
Water monthly bill	−0.56	Child's jeans	0.07
Taxi: airport to city center	−0.56	Ground coffee (500 g)	0.04
Potatoes (2 kg)	−0.55	Business shirt white	0.04
Unfurnished residential apartment: 2 bedrooms	−0.55	Compact disc album	0.04
		Batteries (two size D/LR20)	0.02
Frozen fish fingers (1 kg)	−0.49		
Lowest price dispersion	**IQR**	**Highest price dispersion**	**IQR**
Compact disc album	0.28	Routine checkup at family doctor	1.48
Lipstick (deluxe type)	0.29		
Personal computer (64 mb)	0.30	Gas monthly bill	1.44
Low priced car (900–1299 cc)	0.32	Entrance fee to a public swimming pool	1.22
Child's shoes sportswear	0.35		
Compact car (1300–1799 cc)	0.36	Cigarettes local brand (pack of 20)	1.17
Chicken: Frozen (1 kg)	0.38		
Electric toaster (for two slices)	0.38	Taxi rate for a 5 km ride	1.12
		One X-ray at doctor's office or hospital	1.06
Coca-Cola (1 l)	0.39		
Television color (66 cm)	0.41	Tomatoes (1 kg)	1.05

Table 8.1. (*Continued*)

Lowest price dispersion	IQR	Highest price dispersion	IQR
Toilet tissue (two rolls)	0.43	Veal: fillet (1 kg)	1.04
Shampoo & conditioner in one (400 ml)	0.43	Hire of tennis court for 1 hour	1.03
		Beef: filet mignon (1 kg)	0.99
Peas canned (250 g)	0.43	Veal: chops (1 kg)	0.99
Instant coffee (125 g)	0.44	Cigarettes Marlboro (pack of 20)	0.98
Family car (1800–2499 cc)	0.45		
Butter (500 g)	0.45	Electricity monthly bill for a family of 4	0.97
Child's jeans	0.45		
Sliced pineapples canned (500 g)	0.45	Lemons (1 kg)	0.95
		Green fees on a public golf course	0.93
Batteries (two size D/LR20)	0.46	Daily local newspaper	0.92
Insect-killer spray (330 g)	0.46	White rice (1 kg)	0.92
		Dry cleaning woman's dress	0.90
		Mushrooms (1 kg)	0.88
		Aspirins (100 tablets)	0.88

Note: Medians and inter-quartile ranges (IQR) are computed separately for each good g across cities for the log difference between the dollar price of good g in city c and the median price of good g in U.S. cities. The overall median and IQR are, respectively, -0.15 and 0.69. Goods in bold appear in both the upper left and lower right (or in the upper right and the lower left) sections of the table.

Table 8.2. *Price comparisons across cities, 2001*

Lowest prices			Highest prices		
City	Country	Median	City	Country	Median
Tehran	Iran	−1.12	Tokyo	Japan	0.52
New Delhi	India	−1.02	Osaka/Kobe	Japan	0.47
Karachi	Pakistan	−0.89	Libreville	Gabon	0.28
Belgrade	Yugoslavia	−0.85	Hong Kong	Hong Kong	0.23
Mumbai	India	−0.85	Beijing	China	0.20
Budapest	Hungary	−0.83	Tel Aviv	Israel	0.19
Tripoli	Libya	−0.76	Seoul	Korea	0.12
Bucharest	Romania	−0.74	Chicago	U.S.	0.12
Manila	Philippines	−0.73	Reykjavik	Iceland	0.12
Harare	Zimbabwe	−0.64	Oslo	Norway	0.11
Johannesburg	South Africa	−0.64	New York	U.S.	0.10
Colombo	Sri Lanka	−0.59	Buenos Aires	Argentina	0.09
Jakarta	Indonesia	−0.59	Los Angeles	U.S.	0.08
Tunis	Tunisia	−0.58	Zurich	Switzerland	0.07
Asuncion	Paraguay	−0.54	Mexico City	Mexico	0.07
Dhaka	Bangladesh	−0.54	Vienna	Austria	0.06

Table 8.2. (*Continued*)

Lowest prices			Highest prices		
City	Country	Median	City	Country	Median
Bangkok	Thailand	−0.53	London	Great Britain	0.06
Kuala Lumpur	Malaysia	−0.48	Moscow	Russia	0.06
Bogotá	Colombia	−0.47	Taipei	Taiwan	0.04
Prague	Czech Republic	−0.47	Tianjin	China	0.04

Lowest price dispersion		IQR	Highest price dispersion		IQR
Washington, DC	U.S.	0.18	Karachi	Pakistan	1.21
Los Angeles	U.S.	0.18	New Delhi	India	1.17
Pittsburgh	U.S.	0.22	Mumbai	India	1.13
Boston	U.S.	0.23	Dhaka	Bangladesh	1.13
Houston	U.S.	0.24	Harare	Zimbabwe	1.11
Detroit	U.S.	0.25	Tehran	Iran	1.11
San Francisco	U.S.	0.26	Bucharest	Romania	1.03
Chicago	U.S.	0.26	Tripoli	Libya	1.01
New York	U.S.	0.27	Libreville	Gabon	0.99
Seattle	U.S.	0.28	Asuncion	Paraguay	0.98
Miami	U.S.	0.30	Colombo	Sri Lanka	0.95
Minneapolis	U.S.	0.31	Belgrade	Yugoslavia	0.94
Lexington	U.S.	0.31	Shenzhen	China	0.92
Cleveland	U.S.	0.32	Lagos	Nigeria	0.91
Atlanta	U.S.	0.35	Hanoi	Viet Nam	0.91
Honolulu	U.S.	0.35	Cairo	Egypt	0.90
Montreal	Canada	0.39	Nairobi	Kenya	0.88
Toronto	Canada	0.42	Amman	Jordan	0.86
Melbourne	Australia	0.43	Dakar	Senegal	0.86
Vancouver	Canada	0.44	Baku	Azerbaijan	0.86

Notes: Medians and inter-quartile ranges (IQR) are computed separately for each city c across goods for the log difference between the dollar price of good g in city c and the median price of good g in U.S. cities. The overall median and IQR are, respectively, −0.15 and 0.69. Cities in bold appear in both the upper left and lower right (or in the upper right and the lower left) sections of the table.

($r = -0.55$), and eleven of the least expensive cities are also among the twenty with the most variable prices.[11]

The remarkable dispersion of prices associated with the presence of cities belonging to countries with very different levels of development motivates the inclusion as explanatory variables of the mean GDP per capita and the measure

[11] Although it is not surprising that U.S. cities have the lowest price dispersion (because prices are compared to the median U.S. prices), notice that this dispersion is not trivial.

of inequality in GDP per capita described above. Based on the information presented in Tables 8.1 and 8.2, it is to be expected that price dispersion is inversely related to GDP per capita and directly related to the measure of inequality in GDP per capita.

8.3 Results

Before estimating Eq. (3), I present in Table 8.3 the results of a more parsimonious specification with only five dummy variables: Same currency, same regional trading area, same country, same language, and same historical links. These dummy variables take a value of one whenever cities i and j share each of those characteristics. For example, the same currency dummy is coded as one for cities that share the use of either the euro, the CFA franc, or the dollar (or that have a hard peg regime to the dollar). These regressions show that sharing the currency leads to a reduction of the order of 2–3 percent in the standard deviation of log price differences across city pairs, depending on the panel. This effect is significantly larger than the effect of language or historical links, which have the expected negative signs. Somewhat surprisingly, the effect of sharing the currency is also larger than the effect of belonging to the same

Table 8.3. *Determinants of price dispersion across city pairs – abridged regressions*

Variable	Diverse panel		OECD panel		P&W panel	
	Estimate	T-stat	Estimate	T-stat	Estimate	T-stat
Intercept	0.051	−0.8	0.187***	−2.7	0.13	−1.3
Log distance	0.161***	−10.5	0.119***	−7.2	0.151***	−6.3
Log distance squared	−0.009***	−9.6	−0.007***	−6.7	−0.008***	−5.6
Log mean GDPPC	−0.042***	−34.4	−0.028***	−10.6	−0.049***	−30.0
Inequality in GDPPC	0.153***	−42.4	0.114***	−20.7	0.155***	−31.2
Nominal ER volatility	0.056***	−13.1	0.067***	−15.3	0.044***	−8.8
Same currency/Hard peg	−0.021***	−3.5	−0.021***	−4.0	−0.032***	−4.2
Same regional trading area	0.001	−0.2	−0.016***	−3.5	0.01**	−2.4
Same country	−0.064***	−7.8	−0.043***	−5.7	−0.065***	−5.6
Same language	−0.002	−0.6	−0.04***	−11.7	−0.005	−1.3
Same historical links	−0.007**	−2.6	−0.031***	−8.7	−0.007**	−2.0
n	6,670		3,081		3,403	
Adj. R^2	0.497		0.601		0.539	

Notes: The dependent variable is the standard deviation of the log price differences between a pair of cities. The number of goods and services prices and the number of city pairs vary in the three panels.
** and *** indicate that coefficients are significantly different from zero at the 5% and 1% level, respectively.

Table 8.4. *Determinants of price dispersion across city pairs – base regressions*

Variable	Diverse panel		OECD panel	
	Estimate	*T*-stat	Estimate	*T*-stat
Intercept	0.024	0.3	0.170**	2.3
Log distance	0.177***	10.5	0.112***	6.4
Log distance squared	−0.010***	−10.1	−0.006***	−5.8
Log mean GDPPC	−0.044***	−38.4	−0.029***	−10.4
Inequality in GDPPC	0.155***	47.2	0.131***	28.8
Nominal ER volatility	0.058***	13.4	0.064***	14.9
Currency / Hard peg				
Euro	−0.056***	−4.8	−0.041***	−4.5
CFA	−0.062	−1.4		
Dollar	−0.025**	−2.4	−0.008	−1.0
Regional trading area				
EU	0.015	1.5	−0.022**	−2.6
NAFTA	−0.052***	−5.3	−0.018*	−1.9
EFTA	0.027	0.7	−0.016	−0.6
ASEAN	−0.029	−1.5	−0.035	−1.3
ANZCERTA	−0.203***	−7.7	−0.124***	−5.9
MERCOSUR	−0.058**	−2.0	−0.040	−1.6
Andean common mkt.	−0.015	−0.4	−0.029	−0.4
CACM	−0.034	−0.4		
Same country				
Australia	0.041	1.1	0.017	0.6
Brazil	−0.041	−0.4	−0.169**	−2.1
Canada	−0.021	−0.6	−0.010	−0.4
China	−0.091**	−2.0		
Germany	0.051	1.6	0.024	1.0
U.K.	−0.024	−0.3	0.028	0.4
India	−0.139*	−1.7		
Italy	−0.129	−1.6	−0.147**	−2.3
Japan	−0.102	−1.2	−0.171***	−2.6
New Zealand	0.008	0.1	−0.005	−0.1
Russia	−0.194**	−2.3		
Saudi Arabia	−0.036	−0.7		
Spain	−0.219***	−2.6	−0.243***	−3.7
Switzerland	−0.187**	−2.0	−0.177**	−2.5
U.A.E.	0.075	0.9	−0.035	−0.5
U.S.A.	−0.024	−1.5	−0.012	−0.9
Vietnam	−0.145*	−1.7		
Common language				
Spanish	−0.057***	−4.7	−0.042***	−3.2
English	0.010**	2.5	−0.084***	−19.4
French	−0.013	−0.4		
German	0.009	0.5	−0.015	−1.1

Table 8.4. (*Continued*)

Variable	Diverse panel		OECD panel	
	Estimate	T-stat	Estimate	T-stat
Dutch	0.027	0.3	0.047	0.7
Chinese	−0.008	−0.3	−0.011	−0.2
Arabic	−0.078***	−5.5	−0.030	−1.0
Portuguese	−0.079	−1.4	−0.004	−0.1
Malay	0.013	0.2		
Historical link				
Spain / Portugal	0.024**	2.1	0.035**	2.6
England	−0.017**	−2.4	−0.026	−1.5
France	0.062***	3.3		
Former Soviet Block	−0.060***	−3.7	0.018	0.5
China	−0.025	−0.3		
n	6,670		3,081	
Adj. R^2	0.512		0.641	

Notes: The dependent variable is the standard deviation of the log price differences between a pair of cities. The number of goods and services prices and the number of city pairs vary in the two panels.
*, **, and *** indicate statistical significance at the 10%, 5%, and 1% level, respectively.

regional trading area, which has the wrong sign in two of the panels. Moreover, the effect of sharing the currency on price dispersion is significant even while the regressions control for cities that are located in the same country. The "same currency" effect represents between a third and a half of the "same country" effect.

Table 8.4 shows estimation results for Eq. (3) for the diverse and OECD panels, with the dependent variable measured as the standard deviation of log price differences across city pairs. In these regressions, the effect of distance is the usual one. Cities that are further apart are less commercially integrated, and, therefore, their prices are less similar. The effect of the developmental variables is very important statistically, in particular the effect of income inequality among the countries where the cities are located. An increase of one standard deviation in the inequality measure (about 0.33) leads to an increase in the standard deviation of prices of 5 percent. This increase in price dispersion is roughly equivalent to an increase of between 200 and 300 percent in the physical distance between the cities, depending on the estimate. This suggests that the economic distance is as or more important than the geographical distance.

As for the effect of currency areas, use of the euro leads to a significant reduction in the standard deviation of price differences, of around 5 percent. As noted by Parsley and Wei (2001) the effect of currency unions is one order of magnitude more important than a mere reduction in exchange rate volatility. This is verified in the regressions, where an important reduction of 10 percent in the nominal bilateral exchange rate volatility is associated with a reduction of only around

0.6 percent in price dispersion. Countries of the dollar area, including the United States, and those that have a hard peg with the U.S. dollar (such as Argentina up to 2001 and Hong Kong) or that use the dollar (such as Panama and Ecuador) have smaller price dispersion in the diverse panel, but the effect is small and insignificant in the OECD panel. Finally, the effect of the CFA franc on price dispersion is close to zero.

Regional trading areas tend to reduce price dispersion among their countries, as would be expected. The effect is particularly strong for the free trade area between Australia and New Zealand, followed in importance by NAFTA and MERCOSUR. The effect of the European Union varies according to the panel used, being economically important and statistically significant in the OECD panel but positive and insignificant in the diverse panel. Finally, ASEAN countries have lower price dispersion among them, but the effect is not statistically significant.

With almost no exception, the country dummies have the expected negative sign, meaning that prices are more alike within a country than across countries. This effect is important in both developed and developing countries. In the order of importance, the effect is the strongest in Russia, Spain, Switzerland, India, and China. It is also important for Japan, Brazil, and Italy in the OECD panel. The only positive coefficients are for Australia and Germany, but they are not statistically significant.

When people speak Spanish in both cities price dispersion is significantly reduced, and the same is true for cities where people speak Arabic. This similarity might reflect both the effect of language on trade links or the fact that both languages are spoken in regions that are relatively homogeneous in economic terms. Use of the English language is associated with lower price dispersion only in the OECD panel, but with more price dispersion in the diverse panel. As far as historical links are concerned, developing countries that were colonies of England or that were under the hegemony of the former Soviet Union have lower price dispersion (though the effect is only significant in the diverse panel). In contrast, countries that were former colonies of France, Spain, or Portugal tend to have less similar prices.

Because outliers in the price data might lead to artificially high standard deviations, I repeat the regression analysis using the IQR of log price differences across cities as an alternative dependent variable. The results are shown in Table 8.5, which includes for comparison purposes estimates for the Parsley and Wei panel. The results do not change much qualitatively. Although the goodness of fit is reduced and the standard errors are larger, the basic picture presented above is not dramatically changed.

Some of the coefficients become larger in absolute value. For example the inequality measure increases in both the diverse and the OECD panels. Now a one standard deviation increase in this measure leads to an increase in price dispersion of somewhat more than 6 percent. In addition, many of the country dummies coefficients increase noticeably, in some cases doubling the values of

Table 8.5. *Price dispersion across city pairs–dispersion measured as the IQR in log price differences*

Variable	Diverse panel		OECD panel		P&W panel	
	Estimate	*T*-stat	Estimate	*T*-stat	Estimate	*T*-stat
Intercept	−0.064	−0.6	0.180	1.5	0.362**	2.1
Log distance	0.221***	8.0	0.092***	3.2	0.158***	3.8
Log distance squared	−0.012***	−7.4	−0.005***	−2.7	−0.009***	−3.6
Log mean GDPPC	−0.053***	−28.2	−0.015***	−3.3	−0.063***	−23.9
Inequality in GDPPC	0.224***	41.4	0.193***	25.9	0.213***	27.4
Nominal ER volatility	0.032***	4.5	0.060***	8.6	0.054***	6.5
Currency/Hard peg						
Euro	−0.074***	−3.9	−0.050***	−3.3	−0.018	−0.7
CFA	−0.105	−1.4			−0.108	−1.4
Dollar	−0.025	−1.5	−0.034**	−2.6	−0.043**	−2.4
Regional trading area						
EU	−0.002	−0.1	−0.065***	−4.7	−0.067***	−2.9
NAFTA	−0.092***	−5.7	−0.039**	−2.5	−0.060**	−2.3
EFTA	0.029	0.5	−0.058	−1.2	0.010	0.1
ASEAN	−0.059*	−1.9	−0.039	−0.9	−0.113**	−2.5
ANZCERTA	−0.283***	−6.5	−0.172***	−5.0	−0.323**	−2.4
MERCOSUR	−0.094*	−2.0	−0.058	−1.4	0.036	0.6
Andean common mkt.	0.021	0.4	−0.068	−0.6	0.005	0.1
CACM	0.039	0.3			0.009	0.1
Same country						
Australia	0.011	0.2	−0.030	−0.6		
Brazil	−0.082	−0.5	−0.333**	−2.5		
Canada	−0.121**	−2.1	−0.061	−1.3		
China	−0.207***	−2.8				
Germany	0.034	0.7	0.006	0.1		
U.K.	−0.009	−0.1	0.095	0.9		
India	−0.348**	−2.6				
Italy	−0.120	−0.9	−0.217**	−2.0		
Japan	−0.239*	−1.8	−0.370***	−3.5		
New Zealand	−0.020	−0.1	−0.034	−0.3		
Russia	−0.215	−1.6				
Saudi Arabia	−0.077	−1.0				
Spain	−0.341**	−2.5	−0.433***	−4.0		
Switzerland	−0.276*	−1.8	−0.242**	−2.0		
U.A.E.	0.009	0.1	−0.191	−1.6		
U.S.A.	−0.045*	−1.8	−0.002	−0.1	−0.076**	−2.2
Vietnam	−0.251*	−1.8				
n	6,670		3,081		3,403	
Adj. R^2	0.419		0.565		0.427	

Note: The dependent variable is the IQR of the log price differences between a pair of cities. The regressions include language and historical links dummies, but they are not shown to save space.
*, **, *** indicate statistical significance at the 10%, 5%, and 1% level, respectively.

the previous estimates, and some estimates that were previously insignificant become now significant.

Table 8.5 also includes results using the P&W panel. One noticeable difference with the previous diverse and OECD panels is that the euro becomes insignificant. A possible explanation of this result is that the P&W panel includes only one city per country, with the exception of the United States. Therefore, the sample of city pairs where the euro is used is significantly reduced in the P&W panel. On the other hand, it is important to note that the euro is significant in the diverse and OECD panels after controlling for the effect of cities located in the same country.

As for the dollar area, although cities that use the dollar or have a hard peg regime with the dollar have less price dispersion, the effect is not always significant. Using the IQR, the coefficient on the dollar dummy decreases to -3.4 percent and becomes statistically significant in the OECD panel, but the same coefficient turns insignificant in the diverse panel. In the next two regressions we explore possible explanations for this lack of robustness.

Table 8.6 presents regression results using the original dependent variable but excluding pairs of cities located in countries that have little or no bilateral trade. The rationale for excluding these observations is that without trade links, there is little reason to believe that the goods markets of these countries would be integrated. As a result, there is little reason to expect good prices in these countries to be similar.

By eliminating the countries with few commercial links, the size of the diverse panel is cut almost in half, while the OECD panel is reduced by a third. The reduced panels include city pairs that are somewhat closer of each other. The mean distance is reduced from 6,400 to 5,400 km in the diverse panel, and from 6,000 to 5,000 km in the OECD panel. More importantly, the average income of the countries of the city pairs included increases from $11,000 to $16,000 in the diverse panel, and from $18,500 to $22,000 in the OECD panel. Finally, the proportion of city pairs located in the same country increases from 2.5 to 4.6 percent in the diverse panel, and from 5.1 to 7.7 percent in the OECD panel.

The regression results show an improvement in the adjusted R^2's, from 0.51 to 0.58 for the diverse panel and from 0.64 to 0.66 for the OECD panel. The effect of distance on price dispersion, while still important, is significantly less so than when using the full sample. This reflects that fact that the countries included are closer to each other. Similarly, because the included countries are more economically homogeneous, the mean income variable becomes statistically insignificant in the OECD panel, though the inequality in per capita GDP variable remains very significant and with similar coefficients in both panels.

In these regressions the use of the euro continues to be an important factor in reducing price dispersion, and the use of the dollar is now significant in both panels.

In a final refinement, I compute the price dispersion measure separately for goods and services. Because the services included in the database are non-tradable, their inclusion in the data might be a source of noise, since it is known that

Table 8.6. *Determinants of price dispersion across city pairs – pairs of cities in countries with little or no trade excluded*

Variable	Diverse panel		OECD panel	
	Estimate	T-stat	Estimate	T-stat
Intercept	0.348***	4.2	0.145	1.2
Log distance	0.088***	4.6	0.052***	2.7
Log distance squared	−0.005***	−3.7	−0.002*	−1.8
Log mean GDPPC	−0.044***	−20.6	−0.006	−0.8
Inequality in GDPPC	0.164***	37.9	0.139***	17.6
Nominal ER volatility	0.063***	8.2	0.075***	11.5
Currency/Hard peg				
Euro	−0.062***	−5.2	−0.043***	−4.6
CFA	−0.044	−0.8		
Dollar	−0.037***	−3.5	−0.017**	−2.0
Regional trading area				
EU	0.022**	2.1	−0.012	−1.4
NAFTA	−0.048***	−4.9	−0.013	−1.4
EFTA	0.037	0.8	−0.009	−0.2
ASEAN	−0.043**	−2.2	−0.001	0.0
ANZCERTA	−0.195***	−7.6	−0.109***	−5.3
MERCOSUR	−0.051*	−1.7	−0.014	−0.5
Andean common mkt.	0.005	0.1	0.007	0.1
CACM	−0.012	−0.2		
Same country				
Australia	0.041	1.2	0.016	0.6
Brazil	−0.138*	−1.7	−0.176***	−2.7
Canada	−0.018	−0.5	−0.002	−0.1
China	−0.071	−1.6		
Germany	0.034	1.1	0.017	0.7
U.K.	−0.045	−0.6	0.018	0.3
India	−0.146*	−1.8		
Italy	−0.136*	−1.7	−0.147**	−2.4
Japan	−0.111	−1.4	−0.176***	−2.8
New Zealand	−0.002	0.0	−0.002	0.0
Russia	−0.217***	−2.7		
Saudi Arabia	−0.031	−0.6		
Spain	−0.203**	−2.5	−0.224***	−3.5
Switzerland	−0.211**	−2.3	−0.190***	−2.6
U.A.E.	0.040	0.5	−0.028	−0.4
U.S.A.	−0.009	−0.6	−0.006	−0.5
Vietnam	−0.064	−0.8		
n	3,594		2,034	
Adj. R^2	0.579		0.663	

Notes: The dependent variable is the standard deviation of the log price differences between a pair of cities. Pairs of cities located in countries with little or no trade have been excluded in the estimation. The regressions include language and historical links dummies, but they are not shown to save space. Pairs of cities in countries with little or no trade excluded.
*, **, and *** indicate statistical significance at the 10%, 5%, and 1% level, respectively.

Table 8.7. *Determinants of price dispersion across city pairs–dispersion computed separately for tradables and non-tradables in the OECD panel*

Variable	Tradables		Non-tradables	
	Estimate	*T*-stat	Estimate	*T*-stat
Intercept	0.271**	2.1	−0.072	−0.3
Log distance	0.073**	2.4	0.234***	3.5
Log distance squared	−0.004*	−2.0	−0.014***	−3.4
Log mean GDPPC	−0.017***	−3.5	−0.035***	−3.2
Inequality in GDPPC	0.183***	23.4	0.176***	10.0
Nominal ER volatility	0.053***	7.1	0.086***	5.2
Currency/Hard peg				
Euro	−0.047***	−2.9	−0.010	−0.3
Dollar	−0.050***	−3.5	0.043	1.4
Regional trading area				
EU	−0.073***	−5.0	−0.019	−0.6
NAFTA	−0.029*	−1.8	−0.127***	−3.4
EFTA	−0.110**	−2.2	0.011	0.1
ASEAN	−0.059	−1.3	0.059	0.6
ANZCERTA	−0.154***	−4.2	−0.372***	−4.5
MERCOSUR	−0.036	−0.9	−0.324***	−3.4
Andean common mkt.	−0.001	0.0	−0.122	−0.5
Same country				
Australia	−0.043	−0.9	0.071	0.6
Brazil	−0.347**	−2.4	−0.092	−0.3
Canada	−0.055	−1.1	−0.012	−0.1
Germany	−0.003	−0.1	0.095	1.0
U.K.	0.101	0.9	0.039	0.2
Italy	−0.246**	−2.2	−0.229	−0.9
Japan	−0.354***	−3.2	−0.204	−0.8
New Zealand	−0.033	−0.3	−0.015	−0.1
Spain	−0.430***	−3.8	−0.304	−1.2
Switzerland	−0.219*	−1.8	−0.140	−0.5
U.A.E.	−0.142	−1.1	−0.019	−0.1
U.S.A.	0.006	0.3	−0.021	−0.4
n	3,081		3,081	
Adj. R^2	0.542		0.156	

Notes: The dependent variable is the standard deviation of the log price differences between a pair of cities. The standard deviation is computed separately for prices of goods and services. The regressions include language and historical links dummies, but they are not shown to save space.
*, **, and *** indicate statistical significance at the 10%, 5%, and 1% level, respectively.

deviations in services prices from PPP are much more long-lasting than for goods (see, for example, Parsley and Wei 1996). Because of data availability, the split between tradables and non-tradables is performed only for the OECD panel. I use the IQR measure of price dispersion for these regressions, because the small

number of services available makes the standard deviation particularly susceptible to the influence of outliers.

The results presented in Table 8.7 are somewhat surprising. As a matter of fact
there are not such striking differences between tradables and non-tradables. The
coefficients of the main explanatory variables are similar and similarly significant. There are, though, some important differences. In particular, the effect of
shared currencies on price dispersion is strong and significant only for tradables.
For example, the coefficient on the dollar is now stronger for tradable, decreas-
ing from -3.4 percent (Table 8.5) to -5 percent, but it becomes positive and
insignificant for non-tradables.

8.4   Conclusions

This chapter examines the link between the use of a shared currency and the extent
of integration in consumer goods and services markets across cities. It extends previous work by Parsley and Wei (2001) in several directions. First, it combines a
more complete cross section of goods and cities into two balanced panels that maximize, respectively, the geographical diversity of the cities included and the size of
the basket of goods and services used to compute measures of price dispersion
across city pairs. Second, it explores the effect of eliminating city pairs located in
countries that have little or no commercial links with each other. Third, it decom-
poses price variability into tradables and non-tradables. And finally, it includes
explanatory variables that, to the best of my knowledge, have not been previously
employed in studies of price dispersion across cities.

The results confirm many of the results of Parsley and Wei (2001), while
adding some new insights that deserve more research in future. Geographical
distance continues to be an obvious impediment to market integration, but so is
economic distance, as measured by the inequality in per capita GDP of the countries where the cities are located. This suggests that development-related variables should be considered more closely in studies of international economic
integration. As far as currencies are concerned, the effect of the euro in reducing
price dispersion across cities is robust and significant, even controlling for trade
integration and for unobserved institutional features shared by cities located in
the same country. Cities located in countries that use the dollar or that have
currencies pegged to the dollar by a currency board system also have reduced
price dispersion, though the effect is not always statistically significant.

Finally, the results show that some of the results may be affected by the selection of the sample of city pairs, by the goods and services included in the measure
of price dispersion, and by the measure of dispersion itself. For example, the
effect of the dollar use in reducing price dispersion across city pairs is stronger
and statistically significant when we drop pairs of cities located in countries with
little or no trade or when we consider only goods. Also, the use of a robust measure such as the IQR is clearly preferable to the standard deviation, for outliers
(which are not unusual in price data) can greatly distort the results.

REFERENCES

Engel, C. and Rogers, J. H. (1996). "How Wide is the Border?" *American Economic Review*, 86 (December): 1112–38.

Freeman, R. B. (1995). "Are Your Wages Set in Beijing?" *Journal of Economic Perspectives*, 9 (Summer): 15–32.

Glick, R. and Rose, A. K. (2002). "Does a Currency Union Affect Trade? The Time Series Evidence." *European Economic Review*, 46 (June): 1125–57.

Helliwell, J. F. (1998). *How Much Do Borders Matter?* Washington, DC: Brookings Institution Press.

McCallum, J. (1995). "National Borders Matter: Canada–U.S. Regional Trade Patterns." *American Economic Review*, 85 (June): 615–23.

Parsley, D. C. and Wei, S.-J. (2001). "Limiting Currency Volatility to Stimulate Goods Market Integration: A Price-Based Approach." *NBER Working Paper* No. 8468, September.

—— and —— (1996). "Convergence to the law of one price without trade barriers or currency fluctuations." *Quarterly Journal of Economics*, 111 (November): 1211–36.

Rose, A. K. (2000). "One Money, One Market: The Effect of Common Currencies on Trade." *Economic Policy*, 30 (April): 7–33.

—— and van Wincoop, E. (2001). "National Borders as a Barrier to Trade: The Real Case for Monetary Union." *American Economic Review*, 91 (May): 386–90.

Appendix 8.A1. *Dummy variables defined at the country level*

Variable	Countries included
Currency area	*Euro*: Austria, Belgium, Finland, France, Germany, Greece, Ireland, Italy, Luxembourg, Netherlands, Portugal, Spain
	CFA franc: Cameroon, Cote d'Ivoire, Gabon, Senegal
	Dollar: Argentina, Ecuador, Hong Kong, Panama, United States
Regional trading area	*European Union*: Euro countries plus Denmark, UK, Sweden
	EFTA: Iceland, Norway, Switzerland
	ANZCERTA: Australia, New Zealand
	ASEAN: Indonesia, Malaysia, Philippines, Singapore, Thailand, Vietnam
	NAFTA: Canada, Mexico, USA
	MERCOSUR: Argentina, Brazil, Paraguay, Uruguay
	Andean Common Market: Colombia, Ecuador, Peru, Venezuela
	CACM (Central American Common Marker): Guatemala, Costa Rica
Common language	*Arabic*: Bahrain, Egypt, Jordan, Kuwait, Libya, Morocco, Saudi Arabia, United Arab Emirates
	Chinese: China, Hong Kong, Taiwan
	Dutch: Belgium, Netherlands
	English: Australia, Canada, Great Britain, India, Kenya, New Zealand, Nigeria, Pakistan, Singapore, South Africa, Sri Lanka, United States, Zimbabwe, Ireland
	French: Cameroon, Cote d'Ivoire, Gabon, Senegal, Tunisia, France
	German: Switzerland, Austria, Germany, Luxembourg
	Malay: Indonesia, Malaysia
	Portuguese: Brazil, Portugal
	Spanish: Argentina, Chile, Colombia, Costa Rica, Ecuador, Guatemala, Mexico, Panama, Paraguay, Peru, Uruguay, Venezuela, Spain
Common historical link	*China*: Honk Kong, Taiwan
	England: Bahrain, Bangladesh, Egypt, India, Jordan, Kenya, Kuwait, Malaysia, Nigeria, Pakistan, Papua New Guinea, Saudi Arabia, Singapore, South Africa, Sri Lanka, United Arab Emirates, Zimbabwe
	France: Cameroon, Cote d'Ivoire, Gabon, Morocco, Senegal, Tunisia, Vietnam
	Former Soviet Block: Azerbaijan, Croatia, Czech Republic, Hungary, Poland, Romania, Russia, Yugoslavia
	Spain/Portugal: Argentina, Brazil, Chile, Colombia, Costa Rica, Ecuador, Guatemala, Mexico, Panama, Paraguay, Peru, Philippines, Uruguay, Venezuela

PART III

Monetary Integration in Latin America

9

Trade Agreements, Exchange Rate Disagreements

EDUARDO FERNÁNDEZ-ARIAS, UGO PANIZZA,
AND ERNESTO STEIN

We show that the negative effects on exports and FDI flows of an exchange rate misalignment are amplified when the misalignment is among countries that share a regional integration agreement (RIA). Regional integration agreements strengthen the well-established relationship between real appreciation and currency crises. We conclude that coordination to achieve real exchange rate consistency within blocs is key to macro stability and, *a fortiori*, sustainable trade agreements.

9.1 Introduction

The recent events in Mercosur have brought to the forefront the problems that may arise when countries have trade agreements and exchange rate disagreements. The January 1999 devaluation of the Brazilian real strained the relationship between Argentina and Brazil. It led to protectionist pressure in Argentina, business relocation from Argentina to Brazil, and put additional pressures on the Argentine peso, which contributed to the ultimate demise of convertibility in December 2001. Developments such as these, however, are not unique to Mercosur. They have occurred repeatedly between Venezuela and Colombia, or even in the European Union after the ERM crisis of 1992.

In this chapter, we look at the circumstances and the type of RIA under which these problems may arise, and the policy responses that may help alleviate them. Throughout the discussion of the potential problems, it is important to ask whether there is something special about being members of the same RIA that makes exchange rate disagreements particularly damaging. The classes of problems we will discuss are the following:

Increased protectionism/Scaling back or elimination of trade arrangements The country that loses competitiveness as a result of a real exchange rate appreciation

The authors gratefully acknowledge Ari Aisen, Christian Daude, Josefina Posadas, and Alejandro Riaño for superb research assistance, and Juan Blyde, Alejandro Micco, and Ernesto Talvi for helpful comments and suggestions. The usual caveats apply. The views expressed in this chapter are the authors' and do not necessarily reflect those of the Inter-American Development Bank.

This chapter is based in part on the 2002 IADB Report on *Economic and Social Progress in Latin America*.

vis-à-vis its trade partners may resort to increased protectionism. The existence of a RIA may preclude the country from increasing tariffs within the bloc. As a result, the country may increase protection *vis-à-vis* the rest of the world, resulting in trade diversion, or it may increase protection *vis-à-vis* the bloc partners, resorting to less transparent methods such as anti-dumping or other administrative measures.

Reduction in trade flows Exchange rate disagreements could lead to reduced exports from the country that loses competitiveness to its partner. If the disagreement occurs in the context of a RIA with high external protection, it may be difficult for the country that loses competitiveness to redirect at least some of its exports to alternative markets.

Relocation of investments Regional trade arrangements may spark intense competition for the location of investment. Provided there are economies of scale, eliminating trade barriers will induce firms to produce in just one location within the bloc, and serve the extended market from this location. Under these conditions, swings in the bilateral real exchange rates may have important consequences for the location of new investment and in some cases shift the location of existing investment as well.

Exchange rate crises Depreciation in a RIA country may reduce the credibility of its partners' commitment to a fixed parity, and can generate speculative attacks on its currency. A country may thus be forced to abandon its preferred exchange rate policy due to the exchange rate disagreement.

In order to study these problems, we draw from the experience of 37 countries that belong to six different RIA: NAFTA, Mercosur, the Central American Common Market, the Andean Community, ASEAN, and the European Union. Our sample, which covers the period 1989 through 2000, thus includes several South–South regional integration agreements, as well as a North–South one (NAFTA) and a North–North one (the European Union). This allows us to study whether the set of problems identified above are equally relevant for all types of regional integration agreements, or whether they are particularly damaging in some of them.

9.2 Exchange Rate Disagreements and Protectionism

One of the reasons why exchange rate disagreements may harm members of RIAs is that they may lead to protectionist pressures, thus preventing the gains from trade from being realized, and defeating the purpose of the RIA. In the context of the European Union, in fact, Eichengreen (1993) has argued that this political economy argument represents the only compelling reason for monetary unification to follow the economic integration provided in the Single European Act.

There are plenty of examples of protectionist pressures following large exchange rate swings in the context of the European Union. Example of these were the events following the September 1992 ERM crisis, which gave rise to considerable tensions among the EU member countries. France accused the United Kingdom and Italy of harming the overall stability of the European Union.

French public officials went so far as to threaten the British with exclusion from the single market, and even EC Commission president Jaques Delors got into the act, warning the British about the incompatibility of their exchange rate policies with the single market (Eichengreen 1993). French entrepreneurs started calling for protectionist measures, while Belgium's Finance Minister warned of retaliatory trade actions against countries resorting to competitive devaluations.

Eichengreen (1997) argues that the danger of a protectionist backlash following a large exchange rate realignment does not necessarily carry over to RIA such as Mercosur which, unlike the European Union, are imperfect custom unions. Bevilaqua (1997) and Rozemberg and Svarzman (2002), however, provide detailed accounts of how episodes of large real exchange rate swings led to protectionist measures in the context of Mercosur.

There are, in fact, a number of arguments that suggest that exchange rate disagreements may be particularly damaging in South–South agreements. First, developing countries have more limited access to financial markets, particularly in periods of financial turmoil, and higher exchange rate volatility. While their experiencing *similar* swings in exchange rates might have given rise to less protectionist pressure under conditions of shallow integration, recent experience shows that exchange rate swings have not really been similar among them. By focusing on the average volatility of real bilateral exchange rates for the 1990s it is possible to see that the European Union is by far the RIA with the lowest volatility, while Mercosur is at the highest end of the spectrum (see Figure 9.1).

Second, the European Union has much more power to enforce trade rules among its member countries than do countries in other RIAs, particularly those formed by developing countries. Thus, even if exchange rate swings were

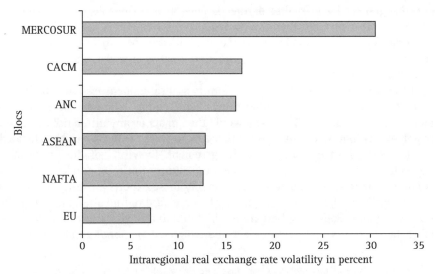

Figure 9.1. *Intraregional volatility of real multilateral exchange rate*

Source: Authors' calculations based on IFS-IMF.

comparable, more lobbying in the case of the European Union need not result in more protectionism. In fact, the discussion in Bevilaqua (1997) and Rozemberg and Svarzman (2002) suggests that, beyond the rhetoric, actual protectionist measures have been more prevalent in the case of Mercosur.

9.3   Real Exchange Rate Misalignments and Exports

Most of the literature on the links between exchange rates and trade has focused on the role of exchange rate volatility. In general, studies find that volatility has negative effects on trade, although the impact is quite small, and declining over time (Frankel and Wei 1998). This decline, combined with evidence showing that effects are larger in developing countries has been explained by the growing availability of hedging mechanisms, particularly for developed countries (Panizza et al. 2003). Currency Unions, on the other hand, have been shown to have large effects on trade (Glick and Rose 2002; see also Rose, this volume, Part II). Rather than focusing on the effects of volatility, this section focuses on the effects of exchange rate misalignments on exports.

The concerns regarding exchange rate disagreements on the part of tradable goods producers in the country that "suffers" the misalignment are generally twofold: They worry about an avalanche of imports from the depreciating country; and they worry about the effect of the exchange rate swing on their capacity to export. Are these concerns justified? A look at the behavior of bilateral trade during episodes of exchange rate realignments suggests that the concern regarding an avalanche of imports is unwarranted but that the concern about the effect on exports is justified (Fernández-Arias et al. 2002). But how costly is this reduction in exports? The answer is that it depends. If a country that suffers an exchange rate realignment by a trading partner is able, at a reasonable cost, to shift its exports to other markets, then the consequences for exporters need not be harsh. If, on the contrary, exports to the partner cannot easily be relocated to other markets, exporters will suffer. This suggests that what is crucial is the evolution of total exports, not just bilateral exports.[1]

In this section, we test whether a country's misalignment *vis-à-vis* their RIA partners has a larger impact, other things being equal, than a similar misalignment *vis-à-vis* non-members. Why would the impact be any different? Our main hypothesis is that RIAs can affect the degree to which exports can be relocated in the event of an exchange rate disagreement. By virtue of the preferential access to its RIA partners, it is possible for a country to export goods in which it is not internationally competitive. If suddenly these exports are curtailed due to a depreciation in the RIA partner, it may be very hard to find alternative markets for these goods. Following Bergara et al. (1995) and Bevilaqua et al. (2001), we label these exports that cannot easily be redirected "regional goods." Consider

---

[1] For an analysis of the impact of exchange rate swings on *bilateral* trade, in the context of Mercosur, see Bevilaqua (1997).

the case of trade in agricultural products in the European Union, or automobile trade in Mercosur. Argentine car exports to (and from) Brazil are made possible by the preferential access, and by a special regime that translates into high protection on car imports from the rest of the world. If for whatever reason (say, a depreciation) Brazil stops demanding Argentine cars, it will be difficult for Argentine producers to find alternative markets. Consider instead a commodity such as oil, another one of Argentina's main exports to Brazil, and a product in which Argentina is internationally competitive. If for whatever reason Brazil's demand for oil declines, oil producers in Argentina will be able to export to other countries, even if this relocation is not costless.[2]

If RIAs increase the importance of regional goods, we would expect the elasticity of total exports with respect to exchange rate misalignments to be higher when the source of the misalignment lies within the RIA. To test this hypothesis, we start from a basic model in which a country's level of total exports depends on the misalignment of its real exchange rate and a set of other controls:

$$\ln(EXP_{i,t}) = \alpha + \beta RER_{i,t} + \theta \ln(Y_{i,t}) + a_i + t_t + u_{i,t} \tag{1}$$

Here $EXP_{i,t}$, $RER_{i,t}$, and $Y_{i,t}$ are total exports, multilateral real effective exchange rate misalignment, and total GDP for country i at time t (exports and GDP are measured in current dollars), a_i is a country fixed effect that controls for country specific factors that do not vary over time and t is a time-fixed effect that controls for dollar inflation and for the fact that trade has been increasing over time. We compute real exchange rate misalignments as the percentage difference between the actual real exchange rate and the trend exchange rate, obtained with a Hodrick–Prescott decomposition.

Equation (1) implicitly assumes that the elasticity of exports with respect to real exchange rate misalignments is independent of the source of the misalignment (within or outside the RIA). As we are interested in testing whether these elasticities differ, we decompose the multilateral real effective exchange rate misalignment into a within-RIA (or regional) component and an outside-RIA (or non-regional) component as follows:

$$RER_{i,t} \cong w_i R\_RER_{i,t} + (1 - w_i) NR\_RER_{i,t}, \tag{2}$$

where w_i is the share of RIA partners in total trade of country i and $R\_RER_{i,t}$, $NR\_RER_{i,t}$ are the exchange rate misalignments of country i with respect to regional and non-regional trading partners respectively.[3] Next, we define

---

[2] The example of cars and oil in trade between Argentina and Brazil was borrowed from Bevilaqua et al. (2001). Regional goods might also exist in the absence of RIAs. However, RIAs are likely to increase the importance of regional goods, because preferential access may create a demand for goods that are not internationally competitive.

[3] $R\_RER_{i,t}$ and $NR\_RER_{i,t}$ are weighted averages of bilateral exchange rate misalignment, with $\sum_i \omega_{fta,i} = 1$ and $\sum_i \omega_{nofta,i} = 1$, where $\omega_{fta,i}$ and $\omega_{nofta,i}$ are weight within and outside RIA, respectively. The misalignments are measured as percentage of the multilateral equilibrium level, that is, $R\_RER_{i,t} = (R\_RE_{i,t} - \overline{R\_RE}_{i,t})/\overline{RE}_{i,t}$, and $NR\_RER_{i,t} = (NR\_RE_{i,t} - \overline{NR\_RE}_{i,t})/\overline{RE}_{i,t}$.

$REG_{i,t} = w_i R\_RER_{i,t}$ and $NOREG_{i,t} = (1-w_i)NR\_RER_{i,t}$. By weighting the regional and non-regional misalignments by their respective shares in total trade, we can interpret $REG_{i,t}$ as the contribution of the regional misalignment to the multilateral misalignment, and $NOREG_{i,t}$ as the contribution of the non-regional misalignment to the multilateral misalignment of country i at time t. We then estimate the following model:

$$\ln(EXP_{i,t}) = \alpha + \beta REG_{i,t} + \gamma NOREG_{i,t} + \theta \ln(Y_{i,t}) + a_i + t_t + u_{i,t}, \qquad (3)$$

and test whether $\beta > \gamma$. In other words, we test whether the impact of an overall misalignment originated within the RIA (β) is larger than that of a similar overall misalignment originated outside the region (γ).

The results are reported in Table 9.1. The first column of the table reports the results obtained by estimating Eq. (1) and confirms that real exchange rate misalignments are a statistically significant and quantitatively important determinant of exports. In particular, the results indicate that a 1 percent appreciation is associated with a 0.6 percent decrease in exports. Columns (2) through (4) report the results obtained by estimating Eq. (3) and confirm that there are large and significant differences in the effect of regional and non-regional misalignments over exports. Column (2), which includes the whole sample, shows that a one-percentage point contribution of the regional real exchange rate to multilateral appreciation is associated with a significant decrease in exports of approximately 1.4 percent. In contrast, the correlation between non-regional misalignments and exports has the expected sign, but is not significant. In Column (3), we restrict the sample to developing countries. The coefficient attached to the regional misalignment is statistically significant and economically important. In this case, a one-percentage point contribution of the regional real exchange rate to multilateral appreciation is associated with a 2.6 percent decrease in exports, much larger than that for the whole sample. The coefficient attached to the non-regional misalignment is not statistically significant and the difference between the two is statistically significant. Column (4) shows that when we focus on developed countries, the coefficient for the regional misalignment is much smaller, and not statistically significant.

If the presence of regional goods is a function of the degree of preferential access a country has *vis-à-vis* its RIA partners, then the impact of regional misalignments on total exports should be a function of this preferential access. To test this hypothesis, we build an index that measures, for each country, the average level of protection of its RIA partners.[4] Next, we generate a dummy variable

---

[4] The index is constructed as follows:

$$P_i = \sum_{j=1}^{n-1} t_{j,1995} \times \frac{trade_{ij}}{\sum_{j=1}^{n} trade_{ij}},$$

where $trade_{ij}$ is the average trade between country i and country j between 1989 and 2000, t_j, 1995 is the average external tariff of country j in 1995, and n is the number of countries that form the RIA of which country i is a member.

Table 9.1. *Exports and real exchange rate misalignments*

Dependent variable: log(exports)	(1) All countries	(2) All countries	(3) Developing countries	(4) Developed countries	(5) All countries
Log(GDP)	0.433 (6.89)***	0.433 (6.85)***	0.230 (1.93)*	0.420 (7.30)***	0.429 (6.81)***
Total misalignment	0.613 (3.09)***				
(a) Regional misalignment		1.449 (2.19)**	2.649 (2.31)**	0.602 (1.20)	
(b) Non-regional misalignment		0.347 (1.35)	−0.115 (0.30)	−0.304 (0.86)	0.321 (1.25)
(c) High protection × regional misalignment					2.900 (2.93)***
(d) Low protection × regional misalignment					0.572 (0.72)
Constant	−1.263 (0.81)	−1.255 (0.80)	2.772 (0.98)	−0.010 (0.01)	−1.159 (0.74)
Observations	394	394	208	185	394
Number of groups	36	36	19	17	36
R-squared	0.79	0.80	0.79	0.91	0.80
Tests on difference between coefficients					
(a) − (b)		1.102 [0.18]	2.764 [0.04]**	0.906 [0.18]	
(c) − (d)					2.328 [0.05]**
(c) − (b)					2.579 [0.02]**
(d) − (b)					0.251 [0.79]

* Significant at 10% level.
** Significant at 5% level.
*** Significant at 1% level.

Notes: Absolute value of *t*-statistics in parentheses, one tail *p*-values in brackets. Year dummies and country fixed effects included in all regressions not reported.

that assigns a value of one to countries that have RIA partners with average protection above the sample mean, and zero to countries that have partners with average protection below the sample mean. We call this the high protection dummy. Likewise, we also generate a symmetrical dummy variable that takes value one for low protection countries (the low protection dummy). Finally, we let each of these two dummies interact with our measure of regional misalignment and estimate Eq. (3) with these interactions. Column (5) of Table 9.1 shows that regional misalignments are significantly more important for countries with highly protected RIA partners. The results indicate that a one-percentage point contribution of the regional real exchange rate to multilateral appreciation is associated with a 2.9 percent decrease in exports in countries with highly preferential access to their RIA partners and with a 0.6 percent decrease in exports in countries with low preferential access. Interestingly, the last row of the table shows that there is no significant difference between the coefficient associated with low-protection regional misalignment and the coefficient associated with non-regional misalignment. These last results are important, because they lend support to the hypothesis that regional goods play an important role in magnifying the impact of exchange rate misalignments within RIAs.

9.4   Exchange Rate Disagreements and the Location of Foreign Direct Investment

Firms in the North usually engage in multinational activity in the South for one of two reasons: Either to take advantage of the difference in relative factor endowments (vertical FDI) or to serve a market that would be too expensive to serve through trade (horizontal FDI). In the case of vertical FDI, firms that produce for the world market locate different stages of production in different countries in order to reduce costs. As, other things being equal, the level of the real exchange rate affects the cost of land and labor, a depreciated exchange rate will attract FDI in activities that are intensive in these factors.[5]

In the case of horizontal "tariff-jumping" FDI, whether a firm engages in FDI in a particular country depends on the relative cost of serving this market via trade or via domestic production. Other things equal, an exchange rate depreciation in the host country will reduce the cost of producing the good there, and thus may result in higher FDI.

These channels suggest that movements in the bilateral exchange rate between two countries will affect the relative amounts of FDI these two countries receive. But are exchange rate swings more likely to have large effects among countries with trade agreements? In the case of vertical FDI, in which a firm produces for the world market, a depreciation may favor location in the depreciating country at the expense of all other potential hosts with similar factor endowments. If production is for a regional market, however, countries that are both similar and near each other should suffer more from another country's depreciation. To the extent that RIAs include countries that are both similar and near each other (as in South–South and North–North RIAs), RIA partners may be more sensitive to exchange rate swings. But, through this vertical FDI channel, sensitivity will be due mostly to proximity, not to the RIA itself.

---

[5] For studies of the relationship between real exchange rate volatility and the determinants of North–North FDI see Froot and Stein (1991) and Blonigen (1997).

In the case of horizontal FDI, however, RIAs create an enlarged internal market protected from the outside world. Provided there are economies of scale, the elimination of trade barriers within the bloc will induce firms to produce in a single location, and serve the extended market from this location. Regional trade arrangements may thus create a space of intense competition for the location of investment, not unlike that which often exists among subnational units in a single country. Under these conditions, swings in the bilateral real exchange rates among countries in the bloc that affect relative costs of production, may have important consequences for the location of new investment, and in many cases may shift the location of existing investment as well. This argument suggests that swings in the real bilateral exchange rate will have larger effects among members of an RIA. For this to matter, however, external protection for the RIA has to be high enough to support horizontal FDI.

In order to evaluate this hypothesis, we study the effects of real bilateral exchange rates on relative inflows of FDI, and check whether the response of relative FDI to bilateral swings in exchange rates is larger among RIA partners. Moreover, we study whether the results depend on the type of the country pair involved (North–North, North–South, or South–South).

Figure 9.2 summarizes our main results. After accounting for other determinants of relative FDI inflows (such as relative income or openness), a 1 percent depreciation of the real bilateral exchange rate increases relative inflows by 1.3 percent when both countries are members of the same RIA. In contrast, the impact is not statistically significant in the case of outside countries. If we limit

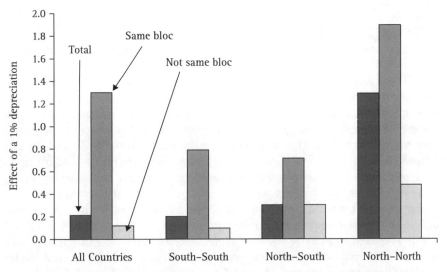

Figure 9.2. *Effect of exchange rate misalignments on FDI inflows (in percent)*
Source: Authors' calculations.

the exercise to South–South country pairs, we obtain similar results, but the impact is smaller (0.8 percent) among countries with RIAs. The largest impact is obtained for the case of North–North country pairs with common membership in RIAs, in which case a 1 percent depreciation increases relative FDI by 1.9 percent. This may be due to the fact that the EU, which accounts for most North–North RIA pairs, is much more deeply integrated than other RIAs. It should be pointed out that the results described in Figure 9.2 are based on regressions that do not control for the interaction between exchange rate misalignment and distance. In future work, we plan to control for distance and extend our sample to the whole world.

9.5 Trade Agreements and Currency Crises

In this section we show that RIAs with exchange rate disagreements may be prone to produce strong depreciation pressures and currency crises in their member countries. Once again, the pressure experienced by the Argentine peso after the depreciation of the Brazilian real since the beginning of 1999 is an excellent illustration of this effect. While the currency crisis experienced in Argentina that eventually led to the repeal of the Convertibility Law was caused by a number of factors, the sudden misalignment with the real played an important part in weakening the Argentinean peg to the dollar. Europe also had its share of remarkable currency crises between close trade partners. For instance, the exit of the Italian lira from the European Monetary System in 1992 was almost immediately followed by the abandonment of the peg by the United Kingdom and caused enormous pressure on the French franc (Buiter et al. 1998).

The connection between currency crises and prior misalignment of the real exchange rate is well established in the empirical literature on leading indicators of such crises (see Frankel and Rose 1996; Goldfajn and Valdés 1997; Kaminsky et al. 1998; Kaminsky and Reinhart 1999). Our specific question is whether the presence of a RIA makes this problem any different than the analysis shown in previous sections suggests. First, the overall balance of payments impact of a given exchange rate misalignment with respect to a trading partner is larger if it happens within a RIA. This was shown to be true both for trade and for FDI inflows. Second, RIAs constrain the ability of member countries to adjust to an adverse shock to competitiveness by use of import tariffs and other offsetting trade policies. In other words, RIAs enlarge the balance of payments shock of exchange rate overvaluation, and reduce the ability to offset it in ways that diffuse the downward pressure on the currency.

Our approach to analyze whether overvaluations *vis-à-vis* RIA partners may be especially risky concerning currency crises builds on Goldfajn and Valdés (1997). They express the probability of a crisis episode in country i at period t ($EP_{i,t}$) as a function of its multilateral real exchange rate misalignment in the period before ($RER_{i,t}$), a set of control variables ($X_{i,t}$), and an error term ($\varepsilon_{i,t}$):

$$EP_{i,t} = \alpha + \beta RER_{i,t} + \delta X_{i,t} + \varepsilon_{i,t} \tag{4}$$

As in previous sections, to address our question, we decompose the multilateral effective real exchange rate misalignment $RER_{i,t}$ into two components: The contribution of countries within the RIA ($REG_{i,t}$) and the contribution of countries outside the RIA ($NOREG_{i,t}$). We then use an expanded specification to capture the differential effect of within-RIA misalignments on the probability of a currency crisis:

$$EP_{i,t} = \alpha + \beta REG_{i,t} + \gamma NOREG_{i,t} + \delta X_{i,t} + \varepsilon_{i,t} \tag{5}$$

If the existence of a RIA is irrelevant for the risk of currency crises, then a given exchange rate misalignment should have the same effect, independently of the source of the misalignment (within or outside the RIA). This would imply that $\beta = \gamma < 0$ and the specification collapses to the one in Goldfajn and Valdés based on the overall misalignment (Eq. 4). If, alternatively, misalignments coming from inside a RIA are riskier, we should obtain $\beta < \gamma < 0$.

As is customary, episodes of currency crisis are identified by a binary variable taking the unit value. In this section, we concentrate on a simple definition of a currency crisis: A country experiences a currency crisis in a given month when its multilateral real exchange rate depreciates by more than either 5 or 10 percent.[6] Perhaps surprisingly, this definition is not common in the literature which concentrates on nominal depreciation (Frankel and Rose 1996; and Kaminsky and Reinhart 1999) instead. In our view, the traditional approach does not capture the real nature of the misalignment and adds the unnecessary complication of how to control for inflation to determine what level of depreciation ought to be considered a crisis.[7]

The key explanatory variable is the real exchange rate misalignment during the previous month. We start with the customary specification in which the misalignment is specified linearly within a probit structure. This linear assumption, however, may not be the most adequate for the problem we face. When the exchange rate is undervalued, for example, we would not expect currency

---

[6] We use a two-month window as in Goldfajn and Valdés (1997), so that the two months following a crisis are assigned a missing value to ensure that a spurious second episode is not accounted for. Wider windows do not change results qualitatively.

[7] An exception is Goldfajn and Valdés (1997), who utilize a definition based on real depreciation. However, they classify as crisis any real depreciation that appears exceptionally large in each country's experience, rather than a uniform threshold across countries like we do. As a result of this definition, every country is imputed a similar number of crises (those depreciation events exceeding two standard deviations), irrespective of whether the country is intrinsically stable or in permanent crisis (irrespective of the size of the standard deviation). Our uniform threshold eliminates this element of arbitrariness. In our sample, the use of Goldfajn and Valdés (1997) definition of currency crises would include among the episodes of crises observations in which the real exchange rate depreciation was below 1.5 percent (e.g. in Luxembourg).

crises to occur. When the exchange rate is grossly overvalued, the degree of overvaluation may mostly affect the size of crisis rather than its likelihood, which is not reflected in a binary probit model. This would justify using a dummy variable for overvaluation, which would match the binary nature of a currency crisis as modeled. We, therefore, test the robustness of our results by replacing our regional and non-regional misalignments by dummies that take a value of one when the contribution of the regional (or non-regional) overvaluation to the overall misalignment is above 4 percent.[8]

Table 9.2 shows results when the thresholds for a real monthly depreciation of the multilateral exchange rate to be classified as a currency crisis are set at either 5 or 10 percent. In each case, we present probit regressions with country fixed effects and three sets of explanatory variables: (*a*) the multilateral real exchange rate misalignment (columns 1 and 4); (*b*) the contribution to the real exchange rate misalignment from countries within and outside the RIA (columns 2 and 5); (*c*) the discrete measures of misalignment represented by the dummies described above (columns 3 and 6). All specifications also include two variables that control for access to credit and recent government changes (all results are robust to dropping these two controls). The regressions with the multilateral real exchange rate misalignment in the first and fourth columns confirm that the effect of this variable, under both definitions of crisis, has the correct sign and is highly significant statistically. It is also substantial in economic terms. In fact, other things being equal, a 10 percent real appreciation doubles the probability of a crisis (from 2.3 to 4.6 percent in the first definition of crisis). Notice that these are monthly probabilities. A 4.6 percent monthly probability implies a 43 percent probability that a crisis will occur within the next year.

When the misalignment contributions are split into its regional and non-regional components (columns 2 and 4), we find that, while both sources of misalignment are statistically significant, the impact of misalignments from within the RIA is at least twice as large as from outside, everything else being equal. Furthermore, the difference between the coefficients for regional and non-regional misalignments is always statistically significant. Thus, the hypothesis of equal coefficients is rejected.

The results just described are robust to substituting the continuous measure of misalignment for the discrete measure described above. In particular, column 3 shows that the presence of a large overvaluation with respect to RIA partners increases the probability of a currency crisis by 14 percentage points while a large overvaluation with respect to non-related countries increases the probability of a currency crisis by 7 percentage points. The results are qualitatively similar when we use the second definition of crisis (column 6). Fernández-Arias et al. (2002) show that the results are robust to several alternative definitions of currency crisis.

---

[8] Approximately equal to two standard deviations in the case of the regional misalignment.

Table 9.2. *Real misalignments and currency crisis, probit estimates*

	A crisis is a real devaluation greater than 5%			A crisis is a real devaluation greater than 10%		
	(1)	(2)	(3)	(4)	(5)	(6)
(a) Multilateral misalignment	−0.2288 (8.180)***			−0.127 (6.591)***		
(b) Regional misalignment		−0.4046 (4.183)***			−0.3388 (3.800)***	
(c) Non-regional misalignment		−0.1652 (4.285)***			−0.0598 (2.298)**	
(d) Dummy regional misalignment			0.1459 (6.435)***			0.1242 (5.146)***
(e) Dummy non-regional misalignment			0.0719 (7.835)***			0.0457 (6.375)***
(f) Access to foreign credit	−0.0194 (3.040)***	−0.0188 (2.977)***	−0.0172 (2.888)***	−0.0049 (1.075)	−0.0035 (0.868)	−0.0027 (0.845)
(g) Government change	0.0157 (1.486)	0.0166 (1.563)	0.0162 (1.623)	0.0162 (1.817)*	0.0147 (1.814)*	0.0136 (1.997)*
Observations	3,848	3,848	3,848	2,716	2,716	2,716
Number of groups	28	28	28	19	19	19
R-squared	0.1368	0.137	0.173	0.1436	0.1577	0.2248
Tests on difference between coefficients						
(b) – (c)		−0.24 [0.023]**			−0.28 [0.005]***	
(d) – (e)			0.07 [0.069]*			0.08 [0.090]*

* Significant at 10% level.
** Significant at 5% level.
*** Significant at 1% level.

Notes: The coefficients reported in the table are marginal effects. Absolute value of *t*-statistics in parentheses, one tail *p*-values in brackets. Year dummies and country fixed effects included in all regressions not reported.

9.6 Conclusions and Policy Issues

Traditional analyses of RIAs have focused mainly on trade issues, such as the changes of trade patterns and their welfare implications. Here, we have focused on the potential problems caused by exchange rates misalignments within RIAs, which may also have important welfare implications. We find that exchange rate disagreements may have more serious consequences when they occur among countries bound by trade agreements. They have a larger impact on exports, on FDI, and on crises and contagion. Furthermore, exchange rate disagreements have the potential to break up or weaken support for RIAs. So, if for no other reason, they need to be considered seriously.

One caveat with the results of this chapter is that our statistical exercises did not control for the interaction among exchange rate misalignments, geographic proximity, and RIAs.[9] One may claim that geographic proximity is the true cause of our results and, if trade among neighboring countries is "different" from trade among faraway countries, the existence of a RIA could play no role in the "regional good" effect discussed in this chapter. While we attempt to disentangle the effect of geographic proximity by showing that the effect of exchange rate disagreements is stronger in RIAs with higher external protection, more work needs to be done to separate the roles of geography and RIAs. In future work, we plan to extend our sample to the whole world and explore in detail the interactions among exchange rate misalignments, RIAs, and geographic proximity. Differentiating between proximity and RIA effects is extremely important in light of the policy issues discussed below. In particular, if the negative impact of exchange rate misalignments are independent from the existence of a RIA and are due only to geographic proximity, then the existence of a RIA may play an important role in generating institutions aimed at limiting damaging episodes of exchange rate volatility. If this were the case, neighboring countries that are part of a RIA would be better positioned to deal with exchange rate disagreements than neighboring countries that are not part of a RIA.

Policy issues in connection with risks emerging from exchange rate disagreements can be grouped into three classes: (*a*) unilateral policies countries may choose to make themselves less vulnerable to exchange rate disagreements within RIAs; (*b*) macroeconomic policy coordination among RIA members; and (*c*) an adequate international financial architecture to support RIAs.

---

[9] We did not control for geographic proximity because, within our restricted sample of thirty-seven countries, the latter is highly correlated with the RIA dummy and its inclusion in the regression causes multicollinearity problems. It should also be pointed out that, even with a larger sample, separating the effect of RIA and geographic proximity could be problematic because in most cases the former depends on the latter.

Unilateral policies   The most direct way to reduce the risks associated with exchange rate disagreements within RIAs is for countries to take into account the potential divergence in exchange rate regimes when choosing partners. Hence, from the point of view of an individual country, countries with lower volatility and countries with similar (convergent) exchange rate regimes and cyclical macroeconomic patterns would make better partners. Another important consideration may be the term structure and currency composition of financial liabilities in both countries. Naturally, and for good reason, countries often decide to join RIAs out of geopolitical considerations, so the scope for this policy may be somewhat limited.

Given its RIA partners, a country can adapt its policies to reduce vulnerability to exchange rate disagreements. For example, it could relax or abandon an exchange rate commitment potentially inconsistent with its partners' exchange rate policies. Industrial policy could also be adapted to protect the country against excessive specialization in "regional goods," that is, goods that are difficult to redirect to alternative markets outside the RIA bloc.

Macroeconomic policy coordination   The deeper and more comprehensive RIAs are, the more important the question of macroeconomic policy coordination. The European Union has always placed great importance on this issue. At what point ought countries to engage in stronger coordination in conjunction with their RIA partners? And then, how deep should it be? While some may argue against forming a monetary union on the ground that such an arrangement does not allow for an independent monetary policy, others may point out that "Independent national policies are neither necessary nor desirable if exchange rate changes can upset carefully negotiated tariff, tax, and pricing policies" (McKinnon 1973: 85–6).[10]

Supporting international financial architecture   A supporting international financial architecture could facilitate international trade and reduce the risks associated with exchange rate disagreements in RIAs. It is well recognized that there is a common interest in reducing exchange rate instability, of which competitive devaluations are an extreme example. However, global institutions in charge of monitoring and advising on exchange rate matters, such as the International Monetary Fund, have a national focus in dealing with each country's program. Given this focus, country programs may support divergent exchange rate regimes within RIAs. Should global institutions be encouraged to expand their scope to the RIA level for the purpose of advising and for program conditionality? Conversely, should regional financial initiatives like the recent Chiang Mai initiative of the ASEAN plus three (China, Korea, and Japan) be encouraged to reduce the frequency and size of exchange rate misalignments within RIAs? In view of the findings of this chapter, questions such as these deserve to be treated with greater urgency.

---

[10] We would like to thank George von Furstenberg for suggesting this passage.

REFERENCES

Bergara, M., Dominioni, D., and Licandro, J. (1995). "Un modelo para comprender la 'enfermedad Uruguaya'." *Revista de Economía*, Segunda Epoca, Banco Central del Uruguay, Montevideo, 2 (November): 39-76.

Bevilaqua, A. (1997). "Macroeconomic Coordination and Commercial Integration in Mercosur." *PUC-Rio Department of Economics Working Paper* 378, October.

—, Catena, M., and Talvi, E. (2001). "Integration, Interdependence, and Regional Goods: An Application to Mercosur." *Economía*, 2 (Fall): 153-207.

Blonigen, B. (1997). "Firm-Specific Assets and the Link Between Exchange Rates and Foreign Direct Investment." *American Economic Review*, 87 (June): 447-65.

Buiter, W., Corsetti, G., and Pesenti, P. (1998). *Financial Markets and European Monetary Cooperation. The Lessons of the 1992-93 ERM Crisis*, Cambridge, UK: Cambridge University Press.

Eichengreen, B. (1993). "European Monetary Unification." *Journal of Economic Literature*, 31 (September): 1321-57.

— (1997). "Free Trade and Macroeconomic Policy." In S. Burki, G. Perry, and S. Calvo (eds.), *Trade: Towards Open Regionalism*. LAC ABCDE Conference, World Bank, Montevideo, Uruguay.

Fernández-Arias, E., Panizza, U., and Stein, E. (2002). "Trade Agreements and Exchange Rate Disagreements." Paper presented at the Annual Meetings of the Board of Governors, Inter-American Development Bank and Inter-American Investment Corporation.

Frankel, J. and Rose, A. (1996). "Currency Crashes in Emerging Markets: An Empirical Treatment." *Journal of International Economics*, 41 (November): 351-66.

— and Wei, S.-J. (1998). "Regionalization of World Trade and Currencies: Economics and Politics." In J. Frankel (ed.), *The Regionalization of the World Economy*. University of Chicago Press, pp. 189-226.

Froot, K. and Stein, J. (1991). "Exchange Rates and Foreign Direct Investment: An Imperfect Capital Markets Approach." *Quarterly Journal of Economics*, 106 (November): 1191-217.

Glick, R. and Rose, A. K. (2002). "Does a Currency Union Affect Trade? The Time Series Evidence." *European Economic Review*, 46 (June): 1125-51.

Goldfajn, I. and Valdés, R. (1997). "Are Currency Crises Predictable?" *IMF Working Paper* No. 97/159. Washington, DC: International Monetary Fund.

Kaminsky, G., Lizondo, S., and Reinhart, C. (1998). "Leading Indicators of Currency Crisis." *IMF Staff Papers*, 45 (March): 1-48.

— and Reinhart, C. (1999). "The Twin crises: The Causes of Banking and Balance-of-Payments Problems." *American Economic Review*, 89 (June): 473-500.

McKinnon, R. I. (1973). "The Dual Currency System Revisited." In H. G. Johnson and A. K. Swoboda (eds.), *The Economics of Common Currencies*. Cambridge, MA: Harvard University Press, pp. 85-90.

Panizza, U., Stein, E., and Talvi, E. (2003). "Assessing Dollarization: An Application to Central American and Caribbean Countries." In E. Levy Yeyati and F. Sturzenegger (eds.), *Dollarization: Debates and Policy Alternatives*. Cambridge, MA: MIT Press, pp. 133-200.

Rozemberg, R. and Svarzman, G. (2002). "El proceso de integración Argentina-Brasil en perspectiva: conflictos, tensiones y acciones de los gobiernos." Documento elaborado para la División de Integración, Comercio y Asuntos Hemisféricos del Banco Interamericano de Desarrollo.

10

Sudden Stops, the Real Exchange Rate, and Fiscal Sustainability: Argentina's Lessons

GUILLERMO A. CALVO, ALEJANDRO IZQUIERDO, AND
ERNESTO TALVI

We offer an alternative explanation for the fall of Argentina's Convertibility Program based on the country's vulnerability to Sudden Stops in capital flows. Sudden Stops are typically accompanied by a substantial increase in the real exchange rate that wreaks havoc in countries that are heavily dollarized in their liabilities, making otherwise sustainable fiscal and corporate sector positions unsustainable. In particular, we stress that the required change in relative prices is larger the more closed an economy is in terms of its supply of tradable goods. By contrasting Argentina's performance with that of other Latin American countries that were also subject to the Sudden Stop triggered by the Russian crisis of 1998, we identify key vulnerability indicators that separated Argentina from its peers. We provide an explanation for the political maelstrom that ensued after the Sudden Stop, based on a War of Attrition argument related to the wealth redistribution conflict triggered by the Sudden Stop and fiscal collapse. This framework also provides elements to rationalize the banking crisis that accompanied the fall of Convertibility.

10.1 Introduction

The fall of the Convertibility Program (i.e. the currency board regime) in Argentina has stirred a lively discussion about the causes for its collapse. Several explanations have been offered. The most popular one relates to the unholy combination of a fixed exchange rate and large fiscal deficits that led to a rapid growth in public debt, severe fiscal sustainability problems, and eventually, a loss of access to the credit markets. Another popular view stresses the impact of a fixed exchange rate regime coupled with devaluation by Argentina's major trading partners as an

The authors thank Ricardo Caballero, Enrique Mendoza, and Rick Mishkin for very useful comments and Luis Fernando Mejía for excellent research assistance. The views expressed in this document are the authors' and do not necessarily reflect those of the IDB.

important cause of real exchange rate (RER) misalignment, which reduced profitability in the tradable sector. This, in turn, slowed down investment and led the economy into a protracted recession as it deflated away the RER disequilibrium.

The purpose of this chapter is to provide a different interpretation of the collapse of Convertibility, which places special emphasis on two key structural characteristics of Argentina's productive and financial structure and on political economy considerations.

Our point of departure is the Russian crisis of August 1998, which drastically changed the behavior of capital markets. We believe that developments at the center of capital markets were key to producing an unexpected, severe, and prolonged stop in capital flows (herein referred to as Sudden Stop) to Emerging Market economies, and Latin America was no exception.

We will argue that in the case of Argentina two considerations played a crucial role in magnifying the effect of the Sudden Stop in capital flows and in creating the fiscal and financial problems that eventually Argentina had to confront, namely

(1) a relatively closed economy, that is, an economy with a small share of tradable goods output (more specifically, output that could swiftly be transformed into exports) relative to domestic absorption of tradable goods;
(2) liability dollarization (more specifically, large financial currency–denomination mismatches) in both the private and public sector.

Being closed implies that the Sudden Stop may call for a sharp increase (i.e. a real depreciation) in the equilibrium level of the RER. Liability dollarization, in turn, entails foreign-exchange-denominated debt in "peso producing" sectors (mostly non-tradables) including the government, which implies large balance sheet effects when the RER rises. Thus, these two factors represented a dangerous financial cocktail for both the private sector and the government.

Argentina's fall from Paradise could be rationalized by its commercial closedness, and penchant for dollar indexation in its corporate sector. To that extent, the tragedy needs no fisc to come about. Under liability dollarization, the sharp (equilibrium) real devaluation that was needed in the aftermath of the Sudden Stop hit first and foremost corporate balance sheets. Perhaps more importantly, it lowered the collateral of non-tradable sectors, which, by and of itself, brings about a *stock* retrenchment of credit to the non-tradable sector (see, for example, Izquierdo 1999).[1] Hence, after the first exogenous Sudden Stop, a second round follows, which validates and likely deepens the impact of the first.

This kind of shock can only be met by a sale of assets, financial restructuring, or the initiation of bankruptcy procedures. No flow "belt-tightening" of the corporate

---

[1] This model assumes that non-tradable collateral is accepted by foreign creditors. In other models, such as Caballero and Krishnamurthy (2003), where only tradable collateral is accepted and assumed to be fixed, falls in the price of non-tradables do not have an effect on output because tradable collateral remains unaffected. Even if this were the case, crises of this magnitude, which bring along fiscal unsustainability, could also alter the amount of tradable collateral since the non-tradable sector may be exposed to confiscation from the public sector.

sector could probably do the trick. The problem here, though, is that the shock hits a whole sector, not just an individual firm. Prospects for individual firms are hard to assess when they belong to a network immersed in financial difficulties. Thus, assets can only be sold at rock-bottom prices, and financial restructurings and bankruptcy procedures are especially hard and time-consuming, which precipitate the economy into a protracted recession. Under these circumstances, cries for help will likely rise from every corner, and it will be politically very difficult for the government to stay put and wait for the dust to settle—thus, unavoidably bringing into play strong and complex political economy factors.

A strong fisc could have come to the rescue by *effectively* socializing private debts or providing additional collateral (such as in Korea's IMF-orchestrated bank negotiations with external creditors in 1997, which eventually resulted in a rise in public debt equivalent to more than 30 percent of GDP). As argued in Calvo (2002*b*), the government can play an important role in cases in which the economy is hit by *low-probability* shocks, like the aftermath of the Russian 1998 crisis.[2] However, and this is when the fiscal impact kicks in, given the financial structure of the public sector, Argentina's government was exposed to exactly the same financial problems as the private sector following the Sudden Stop and the increase in the RER. The government thus became part of the problem rather than (as in Korea) part of the solution. But we do not share the fiscalist view of the Convertibility's demise. Argentina was fiscally weak (i.e. vulnerable to a Sudden Stop) not because it had an unreasonably large current (flow) fiscal deficit that would be inconsistent with the fixed exchange rate regime. It had no such deficit. Instead, Argentina's fiscal weakness lay in that the government being unable to offset the fundamental vulnerabilities associated with the country's closedness and liability dollarization, the latter impinging upon both public and private debt.

Adding together private and public debt, and computing its share in GDP after the Sudden Stop (involving a higher RER), it is clear that Argentina's debt was dangerously high, as early as 1999. For the sake of the argument, consider the case in which the government socializes the larger GDP-equivalent debt incurred by corporates after such change in the RER (which, as will be argued, hovers around 50 percent). Under those circumstances, we will argue that the government would have been required to produce a permanently larger primary surplus in excess of 3 percent of GDP. *Permanently* is the key requirement. Sustaining higher levels of debt by implicitly collateralizing it with future flows of primary surpluses is an extraordinarily difficult task because, for starters, future flows depend on future governments. If credibility on future surpluses is at stake, the ability to roll over the stock of debt would be severely hampered, creating a *stock* retrenchment problem for the government, potentially as severe

---

[2] The Russian crisis was not a low probability event. Savvy investors knew that sooner or later a crisis was likely to erupt. Our claim, however, is that it was hard to even imagine, *ex ante*, that a crisis in a country that represents less than 1 percent of world output would have such devastating effect on the world capital market.

as that suffered by the private sector. To illustrate this point, it is sufficient to say that a failure to produce such an adjustment of the primary surplus on a permanent basis would have implied a 75 percent haircut on the existing debt.

To avoid a painful default, Argentina had to raise its primary surpluses permanently and credibly. This could only occur by raising taxes or reducing primary spending. Raising taxes is particularly problematic when the corporate sector itself is under severe financial stress and arrears with the public sector become very significant as a source of financing. Moreover, under the corporate bailout scenario assumed above, this option would simply not be available. As a result, raising taxes on the non-corporate sector and/or reducing primary expenditures were the only options available, absent debt restructuring.

The government thus was forced to engage in *wealth redistribution* policies across sectors. This is where politics kicks in with full force, and phenomena like War of Attrition among different groups in society develop. Wealth redistribution sets in motion a tug-of-war in which decisions are *delayed* and, as the War of Attrition literature shows (see Sturzenegger and Tommasi 1998), can be highly disruptive. Thus, unless a supranational entity generates a *cooperative* equilibrium, the impasse may take a long time to resolve and may seriously deepen the extent of the crisis. Since no positive rate of return can match losing a chunk of capital to the tax collector's ax, this impasse in resolving which sectors would ultimately sustain the losses, brought about a grinding stop to all investment projects, except for those few that could be safely shielded from the bloodbath (e.g. black-market transactions). Under these circumstances, tax revenue falls, further weakening the government's fiscal situation. This, in turn, increases the expected devaluation and sets in motion a new wave of credit cuts.

At this stage, politically feasible solutions were inevitably going to involve spreading the cost of adjustment among all players, making some type of debt restructuring inevitable. In turn, expectations of debt restructuring would severely hit the banking system to the extent that most of its assets consisted of government debt and dollar loans to non-tradable sectors. It should, therefore, come as no surprise that a bank run materialized as a corollary of the Sudden Stop.

Finally, a word on the role of the Convertibility regime itself. Argentina's adherence to its hard peg to the dollar probably made things worse, but for reasons not necessarily related to competitiveness. As argued in Talvi (1997), incomplete but inevitable adjustments can mask the gravity of the underlying fiscal situation. In the case of Argentina, maintaining the peg and delaying the inevitable adjustment of the RER may have contributed to concealing the true nature of its financial problems for a long period of time, leaving politicians and the general public largely unaware of the gravity of the financial situation. This, in turn, may have contributed to undermining political support for the necessary fiscal and financial adjustments. Furthermore, maintaining the peg left Argentina without a valuable instrument of the adjustment package, namely, inflation, which has proven, time and again, to be a very powerful tool for lowering government expenditure (in real terms).

The chapter is organized as follows: Section 10.2 examines capital market trends in Latin America following the Russian crisis of 1998 and provides a rationale for Sudden Stop behavior. Specifically, we show that the nature of Sudden Stops has typically been large and persistent. Section 10.3 dwells on conditions under which Sudden Stops lead to a sharp depreciation of the RER, and ranks a set of Latin American countries in terms of vulnerability to these shocks. Section 10.4 focuses more closely on Argentina. It discusses fiscal sustainability and determines the sources of vulnerability to swift changes in the RER, and computes how those changes affected Argentina's fiscal position. Section 10.5 dwells on the effects of RER adjustment on the materialization of contingent liabilities (particularly those arising from currency–denomination mismatches in the corporate sector). We compute how Argentina's fiscal position would have deteriorated even further under the assumption that the government would attempt (as it eventually did) to bail out the corporate sector. Section 10.6 briefly touches upon the concealment of the financial problems under Argentina's hard peg, and it analyzes likely performance under a floating exchange rate regime following a Sudden Stop. The chapter concludes with some policy lessons for Latin America that emerge from Argentina's experience (Section 10.7), and an appendix that reviews the policies followed by Argentina.

10.2 The World Scene After Russia

Russia's August 1998 crisis represents a milestone in the development of emerging capital markets. Massive capital inflows that went to Latin America in the early 1990s, financing high growth rates and large current account deficits, came all of a sudden to a standstill following Russia's partial foreign debt repudiation in August, 1998. It was hard to imagine how a crisis in a country with little if any financial or trading ties to Latin America could have such profound effects on the region. This puzzle cast doubt on traditional explanations for financial crises (based on current account and fiscal deficits) and led analysts to focus on the intrinsic behavior of capital markets. Thus, it was argued that prevailing rules for capital market transactions may have been responsible for the spread of shocks from one country to other regions (Calvo 1999).[3]

---

[3] As the argument goes, to the extent that there exist large fixed costs (relative to the size of projects) in obtaining information about a particular country, resulting economies of scale lead to the formation of clusters of specialists, or informed investors, who lead capital markets. These investors leverage their portfolios to finance their investments and are subject to margin calls in the event of a fall in the price of assets placed as collateral. Remaining investors, the uninformed, observe transactions made by informed investors, but are subject to a signal-extraction problem, given that they must figure out whether sales of the informed are motivated by lower returns on projects or by the informed facing margin calls. As long as the variance of returns to projects is sufficiently high relative to the variance of margin calls, uninformed investors may easily interpret massive asset sales as an indication of lower returns and decide to get rid of their holdings as well, even though the cause for informed investors' sales was actually due to margin calls.

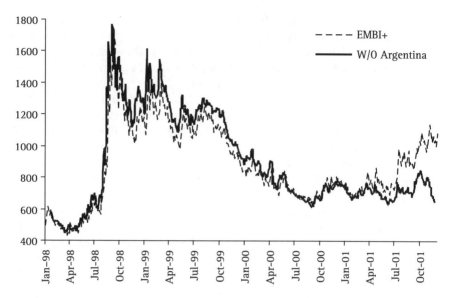

Figure 10.1. *External financial conditions, EMBI+ spread over U.S. Treasuries*
Source: JP Morgan Chase.

Table 10.1. *Difference in bond spreads with minimum pre-crisis levels*

	1999	2000	2001
EMBI+	666	307	393
EMBI+ W/O Argentina	757	315	259

Note: Values are yearly averages.
Source: JP Morgan Chase.

In Figure 10.1, spreads measured by the EMBI+ index show a dramatic increase following the Russian crisis. Although they have since declined, spreads continue to be large compared with pre-crisis levels, exceeding 250 basis points for 2001.[4] This gap was much higher for 1999 and 2000 (over 700 basis points and 300 basis points, respectively, see Table 10.1).

Latin American markets were not the only ones hit by the higher cost of capital. For most EMs higher interest rates were accompanied by a large reduction in capital inflows. Figure 10.2 and Table 10.2 show that, for the seven biggest Latin

---

[4] We compare the lowest 1998 pre-crisis spread level to yearly averages of the spread measure in following years.

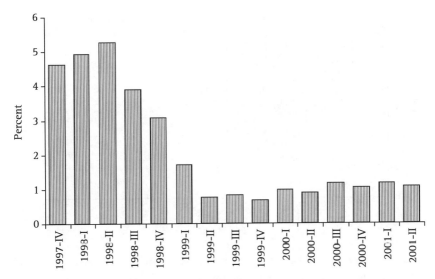

Figure 10.2. *Sudden Stop in LAC (Capital flows, % of GDP)*

Note: Argentina, Brazil, Chile, Colombia, Mexico, Peru, and Venezuela.

Source: Corresponding Central Banks.

Table 10.2. *Capital flows, % of GDP*

	1998.II	2001.III	Reversal
Capital	5.6	1.6	−4.0
Non-FDI Capital	2.0	−0.9	−2.9
FDI	3.6	2.5	−1.1

Note: Argentina, Brazil, Chile, Colombia, Mexico, Peru, and Venezuela.

Source: Corresponding Central Banks.

American economies, the decline in net capital inflows was steep, particularly for portfolio flows, and linked with a steep hike in interest rates. The fact that the root of this phenomenon lay in Russia's crisis indicates that the capital-inflow slowdown contained a large *unexpected* component. "Large and highly unexpected" are the two defining characteristics of what the literature calls "Sudden Stop" (Calvo and Reinhart 2000). New information that a standstill in the capital account can materialize for rather exogenous reasons, and for a whole region, emerged gradually in the wake of the Russian crisis and generated drastic effects on fiscal sustainability; either because of debt revaluation effects or the emergence of contingent liabilities. This worsening news may well have produced a lengthy halt in capital flows because it reduced investor appetites for holding

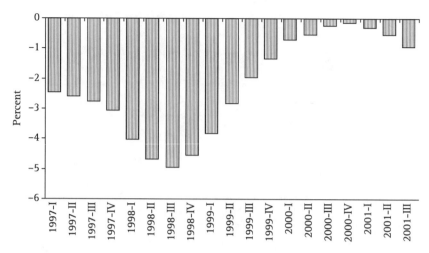

Figure 10.3. *Sudden Stop and the current account in LAC (four quarters, % of GDP)*
Note: Argentina, Brazil, Chile, Colombia, Mexico, Peru, and Venezuela.
Source: Corresponding Central Banks.

assets of countries subject to large swings in RER and high degrees of liability dollarization. Sudden Stops usually lead to a significant cut in current account deficits. Starting in the fourth quarter of 1998, key Latin American countries showed a steady decline in their current account deficits, which eventually reached a zero balance by the end of 2000.[5] This adjustment of the current account was on average equivalent to 5 percentage points of GDP for the seven biggest Latin American economies (see Figure 10.3).

10.3   Sudden Stops and Real Exchange Rate Adjustment

So far we have made a case for the large external component accounting for the observed fall in capital inflows. But what are the consequences of this event in terms of RER behavior and debt sustainability analysis? Two key elements in this discussion are the unexpected component of the Sudden Stop and its duration.

---

[5] Although FDI flows fell on average in the aftermath of the Russian crisis, they did increase significantly in Brazil, where FDI flows rose 80 percent in dollar terms from the second quarter of 1998 to the second quarter of 2001. We follow up on this fact because it may be an important element behind the resumption of capital flows to Brazil. A possible explanation is that higher interest rates led to sharp declines in domestic collateral, adding to the perception that this asset class was more risky than expected. Thus, domestic firms found it more difficult to finance the current operations and expansion plans, further depressing their plants' market value. This may have opened attractive investment opportunities for G7-based firms whose collateral was insulated from EM financial turmoil, leading to a sharp increase in FDI.

It is clear that expectations prevailing before the Russian crisis are unlikely to have factored in the widespread effects on EMs that followed, so the unexpected element required for a Sudden Stop is met. A different question is whether this shock was perceived as temporary or highly persistent, which is quite relevant from a policy perspective. With the benefit of hindsight it is easy to argue that the shock had a large permanent component, since capital inflows remained stalled for at least four years after the August 1998 Russian crisis. But it is not clear that this high degree of persistence was correctly anticipated from the very beginning (this is an important point that we will revisit when we discuss Argentina in greater detail). Indeed, investors and policymakers had witnessed a quick recovery of capital flows following the Mexican (Tequila) crisis in 1995, which could have led them to expect a similarly fast recovery after the Russian collapse. But things turned out differently. Figure 10.4 shows that, two years after the Mexican crisis, there was more than a complete recovery of capital flows, whereas there has been no recovery in capital flows to the region since 1998 following the Russian crisis.

Sudden Stops are also typically accompanied by large contractions in international reserves *and* declines in the relative price of non-tradables with respect to tradables (i.e. real currency depreciation). By way of illustration, consider the case of a small open economy that experiences a current account deficit before

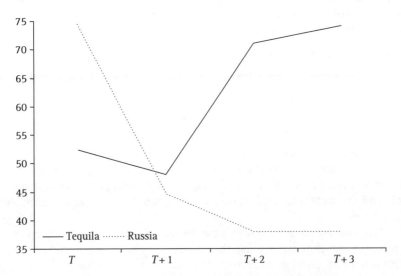

Figure 10.4. *Sudden Stop and the current account in LAC (Net private capital flows, U.S. $ billion)*

Note: "LAC" refers to Western Hemisphere countries, according to IMF definition, "*T*" denotes the year of occurrence of the crisis.

Source: IMF.

Table 10.3. *Current account adjustment*

	ARG	BRA	CHL	COL	ECU
Current account balance, US$ billions					
1998	−14.5	−33.4	−4.1	−5.2	−2.2
1999	−11.9	−25.4	−0.1	0.2	0.9
2000	−8.9	−24.6	−1.0	0.3	0.7
2001	−5.6	−23.2	−0.9	−2.1	−0.8
Current account change, % of 1998 imports					
1999 vs. 1998	6.1	10.6	18.8	31.3	49.0
2001 vs. 1998	21.1	13.5	14.9	18.0	21.3

Source: IMF.

a Sudden Stop takes place. By definition

$$CAD = A^* + S^* - Y^*, \qquad (1)$$

where CAD is the current account deficit, A^* is absorption of tradable goods, S^* represents net non-factor payments to foreigners, and Y^* is the supply of tradable goods. If financing of the current account deficit is stopped, the full amount of that imbalance needs to be cut. Table 10.3 shows that current account adjustment can be sharp. Indeed, it is not uncommon to see an abrupt adjustment towards current account balance within a year following the Sudden Stop.

A measure of the percentage fall in the absorption of tradable goods needed to restore equilibrium is given by

$$\eta = CAD/A^* = 1 - \omega, \qquad (2)$$

where ω is a measure of the unleveraged absorption of tradable goods, defined as

$$\omega = (Y^* - S^*)/A^*. \qquad (3)$$

Notice that this measure captures the share of absorption of tradable goods that is financed by the domestic supply of tradable goods.[6] The lower this value, the higher will be the share of absorption of tradables financed from abroad. In other words, relatively closed economies with a small supply of tradable goods running a current account deficit will be highly leveraged. As we will see later, this is an important consideration regarding RER behavior after a sudden stop in capital flows.

To obtain an estimate for η which can be used for cross-country comparisons, we proxy A^* by imports. We use the observed current account adjustment for different periods, taken as a share of imports at the time of the crisis, in order to illustrate the observed percentage fall in absorption of tradable goods that was required to accommodate the change in the current account. Results are shown in Table 10.3 for 1999 and 2001. Countries like Chile, Colombia, and Ecuador,

[6] Net of factor payments.

where the percentage fall ranged anywhere from 18.8 to 49 percent, experienced a quick and substantial adjustment in absorption of tradable goods by 1999. Adjustment in Brazil and Argentina has taken longer, a phenomenon that we will analyze in more detail later.

Having shown that the percentage fall of tradable goods absorption can be substantial after a Sudden Stop, we now consider effects on non-tradable goods. A common assumption in the literature is that preferences are homothetic, implying that the income expansion path of tradable *vis-à-vis* non-tradable goods is linear. Under this assumption, for a given RER, consumption of non-tradable goods is, therefore, proportional to that of tradable goods.[7] As a result, a decline in demand for tradable goods of size η must be matched by a proportional fall of equal size in the demand for non-tradable goods. Now consider the effects of this fall in demand on the RER. Given that the price of tradable goods is determined from abroad, all we need to take into account is the behavior of the non-tradable goods market. Define demand for non-tradables as

$$h = a - \chi p, \tag{4}$$

where h is (the log of) demand for non-tradable goods, p is (the log of) the relative price of non-tradable to tradable goods, that is, the inverse of the RER, χ is a parameter, and a captures the income effect. Then, for a given RER, the fall in demand following a Sudden Stop is simply

$$da = \eta = 1 - \omega. \tag{5}$$

Assuming, for simplicity, that the supply of non-tradable goods is fixed (so that $dh = 0$), the required percentage change in the real exchange, after differentiation of Eq. (4), is

$$-dp = (1 - \omega)/\chi; \tag{6}$$

That is to say, the higher is the leveraged absorption of tradables, that is, the lower is ω, the higher the impact on the RER needed to restore equilibrium after a Sudden Stop. The intuition for this result is that, in the short run, the ability to generate purchasing power in terms of tradables is exports minus debt service. Thus, a Sudden Stop that requires a larger *proportional* sacrifice in absorption in terms of tradables, the smaller is ω. Another element that affects our measure of absorption leverage is non-factor payments (S^*), typically composed of interest payments, which implicitly capture indebtedness levels. High external indebtedness, therefore, reduces available resources to finance absorption of tradable goods, requiring greater RER realignment following the elimination of the current account deficit. Given these characteristics, ω is a good summary statistic to measure the impact on RER realignment. A further simplifying assumption we make is that the supply of tradable goods can be measured by exports whereas,

---

[7] In what follows we abstract from investment. This is indeed a major omission, which is, however, likely to be less misleading in a steady-state context such as the present one. Catena and Talvi (2001) reach similar results in terms of a full-fledged dynamic model.

Table 10.4. *Unleveraged absorption coefficient (ω)*

BRA	ARG	ECU	COL	CHL
0.56	0.66	0.66	0.70	0.81

Note: Values are given for 1998.
Source: IMF.

as earlier noted, imports serve as a proxy for absorption of tradables. Table 10.4 contains a list of Latin American EMs ranked by this measure in 1998. Chile clearly leads the ranking in terms of unleveraged absorption. Argentina, although not the lowest ranked in the group, stands 15 percentage points below Chile, indicating that it would need greater RER realignment following a Sudden Stop.

Another key element in determining the size of the required change in the RER is given by the price elasticity of the demand for home goods, χ. Estimates for developing countries are typically much lower than those for industrial countries, implying that Sudden Stops can be much more devastating for EMs. Thus, not only are Sudden Stops a much more common feature of developing countries (Calvo and Reinhart 2000), but their effects can be more dangerous as well. Actually, the higher vulnerability of EMs to Sudden Stops could partly explain their higher recurrence.

Given this framework, we next ask what should be the size of RER realignment following a Sudden Stop that requires a full adjustment of the current account deficit, using 1998 as a starting point. To compute this, we make use of Eq. (6), taking a value of $\chi = 0.4$ (the lowest point estimate in the literature). Given that we measure the RER as the inverse of (antilog of) p, the rate of depreciation is $-dp$. Obviously, these figures should not be taken at face value, but as a way of ranking the effects of a Sudden Stop across countries.[8] Table 10.5 shows the results. As it stands, this exercise indicates that Argentina would have needed to depreciate its RER by 46 percent in order to bring down its current account to zero, whereas Chile, for example would only have needed to depreciate its RER by 32 percent. This means that Argentina would have needed to depreciate its RER about 43 percent more than Chile in order to close the current account gap.

Moreover, since the Russian crisis, between 1998 and 2001, Chile depreciated its currency *vis-à-vis* the dollar by about 45 percent in real terms, and closed a current account gap that had been equal to almost 19 percent of imports. Chile's current account deficit was equivalent to 6 percent of GDP in 1998 and fell to zero in 1999. In this respect, it would look like Chile's adjustment was larger than that of Argentina, whose current account deficit fell from 4.9 percent of

---

[8] Here, we have made several strong assumptions, such as that the supply of both tradable and non-tradable goods are constant, and that the price elasticity of demand of non-tradables is low and the same across countries. Again, these figures do not attempt to match observed figures, but to illustrate the main transmission channels behind Sudden Stops.

Table 10.5. *Required % change in equilibrium RER*

BRA	ARG	ECU	COL	CHL
52.5	46.2	46.1	43.0	32.4

Note: Values are given for 1998.
Source: IMF.

GDP in 1998 to 2.4 percent of GDP in 2001. However, if Argentina's reduction in the current account gap is measured as a share of imports (the relevant measure from our perspective), the reduction was also 19 percent, similar to the adjustment observed in Chile. According to our model, Argentina's depreciation should have been at least as large as Chile's 45 percent, clearly indicating that its RER depreciation of only around 14 percent was far from sufficient for the required adjustment in the current account.[9] The slow adjustment of RER observed in Argentina can be explained by the combination of a fixed exchange rate and price stickiness (a relevant feature given the weight of public wages and public utility fees in price behavior), which retarded the adjustment of the RER.

10.4 Debt Valuation and Fiscal Sustainability

We now turn our attention to the effects of RER depreciation on fiscal sustainability. It is not uncommon to find countries where public sector debt is largely denominated in terms of tradables (see Table 10.6) and government revenue comes to a large extent from non-tradable activities. This introduces a currency mismatch in the public sector balance sheet, which makes any sustainability analysis highly susceptible to RER swings.

Consider the typical sustainability calculation, where the size of the primary surplus necessary to keep a constant ratio of debt to GDP is computed, given a cost of funds, and a growth rate for the economy. Take the standard asset accumulation equation:

$$b_{t+1} = b_t \frac{(1+r)}{(1+\theta)} - s_t, \tag{7}$$

where b is the debt to GDP ratio, r is the real interest rate on debt, θ is the GDP growth rate, s is the primary surplus as a share of GDP, and t denotes time. To obtain a constant debt to GDP ratio ($\bar{b}$), the budget surplus must satisfy, assuming constant r and θ:

$$s = \bar{b}\left[\frac{(1+r)}{(1+\theta)} - 1\right]. \tag{8}$$

[9] Had Argentina reduced its current account balance to zero, the required adjustment should have been higher than that of Chile, as illustrated in Table 10.5.

Table 10.6. *Public sector debt mismatch measure*

	ARG	ECU	COL	BRA	CHL
$B/e\ B^*$	0.08	0.02	0.59	1.76	1.30
$Y/e\ Y^*$	8.63	2.94	6.36	12.34	2.85
$(B/e\ B^*)/(Y/e\ Y^*)$	0.01	0.01	0.09	0.14	0.45

Note: Values are given for 1998.

Source: Own estimates.

Key to this analysis is the initial debt to GDP ratio $(\bar{b})$, which, in turn, depends on its denomination in terms of tradables and non-tradables. This ratio can be expressed as

$$\bar{b} = \frac{B + eB^*}{Y + eY^*},\tag{9}$$

where e is the RER (defined as the price of tradables relative to non-tradables), B is debt payable in terms of non-tradables, B^* is debt payable in terms of tradables, Y is output of non-tradables, and Y^* is output of tradables. Obviously, debt composition, as well as output composition, matter a great deal for sustainability analysis, because mismatches between debt and output composition can lead to substantial differences in valuation of the debt/GDP ratio following a real currency depreciation.

For example, consider the limit case in which $b = eB^*/Y$, where valuation effects apply to debt only. This is the worst scenario in which RER depreciation has the greatest impact on sustainability. Another case that is particularly relevant is that in which $(B/eB^*)/(Y/eY^*)=1$, that is, when the composition of debt and output is perfectly matched. When this condition holds, a change in the RER has no effect on fiscal sustainability. Table 10.6 shows how countries ranked in terms of mismatch at the time of the Russian crisis.[10] A value of 1 would indicate a perfect match, and a value of zero would indicate the highest degree of mismatch. Clearly, the highest mismatch holds for Argentina. On the other side of the spectrum lies Chile, the best-matched economy, with a value of 0.45.

For comparison purposes, we consider the effects of a RER rise of 50 percent on debt valuation and fiscal sustainability for all the countries we selected, as of 1998. The results are presented in Table 10.7.[11] We see clearly that under this

[10] We proxy output of tradable goods (Y^*) with exports. This measure is particularly relevant in the short run, although it could underestimate tradable output in the long run.

[11] Calculations were made assuming that debt is issued either in terms of tradable goods, or in terms of non-tradable goods. When debt is issued in domestic currency, the relevant price index for valuation purposes is the consumer price level, which typically includes a share of tradable goods in the basket it values. In this respect, real depreciation should affect the valuation of domestic-currency-denominated debt through the tradable component of the price level, making the effects of a RER rise larger than estimated here. This can be interpreted as the case where a portion of this debt is issued in terms of tradable goods, so that the valuation effects of RER depreciation are larger.

Table 10.7. *Fiscal sustainability under a 50% RER depreciation*

	ARG	BRA	CHL	COL	ECU
(a) Base exercise					
Observed public debt (% of GDP)	36.5	51.0	17.3	28.4	81.0
Real interest rate	7.1	5.8	5.9	7.3	6.3
Real GDP growth	3.8	2.0	7.5	3.6	2.6
Observed primary surplus (% of GDP)	0.9	0.6	0.6	−3.0	−0.2
(i) Req. primary surplus (% of GDP)	1.2	1.9	n.a.	1.0	2.9
(b) Change in relative prices					
Real exchange rate depreciation	50.0	50.0	50.0	50.0	50.0
Imputed public debt (% of GDP)	50.8	58.1	18.7	34.9	107.2
Real interest rate	7.1	5.8	5.9	7.3	6.3
Real GDP growth	3.8	2.0	7.5	3.6	2.6
(ii) Req. primary surplus	1.6	2.2	n.a.	1.2	3.9
NPV of (ii)–(i) (% of GDP)	14.3	7.1	n.a.	6.5	26.3
Corresponding debt reduction (%)	28.2	12.2	n.a.	18.7	24.5
(ii)–(i) (% of Government expenditures)	2.3	1.0	n.a.	1.3	4.5

Note: Values are given for 1998. n.a.: Not applicable given that the real interest rate is smaller than the growth of GDP, so sustainability is not a concern.

Source: Own estimates.

scenario, Argentina, together with Ecuador, would be the hardest hit economy in terms of debt revaluation. Just because of the relative price adjustment (holding the assumption that interest rates on public debt and GDP growth remain unchanged), Argentina's debt/GDP ratio would jump from 36.5 percent of GDP to 50.8 percent of GDP, an increase of nearly 40 percent on impact. Quite a different scenario plays out for Chile, where the debt revaluation effect is minimal: Public sector debt as a share of GDP increases from 17.3 to 18.7 percent. It is interesting to see that in the case of Brazil, a 50 percent rise in the RER only affects the debt/GDP ratio by 14 percent. As we shall see later, in our view this was a key element, together with a substantial adjustment in the primary surplus, to explain Brazil's success in controlling its fiscal position after the real currency depreciation it experienced in 1999.

We also consider the effects on the required primary surplus following a rise in the RER. Making use of Eqs (8) and (9), we calculate the required primary surplus after revaluation of the debt/GDP ratio.[12] It is important to note that these calculations implicitly assume that the shock is permanent. Had the shock been temporary, the effects on sustainability would be far less and, consequently, the

---

[12] Assuming interest rates and GDP growth remain at initial levels, which underestimates the required primary surplus.

need for adjustment would be smaller. But as became apparent after the 1998 Russian crisis, this shock was highly persistent, implying that the adjustment in the RER and its effect on debt valuation were large as well. Of course, this was not clear at the time of the crisis, which led to underestimating the necessary fiscal adjustment.

Taking as a benchmark the case in which the RER depreciation is permanent, we estimate changes in the required primary surplus needed for sustainability. The biggest correction is for Ecuador (about 1 point of GDP). Argentina, for example, would require an adjustment of 0.4 points of GDP. In order to assess the significance of this adjustment, we estimate the net present value of the difference between the required primary surplus before and after the RER depreciation, which is equivalent to the change in debt before and after the shock, measured in percentage points of GDP.[13] This figure would be equivalent to 14.3 points of GDP for Argentina, and as much as 26.3 points of GDP for Ecuador. Besides, these figures only represent changes in the required primary surplus, and, in most cases, countries had much lower observed primary surpluses than those required, meaning that the need for adjustment was much higher. In summary, once again we see that highly indebted, dollarized, and closed economies are bad candidates to accommodate RER swings that will be fiscally sustainable.

Given that we have used exports as a proxy for tradable goods output in these calculations, we run the risk of overestimating the effects of RER depreciation because tradable goods output will typically be higher than exports. In order to assess the significance of this shortcut, we compare results against a more thorough measure of tradable output typically used for this calculation. This measure defines a category of output as tradable when the sum of imports and exports of goods in that one-digit category exceeds domestic output from the national income accounts in that same category by more than 5 percent. Results are shown in Table 10.8.[14]

As can be seen by comparing Table 10.8 with Table 10.7, although there are some differences in debt to GDP ratios, the required primary surplus following an adjustment in relative prices does not change substantially, implying that our first approximation is indeed a good one to evaluate the effects of a Sudden Stop.[15]

Now that we have provided examples of the effects on the RER of closing the current account gap, and examples of debt revaluation for a given depreciation

---

[13] This is computed as $(s^* - s)(1 + \theta)/(r - \theta)$, where s^* is the required primary surplus after the rise in RER (real currency depreciation), s is the required primary surplus before the rise in RER, r is the real interest rate, and θ is the growth rate of the economy. This is obtained by solving (7) forward and taking the difference between the stream of flows valued at s^* with respect to the stream of flows valued at s. In other words, it measures the change in debt (in percentage points of GDP) that corresponds to the permanent increase in the primary surplus.

[14] Results for Brazil could not be computed, given that national accounts data is not split according to standard classification.

[15] Even more thorough measures that split national accounts data at two or more digit levels may yield different results, but that information was not available for all countries in our sample, so we rely on calculations at a one digit level only.

Table 10.8. *Fiscal sustainability under a 50% depreciation*

	ARG	BRA	CHL	COL	ECU
(a) Base exercise					
Observed public debt (% of GDP)	36.5		17.3	28.4	81.0
Real interest rate	7.1		5.9	7.3	6.3
Real GDP growth	3.8		7.5	3.6	2.6
Observed primary surplus (% of GDP)	0.9		0.6	−3.0	−0.2
(i) Req. primary surplus (% of GDP)	1.2		n.a.	1.0	2.9
(b) Change in relative prices					
Real exchange rate depreciation	50.0		50.0	50.0	50.0
Imputed public debt	47.2		18.1	32.3	98.9
Real interest rate	7.1		5.9	7.3	6.3
Real GDP growth	3.8		7.5	3.6	2.6
(ii) Req. primary surplus	1.5		n.a.	1.1	3.6
NPV of (i)–(ii) (% of GDP)	10.7		n.a.	3.9	17.9
Corresponding debt reduction (%)	22.7		n.a.	12.1	18.1
(i)–(ii) in (% of Government expenditures)	1.7		n.a.	0.8	3.1

Note: Values are given for 1998.

Source: Own estimates.

of the RER, we put both pieces together for the case of Argentina, and analyze the effects of a sudden stop in capital inflows in 1998. Results are summarized in Table 10.9. In our example, following a Sudden Stop, Argentina's RER would have to rise by about 46 percent. Had this depreciation occurred, the country would have displayed a debt/GDP ratio of 49.7 percent, a considerably larger value than that observed in 1998 (which was 36.5 percent of GDP). Under favorable growth and interest rate assumptions,[16] the *permanent* primary surplus needed to sustain the new (and higher) debt/GDP ratio would have been equivalent to 1.6 points of GDP, 0.7 percentage points of GDP higher than the observed figure (0.9 percent of GDP).

The above analysis only considers valuation effects, but Table 10.9 also examines two other factors associated with the Sudden Stop: Interest rates and economic growth. On the one hand, if our hypothesis that the Russian crisis changed investors' perceptions about the risk associated with EM bonds is correct, then interest rates are likely to rise. On the other hand, the fact that GDP growth rates

---

[16] The growth rate used for this exercise is the geometric average of the previous ten years. Interest rates are average rates on public debt prevailing in 1998. Both measures do not account for the fact that following a sudden stop in capital flows interest rates typically increase and growth prospects decline. Thus, sustainability calculations are less demanding than those that would prevail had these additional effects been incorporated. We account for this later on.

Table 10.9. *Fiscal sustainability in Argentina under alternative scenarios in 1998*

	Debt to GDP ratio (%)	(*i*) Adjustment in prim. surplus[a]	NPV of (*i*) (% of GDP)	(*i*) % of Gov. expenditures	Debt reduction (%)
(a) Baseline[b]	36.5	0.3	9.3	1.5	25.6
(b) Change in relative prices to close current account deficit (RER depreciation of 46.2%)	49.7	0.7	22.6	3.6	45.4
(c) (b) + 200 BPS increase in real interest rate	49.7	1.7	32.8	8.3	66.0
(d) (c) + 1% Reduction in real GDP growth	49.7	2.2	35.6	10.8	71.7
(e) (d) + Contingent liabilities	58.6	2.7	44.5	13.5	75.9

[a] The observed primary surplus for 1998 was 0.9 percent of GDP.
[b] The baseline scenario assumes a long run rate of growth of 3.8% and a 7.1% real interest rate.
Source: Own estimates.

fell all over Latin America may have increased expectations of much lower growth than originally expected.

Recomputing our estimates under the assumption that interest rates remained 200 basis points higher than in 1998 (an increase similar to the observed increase in EMBI spreads in 2001 compared to pre-Russian crisis levels) and growth estimates fell by 1 percent, the primary surplus needed to achieve fiscal sustainability following a Sudden Stop, jumps to 3.1 percent of GDP. This is about 2.2 percentage points above the value observed for 1998 (see Table 10.9). The needed adjustment is equivalent to 13.5 percent of total expenditures, a tall order from a political perspective. Alternatively, keeping the primary surplus at its 1998 level, debt would have had to be 75 percent below its actual level for sustainability once we factor in all the different elements of a Sudden Stop that affect the fisc. From a credit risk perspective, this is also a large figure that helps us understand why under imperfect credibility on future primary surpluses, the ability to roll over the existing stock of debt was severely hampered after the Sudden Stop. It is worth noting that under the 1998 baseline scenario[17] it is not evident that Argentina's fiscal position was out of control. Indeed, standard sustainability analysis indicates that the difference between the required and observed primary surplus was 0.3 percentage points of GDP at prevailing RER, growth and real interest rate levels (see Table 10.9). Undoubtedly, Argentina was quite vulnerable to RER swings, but it was not clear before the Russian crisis that Argentina's fiscal position was out of hand in the absence of a Sudden Stop.[18] This points up the need to obtain risk-weighted measures of fiscal sustainability that account for the occurrence of events such as a Sudden Stop. Used as part of

[17] That is when we take the prevailing average interest rate, growth rate, and RER instead of imputed post-shock levels.
[18] This assertion is made without considering the possibility that the RER was appreciated by 1998.

fiscal stress testing, such measures could prove beneficial to internalize the need for more conservative fiscal policy.

This experience highlights two relevant aspects pertaining debt: both debt levels and indexation clauses are crucial in determining the effects of Sudden Stops on sustainability. High debt levels imply little room for cushioning valuation effects. Higher debt service, in turn, may imply higher RER swings. And dollarization (or indexation to the dollar) can trigger substantial valuation effects that may compromise solvency.

It is useful to contrast the Chilean and Argentine experiences in terms of sustainability. Chile was subject to a Sudden Stop that forced the country to bring the current account to almost a zero balance, an adjustment equivalent to 18.8 percent of imports. Yet, it fared much better in terms of fiscal sustainability. Chile differed from Argentina in two respects. First, as we already argued in the previous section, Chile required a smaller RER realignment given the country's openness and low indebtedness position. Second, recalling the valuation effects, shown in Table 10.7, that were previously deduced from an assumed rise of 50 percent in the RER (close to Chile's effective depreciation of 45 percent), explains why Chile's debt/GDP ratio remained almost unchanged. Chile's relatively high share of tradables in GDP, and relatively low ratio of debt in tradables to total debt, helped dampen the effect of the rise of the RER on sustainability. Thus, in terms of sustainability very little changed for Chile after the Sudden Stop. Moreover, the RER shift was successful in switching production to tradables (an effect that we do not consider in our model), thus compensating in part for the standstill in capital flows. Table 10.10 shows the change in exports relative to the change in the current account deficit observed one year and three years after the Russian crisis, as an indication of the contribution of exports in closing the current account gap. It clearly shows that Chile was highly successful in switching production to tradables, something that did not occur in Argentina, in part because the RER misalignment was providing little incentive to do so.

Another interesting case to contrast with Argentina is that of Brazil. Why was the rise in the RER in Brazil successful? Three factors contributed to its success.

Table 10.10. *Change in exports relative to change in the current account deficit*

	ARG	BRA	CHL	COL	ECU
Exports change/current account change, %					
1999 vs. 1998	−127.5	−47.6	11.1	8.7	8.0
2001 vs. 1998	−1.8	82.7	79.1	43.8	41.8
Exports change, %					
1999 vs. 1998	−10.6	−6.5	2.4	3.5	5.0
2001 vs. 1998	−0.5	14.3	13.4	10.2	11.3

Source: IMF.

First, by 1999, the country's adjustment of the current account was equivalent to only 10.6 percent of imports, far below the 44.2 percent that would have occurred had the current account deficit been completely eliminated. So what made Brazil avoid a bigger adjustment? Contrary to the experience of other countries, the Sudden Stop in Brazil was short-lived and quickly compensated by FDI flows, which increased 80 percent in dollar terms between the second quarter of 1998 and the second quarter of 2001. According to our view, this prevented an even larger currency meltdown.[19] Second, Brazil's level of indebtedness was quite high in 1998 (51 percent of GDP) and a sustainability analysis along the lines presented here would have shown that large fiscal adjustment was also needed. After the 1999 crisis and in contrast to Argentina, Brazil responded with a severe fiscal adjustment, which increased its primary balance considerably by 3.5 percent of GDP in 1999. This adjustment proved to be politically feasible and long-lasting, two factors that are crucial in explaining Brazil's success in weathering the Sudden Stop, something that was unattainable by Argentina. And third, a crucial difference with Argentina is that by 1998, although Brazil's public debt was higher in percent of GDP than that of Argentina, Brazil's debt was only partially dollarized, as Table 10.6 shows. Since the level of dollarization was also relatively low in the private sector, contingent liabilities were kept in check, an issue we will discuss further in the next section. Therefore, liability-revaluation effects of an RER depreciation on the ratio of public debt to GDP were not substantial in Brazil.

10.5   Real Exchange Rate Adjustment and Contingent Liabilities

So far we have not discussed another issue that further raises the hurdle for any type of sustainability analysis following a Sudden Stop, namely, the existence of contingent liabilities of the public sector, originated in the corporate and banking sectors. Here the financial system becomes an element of extraordinary importance. It is not uncommon, as was the case of Argentina recently (and in Thailand, e.g. in previous crises), to find that commercial bank loans are heavily dollarized, whereas a large proportion of bank debtors obtain income from non-tradable activities. The currency mismatch between debtors' revenues and liabilities can easily lead to financial distress following large swings in the RER, as balance sheets deteriorate dramatically, with the increased face value of debts to banks usually rendering these sectors bankrupt. To the extent that expectations concur that the public sector is willing to bail out banks and/or the corporate sector in the event of a crisis (another common feature of recent crises), the prospective costs of this bailout ought to be added to the sustainability analysis of the fisc. The combination of big RER swings, highly-dollarized public debt,

---

[19] One can only conjecture that to the extent that FDI flows were due to opportunities facing foreign investors given the low valuation of Brazilian firms after the devaluation of the Real (a one time shot), Brazil should be ready for additional fiscal adjustment in case FDI flows do not proceed at the previously observed pace.

and the activation of contingent liabilities of this sort can send debt/GDP ratios skyrocketing, rendering public sector accounts bankrupt. Argentina suffered from all of these additional fiscal exposures. Rough estimates of the bank bailout yield anywhere between US$7bn and US$13bn, and this excludes previous rediscounts and repos placed with public banks to finance their deposit losses equivalent to about US$6bn. Putting it all together yields an additional burden of US$13–19bn, which raises the debt/GDP ratio after the shock to anywhere between 55.8 and 58.6 percent, almost two-thirds higher than the pre-crisis 1998 measure!

Obviously, public debt surges of this magnitude are the prelude to a wealth redistribution conflict given the size of the required adjustment. Once all elements triggered by the Sudden Stop are factored in,[20] the primary balance needed to regain sustainability would have exceeded 3 percent of GDP, a figure never attained by Argentina in its recent history (see Table 10.9). In order to achieve this, the government would have needed to come up with new sources of financing or a cut in expenditures. It is evident from our previous discussion that the corporate sector could not be considered a good candidate for taxation, given that it was facing the same balance sheet breakdown and credit crunch confronted by the government. Thus, abstracting from default, the government was left with basically two alternatives: Taxing consumers or reducing expenditures via wage cuts.

Both instruments were used to some extent by different Ministers during the de la Rua administration, but they proved to be politically very tricky because both were mostly placing the burden on the shoulders of the middle class, de la Rua's main political constituency. Besides, these losing groups in the wealth redistribution game strongly challenged the implicit decision of the government to leave external creditors unscathed. The redistribution conflict gave rise to a War of Attrition in which decisions were delayed, deepening the extent of the crisis and the credibility of the public sector in terms of its ability to generate fiscal surpluses of the magnitude needed to regain sustainability. This, of course, closed any remaining open doors to government financing from abroad, thus making it clearer that the solution to this conundrum would most likely involve debt restructuring, something that lay at the heart of the bank run experienced in 2001. Most bank assets comprised loans to the private sector (most of them exhibiting currency mismatch) as well as government bonds. Both types of assets would be severely hit at the time of the crisis. This realization precipitated a run by depositors in order to avoid the expected confiscation of their deposits.

In summary, when judging sustainability by taking into account the valuation impact of a Sudden Stop and the cost of a bailout of the corporate sector on the balance sheet of the government, it would become apparent that by late 1999 Argentina had acquired a large debt problem as summarized in Table 10.9.

---

[20] That is, valuation effects, interest rate increases, growth slowdown and the emergence of contingent liabilities.

To "fix" this problem would have required very large cuts in government expenditures at a time when the fixed peg to the dollar left Argentina without a valuable instrument, that is, inflation, to engineer large government expenditure reductions which are politically very costly to implement in an explicit way.

Considering the requirements imposed by the new equilibrium level of the RER, the de la Rua administration was facing an uphill battle in order to restore credit-worthiness. It is fair to ask whether adjustments of such magnitude would have been feasible with standard fiscal policy instruments. Under lack of credibility, Argentina was definitely facing a stock problem. Such a problem can hardly be resolved with a tool such as the public sector deficit, which represents a flow, unless the reduction in the deficit is expected to be long-lasting. This was a tall order given the weak political structure underlying de la Rua's administration. Indeed, at this stage it would have been extremely difficult for any government to search for a solution that did not involve some form of debt restructuring.

Before concluding this section, let us revisit the issue of the expected duration of the Sudden Stop and expectations about Argentina's lack of fiscal sustainability. As previously noted, all sustainability calculations presented here were made under the assumption that the shock was permanent, but it is not clear that the shock was initially perceived as such by capital markets. Figure 10.5 shows Argentina's public bonds' spread measured by the EMBI index relative to the EMBI average for emerging markets. The fact that for the period starting with the Russian crisis through early August of 2000, Argentina's relative spread was lower than the average spread, indicates that the market had not yet rated Argentina as about to become insolvent.

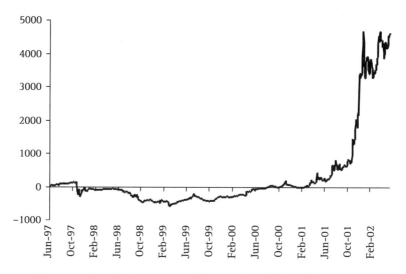

Figure 10.5. *Argentina: Relative external financial conditions (EMBI Arg − EMBI+)*
Source: Bloomberg.

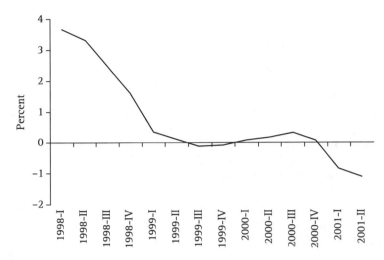

Figure 10.6. *Sudden Stop in Argentina (Private Capital Flows, % of GDP)*
Source: Central Bank of Argentina (BCRA).

Although private capital flows had already dried up by early 1999 (see Figure 10.6), two factors may have contributed to holding off bankruptcy expectations. First, it was not clear that the shock would be permanent so that the size of the required adjustment in relative prices and the fiscal outlook remained uncertain. Hence, it also had not yet become clear that Argentina's position would become unsustainable. But to the extent that investors were updating their expectations about the duration of the shock based on past and present behavior of capital flows, they had to infer from the observed persistence of the initial Sudden Stop that Argentina's fiscal solvency was deteriorating and this contributed to the increase in spreads. Second, although lower output levels resulting from the sudden stop in capital private flows depressed tax collections, putting additional strain on the fiscal balance, multilaterals, in particular, International Financial Institutions (IFIs), provided financing to the public sector during this period. Had the shock been temporary, this additional financing would have been sufficient to cover the government deficit and avoid default since there would be no underlying sustainability problem. But as time went by and it became clear that capital inflows were not returning, real currency depreciation (i.e. a rise in RER) was unavoidable and sustainability was at stake.

10.6 Nominal Exchange Rate Issues

We now briefly turn to the implications of having kept a fixed exchange rate regime in place when the sudden stop in capital flows hit Argentina (requiring substantial changes in the RER), and contrast this with a scenario where the exchange rate is allowed to float. The Argentine experience shows that under certain conditions, fixed exchange rates can help conceal fiscal disequilibrium. In particular, if prices are sticky, the RER may take time to reach its new equilibrium, revealing very little about the true magnitude of the necessary fiscal adjustment. The problem is that under those circumstances, it would be politically very hard to justify the need for a substantially larger fiscal retrenchment. This would be true even if we assume (unrealistically) that the International Monetary Fund (IMF) and policymakers were aware of the yawning misalignment.

The fact that the true magnitude of the fiscal adjustment was not evident may also be relevant in explaining the political turmoil that took place in 2000 in Argentina. Faced with the dilemma of deciding whether it was necessary to proceed with fiscal adjustment, the ruling alliance experienced substantial tension. This may very well have been the underlying force behind the resignation of several cabinet members and its implicit breakup following the vice-president's resignation. Even if sluggish RER adjustment was concealing the need for fiscal adjustment, one may ask whether other variables such as central bank reserves could have revealed that information. Under a fixed exchange rate regime, reserve loss would be a signal for adjustment. But this variable can be a very noisy signal. For example, to the extent that the crisis is anticipated, consumption will be higher before than after the crisis (see Calvo 1986), and so will money holdings and reserves in a cash-in-advance model. Thus, reserves may actually conceal the need for adjustment. Also, to the extent that reserves are supported by multilateral loans, they may mask the needed corrections (for a discussion of reserves as noisy signals, see Talvi 1997; Calvo 1998).

These considerations immediately raise the question: Would it have been very different had Argentina floated its exchange rate instead in January 2000? Leaving any initial overshooting aside, the floating rate may have revealed that Argentina was in the dumps. The de la Rua administration would have faced some of the same difficulties subsequently faced by the Duhalde administration, such as dealing with a banking system bailout. However, remedial measures may have been taken then, avoiding the costly financial engineering that was undertaken later in 2001. Moreover, the alliance was supported by a strong popular vote that could have provided the backing for quickly implementing an expeditious resolution of the crisis.

However, the above scenario is unrealistic. Authorities would likely have been reluctant to let the exchange rate go as far up as required to reach equilibrium RER. Be it because of high liability dollarization, high pass-through from the exchange rate to inflation, or lack of credibility, the authorities would likely have suffered from "fear of floating" (Calvo and Reinhart 2002). For these reasons, we conjecture that devaluation would have gone only half way. Thus, although the RER would have adjusted more rapidly at the beginning, interest rates would have exhibited a sharp increase. Surging interest rates are the result of incomplete devaluation and, thus, the expectation of more devaluation to come (*peso problem*). Higher future devaluation, implying a lower expected price of consumption today *vis-à-vis* tomorrow, may lead to a temporary increase in aggregate spending, but inevitably this boomlet gives way to bust as the intertemporal budget constraint presses in. Therefore, it is not clear that a more flexible exchange rate system would have cleared the air in 2000. Even if the nominal exchange rate had been allowed to float freely, results would not have been much different. Argentina's high vulnerability to big swings in the RER following a Sudden Stop and their detrimental effects on corporate balance sheets and fiscal sustainability were basically unaffected by whether the exchange rate was kept fixed at that stage or was allowed to float.

On the other hand, it is clear that floating the exchange rate was indeed a solution to the problem of nominal wage inflexibility faced by the government in the last few months before the collapse of Convertibility, a key element in bringing down real expenditure levels through inflation.[21] But this clear benefit in "facilitating" the fiscal adjustment would probably have been insufficient to compensate for the balance sheet breakdown caused by liability dollarization. As a result, a debt restructuring process to resolve the dynamics set in motion by the Sudden Stop became inevitable.

10.7   Lessons and Policy Issues

We now take stock and use what we have learned to list a set of lessons/policies for Latin America that are derived from our analysis of vulnerability to Sudden Stops. An overview of the specific attempts made in Argentina to escape the crisis, and the reasons why we believe they failed, are left for the Appendix.

Argentina was extremely vulnerable to a sudden stop in capital inflows such as the one that followed the Russian crisis due to three characteristics: It was extremely closed to international trade (C), highly indebted (D), and had a high degree of de facto dollarization both in the public and private sectors and, as a result, large financial currency mismatches (M). For future reference we will call an economy with these characteristics a *CDM* economy. Without any pretense of being exhaustive, in what follows we list the main policy lessons that logically emerge from our analysis:

Systemic Vulnerability
1. *CDM* economies are vulnerable to changes in international conditions that require an adjustment in the current account deficit since they may require correspondingly large increases in equilibrium RER.
2. In *CDM* economies, large changes in the RER could generate deep financial distress in the corporate sector and/or turn a sustainable fiscal position into an unsustainable one, leading to financial problems for the public sector as well.

---

[21] A floating exchange rate regime is a solution to a fixed exchange rate regime facing serious difficulties, such as a Sudden Stop. But this does not necessarily point to floating exchange rates as a better regime, since the advantages of such a regime should be evaluated *ex ante*.

3. A banking crisis may be the inevitable corollary, either because banks are themselves exposed to RER changes and/or because they are exposed to the public sector through large holdings of public debt.

Exchange Rate Policy

4. CDM economies are vulnerable, regardless of the exchange rate regime that is adopted. Sudden Stops are shocks to credit that generate real effects, with long-run outcomes that are independent of nominal exchange rate arrangements (although short-run dynamics can vary substantially depending on nominal arrangements).

5. Exchange rate flexibility could play a useful role if the C, D, or M are dropped (as was the case of Chile). It may be particularly useful if nominal wage inflexibility in the public sector is an issue. Otherwise, however, exchange rate flexibility could give rise to non-transparent policies, which might do more harm than good. In the short run, the C is hard to drop, and dropping D or M could be traumatic (as exemplified by Argentina's default and pesofication).

Fiscal Policy

6. Prima facie, in CDM economies it is dangerous to have high levels of public indebtedness. Governments should decide on lower debt levels (based on their degree of openness and liability dollarization) that create the necessary space for the public sector to respond in times of crisis while securing sustainability.

7. Dealing with an unsustainable fiscal position involves wealth redistribution across sectors. The way and the speed at which that redistribution is made are crucial in determining how fast a crisis is resolved. Ideally, wealth redistribution should be contracted *ex ante*.[22]

Trade Policy

8. Increasing trade openness (i.e. dropping the C) may be relevant not just because it reduces the size of RER swings after a Sudden Stop, but also because, from a financial perspective, a higher share of tradable sectors in output composition may reduce the risk of currency mismatches in private sector balance sheets. This effectively reduces the vulnerability of the banking sector following RER swings, as well as the size of potential bailouts that may worsen the fiscal position. Although the literature has focused on the benefits of openness for growth, the financial channels described above may be equally important.

Debt Management Policy

9. Efforts should be made to create markets for the issuance of debt in domestic currency not indexed to the exchange rate (i.e. dropping M).[23] Any debt contract that is contingent on RER fluctuations could be highly beneficial, not only

---

[22] For example, Brazil sold exchange rate insurance to private firms (and its cost was budgeted). This avoided a costly redistribution process by the time Brazil faced devaluation in 1999.

[23] Indeed, this is just one instrument to insulate the economy from the effects of external shocks. Other instruments, contingent on indicators of external shocks (such as main export commodity prices), could be just as beneficial. For more on this, see Caballero (2002).

because it may soften valuation effects, but because it specifies *ex ante* the redistribution process generated by a Sudden Stop, thus avoiding the costly resolutions and the associated political turmoil. But this must be done in such a way that two common weaknesses are avoided: First, debt should be issued under terms that eliminate incentives to inflate it away through money creation (such as CPI indexing). Second, issuance should be made at sufficiently long maturity to avoid vulnerability to liquidity shocks. Typically, attempts to issue debt with these characteristics have not been successful. But a recurrent characteristic of these attempts has been the fact that issuance was made under domestic law instead of international law. Thus, there may be a significant difference in risk other than that associated with exchange rate risk, which may further complicate currency-matching strategies.

Appendix 10.A1   Domestic Policies in Argentina under the Perspective of the Sudden Stop

Here, we will present and briefly discuss policies that were pursued in Argentina prior to the fall of the Convertibility Program.

Fiscal policy   From the previous discussion, it is clear that fiscal restraint introduced in late 1999 and early 2000, although in the right direction, was not sufficient to cope with the sustainability demands raised by the new equilibrium RER and the expected bailout of the private sector, making it difficult for the government to sustain the higher levels of debt, thereby creating a stock problem. The IMF was not immune to this misunderstanding. Under the assumption that Argentina was facing a liquidity problem, the initial program agreed upon with the de la Rua administration was followed by the *blindaje*.[24] Fiscal policy was relaxed and the original program was buttressed by a larger package. This failed, as the program was now heading in the wrong direction. The mistaken diagnosis could help explain why there was a lack of consensus about the degree of fiscal adjustment needed to restore credibility. When the size of adjustment reaches the magnitude required by the Sudden Stop, it is easy to see why a heterogeneous political alliance can break up. Disunity was exacerbated by the fact that economists did not offer a clear explanation to politicians about the reasons and urgency for adjustment, and particularly about the need to regain solvency if the capital flow standstill was ever to be reversed. This conceptual and political maelstrom was a clear source of uncertainty for the private sector about the future. Hence, it is not surprising that investment projects were suspended, resulting in higher unemployment.

An attempt to introduce a fiscal package in early 2001 by a new minister[25] (which again would not have been sufficient to recover solvency) was quickly

---

[24] A package of about US$40bn provided by official creditors.
[25] Ricardo Lopez-Murphy, a respected macroeconomist known for being fiscally strict was appointed to the Ministry of Economy.

ruled out given that an agreement could not be reached either with some members of the alliance or with the opposition party. After this failed attempt, fiscal adjustment was rejected by the new incoming minister[26] (a big error in a situation in which sustainability was at stake), and replaced by a bewildering variety of stimulating fiscal arrangements (competitiveness plans), which were subject to several changes (another big error regarding credibility). Fiscal policy was swiftly changed in mid-2001, when it became clear that no additional external financing was going to materialize, by adopting a zero-deficit rule, and cutting transfers to provincial governments. Both measures put the political system to the test, and came too late to stop the crisis. Even though these announcements were made in an attempt to send a signal of improved sustainability, they were probably not credible inasmuch as political support was dim and the wealth redistribution struggle previously alluded to was already developing.

Debt management   On the debt management side, under the perception that the country was only facing liquidity problems, the government engineered a massive debt swap in June 2001 to extend the maturity of the debt profile, but ended up validating extremely high interest rates which, in turn, confirmed expectations about an unsustainable fiscal position. This quickly led to expectations of a balance of payments crisis, which in the case of Argentina would be much more devastating given the existence of highly dollarized liabilities in the banking system.

Another measure aimed at improving the fiscal position was the "voluntary"[27] debt exchange introduced in late 2001, which reduced interest rates and extended debt maturity. But even if it was the right way to go because this policy was addressing the debt stock problem by reducing its present value, such measures should have been introduced much earlier. By then, the attack on the banking system and reserve loss were underway.

Exchange rate policy   To correct for RER misalignment, the *convergence factor* was introduced in mid-2001, basically a peg to a basket composed of dollars and euros in equal proportions[28] that would become effective for all transactions when the parity between these currencies reached one. For trade transactions, though, dollars were exchanged at the ongoing dollar/euro basket rate, which amounted to a (fiscal) devaluation of about 8 percent. Unfortunately, the prevailing view was that misalignment stemmed exclusively from trade factors like the devaluation of the real and the euro—which ignored misalignment due to

---

[26] Domingo Cavallo, the father of the convertibility plan introduced in 1991, who had been highly successful in the fight against inflation and making the economy grow fast during the first presidency of Carlos Menem.

[27] Banks and pension funds were the main bondholders of the debt to be exchanged. Banks were persuaded to enter the exchange under pressure that their assets would otherwise have to be marked to market, something that could threaten their net worth position. Pension fund limits for holdings of public debt were increased to allow for placement of additional bonds.

[28] But surprisingly, not the real, which would have been a key price to include if the main reason behind this change was to increase trade competitiveness.

country risk considerations. From the previous analysis, it is clear that the peso's real depreciation obtained through fiscal devaluation, although in the right direction, was far from enough to correct the existing misalignment. The implementation of the convergence factor also had implications for exchange rate policy that may have contributed to the deposit run that would take place later, and the emergence of contingent liabilities that would further compromise the fiscal position. The *convergence factor* was mired in messy implementation, as there was no clear indication about when this new rule would become operational for all transactions. All that agents knew was that it would materialize whenever the dollar and the euro reached a parity of one to one. Moreover, this policy signaled to the market that the government was ready to loosen the shackles of the currency board and devalue. Fearful of the detrimental effects on bank assets that devaluation would cause via massive bankruptcies, depositors figured out that their assets (even if dollarized) were at stake, particularly given that the burden of a bank bailout was probably perceived as too big for the government to handle with its own resources. In this context, the signal given by the change in the currency board worsened expectations, something that would later lead to a massive deposit withdrawal and even larger loss of international reserves.

Monetary policy   Perhaps the policy that most swiftly precipitated the balance of payments crisis (which, in turn, would weaken the fiscal position even further when the contingent liabilities materialized) was the expansionary monetary stance adopted by the administration even while the Currency Board still kept the exchange rate firmly tied to the dollar.[29] Expansionary reserve-requirement policies were introduced,[30] but quickly compensated for as a result of IMF pressure. The second tool available was domestic credit to commercial banks, which increased sharply (see Figure 10.7). Central bank credit expansion explains about 53 percent of the staggering loss of reserves that took place from April to December 2001.[31] As discussed in Calvo (2002a), under a Sudden Stop, a Central Bank will have incentives to hand its reserves to the credit constrained non-tradable corporate sector via credit expansion (a strategy that requires keeping a fixed exchange rate); but this may be a risky policy because it is not at all clear that reserves will end up in the hands of those who need them the most. There is a high chance that the sectors more likely to receive the proceeds from credit expansion (the public sector and prime borrowers with access to international markets, who represent a lower risk to banks) will end up unwinding their dollar

[29] This policy was implemented after the dismissal of the central bank president, Pedro Pou. Although Convertibility required that the monetary base be backed by foreign assets, a share of these foreign assets could be composed of government paper in foreign currency, thus providing room for expansionary monetary policy.

[30] Bank excess reserves were accepted as part of reserve requirements, implying an expansion of lending capacity, but this was compensated for by increases in reserve requirement rates.

[31] Reserves are net of US$4bn in new IMF loans.

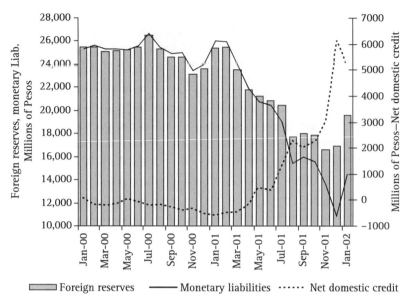

Figure 10.7. *Increase in domestic credit and foreign reserve loss*
Source: Central Bank of Argentina (BCRA).

debts, something that could be highly beneficial in light of upcoming devaluation. Thus, reserves are lost and there is little relief for those originally targeted by the Central Bank.

Not all credit expansion reflected the heterodox monetary position. As it turns out, soon after the government gave these expansionary signals, deposits began to decline sharply (about 18 percent between April and December 2001), which allegedly demanded Central Bank intervention in order to prevent a massive crash of the banking system. But, in any case, the question still remains as to what led the Central Bank to accommodate deposit withdrawal so swiftly, when the dominant theory was that foreign-owned banks would provide the necessary liquidity.

As the crisis was brewing, deposits fled the system and composition changed in favor of private banks, most of which are foreign-owned. Thus, depositors seem to have bought the theory—which constituted the intellectual basis behind bank denationalization since at least 1995—that foreign-owned banks would not let their subsidiaries go under. The Central Bank responded by providing support to the official sector. Deposits in those banks far exceeded international reserves. Thus, the realization that the Central Bank was ready to bail out state-owned banks reinforced the expectation that the currency board's days were numbered. To further complicate matters, the Central Bank increased the reserve requirement of deposit-receiving banks in order to sterilize credit expansion (marginal reserve requirements were set at 75 percent). This sent a clear signal to foreign banks that they might be treated differentially, and their assets eventually confiscated, completely neutralizing the "lender-of-last-resort" role that those banks were supposed to play.[32]

REFERENCES

Caballero, R. (2002). "Coping with Chile's External Vulnerability: A Financial Problem." http://web.mit.edu/caball/www/Chile_11Jan2002.pdf.

— and Krishnamurthy, A. (2003). "A 'Vertical' Analysis of Monetary Policy in Emerging Markets." http://web.mit.edu/caball/www/verticalaer.pdf.

Calvo, G. A. (1986). "Temporary Stabilization: Predetermined Exchange Rates." *Journal of Political Economy*, 94 (December): 1319–29.

— (1998). "Growth, Debt, and Economic Transformation: The Capital Flight problem." In F. Coricelli, M. Di Matteo, and F. Hahn (eds.), *New Theories in Growth and Development*. Basingstoke, UK: Palgrave Macmillan, pp. 251–69.

— (1999). "Contagion in Emerging Markets: When Wall Street is a Carrier." www.bsos.umd.edu/econ/ciecrp8.pdf.

— (2002*a*). "Explaining Sudden Stop, Growth Collapse, and BOP Crisis: The Case of Distortionary Output Taxes." www.imf.org/external/pubs/ft/staffp/2002/00-00/pdf/calvo.pdf.

— (2002*b*). "Globalization Hazard and Delayed Reform in Emerging Markets." *Economía*, 2 (Spring): 1–29.

— and Reinhart, C. (2000). "When Capital Flows come to Sudden Stop: Consequences and Policy." In P. K. Kenen and A. K. Swoboda (eds.), *Reforming the International Monetary and Financial System*. Washington, DC: International Monetary Fund, pp. 175–201.

— and — (2002). "Fear of Floating." *Quarterly Journal of Economics*, 117 (2): 379–408.

Catena, M. and Talvi, E. (2001). "Sudden Stops in a Dynamic General Equilibrium Model: An Application to Latin American Countries." http://ceres-uy.org/.

Izquierdo, A. (1999). "Credit Constraints, and the Asymmetric Behavior of Output and Asset Prices under External Shocks." Ph.D. dissertation, University of Maryland.

Sturzenegger, F. and Tommasi, M. (eds.) (1998). *The Political Economy of Reform*. Cambridge, MA: MIT Press.

Talvi, E. (1997). "Exchange Rate Based Stabilization with Endogenous Fiscal Response." *Journal of Development Economics*, 54 (October): 59–75.

---

[32] Although many feared that foreign banks typically would not behave as shock smoothers, bringing along necessary resources to finance a bank run, the case of Uruguay may be relevant proof that when rules of operation are not changed and contracts are not repudiated, foreign banks may have incentives to come up with the necessary resources.

11

Living and Dying with Hard Pegs: The Rise and Fall of Argentina's Currency Board

AUGUSTO DE LA TORRE, EDUARDO LEVY YEYATI, AND
SERGIO L. SCHMUKLER

The rise and fall of Argentina's currency board illustrates the extent to which the advantages of hard pegs have been overstated. The currency board did provide nominal stability and boosted financial intermediation, at the cost of endogenous financial dollarization, but did not foster fiscal or monetary discipline. The failure to adequately address the currency–growth–debt (CGD) trap, into which Argentina fell at the end of the 1990s, precipitated a run on the currency and the banks, followed by the abandonment of the currency board and a sovereign debt default. The crisis can be best interpreted as a bad outcome of a high-stakes strategy to overcome a weak currency problem. To increase the credibility of the hard peg, the government raised its exit costs, which deepened the crisis once exit could no longer be avoided. But some alternative exit strategies would have been less destructive than the one adopted.

11.1 Introduction

The rise and fall of Argentina's currency board (a textbook model of a rigid exchange rate regime for more than ten years) and the subsequent financial system collapse yield important lessons for the debate on exchange rate regimes for

Reprinted from the July 2003 issue of *Economía*, by kind permission of the Brookings Institution Press.

We are grateful to Alberto Ades, Javier Bolzico, Jerry Caprio, José De Gregorio, Graciela Kaminsky, Paul Levy, Sole Martinez Peria, Guillermo Perry, Andrew Powell, Roberto Rigobón, Luis Servén, Federico Sturzenegger, Ted Truman, Andrés Velasco, Charles Wyplosz, as well as participants at seminars held at Columbia University, the LACEA Annual Meeting (Madrid), and Universidad Torcuato Di Tella for helpful comments. We thank Tatiana Didier, Mariano Lanfranconi, Ana Maria Menendez, Josefina Rouillet, and particularly Marina Halac for excellent research assistance. We thank Laura D'Amato, Fernanda Martijena, and Maria Augusta Salgado for help with the data. The views expressed in this paper are entirely those of the authors and do not necessarily represent the views of the World Bank.

developing countries.[1] As expected, the Argentine case has already generated an extensive debate on the causes and policy implications of the crisis.[2] Current explanations, however, concentrate too much on the latest years and do not pay enough attention to the underpinnings of the currency board and to its implications for the financial system and the economy at large.

In this paper, we study the Argentine experience from a perspective that links money (in its function as store of value) and financial intermediation. This approach has important advantages. By organizing the discussion of the different intervening factors around a main motive, it allows us to balance the broadness of a comprehensive survey with the focus needed to extract fairly general lessons. More importantly, it enables us to highlight the role played by the currency board in the development of the financial sector during the 1990s and in the genesis of its collapse. It also allows us to better understand the nature of the CGD trap into which Argentina fell during the late 1990s, and how it eventually led to a currency and bank run that precipitated a devastating economic crisis.

In light of the Argentine experience, we argue that the benefits of hard pegs have been greatly overstated. To be sure, by providing savers with the dollar as the store of value (directly under dollarization, or via the peg under currency boards), a credible hard peg ensures nominal stability and boosts financial intermediation. But even if credible, a hard peg does not automatically lead to the emergence of alternative nominal flexibility (particularly in wages, fiscal spending, and financial contracting) to compensate for the loss of the nominal exchange rate as a policy instrument. This is particularly problematic in the case of hard peg countries that, like Argentina, do not meet the classical conditions for an optimal currency (dollar) area. Partly as a result, hard pegs do not *per se* induce fiscal or even monetary discipline. The monetary framework of a hard peg, although typically protected by a heavy legal and institutional armor, can be dismantled more easily than expected through the emergence of quasi-monies in response to extreme budgetary cash flow pressures coupled with insufficient nominal flexibility in fiscal spending and public sector wages. Moreover, with its credibility being a positive function of its exit costs, a hard peg creates powerful incentives for the government to raise exit costs further (redouble the bet) when the hard peg is under pressure. A particular way in which hard pegs endogenously raise exit costs is by fostering dollarization, including of the liabilities of debtors in the non-tradable sector—as the government would rather not adopt measures to explicitly discourage dollarization for fear of undermining the credibility of its commitment to the hard peg.

Exiting a hard peg is inherently a very painful affair, given the contradiction between hardening the peg and allowing for a smooth exit. But some ways of exiting can be more disastrous than others. We analyze the Argentine experience

---

[1] See Frankel et al. (2001) for a brief history of this debate.

[2] See among others, Feldstein (2002), Calvo et al. (this part), Perry and Servén (this part), Mussa (2002), Hausmann and Velasco (2003), and Powell (2003).

to draw lessons on alternative exit strategies. With the benefit of hindsight and the caveats of any counterfactual analysis, we argue that the forcible pesofica- tion of existing financial contracts ("stock pesofication") was the most costly choice, for it was bound to cause an excessive destruction of property rights with long-lasting consequences for financial intermediation and, by creating a mas- sive peso overhang in the midst of a currency run, was likely to rekindle the deposit flight and exacerbate the exchange rate overshooting. By contrast, an early (before 2001) exit into full dollarization (of financial contracts *and* money in circulation) might have averted the bank run, thus protecting financial inter- mediation and the payment system, but would have done nothing to mitigate the deflationary and recessionary costs of a protracted adjustment of the real exchange to a more depreciated equilibrium level. In this light, we find support for an intermediate exit option: Dollarization of existing financial contracts ("stock dollarization") to respect the widespread use of the dollar as store of value, combined with "pesofication at the margin" (for instance, via the consol- idation of the existing pesos and quasi-monies into a new national currency) to exploit the use of the peso as means of payment and unit of account, which remained extensive and resilient throughout the convertibility period and even during the run.[3] While this alternative would not have spared Argentina from significant banking system stress and even some individual bank failures, as debtors in the non-tradable sector would have seen their balance sheets and payment capacity adversely affected by the real exchange rate (RER) correction, it might have provided a margin of nominal flexibility while avoiding a systemic financial collapse and the unnecessary destruction of property rights.

Within the terms of the exchange rate debate, the failure of the Argentine cur- rency board is sure to elicit two reactions. On the one hand, bipolar proponents may conclude that currency boards are not hard enough and that sustainable pegs have to go all the way to formal dollarization. On the other, hard peg critics may interpret the case as evidence that the regime debate has been settled in favor of fully floating regimes. We argue that a one-dimensional emphasis on pure fix versus float dilemma is insufficient and can even be misleading. It would be more productive to focus on the weak currency problem that plagues most emerging economies and on the need to build healthy links between money (in its function as store of value) and financial intermediation, while establishing ade- quate flexibility, including in financial contracting, to facilitate adjustment to shocks.[4]

The rest of the paper is organized as follows. Section 11.2 analyzes the rise and fall of convertibility, distinguishing between the good times of financial

---

[3] It is useful to state at this point that we do not favor redollarization of contracts once the costs of pesofication have been largely incurred.

[4] Underscoring this view is the need for institutional building irrespective of the exchange rate regime of choice. The case of Argentina clearly illustrates the difficulties of importing monetary institutions through the adoption of a peg. We conjecture that these difficulties would not have been bypassed by unilateral dollarization.

deepening that were, nonetheless, accompanied by persistent and rising financial dollarization, and the bad times that witnessed the fall of the Argentine economy into a CGD trap from which it could not break free, and the resulting meltdown, triggered by a massive run on the currency that evolved into a deposit run. Section 11.3 draws lessons from the Argentine experience on hard pegs: Their limitations as commitment mechanisms, their specific prudential concerns, and the alternative exit strategies. Section 11.4 offers some final remarks.

11.2   The Rise and Fall of Argentina's Currency Board

It was never a mystery that the rigid peg of the peso to the dollar under convertibility was a highly inconvenient choice from the point of view of Argentina's trade and productive structure. In effect, Argentina is far from meeting the conditions for an optimal currency (dollar) area. It is subject to typically different shocks than the United States, it has a substantial share of its foreign trade with countries whose currencies fluctuate *vis-à-vis* the U.S. dollar and, as a relatively closed economy with a large non-tradable sector, could benefit much more (compared to open economies with relatively small non-tradable sectors) from nominal exchange rate adjustments to correct for misalignments in the relative price of tradables to non-tradables.

Convertibility was chosen in Argentina despite the mentioned reasons and not even in light of long-term growth considerations. It was a decision understandably driven by overriding monetary and financial considerations. Convertibility in fact arose as an extreme response to hyperinflation and the consequent implosion of financial intermediation that had taken place in the 1980s, and against a much longer history of repeated episodes of debasement of the domestic currency and fiscal mismanagement.

From its introduction in April 1991, however, convertibility was much more than a simple peg or an expedient exchange rate arrangement to conquer inflation. For starters, the peg was embedded in a broader monetary arrangement that featured, at its heart, a money issuance rule that legally precluded the creation of pesos not backed by hard dollars, except within a very limited range.[5] Convertibility was intended to produce a nonreversible break away from monetary and financial instability. It was expected to mark for the Argentine psychology a point of no return and a one-way path forward, much like Hernán Cortez's decision to burn the ships had marked for his crew. Moreover, convertibility was from the outset envisioned to have implications well beyond the pure monetary sphere, for it aspired to become an institutional axis that would help put order in other institutions and align incentives among agents, particularly in the economic

---

[5] The law allowed for up to one-third of disposable international reserves to be constituted with internationally traded, dollar-denominated Argentine sovereign bonds, valued at market prices. This proviso enabled a very limited role for the central bank as lender-of-last-resort—it could create and provide peso liquidity to the banking system in exchange for sovereign Argentine bonds, rather than hard dollars.

sphere (fiscal process, bank regulation, labor markets, etc.) but also in the social and political spheres. Convertibility indeed became a central component of the social contract, a key institution in the economic and political life of the country. Convertibility was not a contract like any other; it was rather a core or master contract, one upon which other (financial and non-financial) contracts depended.

Mr. Cavallo, Minister of Economy of Argentina at the beginning and at the end of the convertibility decade (1991–2001), used to insist that there was, by design, only one way to exit convertibility in accordance to the law—that is, once the Argentine peso had established itself as an international currency, and a strong one at that. In effect, the convertibility law stated that the central bank would stand ready to buy and sell dollars at *no more* than one peso per dollar. By implication, the central bank could eventually buy dollars at *less than* one peso per dollar. Obviously, the catastrophic manner in which convertibility collapsed in January 2002 was a far cry from the glorious exit that had been envisioned by its framers in April 1991.

What explains this massive departure of reality from vision? In the remainder of this section we attempt an explanation. Convertibility did deliver broadly according to promise with respect to the deepening of the financial system, although at the cost of a persistent and rising level of financial dollarization.[6] In contrast, convertibility failed to deliver with respect to the expectation that, being a permanent monetary "straightjacket," it would, by itself, discipline the fiscal process and induce reforms that would endow Argentina with adequate nominal flexibility (particularly in fiscal spending and wages) to compensate for the absence of nominal exchange rate flexibility. Such a failure became particularly taxing after 1998, as the country was increasingly caught in what we label a CGD trap that ultimately precipitated the collapse.

11.2.1 Good times: Financial deepening and increased dollarization

Out of the ashes left by hyperinflation and financial disarray in Argentina in the 1980s, the one-peso-one-dollar rule of convertibility quickly restored the function of money as a store of value, thereby enabling a rapid regeneration of financial intermediation as reflected a steep growth of bank deposits and loans throughout 1999 (Figure 11.1).[7] Moreover, the rapid taming of inflation brought

---

[6] By financial dollarization we refer to the holding by residents of foreign currency-denominated assets and liabilities. As argued in Ize and Levy Yeyati (2003), financial dollarization reflects mostly an asset substitution phenomenon (i.e. the use of a foreign currency as store of value), as opposed to currency substitution (i.e. the use of the foreign currency as unit of account and means of payment).

[7] After a major step increase between 1991 and 1994, banks deposits continued rising steadily from 17 percent of GDP by the end of 1994 to 26 by the end of 1998. Calomiris and Powell (2001) show compellingly that convertibility is indeed the key to understanding the rapid growth and strengthening of the financial system in the 1990s.

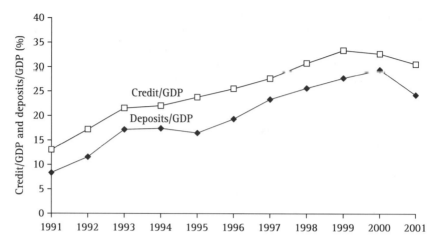

Figure 11.1. *Financial deepening*

Notes: Credit includes loans to private sector, loans to public sector, loans to residents abroad, and private and public securities held by the financial system. Deposits include demand deposits, savings deposits, time deposits, and other deposits, by private sector, public sector, and residents abroad. Figures correspond to end-of-year values.

Sources: Central Bank of Argentina and The World Bank.

about by convertibility greatly enhanced the political viability of a number of first generation reforms that the nominal instability of the past had rendered infeasible. Rapid changes thus swept the Argentine economy in the first phase of convertibility, particularly with the restructuring of the external debt (under the Brady Plan), a tax reform centered on the VAT, a series of privatizations, social security reform, and the deregulation of financial markets. This, combined with a wave of capital flows to emerging economies in which Argentina shared prominently, fueled aggregate demand and boosted GDP growth to a brisk average of 6.4 percent per annum during 1991–98 (9.1 percent during 1991–94), well above the Latin American average of 3.7 percent in 1991–98 (4.3 percent in 1991–94).

The sustainability of convertibility's early successes was transitorily but severely questioned during the Mexican (Tequila) crisis of 1995. The Tequila contagion led to a major run on the Argentine peso and bank deposits. Deposits fell by almost 20 percent in a span of a few weeks, nearly bringing down the financial system and convertibility with it. This crisis marked a turning point in financial sector policy. The authorities responded by affirming convertibility, while recognizing that its viability required a particularly resilient financial system given the limits imposed by the currency board on the central bank to act as lender-of-last-resort. They launched a series of ambitious financial sector reforms to give effect to this conviction, as illustrated in Appendix 11.A1.

Table 11.1. *Consolidation and internationalization of the banking system*

	1994	1998	2000
Number of total banks	166	104	89
Foreign banks			
Number of banks	31	39	39
Number of branches	391	1,535	1,863
(%) Share of total assets	15	55	73
Number of public banks	32	16	15

Note: Figures correspond to end-of-year values.

Source: Central Bank of Argentina.

The results were impressive according to any standard.[8] The banking system consolidated and became internationalized, while many public banks were privatized (see Table 11.1).

By the end of the 1990s, a resilient banking system was the crown jewel of convertibility-induced reform. Convertibility did not lead to strong fiscal institutions,[9] but few doubted that it had led to a shock-resistant banking sector.

The banking system was arguably in a very solid position before the Brazilian devaluation of January 1999, and was still reasonably healthy through the end of 2000, despite the post-1998 continued economic contraction. In effect, common indicators of financial health, shown in Table 11.2, depict a well capitalized, strongly provisioned, and highly liquid banking system through the year 2000, although a system experiencing losses and increasingly burdened by bad loans after 1998.[10]

The Tequila aftermath affirmed convertibility as a central piece in the social contract, with post-1994 reforms creating a banking system that, though costly, appeared convertibility-compatible in most respects. Towards the end of the decade, the financial system's prudential buffers were sufficient to withstand

[8] So much that by 1998 Argentina ranked second (after Singapore, tied with Hong Kong, and ahead of Chile) in terms of the quality of its regulatory environment, according to the CAMELOT rating system developed by the World Bank. This system combined separate rankings for capital requirements (C); loan loss provisioning requirements and definition of past-due loans (A); management (M), defined by the extent of high-quality foreign bank presence; liquidity requirements (L); operating environment (O) as measured by rankings with respect to property rights, creditor rights, and enforcement; and transparency (T), as measured by whether banks are rated by international risk rating agencies and by an index on corruption. Argentina ranked first for C (tied with Singapore), fourth for A, third for M, fourth for L, seventh for O, and second for T. For details see World Bank (1998: 39–61 and appendix A).

[9] See Gavin and Perotti (1997) and Tornell and Velasco (2000).

[10] Profits turned negative already in 1998 and became deeply negative during 1999–2000 partly because of the need to constitute provisions in the face of rising bad loans. NPLs rose to 11.6 percent of total loans in 2000, from 10.5 percent the year earlier (Table 11.2).

Table 11.2. *Selected banking system indicators*

	1997	1998	1999	2000
Net worth/Assets	12.1	11.4	10.7	10.5
Capital/Risk weighted assets	18.1	17.6	18.6	21.2
Non-performing loans (NPLs)/ Total loans (a)	10.1	9.1	10.5	11.6
Provisions/Total loans	6.2	5.5	6.1	7.3
Provisions/Non-performing loans (a)	60.9	60.4	58.4	63.3
Systemic core liquidity (b)	43.0	39.6	40.9	38.7
Return on equity before provisions	22.6	10.6	8.4	7.8
Return on equity after provisions	7.4	−2.2	−6.7	−9.4
Return on assets after provisions	1.0	−0.3	−0.8	−1.0
Leverage ratio (not in percent)	6.1	7.3	7.7	8.3

Notes: (a) NPLs is defined as the sum of loans with problems, loans with high risk and non-recoverable loans. (b) Defined as the ratio of international reserves of the central bank in foreign currency and other liquidity requirements held abroad by banks to total deposits. Figures are in percent and correspond to end-of-year values.

Source: Central Bank of Argentina.

sizable liquidity and solvency shocks—including a flight of about one-third of the deposits as well as further significant decay in the loan portfolio—without endangering convertibility.[11] The important presence of reputable foreign banks (they accounted for over 70 percent of total banking assets in 2000, as shown in Table 11.1) was broadly perceived to implicitly augment these liquidity and solvency cushions. These banks were expected to stand behind the capital and liquidity of their affiliates in Argentina, at least in the context of bad states of the world associated with bad luck. (Few were thinking then of bad states of the world caused directly by confiscatory government policy.)

The remarkable strengthening of the banking system was accompanied by a persistent and rising level of financial dollarization. This phenomenon was not part of the intention of the framers of convertibility. But it was an almost inevitable corollary of policy incentives created by convertibility itself coupled with a stubborn market perception of exchange rate risk that convertibility could not remove, despite its heavy institutional and legal armor.

The founders of convertibility envisioned a strong peso as the way for an elegant and almost natural exit from the one-peso-one-dollar rule. Such an aspiration, however, could not be easily translated into measures to discourage financial dollarization. This was because of the risk that such measures be

[11] Table 11.2 puts systemic core liquidity (disposable international reserves of the central bank plus foreign exchange in cash or near-cash held abroad by banks) at about 39 percent of banking system deposits at end-2000. However, there was a significant variance in the distribution of such liquidity across banks. This may explain why the "corralito" was imposed at the end of 2001 before deposits had fallen by 30 percent.

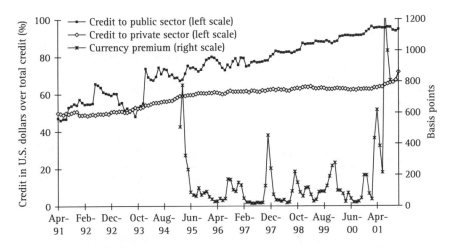

Figure 11.2. *Loan dollarization and currency premium*

Notes: The currency premium is measured by the differential between peso and dollar interbank deposit rates, using daily one-month interest rate premium. Credit to public and private sector correspond to end-of-period values and currency premium is monthly average.

Source: Central Bank of Argentina.

interpreted by the market as an indication that the authorities themselves did not think that the one-peso-one-dollar rule was to endure under most states of the world. Hence, the authorities faced incentives not to adopt prudential norms (e.g. loan classification and provisioning rules, liquidity requirements) that would explicitly discourage the use of the dollar in financial contracts.[12] Similarly, the government did not issue peso debt in domestic markets not just because dollar debt was less costly, but also because incurring the additional cost could only have been interpreted as a hedge against a future devaluation, undermining the confidence in the one-to-one rule that convertibility was meant to inspire.

At the same time, markets did not fully take to heart the mantra of "no more than one peso for one dollar, forever." Instead, they continued to attach a non-trivial probability to the risk of a nominal devaluation of the peso. This perceived currency risk was a key factor behind a peso problem that persisted throughout the 1990s, spiking during turbulent times, as shown in Figure 11.2.[13]

The lasting perception of a residual risk of nominal devaluation, together with the mentioned incentives faced by the authorities (which resulted in an essentially currency-blind prudential framework), constitute an important part of the explanation of the rise in financial dollarization throughout the convertibility

---

[12] We come back to this point in the next section.

[13] The interest rate differential reflected not only exchange rate risk, but also default risk as discussed in Broda and Levy Yeyati (2003) and Schmukler and Servén (2002).

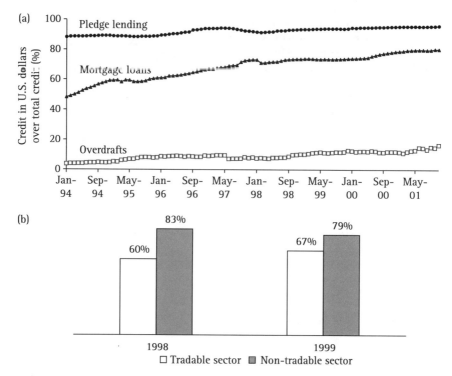

Figure 11.3. *Private sector dollarization (a) by type of credit and (b) firm's balance sheet dollarization*

Notes: (b) shows the average share of U.S. dollar debt across firms.

Sources: Central Bank of Argentina and Buenos Aires Stock Exchange.

decade.[14] Dollarization permeated both private and public sector financial assets and liabilities, and was very significant in loans to the non-tradable sector. Figure 11.2 shows the steady rise in the share of dollar credit in total credit to the private and public sectors. The first panel of Figure 11.3 shows that dollarization of mortgage loans (i.e. loans to an important non-tradable sector) increased significantly since 1994, while the second panel of the same figure shows that dollar debt, as indicated by firms' balance sheets, was even higher for non-tradable firms than for tradable ones.

Dollarization of public sector debt also rose significantly, and not just in terms of bank credit to the public sector. In particular, the public debt made explicit as a result of the reform in the social security system was denominated in dollars. At the same time, certain other policies taken by the public sector encouraged

[14] The peso problem was not independent of the degree of financial dollarization, as explained at the end of this section.

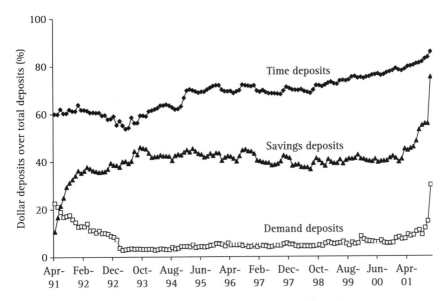

Figure 11.4. *Dollarization by type of deposit*

Source: Central Bank of Argentina.

real dollarization—for instance, the decision to allow public utility tariffs to be denominated in dollars (done to reassure a dollar income to the privatized utility companies, thus recognizing that convertibility was not fully credible in the view of such companies).

Financial dollarization in Argentina reflected an asset substitution phenomenon (a shift to the dollar as a store of value), and was accompanied by currency substitution (a shift to the dollar as a unit of account and means of payment) only to a minor degree. Dollar pricing was limited mostly to internationally traded goods and big-ticket items such as real estate, and use of the dollar for everyday transactions was rather marginal, as reflected in marked differences in dollarization ratios for different types of bank deposits (Figure 11.4).

Time deposits became increasingly dollarized during convertibility. In contrast, the degree of dollarization of passbook saving accounts, albeit high (about 40 percent), remained relatively stable throughout the eight years ending in 2000. Moreover, the degree of dollarization of demand deposits was strikingly low (well under 10 percent) and stable during most of the decade.[15]

[15] The evidence of a resilient transactional demand for pesos was ultimately confirmed by the stability of real peso balances following the abandonment of convertibility, as we show below. Even after the *corralito* was lifted in December 2002, M1/GDP remained slightly above its historical levels. The distinction between currency and asset substitution will play a crucial role when we come back to the exit strategy problem in the next section.

Table 11.3. *Risk indicators*

Date	Annual interest rate (%)	Annual interest rate (%)	Risk
7/1/1993	Peso financing	Foreign currency financing	
	Up to 24	Up to 18	1.00
	More than 24–27	More than 18–21	1.20
	More than 27–30	More than 21–24	1.40
	More than 30–33	More than 24–27	1.60
	More than 33–36	More than 27–30	1.80
	More than 36–39	More than 30–33	2.00
2/1/1996	Peso financing	Foreign-currency financing	
	Up to 18	Up to 14	1.00
	More than 18–21	More than 14–17	1.20
	More than 21–24	More than 17–20	1.40
	More than 24–27	More than 20–23	1.60
	More than 27–30	More than 23–26	1.80
	More than 30–33	More than 26–29	2.00
1/1/2000	Peso and foreign-currency financing: Personal loans, credit card financing, and overdrafts	Other financing	
	Up to 26	Up to 16	1.00
	More than 26–29	More than 16–19	1.10
	More than 29–32	More than 19–22	1.20
	More than 32–35	More than 22–25	1.30
	More than 35–38	More than 25–28	1.40
	More than 38–41	More than 28–31	1.50
	More than 41–44	More than 31–34	1.60
	More than 44–47	More than 34–37	1.90
	More than 47–50	More than 37–40	2.20

Notes: Risk indicator is used in the calculation of the risk value of loans and other financing (excluding credit to financial institutions), which is then used to determine the capital requirements for credit risk. For higher interest rates other risk indicators apply.

Source: Central Bank of Argentina.

To be sure, the authorities tried an indirect avenue to deal with the currency risk associated with financial dollarization through prudential norms—namely, the interest rate factor.[16] As explained in Appendix 11A.1 and shown in Table 11.3, regulatory capital requirements for credit risk were not only determined in line with the typical Basle-type procedure of applying higher weights to riskier loan *classes*. They also tried to take into account the risk of individual loans *within* each loan class. This was operationalized by increasing the weight applied to individual loans that charged higher interest rates—that is, by adding a so-called interest rate factor. The underlying assumption was that if banks price risks

---

[16] We thank Andrew Powell for raising this point.

correctly, these should be fully reflected in the lending interest rate. The norm was initially designed to take into account different interest rate scales and thresholds depending on the currency of loan denomination (Table 11.3). This innovative system was probably effective in capturing some risk differences across loans, but failed at capturing the specific risk of dollar loans to the non-tradable sector (a point further discussed in Section 11.3). Rather, the interest rate factor may have encouraged dollarization because it was in fact higher for peso loans than for dollar loans, given that the peso problem entailed systematically higher peso interest rates (Figure 11.5).

Moreover, in 1999, when currency risk became a source of policy concern, the differentiation in the interest rate factor according to the currency of loan

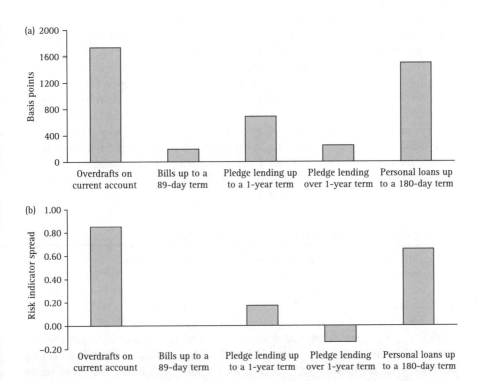

Figure 11.5. *Interest rate and risk spreads by type of loan (a) Peso-dollar interest rate speed (b) peso-dollar risk spread*

Notes: The top figure shows the average spread between peso and dollar financing interest rates. The bottom figure shows the average spread between peso and dollar financing risk indicators. The period covered is July 1993–December 1999, when the risk indicator was different for peso and dollar financing. Mortgage loans are excluded because only few banks in the system granted mortgage loans in pesos during this period. Note that the peso-dollar risk spread for bills up to a 89-day term is zero although the interest rate spread is positive. This is due to the fact that when the interest rate spread is small, the same risk indicator is used for peso and dollar loans.

Source: Central Bank of Argentina.

denomination was eliminated—yet another example of the contradictions inherent in the convertibility game of continuously raising the stakes. At any rate, the increasing level of financial dollarization further affirmed the one-peso-one-dollar but at the expense of the peso—that is, by departing from the admittedly unrealistic vision of a strengthening peso that, as noted earlier, was held by the convertibility framers. As financial dollarization persisted and increased, it also became clearer that a disorderly breakdown of the one-peso-one-dollar rule would be an unmitigated catastrophe—it would wreck the solvency of debtors in the non-tradable sector and, hence, of the banking system. As such, dollarization was not an undesirable side effect but rather a crucial ingredient in the convertibility scheme: By increasing the exit costs, it reinforced the "burning-of-the-ships" effect.

The high level of financial dollarization appears to have been a key factor behind the ambivalence of investor confidence in the currency board and the easy shifts in market sentiment. On the one hand, by raising the stakes and creating incentives in favor of policies that would not undermine convertibility, in tranquil times dollarization seems to have reinforced the perception that convertibility would endure, which was reflected in a peso premium that, at its minimum, was remarkably low (see Figure 11.2 before). On the other, during times of financial turbulence when the sustainability of the currency board was put to test, high dollarization exacerbated investor anxiety and the currency premium spiked sharply. By raising the costs of exit from the currency board to catastrophic levels, dollarization seems to have increased the scope for multiple equilibria and self-fulfilling runs, as manifested in a highly volatile currency premium.

11.2.2   Bad times: A currency–growth–debt trap

Right from the beginning of the de la Rúa administration (which assumed power in December 1999), the Argentine economy was caught in a CGD trap. The currency was overvalued, growth was faltering, and the debt was hard to service. This trap was in no small part due to major external shocks. This section analyzes the elements of the trap and the policy failures in addressing them.

The Argentine peso appreciated sharply relative to most trading partners, in tandem with the revaluation of the U.S. dollar *vis-à-vis* European and emerging market currencies (particularly the Brazilian real).[17] The RER overvaluation, in turn, masked the precariousness of Argentina's sovereign debt position. To be sure, the reported debt-to-GDP ratio, while on the rise (from less than 40 percent in 1997 to over 50 percent by the end of 2000), was not high in comparison to other Latin American countries. However, when measured at the *equilibrium* RER, the debt-to-GDP ratio was very high and assailed by a potentially explosive

---

[17] Perry and Servén (this part), for example, estimate that, by the year 2000, the Argentine RER was overvalued by about 50 percent. While estimates may diverge, the perception of overvaluation was widespread both at home and abroad.

dynamic. Perry and Servén (this part) estimate that, relative to a benchmark analysis of fiscal sustainability, the use of the equilibrium RER in the sustainability calculation adds 24 percentage points to the public sector debt-to-GDP ratio in 2001, and leads to an average increase of about two percentage points in the annual primary fiscal surplus required (in 2000–03) to attain intertemporal fiscal solvency.

After 1998, Argentina slipped into an unyielding economic recession and rising unemployment,[18] triggered by a sudden stop in capital flows that, while regional in its origins, was particularly acute and persistent in Argentina after the 1999 Brazilian devaluation.[19] This capital flow reversal, together with doubts about fiscal viability, was reflected in sharp increases in the marginal cost of capital for Argentina (as measured by the spread of Argentine bonds over U.S. Treasury bonds), reinforcing pessimistic expectations regarding future growth and fiscal revenues, and exacerbating the perception of a potentially explosive debt trajectory. All of this fed doubts about the sustainability of the one-peso-one-dollar commitment.[20]

The government's strategy to break free from the CGD trap focused on reviving growth, although the means to achieve this objective changed dramatically after April 2001, when Mr. Cavallo took the post of Minister of Economy.[21] During 2000, growth resumption was sought indirectly—trying to regain investor confidence through fiscal adjustment, including the tax increase ("impuestazo") enacted in January 2000. It was hoped that improved confidence would eventually lead to more capital inflows and growth, making the debt and current account sustainable. To be sure, the authorities also tried to address the problem of currency overvaluation indirectly, through a rather marginal flexibilization of labor markets.[22] In addition, as confidence was not restored and growth failed to pick up, the authorities shifted their attention towards calming fears of a possible debt default. The December 2000 IMF bailout package (advertised as a US$40 billion package) was negotiated with this latter objective prominently in mind. However, none of these actions achieved the expected results and hopes of reviving growth faded away.

---

[18] GDP shrank by nearly 4 percent in 1999 (although it registered a rather strong, albeit fleeting, revival in the last quarter of 1999). GDP continued to contract at about 2 percent per year in 2000–01. Open unemployment rose from about 13 percent in 1998 to over 15 percent in 2000.

[19] Perry and Servén (this part) provide evidence that: (a) during 1999 Argentina was not affected as severely as other countries in Latin America by the slowdown in capital flows; and (b) the sharp reversal of capital flows to Argentina in 2000–01 was mainly endogenous to domestic factors.

[20] Some people still argue that the currency was not overvalued, as most observers claimed at the time. Note, however, that, even if this was the case, a widespread *belief* that the currency is overvalued is enough to generate a preventive retrenchment of capital flows that could give rise to a CGD trap, as described in this section. See Razin and Sadka (2001) for an analytical discussion.

[21] See the Appendix 12A.1. Argentina's *Via Crucis*, in Perry and Servén (this part) for a chronology of the political and economic events from December 1999 to May 2003.

[22] The approval of the labor market reform was linked to a bribery scandal, in which senators were accused of receiving payments from the government to approve the law. The scandal was unresolved, leading to the resignation of vice-president Carlos Alvarez.

Minister Cavallo banked on his prestige to pull off the rescue. Empowered by Congress with special powers, he focused on rekindling growth, but this time directly, through heterodox measures. These included imposing a tax on imports and subsidizing exports (a fiscal devaluation for trade transactions), lowering reserve requirements, and announcing the eventual peg of the peso to the dollar *and* the euro (with equal weights), once these two currencies reached parity. From hindsight, it is clear that the growth-focused strategy, particularly in Cavallo's heterodox version, was half-blind. It not only did not yield growth, it also *escalated the uncertainty about the debt and currency components of CGD trap.*[23]

Doubts about the maintenance of the one-to-one correspondence of the peso to the dollar soared after April 2001 (see Figure 11.2).[24] This correspondence had already been broken through the back door for trade transactions and it was feared that it could be broken also for financial transactions. In addition, Cavallo had pushed successfully for the resignation of central bank president Pedro Pou, who was viewed by investors as a strict guardian of monetary and banking system soundness.[25] Moreover, Cavallo used his special powers to reform the central bank charter, removing limits on the ability of the central bank to inject liquidity, thereby effectively dismantling the money-issuance rule that underpinned convertibility.[26]

At the same time, uncertainty about the debt component of the CGD trap grew as the government procrastinated in taking a decision on the debt. Instead of accepting that an orderly approach to debt reduction was becoming a necessity following the failed attempts to restore growth, the government averted debt service arrears temporarily by absorbing the liquidity of the financial system— mainly of banks and pension funds. In particular, in April 2001, the government used moral suasion to place US$2 billion of bonds with banks in Argentina, allowing banks to use those bonds to meet up to 18 percent of the liquidity requirement. The banking system, thus, became less liquid and more exposed to a government default. Total banking system claims on the government rose

[23] Whether this risky bet was justified *ex ante* is difficult to ascertain given the foreseeable costs of attempting an early exit. At any rate, the decision illustrates how a government facing a dilemma between a sure loss and an improbable salvation is tempted to gamble by adopting desperate measures that make the loss even larger in the event those measures fail.

[24] For a detailed chronology of the impact of political and economic announcements on the currency premium, see Schmukler and Servén (2002).

[25] At the time of this writing (January 2003), the Argentine Supreme Court was discussing the constitutionality of Mr. Pou's forced resignation.

[26] As mentioned above, prior to the April 2001 amendments to the central bank charter, dollar-denominated, internationally traded Argentine government bonds valued at market prices could be treated as part of the country's disposable international reserves. After the amendments, the claims on the government received by the central bank (in repo or as collateral) in the context of its liquidity operations with the banking system no longer counted as part of the maximum of 33 percent of disposable international reserves. Thus, the April 2001 amendments enabled unlimited injection of lender-of-last-liquidity with the backing of government paper, thereby effectively eliminating the money issuance rule of convertibility. In practice, the claims on the government that the central bank received as part of its lender-of-last-resort activity during 2001 did not exceed the 33 percent limit. Nevertheless, the amendment contributed to increasing the doubts that the currency board would be maintained.

(a)

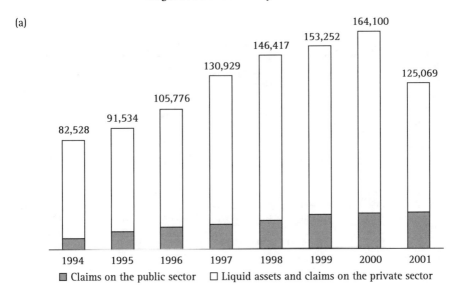

Claims on the public sector   Liquid assets and claims on the private sector

(b)

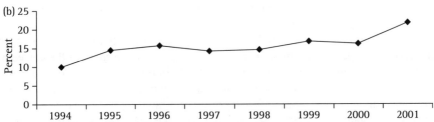

Figure 11.6. *Financial system: Exposure to public sector (a) total assets in millions of dollars and (b) share of claims on the public sector to total assets*

Notes: Financial system is defined to include public banks, private domestic banks, foreign banks, and non-bank financial institutions. Figures correspond to end-of-year values.

Source: Central Bank of Argentina.

gradually from less than 10 percent of total bank assets at the end of 1994 to 15 percent at the end of 2000, and jumped to over 20 percent by end-2001, as shown in Figure 11.6. This, in turn, heightened concerns about a potential abandonment of the currency board. As choices to finance the deficit through debt rapidly shrank, the specter of money printing loomed bigger. In the process, the fate of public finances, the banking system, and the currency became tightly linked.

The elements of the CGD trap reinforced each other in a perverse way. Continued economic contraction, increasing doubts about the sustainability of the public debt, and soaring uncertainty about the permanence of the one-peso-one-dollar rule fell into a vicious circle. This led to capitulation—including a massive run on bank deposits (see Figure 11.7). The run, in turn, precipitated an economic meltdown by the end of 2001, which featured the imposition of limits

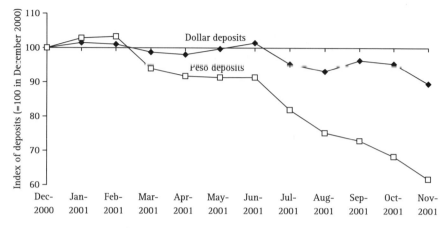

Figure 11.7. *Evolution of private deposits*

Source: Central Bank of Argentina.

on cash withdrawals from bank accounts ("corralito") and the consequent disruption of the payment system.[27]

The "corralito" was immediately followed by angry riots that prompted changes in presidents, a default on the government debt, the abandonment of the currency board into floating (an initial 40 percent devaluation immediately proved insufficient), the forcible conversion of dollar-denominated financial contracts into peso-denominated ones with different conversion rates applied to bank loans and deposits ("asymmetric stock pesofication"), and the lengthening of their maturities.[28] This unprecedented destruction of property rights was compounded later on by new measures (e.g. the de-indexations of part of the pesofied loans, changes in the corporate bankruptcy code, a series of court rulings on "amparos" regarding deposit freeze, etc.).

---

[27] The name *corralito* ("little fence") was initially adopted because deposits could be used freely inside the financial system but could not leave the system. This measure should not be confused with the forcible reprogramming of time deposits that followed in January 2002, referred to locally as the *corralón* ("large fence").

[28] Dollar loans were forcibly converted to pesos at 1 dollar = 1 peso, while bank deposits were converted at 1 dollar = 1.4 pesos. Pesofied loans and deposits were indexed to the CPI, although a part of the loans was subsequently de-indexed. Also, pesofied deposits (loans) were subject to a minimum (maximum), administratively imposed, interest rate. The asymmetric pesofication transferred part of the currency mismatch that had previously resided in the balance sheets of debtors in the non-tradable sector to the balance sheets of their creditor banks, resulting in less losses than otherwise to depositors. However, the (already bankrupt) government undertook to compensate banks for the impact of the asymmetric pesofication on their net worth, through the so-called "compensation bond." On impact, the asymmetric pesofication left banks with a capital loss *and* a major open exposure to foreign exchange risk (because their foreign liabilities cannot be pesofied through a domestic decree). The compensating bond would thus have to offset both problems. The amount of the compensating bond is estimated at 14.6 billion pesos. To close the open foreign exchange position, the equivalent of 13.8 billion pesos (US$9.8 billion) of that total would have to be denominated in dollars.

In the next section we abstract from the stream of ill-advised measures that followed the collapse of convertibility to examine in some detail the salient features of the depositor run that precipitated the collapse.

11.2.3 Meltdown: Currency and deposit run

Understanding the nature of the bank run in Argentina is essential to answering key questions regarding alternative paths to exit convertibility. Could a different exit strategy have enabled the authorities to preserve, and capitalize on, the high quality of the banking system and its regulatory framework, including the large presence of foreign banks? Was the "corralito" a coarse measure mainly aimed at saving the few (mostly public) banks with significant fiscal exposures that were suffering large deposit withdrawals? If so, was the "corralito" a vehicle through which the government exported the crisis to otherwise liquid institutions, leading in the process to a currency run that made the abandonment of convertibility inevitable? Or was the "corralito" rather the consequence of a run on the banking system? What triggered the run, perceived currency risk, perceived country risk, or both? What was behind the run is ultimately an empirical question, to which we now turn.

To better identify the factors that fueled the run, we compiled a rich bank-level data set on deposits that distinguishes both across currencies (peso and dollar), as well as deposit type (demand, savings, and time). We also used banks' balance sheet data to control for bank-specific fundamentals. We analyzed the top fifty banks, which accounted for 98 percent of total private deposits as of December 2000. Our empirical analysis supports the view that it was the rising perception of currency risk that generated a run on the currency, illustrated by a shift from peso to dollar deposits between February 2001 and July–August 2001, which evolved into a run on bank deposits regardless of currency of denomination or bank characteristics, probably out of increasing fears that a major devaluation could lead to bank failures and some form of deposit confiscation.[29]

Figures 11.7 and 11.8 show the evolution of deposits and of the currency premium over time. Regarding demand and savings deposits, while dollar deposits remained stable, even increasing up to the end of 2001, peso deposits started to decline after February 2001. The pattern is more salient in the case of time deposits, with dollar deposits steadily increasing until the second semester of 2001.

The December 2000–November 2001 deposit withdrawal was not just focused on few banks or on certain types of banks (Figure 11.9). It spread to almost all banks as the crisis progressed.[30] By November 2001, forty-seven of the top fifty banks had suffered withdrawals relative to December 2000. Local private, foreign

---

[29] In this regard, the 2001 run presents a striking similarity with the post-Tequila crisis, both in terms of the displayed symptoms as well as the underlying drivers.

[30] Banks differed, however, in their level of liquidity. Towards the end of 2001, as the deposit run intensified, the government put pressure on the most liquid private banks to recirculate their liquidity towards the relatively less liquid (mainly public) banks. This is consistent with the view of the corralito as an extreme (and highly inefficient) way of distributing the burden of the run between liquid and illiquid banks. It does not detract, however, from the fact that the run was systemic in nature and was not directed only to those banks with relatively weak fundamentals.

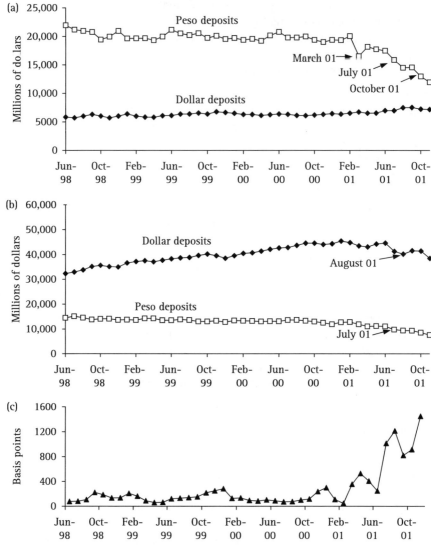

Figure 11.8. *(a) Demand and savings deposits (b) time deposits, and (c) differential of interest rates*

Notes: Deposits include private and public deposits. Differential of interest rates is defined as the spread between domestic interest rates for 30-day time deposits in pesos and U.S. dollars.

Source: Central Bank of Argentina.

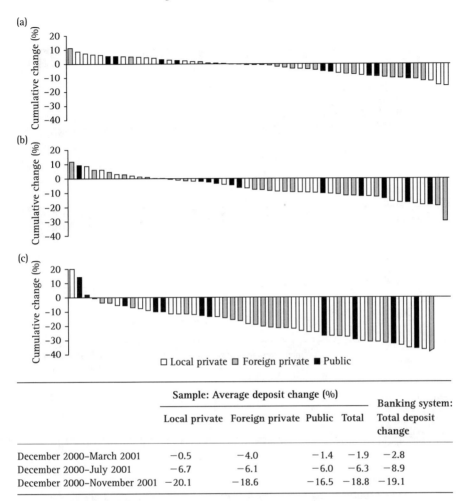

Figure 11.9. *Change in private deposits for fifty largest banks*
(a) December 2000–March 2001 (b) December 2000–July 2001, and
(c) December 2000–November 2001

Notes: Financial system is defined to include public banks, private domestic banks, foreign banks, and non-bank financial institutions. Figures correspond to end-of-year values. The bars in the graphs represent the cumulative change in private deposits sorted from largest positive to largest negative change. A positive (negative) bar means that the bank gains (loses) deposits during the period. The different colors indicate whether the bank is local private, foreign private, or public. The 50 banks in the sample represent 98% of private deposits and 96% of total deposits in December 2000. In the bottom table, banking system total deposit change includes all banks in the system.

Source: Central Bank of Argentina.

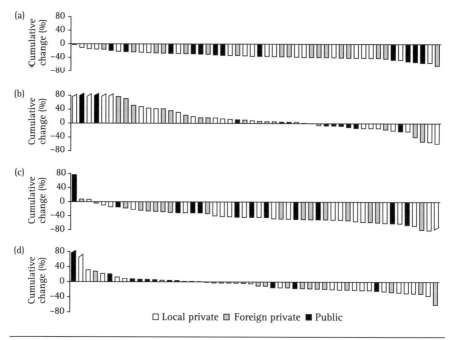

	Sample: Average deposit change (%)				Banking system: Total deposit change (%)
	Local private	Foreign private	Public	Total	
Peso demand and savings deposits	−31.5	−35.7	−36.3	−34.1	−36.0
Dollar demand and savings deposits	35.6	14.4	19.8	24.6	11.3
Peso time deposits	−45.2	−37.3	−32.7	−39.5	−37.7
Dollar time deposits	−6.5	−13.0	7.5	−5.4	−13.9

Figure 11.10. *Change in private deposits for fifty largest banks by deposit type December 2000 to November 2001 (a) Peso and (b) dollar demand and savings deposits by bank and (c) peso and (d) dollar time deposits by bank*

Notes: Financial system is defined to include public banks, private domestic banks, foreign banks, and non-bank financial institutions. Figures correspond to end-of-year values.

The bars in the graphs represent the cumulative change in private deposits sorted from largest positive to largest negative change. A positive (negative) bar means that the bank gains (loses) deposits during the period. The different colors indicate whether the bank is local private, foreign private, or public. The 50 banks in the sample represent 98% of private deposits and 96% of total deposits in December 2000. In the bottom table, banking system total deposit change includes all banks in the system.

Source: Central Bank of Argentina.

private, and public banks were all affected by the run, with no particular ranking by type of bank. A breakdown by currency and deposit type confirms that there was no particular pattern regarding withdrawals by bank type (Figure 11.10). Withdrawals of peso deposits were generalized and substantial. The average withdrawal for the top fifty banks was 34 percent for peso demand and passbook savings deposits and about 40 percent for peso time deposits. But the figures are different for dollar deposits. There were more banks that gained rather than lost dollar demand and savings deposits—on average, the top fifty banks gained close to 25 percent of dollar demand and savings deposits relative to the December 2000 level. By contrast, more banks lost than gained dollar time deposits—on average, the top fifty banks lost 5 percent of their dollar time deposits, although eighteen out of the fifty banks registered an increase in their dollar time deposits. This suggests that whatever flight to quality there may have been, it mainly involved dollar time deposits and did not favor, as expected, foreign-owned over locally owned banks.

A more formal examination of the deposit run yields the same insights. We follow the methodology used in Martinez Peria and Schmukler (2001), which regresses the change in monthly deposits on different bank-specific characteristics to gauge the importance of bank fundamentals. If depositors distinguished between banks with different risks, bank fundamentals would appear as statistically significant in the regression. We run the same regressions for different types of deposits and for different periods, namely, a "pre-crisis" period (1997–99) and a "crisis" period (2000–01). Bank fundamentals are chosen based on standard measures of bank risk characteristics. Since this information is published with a delay of three months, variables are lagged accordingly. We also add bank-type dummies to test whether the crisis affected different types of banks differently.

Table 11.4 reports the results for the monthly change in dollar and peso deposits, and for the pre-crisis and crisis periods. The ratio of capital to total assets and that of non-performing to total loans are bank-specific risk features that had an statistically significant effect (with the expected sign) during the pre-crisis period. The other explanatory variables, including the bank-type dummies, are not significant. However, during the crisis period, almost all bank-specific risk variables become insignificant. Only cash over total assets is significant in the regression for peso deposits, while no variable is significant in the regression for dollar deposits. Table 11.5 shows that the proportion of the R-squared explained by bank fundamentals decreases from 19 percent during the pre-crisis period to less than 4 percent during the crisis period in the case of peso deposits. A similar phenomenon affects dollar deposits, with the proportion falling from 10 to 1 percent. In other words, the importance of systemic effects (relative to bank fundamentals) rose sharply during the crisis period, suggesting that whatever the influence bank-specific fundamentals had on depositors' behavior in the preceding period, it was dwarfed by systemic factors during the 2001 run, and confirming the pattern displayed in Figures 11.7–11.10 examined above.[31]

---

[31] This pattern is similar to those obtained for the Tequila crisis in Argentina and Mexico, and the debt crisis in Chile, as studied by Martinez Peria and Schmukler (2001).

Augusto de la Torre et al.

Table 11.4. *Response of peso and dollar deposits to bank risk characteristics*

	Pre-crisis period 1997–99		Crisis period 2000–01	
	Growth of peso deposits	Growth of dollar deposits	Growth of peso deposits	Growth of dollar deposits
Capital/Total assets $(t-3)$	0.112 *	0.091	0.039	0.051
	[0.068]	[0.062]	[0.053]	[0.059]
NPL/Total loans $(t-3)$	−0.104 **	−0.067 *	0.009	−0.023
	[0.041]	[0.038]	[0.028]	[0.031]
Mortgage loans/Total loans $(t-3)$	−0.009	−0.007	−0.024	−0.003
	[0.032]	[0.029]	[0.027]	[0.029]
Personal loans/Total loans $(t-3)$	−0.010	−0.019	−0.021	0.001
	[0.027]	[0.025]	[0.021]	[0.023]
Cash/Total assets $(t-3)$	−0.112	−0.136	0.167 **	0.081
	[0.094]	[0.086]	[0.075]	[0.083]
Public exposure $(t-3)$	−0.036	0.050	0.002	−0.053
	[0.048]	[0.044]	[0.036]	[0.040]
Dummy public bank	0.010	−0.009	−0.004	0.008
	[0.014]	[0.013]	[0.011]	[0.012]
Dummy private local bank	−0.007	−0.011	−0.007	−0.004
	[0.010]	[0.009]	[0.009]	[0.010]
Overall R-squared	0.05	0.08	0.07	0.15
Number of observations	1,469	1,469	1,144	1,144
Number of banks	50	50	50	50

* Significant at 10%.
** Significant at 5%.
*** Significant at 1%.

Notes: The table reports regressions of growth of deposits on bank fundamentals including time dummies. Public exposure is calculated as public bonds and loans to the public sector over total assets. Robust standard errors are in brackets.

Table 11.5. *Percentage of variance explained by bank risk characteristics*

	Pre-crisis period 1997–99	Crisis period 2000–01
Growth of peso deposits (%)	19.2	3.6
	[0.05]	[0.07]
Growth of dollar deposits (%)	10.3	1.2
	[0.08]	[0.15]

Notes: The figures indicate the percentage of the overall R-squared explained by bank fundamentals, as a proportion of all the time varying variables. They are calculated as the R-squared of the regressions of growth of deposits on bank fundamentals over the R-squared of the regressions of growth of deposits on both bank fundamentals and time dummies. Overall R-squared is in brackets.

Table 11.6. *Private deposit withdrawal by currency and type*
December 2000–November 2001

	Growth of demand and savings deposits		Growth of time deposits	
	(1)	(2)	(1)	(2)
Peso				
Currency risk	−0.006***	−0.012***	−0.011***	−0.011***
	[0.001]	[0.003]	[0.001]	[0.004]
Country risk		0.003		0.000
		[0.002]		[0.002]
Country risk* public exposure		0.003		0.000
		[0.006]		[0.008]
Overall *R*-squared	0.03	0.03	0.05	0.05
Number of observations	1,144	1,144	1,144	1,144
Number of banks	50	50	50	50
Dollar				
Currency risk	0.002	−0.006	−0.005***	−0.001
	[0.003]	[0.007]	[0.001]	[0.002]
Country risk		0.004		−0.003**
		[0.004]		[0.001]
Country risk* public exposure		0.000		0.002
		[0.014]		[0.003]
Overall *R*-squared	0.00	0.01	0.05	0.05
Number of observations	1,140	1,140	1,140	1,140
Number of banks	50	50	50	50

* Significant at 10%.
** Significant at 5%.
*** Significant at 1%.

Notes: The table reports regressions of growth of deposits on bank fundamentals and country and currency risks. Although included in the regressions, bank fundamentals are not reported in the table. Figures correspond to end-of-period values. Standard errors are in brackets.

To further probe on the factors behind the systemic effects, we run regressions by type of deposits in which the time dummies are replaced by time-varying variables. The results are reported in Table 11.6 (bank fundamentals are included in the regressions but omitted from the table). The top panel of Table 11.6 displays the results for peso deposits, divided by demand and passbook savings deposits, on the one hand, and time deposits, on the other. The bottom panel shows similar estimations for dollar deposits. Regarding peso deposits, the currency risk (measured by the interest rate differential) is statistically significant for demand and savings as well as time deposits. This result is robust—it holds even when including country risk and the interaction between country risk and exposure to the public sector.[32] By contrast, systemic variables are not statistically significant in the regression for dollar demand and passbook savings deposits—not too surprising given that these deposits remained flat throughout the crisis. Regarding dollar time deposits, the currency risk is statistically significant when introduced as the only systemic factor, but it becomes non-significant when country risk (measured by bond spreads) is introduced. Thus, while currency risk was the dominant factor behind the generalized withdrawal of peso deposits, country risk appears to be a more precise thermometer of the evolution of dollar time deposits. Overall, the result seems to support the view that the crisis was originated in a currency run that affected banks across the board, regardless of their fiscal exposure or other bank-specific characteristics.

11.3   Living or Dying with Hard Pegs: Lessons from Argentina

This section reviews the salient lessons that can be drawn from the Argentine experience for hard pegs and formally dollarized systems. Three sets of lessons are worth emphasizing. The first relates to the practical limitations of a hard peg (including its extreme version of formal dollarization), particularly in the case of countries that do not meet the conditions for an optimal dollar area. The second set relates to issues in designing appropriate prudential norms *given* the hard peg (i.e. accepting its premise that the exchange rate will not be modified). The third one concerns an issue on which the literature on hard pegs has always been speculative: Strategies to exit hard peg arrangements. While the Argentine case certainly does not provide a blueprint for a smooth exit, it does illustrate the costs of suboptimal strategies.

11.3.1   Limitations of hard pegs as commitment mechanisms

As discussed in Section 11.2.1, one obvious benefit of a hard peg system is that, by providing savers with an unquestionable store of value, it boosts financial intermediation, albeit at the expense of rising financial dollarization. The drawbacks of hard pegs have been extensively discussed in the economic literature, particularly for the case of countries, such as Argentina, that do not meet the conditions for an optimal currency area (see the beginning of Section 11.2). Nonetheless, advocates of hard pegs frequently downplay the practical difficulties of establishing greater nominal flexibility in fiscal spending and wages in light of the limitations imposed by the loss of the nominal exchange rate as an adjustment mechanism, and of establishing a fiscal discipline consistent with the

---

[32] The fact that the latter is never significant contradicts the view that depositors run from those banks most exposed to the public sector.

loss of the inflation tax.[33] Moreover, these advocates tend to overstate the potential disciplining spillovers of hard pegs. They often advertise hard pegs as an irrevocable decision that, inasmuch as it restricts monetary financing of the budget, can help foster fiscal prudence, inducing governments eventually to learn to adjust nominal fiscal spending.[34]

This view is naïve and ultimately wrong, particularly in the case of hard peg countries that are open to capital flows but far from meeting optimal currency area-type conditions, therefore exposed to significant shifts in the *equilibrium* RER. The fact is that no matter how credible, a currency board (or dollarization) *per se* does not create nominal flexibility and fiscal discipline.[35] The Argentine experience illustrates this well. To start with, nominal flexibility in fiscal spending is seldom verified in practice (in either emerging or industrial economies). Political realities of democratic processes severely constrain the margin to reduce nominal fiscal expenditure, especially in the context of a recession. As noted, this was a decisive factor in the evolution of the Argentine CGD trap. Nominal adjustment of the Argentine budget was achieved only to a limited extent and in the context of a protracted recession. Indeed, the reduction in public expenditure that should have accompanied the curtailment of access to external financing did not go beyond an insufficient and politically costly wage cut never meant to be permanent.[36]

The restriction on monetary financing of the deficit was not relevant in practice during the good times of convertibility because Argentina had access to voluntary debt placements in international and local markets. In effect, the pro-cyclicality of access to international capital markets helped create incentives against appropriate fiscal discipline in good times.[37] When foreign markets closed, the restriction imposed by convertibility was violated through a somewhat compulsory placing of domestic debt. And when even compulsory access to local banks and other local sources of financing (like pension funds) was exhausted, the public sector resorted to the issuance of central government and provincial paper that differed from currency only cosmetically.

---

[33] To be sure, hard peg advocates recognize these needs, but tend to simply state them as obvious conditions for the success of hard pegs, without highlighting the practical obstacles to their feasibility. For instance, Calvo (2002) writes that hard pegs have "to be supplemented by adequate institutions and regulatory conditions. For example, it is essential that government wages and regulated prices show a high degree of flexibility."

[34] See, for example, Baliño and Enoch (1997) for a discussion of the pros and cons of currency boards.

[35] See, for example, Levy Yeyati (2001) or, for the case of Panamá, Goldfajn and Olivares (2001).

[36] Public sector wages and contracts in the federal government were cut by 13 percent in the second semester of 2001, but the reduction could not be extended to provincial workers. Moreover, although the cuts were meant to adjust endogenously in order to meet the zero-deficit rule, further reductions were judged to be politically unfeasible and were never implemented.

[37] Perry and Servén (this part) analyze cyclically adjusted measures of (federal government) fiscal stance. They show that fiscal policy, thus, assessed was unduly expansionary in the "good" years of 1996–98, and that fiscal adjustment was actually insufficient during 1999–2001, except in few months leading to the 1999 election.

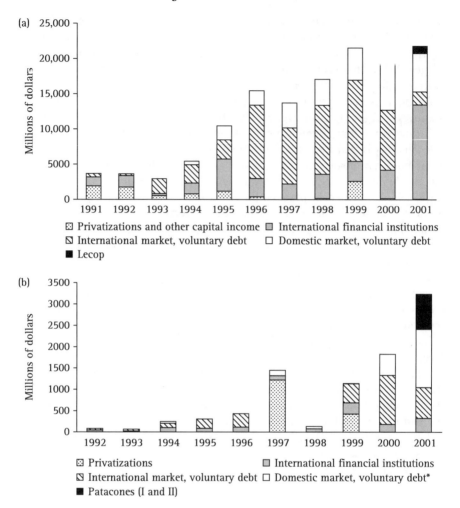

Figure 11.11. *Financing sources (a) federal government and (b) province of Buenos Aires*

* Includes bank debt and national government financing.

Notes: The bars in the graphs represent the cumulative change in private deposits sorted from largest positive to largest negative change. A positive (negative) bar means that the bank gains (loses) deposits during the period. The different colors indicate whether the bank is local private, foreign private, or public. The 50 banks in the sample represent 98% of private deposits and 96% of total deposits in December 2000. In the bottom table, banking system total deposit change includes all banks in the system.

Source: Central Bank of Argentina.

Table 11.7. *Quasi-monies in circulation (millions of Argentine pesos)*

	Denomination	December 2001	March 2002
(a) Federal government	Lecop	1,039	2,543
(b) Provincial "own" securities		1,627	2,591
1. Buenos Aires	Patacón	822	1,591
2. Buenos Aires, City	Porteno	–	–
3. Catamarca	Ley 4,748	26	31
4. Chaco	Quebracho	50	100
5. Cordoba	Lecor	200	300
6. Corrientes	Cecaror	193	185
7. Entre Rios	Bonfe	54	148
8. Formosa	Bocanfor	33	50
9. Jujuy	Patacón	–	6
10. Mendoza	Petróm	–	–
11. La Rioja	Bono de Cancelación	8	8
12. Tucuman	Bocade	98	173
Total quasi-monies (a + b)		2,666	5,134
Total quasi-monies (as percentage of pesos in circulation)		26.2	37.5

Source: Ministry of Economy, Argentina.

Figure 11.11 depicts this process. Growing financing needs were met in the first half of the 1990s by recourse to the sale of state-owned assets and, when this source dried up, by borrowing in international capital markets. After the Tequila crisis, the government started to rely on domestic savings, notably pension funds and local banks, which steadily increased their share up to 2001. Once the funding capacity of the domestic markets was exhausted, the government resorted to the issuance of small-denomination federal bonds (lecop) redeemable for federal tax payments.[38] Similarly, in the case of the province of Buenos Aires, financing needs exceeding local revenues and federal transfers were eventually met by the placement of provincial bonds in domestic markets and the launch of the province's own small denomination paper, the patacón (Table 11.7).[39] Thus, the persistent fiscal imbalance, far from adjusting to the budget constraint presumably imposed by the monetary regime, de facto circumvented it, rendering the regime all but a formal arrangement in this regard.

[38] The figure underestimates the monetary expansion, by excluding indirect deficit financing through central bank lending to Banco Nación, which accelerated substantially during 2001.

[39] Figure 11.1 understates the surge of quasi-money printing. As Table 11.7 indicates, a number of other provinces adopted similar mechanisms to finance their deficits and, as a result, the total stock of quasi-monies reached more than 2.6 billion pesos or about 26 percent of total pesos in circulation by the end of December 2001, and had doubled by the end of March 2002.

Two lessons can be drawn from this evidence. First, there are perils in trying to impose a hard budget constraint when the government is incapable of squaring its fiscal accounts in the short run. One key peril is the spillover of fiscal problems into the financial system. On its way towards outright monetary financing of its budget, the Argentine government dramatically increased the exposure of the banking sector to fiscal default. We discuss the prudential implications of this process in Section 11.3.2 below.

Second, the monetary discipline of hard pegs appears easier to abandon than often believed. This is illustrated by the relative ease with which the Argentine government in need of funds resorted to money printing with another name (lecops, patacones, and the like). It is also clear that the same could have happened under formal dollarization. Dollarization *per se* would not have overcome the CGD trap as long as the fiscal imbalance was a given (at least in the short term); it was not easily reversible by a reduction in nominal public expenditure. Dollarization too would have likely been accompanied by a proliferation of local quasi-monies that would have reflected the simple fact that a fiscal deficit cannot be eliminated merely by a monetary arrangement. Quasi-monies more than a problem in themselves are, therefore, a symptom of a deep inconsistency between a strict monetary framework and the nominal rigidities that this framework cannot magically eliminate.

11.3.2 Prudential lessons

The financial system was not a cause of the Argentine crisis but rather its victim. The evidence clearly indicates that, under convertibility, Argentina was able to build a strong and well-supervised banking system—a model to be emulated by other emerging markets. Moreover, Argentine authorities displayed considerable innovative capacity in developing prudential norms, particularly in terms of liquidity buffers, suitable to a hard peg system (see Appendix 11A.1).

Nonetheless, from hindsight, the Argentine experience reveals some prudential shortcomings and, hence, suggests directions in which prudential policy needs to be tailored further to better deal with risks that are specific not just to hard peg regimes but also, and more broadly, to financial systems that are de facto highly dollarized. Three weaknesses in the otherwise sound Argentine regulatory framework can be identified by taking as given the rules of the convertibility game—that is, by assuming the permanency of the one-peso-one-dollar rule. They have to do with (*a*) the insufficient realization that *general* liquidity buffers do not fully protect the payments system from a run; (*b*) the exposure of the banking system to government default; and (*c*) the link between debtor capacity to pay and the deflationary adjustment to a more depreciated equilibrium RER.

High liquidity requirements, as those in effect in Argentina during the second half of the 1990s, enhance the resiliency of the banking system—they cushion the system *vis-à-vis* liquidity shocks and deter runs, thereby, reducing the scope for multiple equilibria. Thanks to its liquidity requirements, the Argentine banking system withstood a prolonged and severe process of deposit withdrawal in the Tequila and also during 2001. At the same time, however, the Argentine experience suggests that once a run is underway, relaxing liquid reserve requirements can have adverse signaling effects that exacerbate the attack on the peso (instead of spurring credit growth as Minister Cavallo hoped for), further weakening confidence.[40] Moreover, Argentina illustrates that, as confidence collapses, a *general* liquidity requirement (available to all deposits on a first come first served basis) fails to protect the payment system, as liquidity is rapidly consumed by the flight of time deposits.

The lesson is sobering. In the absence of an effective and credible lender-of-last-resort, the payment system is vulnerable and can collapse under a run, even when liquidity is high but still a fraction of deposits equally available to pay *any* deposit withdrawal.[41] It, thus, would appear that, under a currency board or dollarization, the protection of the payment system from bank runs might actually require prudential norms that give some form of priority of claim over available liquidity to transactional deposits, that is, to deposits that are germane to the functioning of the payment system. This does not necessarily require a narrow-bank type structure. It could also be achieved, for instance, by an *ex ante* rule that, under specified conditions, earmarks available liquidity to demand deposits. While the operationalization of this concept does not appear easy, the prudential principle on which it is based warrants serious consideration. The objective of such prudential innovation would be to preserve the functioning of the payment system even in the extreme scenario where banks are unable to honor withdrawals of time deposits.[42]

The second prudential weakness has to do with credit risk. It arises from the Argentine failure to sufficiently isolate the solvency of the banking system from the solvency of the government. As discussed earlier, no matter how credible, a currency board (or dollarization) *per se* does not create fiscal discipline. To the extent that banks hold significant claims on the domestic government, a fiscal and public debt crisis would immediately affect banking system solvency.

---

[40] During the Tequila crisis in the mid-1990s, the Argentine authorities reduced liquidity requirements to help the banking system confront the deposit withdrawals, and this regulatory action did not seem to have exacerbated such withdrawals. The deleterious effect of the relaxation of liquidity requirements during the 2001 run was probably because it contributed to the already high uncertainty about the authorities' commitment to the currency board. Many analysts cautioned about the potential negative effects of using prudential policy as a counter-cyclical instrument in 2001. In effect, this issue was a major cause of dispute between the central bank and the ministry of economy.

[41] See Chang and Velasco (2000) for an argument along these lines.

[42] Developments during the recent crisis in financially dollarized Uruguay are an *ex post* rendition of this concept. In effect, as the run intensified, the Uruguayan authorities decided to concentrate central bank reserves (which were bolstered by an IMF-led emergency package) on fully backing demand deposits in troubled banks. Time deposits of troubled banks were, by contrast, restructured by decree. The same could be achieved in a more orderly manner by imposing *ex ante* a stop-loss clause on the use of bank liquid reserves, forcing automatic restructuring of time deposits once the decline reaches certain threshold.

However, one silver lining of convertibility (or dollarization) is that, in principle, it makes it possible to protect banking intermediation from the vagaries of the fiscal process, including an event of government debt default, *as long as* banks are not significantly exposed to domestic government risk. The reason is that the store of value that underpins financial intermediation in a currency board (or dollarized) country is ultimately the dollar, whose quality does not depend *directly* on the solvency of the domestic government.[43] This feature should have been harnessed through prudential norms in Argentina, all the more considering the country's recurrent fiscal problems. As described in the appendix, the authorities moved in this direction belatedly, in 2000, when they introduced mark-to-market requirements for government bond holdings and established a positive weight for loans to the government for the purposes of determining regulatory capital requirements. It would have been advisable to take this approach more aggressively and much earlier in the decade, and to complement it by limiting the exposure to the public sector of individual banks, and the amount of government debt that could count as part of the assets eligible to meet bank liquidity requirements.

The third weakness has to do, again, with credit risk—the latent NPLs in the context of a misalignment of the RER relative to a more depreciated *equilibrium* level. Convertibility (or formal dollarization), as Roubini (2001) has correctly stressed, does not immunize a country from the balance sheet effects of a RER adjustment. In particular, RER overvaluation is corrected under convertibility (or dollarization) slowly, through painful deflation and unemployment (particularly if rigidities in the labor market are significant), which certainly erodes the capacity to pay of debtors whose earnings come from the non-tradable sector.[44] Under a hard peg or a de facto highly dollarized financial system that breeds a systematic and severe "fear of floating," the erosion of capacity to pay of debtors in the non-tradable sector occurs *regardless of whether the loans in question are denominated in dollars or in pesos.*

The lesson here has much less to do with the Argentine failure to single out the currency of loan denomination in the design of its prudential norms, than with the failure to explicitly recognize the special credit risk of loans to debtors in the non-tradable sector—a credit risk that would materialize in the event of significant adverse shocks that led to a deflationary adjustment of the RER. This risk arises from the simple fact that debtors in the non-tradable sector cannot denominate their debts in terms of non-tradables or hedge when contracting debts in terms of tradables. The implication is that the authorities in fixed-exchange rate economies

---

[43] In contrast, this condition cannot be obtained where the store of value is the domestic currency.

[44] Deflationary adjustment in a currency-board (or dollarized) country lowers the value of non-tradable income in terms of tradables, which implies that the burden of the debt rises (capacity to pay falls) for the non-tradable sector. By contrast, in a country with a flexible exchange rate (i.e. where a fixed parity is *not* part of the social contract) and *without* a substantial problem of dollar debts in the non-tradable sector, the adjustment to a more depreciated equilibrium RER would come through nominal depreciation, which would be associated with an *improvement* (via debt dilution) in the capacity to pay of debtors in the non-tradable sector.

would be well advised to establish relatively tougher loan classification criteria, higher loan-loss provisioning rules, and possibly also a higher weight for the purposes of measuring capital requirements for loans to the non-tradable sector *in either currency.*[45] In addition, the authorities could promote the development of a market for financial contracts indexed to the price of non-tradables.

A final point is useful to clarify how the previous analysis can be extended once the assumption of a permanent peg is relaxed. While the first two lessons are fairly general to any monetary arrangement, a distinction must be made in the third lesson for the case of financially dollarized economies in which changes in the nominal exchange rate have non-zero probability. While the currency of denomination is irrelevant where the peg is preserved, it is crucial in the event of a nominal depreciation of the local currency. In financially dollarized economies under flexible regimes, the considerations discussed in the previous paragraph apply only to dollar loans to non-tradable income producers. The presence of a not fully credible peg in a financially dollarized environment adds an obvious complication. Conditional on the survival of the peg, non-tradable debtors are exposed to RER risk regardless of whether they borrow in pesos or in dollars. However, if the peg is abandoned, their exposure is more dramatic but only if they borrow in dollars. Thus, some degree of currency discrimination in prudential norms may be warranted in countries committed to a hard peg, although these considerations should be weighted against a signaling effect that may weaken the credibility of the peg.

11.3.3   Exit strategies

With the benefit of hindsight, this section focuses on counterfactual analysis: What would have happened if Argentina had adopted different policies in the months *before* the crisis erupted? And, were there superior exit strategies open to Argentina from the CGD trap? By nature, this type of analysis is very difficult to back with real data and hard to substantiate. Nevertheless, a serious consideration of the different arguments presented here may help to draw relevant policy lessons for the future, particularly for countries with weak national currencies and highly dollarized financial systems.

Four alternative courses of action can be identified in relation to the Argentine case, particularly for the period after the January 1999 devaluation of

---

[45] Given that information asymmetry problems in buoyant times lead to rising bank exposure to the non-tradable sector without adequate internalization of risks, a system of counter-cyclical loan-loss provisioning requirements, like the one established at end-1999 by the Bank of Spain (Circular No. 9/1999 of December 17, 1999), could help address risks in loans to the non-tradable sector. This is because lending booms are mainly to the non-tradable sector and, hence, the loan decay after the boom affects primarily loans to non-tradable producers. The Spanish system requires a build-up of counter-cyclical provisions in good times (thereby curbing excessive dividend distributions), which are shifted into specific provisions in bad times (without passing through the income statement) as the loan portfolio decays.

the Brazilian *real*. Those that emphasized the RER overvaluation as the source of the sluggish growth recommended floating the currency, despite its adverse balance sheet effects (for instance, Roubini 2001; Krugman 2001). Those that disbelieved the existence of a demand for a floating peso recommended *de jure* dollarization (for instance, Dornbusch 2001; Calvo 2002). Those concerned about the balance sheet implications of a float but also worried about the RER overvaluation, recommended "stock pesofication cum float"—that is, the forcible conversion of dollar-denominated domestic contracts into CPI-indexed peso-denominated ones, followed by the abandonment of the peg (in particular, Hausmann 2001). In Section 11.3.3.4 below, we submit a fourth alternative: Early dollarization of existing financial contracts ("stock dollarization") complemented by the introduction of a new national currency ("pesofication at the margin") to function as a means of payments.

The main messages from the counterfactual analysis are as follows. The floating alternative could have corrected the overvaluation problem, but would have destroyed the convertibility contract and, by fueling the currency run of peso depositors, would have had a massive and immediate adverse impact on debtor and banking system solvency. Formal dollarization at a 1 : 1 rate would have respected the structure of property rights and would have had a better chance of preventing the run on deposits, but would have done nothing to attenuate the protracted and contractionary RER adjustment.[46] Stock pesofication cum float was probably the most disorderly exit alternative. While in principle it limited the immediate impact on balance sheets of the unavoidable RER adjustment by shifting the losses to depositors, its destructive effect on property rights and institutions will probably have long-lasting costs in terms of financial desintermediation. Moreover, by creating a huge peso overhang in the context of a currency run, it fueled the deposit flight and the unprecedented exchange rate overshooting that followed. For the same reasons, stock dollarization cum pesofication at the margin could have averted the run. It would not have spared debtors in the non-tradable sector from the adverse balance sheet effects of the devaluation. But, by providing a margin for nominal flexibility, it could have facilitated the RER adjustment without unduly disfiguring property rights.

11.3.3.1 *Float*
Floating the peso would have immediately addressed the C component of the CGD trap, albeit at the cost of: (*a*) A run on the currency, as peso depositors moved to protect the real value of their savings, adding to the exchange rate overshooting; (*b*) a sharp and immediate deterioration of the payment capacity of private and public sector debtors in the non-tradable sector, *compounded by the overshooting to be expected from the currency run*; and (*c*) a run on bank deposits, as agents anticipated that banks would become insolvent immediately

---

[46] If done at a much more depreciated rate, formal dollarization would have had similar (immediate) adverse effects on debtor and banking system solvency as the previous alternative.

after the float. Moreover, a disorderly float in the context of widespread dollar debts among non-dollar earners would have likely led to a long period of continued RER depreciation, as Ecuador's experience suggests.[47]

While the second cost was inevitable in the context of a RER adjustment, and may have prompted government action to compensate bank losses and minimize depositors' misgivings about bank solvency, the currency run induced by the floating of the peso was the main drawback of the "just float" exit strategy. The resulting exchange rate overshooting would have not only accelerated the RER adjustment but also exacerbated its balance sheet effects. Even if depositors were allowed to dollarize their savings within the banking system (as Minister Cavallo encouraged by end-2001, once the run was underway), existing limits on foreign exchange open positions would have forced banks to drastically reduce dollar *vis-à-vis* peso deposit rates to balance their positions, which could have resulted in a dollar deposit flight. At any rate, it is not obvious whether an early move to a float would have triggered a run to the dollar bill. But it seems realistic to assume that, once underway, such a run would have only ended once deposits became dollarized, an outcome that could have been achieved in a more orderly fashion through a preemptive *de jure* dollarization of all financial contracts, as explained in Section 11.3.3.4.

From a political economy perspective, a substantive devaluation would have coordinated the actions of debtors (even those in the tradable sector that preserved their to capacity pay) and would have likely triggered an enormous pressure on the government to provide exchange rate insurance or some kind of compensation to private debtors, increasing either the fiscal cost of the bailout, the level of NPLs, or both.[48]

Such likely consequences made the "just float" alternative highly unlikely politically, particularly in 1999 when there was not still a clear perception of the imminence and size of the crisis. From a practical point of view, however, and as the margin to avoid a full-blown crisis narrowed, many analysts came to believe that, in the event of a float, something drastic had to be done to avoid its deleterious impact on balance sheets.

11.3.3.2 *Stock pesofication cum float*
Because of widespread balance sheet mismatches (dollar debts of non-dollar earners), an increasing number of analysts believed that exiting convertibility by floating required the prior pesofication of existing domestic financial contracts by decree. As the argument goes, without prior stock pesofication, a significant and discrete devaluation would have immediately wrecked debtors in

---

[47] Ecuador's 1999 crisis illustrates the dire consequences of floating in the context of a weak fiscal position and widespread currency mismatches (dollar debts of non-dollar earners). The crisis deepened dramatically as nominal devaluation and debtor insolvency were caught in a feedback loop, leading to an excruciatingly long period of a collapsing RER. See de la Torre et al. (2002*a*).

[48] In turn, the perception of a bankrupt financial sector as NPLs mounted, could have re-ignited the run on bank deposits.

the non-tradable sector and, hence, the banking system. A way to deal with the adverse real and financial impact of a devaluation would have been a massive public bailout (of banks and firms), but this possibility was by mid-2001 out of the question for a government on the verge of default. By contrast, stock pesofi-cation cum float promised a way to address the C component of the CGD trap that presumably avoided the adverse balance sheet effect on debtors *by transfer-ring the burden of the expected bailout directly to private creditors.*[49] It was the alternative chosen by the Argentine government under pressure at the beginning of 2002.

The forcible pesofication of domestic financial contracts only created a mass of previously dollarized savings whose owners could not wait to redollarize them before the expected RER adjustment drastically reduced their dollar value. Even after abstracting from the social discontent that such a massive confisca-tion unsurprisingly stirred,[50] one could not ignore the fact that pesofication could only exacerbate the ongoing currency run, fueling the overshooting of the nominal exchange rate, and turning a potential solvency problem into an imme-diate liquidity problem. Stock pesofication was a desperate attempt to escape what Eichengreen and Hausmann (1999) call the "original sin," but it gave way to a graver sin—the murder of money as store of value.[51] Pesofied Argentina now awaits a sort of miracle, that is, the resurrection of the peso as a store of value and, with it, the regeneration of peso financial intermediation.

Was stock pesofication cum float a feasible alternative for earlier, more tranquil times? Would it have been less destructive then? We have serious doubts that there is a yes answer to these questions. Since forcible stock pesofication cum float nec-essarily implied a departure from the one-peso-one-dollar rule, no government had an incentive to implement such a departure in tranquil times. Forcible pesofi-cation cum float was therefore a feasible alternative only for turbulent times.[52] In addition, the massive violation of property rights implied in stock pesofication

---

[49] Not surprisingly, this option appeared late in the crisis process and was originally presented in the context of the debt restructuring debate, with an emphasis on the compulsory conversion of sovereign debt. At the time of this writing, the Supreme Court was considering a ruling stipulating the redollarization of deposits. Since the redollarization of debts appeared politically unlikely, it was widely believed that such an action by the Supreme Court would induce the government to assume the banks' balance sheet losses. Under that scenario, the pesofication adventure would go full circle to become a blanket exchange rate guarantee to be financed by taxpayers in years to come—a massive bailout that stock pesofication was intended to avoid.

[50] This discontent had non-negligible political economy consequences, as witnessed by the subse-quent reluctance of the judicial system to validate the pesofication and the decision of the govern-ment to allow the redollarization of reprogrammed deposits through their swap for dollar government bonds.

[51] As defined by Eichengreen and Hausmann (1999) the "original sin" refers to the condition of a country that is unable to issue peso debt in international markets. As a result, such country is tragi-cally trapped between currency mismatches (it can only issue long-term debt in dollars) and maturity mismatches (local markets only accept short-duration peso debt).

[52] Indeed, it was an alternative that almost by necessity had to be implemented in the context of a change in government.

(and the massive transfer of wealth involved) meant that any anticipation of it would have triggered a run. Hence, stock pesofication cum float would have required the simultaneous establishment of a deposit freeze or securitization as well as widespread capital controls in order to keep depositors and investors from fleeing.

In sum, stock pesofication cum float was arguably: (*a*) Not an alternative that could have been feasibly implemented in tranquil times or without a change of government; (*b*) an alternative that would have in any case provoked a run, requiring a deposit freeze of some form; and (*c*) a deleterious alternative for financial intermediation. All these reasons lead us to believe that stock pesofication was the least desirable alternative.

11.3.3.3 *Formal dollarization*
Was formal dollarization then a better option? Dollarization would have been consistent with the Argentine social contract based on the long-term commitment to one-peso-one-dollar, with salutary implications for depositor confidence, which would have been boosted not just because the perceived risk of deposit confiscation would have been dimmed significantly, but also because the option-value of foreign bank access to their parent's capital and liquidity would have been better protected. That is, even if a run would have occurred, foreign banks would have likely been more willing to stand behind their Argentine affiliates, compared to the current situation marked by confiscatory (and asymmetric) stock pesofication.

Dollarization, though clearly not easy politically, would have not necessarily entailed a change of government—it would have arguably been within the scope of the government in power, inasmuch as it respected the one-peso-one-dollar rule. In this sense, there is an asymmetry in the political economy of dollarization versus stock pesofication. It is generally less costly politically for developing-country governments to maintain an exchange rate parity than to break it. This argument is *a fortiori* stronger in the case of Argentina, given the crucial relevance of the currency board to the operation of the financial system.

The dollarization alternative would have been more likely to avert a run if adopted early in the game—that is, before 2001. It was in fact considered by the Argentine government in 1999–2000, but it lost ground afterwards partly due to political polarization: It was construed as a symbol of support for Mr. Menem. By contrast, against a background of continued recession and increasing RER overvaluation, the proposal of stock pesofication cum float gained ground.[53] The feasibility and potentially salutary effects on depositor confidence of dollarization

---

[53] It, in fact, became somewhat popular in academic and policy circles after Prof. Hausmann's public recommendation to Argentina, presented in the October 2001 Latin American and the Caribbean Economic Association Meetings in Montevideo (see Hausmann 2001). This proposal failed to anticipate that it would inevitably lead to a deposit freeze. The proposal, moreover, seriously underestimated the difficulty of establishing the peso as a store of value in order to regenerate financial intermediation going forward.

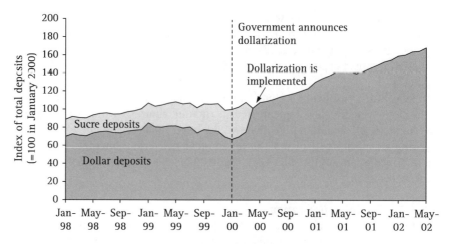

Figure 11.12. *Ecuador: Bank deposits and dollarization*

Notes: Dollarization was announced by President Mahuad in January 2000 but legally entered into effect only in March 2000, with the approval of the respective law, and after President Mahuad was replaced by President Gustavo Noboa. Sucre deposits are scaled by the conversion rate at which dollarization took place (25,000 sucres per dollar).

Source: Central Bank of Ecuador.

clearly narrowed during 2001, but did not disappear. A run became more likely once the government raided the liquidity of the financial system and was clearly headed towards default in the context of no access to capital markets.[54]

Could formal dollarization have still averted the run if adopted belatedly in 2001? Any answer to this question is, of course, highly speculative. Nonetheless, we are inclined to answer with a cautious yes. This is in part because, while deposit withdrawals in 2001 were probably motivated by heterogeneous expectations, much of the depositor activity appears to have reflected fears of a nominal devaluation, as discussed in Section 11.2.3. The possibility of no run under dollarization, even in the face of a default in government debt, appears reasonable in light of Ecuador's experience (Figure 11.12). Thus, the persistent fiscal imbalance, far from adjusting to the budget constraint presumably imposed by the monetary regime, de facto circumvented it, rendering the regime all but a formal arrangement in this regard. In Ecuador, the sole *announcement* of dollarization in January 2000 (formal dollarization was put into law only in March 2000) had an immediate positive impact on deposits even though the Ecuadorian government was in open default (the debt restructuring agreement was signed several months after the dollarization announcement), most banks were highly exposed to the government, and it was no secret that many of the large banks were completely insolvent. There is no obvious reason to believe that developments would have

---

[54] The failure to secure debt rollover in July 2001 was probably the threshold.

been different in Argentina, particularly considering that the Argentine banking system was unquestionably in a substantially better shape than Ecuador's. Moreover, to reinforce the stabilizing effects of dollarization on depositor behavior, Argentina could have taken additional positive steps to relax the link between banking system solvency and fiscal solvency.[55]

In all, it is difficult to escape the conclusion that, from the point of view of increasing the chances for averting a run, preserving healthy links between money and banking, and preventing a disorderly RER adjustment, the more obvious non-traumatic strategy would have implied the dollarization of *financial* contracts. Under this strategy, though painfully, the banking system could have absorbed over time the losses associated with rising NPLs as the RER adjusted towards equilibrium through deflation.[56]

A formal move to full dollarization (of financial contracts *and* money in circulation), however, would have been clearly inadequate to mitigate the fundamental inconsistency between the peg to the dollar and Argentina's trade and productive structure. And it would have not addressed the problem posed by severe practical limits to nominal flexibility in fiscal spending in a recessionary context. Initially, the main function of dollarization would have been to stabilize the financial system and hopefully stem the run. Over time, however, the premium of introducing some nominal flexibility would have risen. As a result, dollarization would have appeared as only one step towards building a viable paradigm that combines the dollar as the store of value with substantive nominal flexibility (particularly in wages and fiscal spending).[57]

11.3.3.4 *Stock dollarization cum pesofication at the margin*

From the previous discussion it follows that dollarization was a better exit strategy *only if it had been followed by greater nominal flexibility*. Indeed, full dollarization would have eliminated two sources of flexibility available at the time: The peso-denomination of most prices and non-financial contracts, and the transactional demand for the local currency. In this section, we argue that the stabilizing benefits of stock dollarization could have been reaped while preserving these two sources of flexibility through "pesofication at the margin"–that is, the introduction of a new domestic currency, initially circumscribed to transaction purposes, either by design or spontaneously, as was already occurring in Argentina, albeit in a disorderly manner, through the issuance of quasi-monies.

---

[55] The decree passed in 2001 (Presidential Decree 1005) to enable the use of the amounts falling due in the government debt to pay taxes would have helped in this regard.

[56] Moreover, as the recent Uruguayan experience illustrates, a securitization of liabilities can be designed selectively (distinguishing across banks and, within them, between deposit and non-deposit claims), without changing the original currency of denomination of bank assets and liabilities.

[57] This paradigm corresponds to what we elsewhere call the "dollar trinity." A key element of such trinity is sound institutions, which we believe are a key precondition irrespective of the exchange rate arrangement in place. See de la Torre et al. (2002b).

The simplest version of this alternative strategy would have implied dollarizing by decree the stock of existing financial contracts (without redeeming the pesos in circulation with dollars), in order to stem the run and stabilize financial conditions, and then consolidating into a single (new) national currency the peso and quasi-monies (such as the lecops and patacones) in circulation. That national currency would have floated against the dollar and would have been voluntarily used for future flows (payments, wage and prices, and *new* financial contracts). It would have had legal tender privileges under the control of the central bank. This process would have provided a much less disruptive way out of the rigid constraint imposed by the one-to-one rule, without unduly violating existing contracts. By offering the government an escape valve out of nominal fiscal rigidities in the face of a drying up in financing, the consolidation of the peso and quasi-monies in circulation into a single currency would have turned the disorderly situation of quasi-monies into an opportunity for recomposing a degree of sustainable flexibility (to adjust the budget as well as real wages) in a financially dollarized economy.

In Argentina, not only did the recourse to printing quasi-monies relax the cash flow constraints faced by the public sector. It also worked as an adjustment mechanism for the private sector, which rapidly embraced the new "bills" as an instrument to reduce labor costs and, thus, circumvent labor market rigidities. However, most of these quasi-monies were accepted for tax payments at face value. This, coupled with the convertibility of the peso in which they were denominated, limited the nominal flexibility that could be achieved through its use to a secondary market discount that never exceeded 10 percent.[58]

To be sure, the introduction of a new currency may find political support only once a crisis is well underway. Even at that stage, it is more likely that the process of pesofication at the margin in a currency board or dollarized country would start with the spontaneous printing of quasi-monies. However, it seems plausible that, as part of crisis management and resolution, once a quasi-money has emerged spontaneously the authorities could shepherd it and eventually formalize it into a new currency. At any rate, while the precise manner in which pesofication at the margin could have been instrumented is a valid matter for debate, the basic process is somewhat of a moot point, given that the emergence of local currencies has to be resolved eventually in some form.[59]

The logic of pesofication at the margin, grounded theoretically and empirically in the distinction between currency and asset substitution discussed above, is reinforced by the post-devaluation experience in Argentina. The legal and political obstacles that hampered the government's strategy to stock pesify exemplify the difficulty of establishing the peso as a store of value. By contrast,

---

[58] The discount was due more to a liquidity premium than to perceived credit risk.

[59] We deliberately abstract from the problem of an unfair wealth transfer between different issuers once currencies are monetized by a central bank. Conceivably, such transfers could be undone either within the monetization scheme or directly through countervailing budgetary transfers.

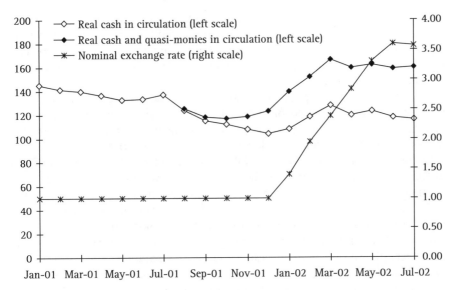

Figure 11.13. *Real cash and quasi-monies in circulation*

Notes: Quasi-monies only include Patacones and Lecop. Cash and quasi-monies in circulation are scaled by CPI. Figures are monthly averages. Financial system is defined to include public banks, private domestic banks, foreign banks, and non-bank financial institutions. Figures correspond to end-of-year values.

Sources: Central Bank of Argentina and IMF *International Financial Statistics*.

the transactional demand for the domestic currency (both for the old peso and the quasi-monies) remained relatively stable even through the depths of the crisis, as the worst devaluation expectations materialized (Figure 11.13).[60] This evidence suggests that stock dollarization cum pesofication at the margin was a viable option for Argentina.

Arguably, reluctant acceptance of the new local currency could have fueled a sharp depreciation that would have defeated the objective of achieving a gradual and less traumatic RER adjustment, prompting central bank foreign exchange intervention and undesired nominal uncertainty. Ultimately, whether dollarization should have been extended, preemptively, to the purchase of pesos in circulation, or be limited to financial contracts only is also a matter for debate, with the answer depending on the estimated demand for the new local currency.

In any event, the new currency would have been, initially, part of a bimonetary system in which the peso would have been used, as before, for transactions and as unit of denomination for most wages and prices, while the dollar would

---

[60] As noted above, the degree of dollarization of deposits in Argentina has historically been inversely related to their transactional nature (Figure 11.4). The flipside of this is the low level of dollarization of bank overdrafts (Figure 11.3).

have retained its role as store of value for financial savings. The new currency would have realistically been externally non-convertible, fluctuating against the dollar. Moreover, in addition to its legal tender status, it could have possibly been granted exclusivity for tax payments purposes, so as to consolidate its transactional demand.

Pesofication at the margin is certainly not a panacea, but it would have allowed a marginal degree of nominal flexibility for a dollarized financial system—flexibility to adjust fiscal spending to income *and*, to the extent that there was less than complete indexation of wages and prices to the dollar, to help correct misalignments in the RER. While the adverse balance sheet effects of RER adjustment on debtors in the non-tradable sector were inevitable, pesofication at the margin would have mitigated the need for a long recessionary and deflationary adjustment of the RER, could have prevented the collapse of the banking sector, and would have avoided the long-lasting effects of the massive violation of the rule of law as a consequence of a forcible stock pesofication. Ultimately, the sustainability of pesofication at the margin would have crucially depended on the re-composition of strong and viable fiscal institutions, financial reforms designed to address the risks of dollar loans to the non-tradable sector, and the strengthening of the local currency through an independent monetary policy credibly focused on price stability.

11.4 Final Remarks

Although now devastated by its crisis, the main challenge for Argentina currently is no different in nature from that faced at the beginning of the convertibility decade: To build a strong and sustainable link between money and financial intermediation, given the initial condition of a weak currency.[61]

Formulating the basic challenge in this way shifts the debate on bi-polar (floating versus hard peg) exchange rate systems to the terrain of financial intermediation and financial globalization. Once in this terrain, it is easy to see that a one-dimensional focus on the fix–float dilemma is insufficient. In effect, having a national currency that floats (freely or dirtily, it does not matter) and thus helps the RER to adjust to shocks is not enough if, at the same time, financial intermediation in that currency is non-existent or shallow and dominated by extremely short-duration contracts. Similarly, having a hard peg (including formal dollarization), and thus enjoying dollarized financial markets that are deeper and with longer-duration contracts could be extremely hazardous in the absence of adequate nominal flexibility.

In the heyday of the currency board, Argentina was able to develop a relatively deep and, by most standard measures, sound banking system, but its

---

[61] de la Torre et al. (2002*b*) define "weak currency" as one not accepted as a reliable store of value by either residents or non-residents, a concept that relates to Eichengreen and Hausmann's (1999) "original sin" and to the widespread financial dollarization observed in numerous developing countries.

inability to generate a minimum degree of nominal flexibility to deal with shocks that resulted in a major depreciation of the equilibrium RER proved to be ultimately devastating. After the collapse of the currency board, Argentina regained a currency that floats and thus facilitates rapid adjustment in the RER. But financial intermediation has been all but wiped out. Argentina, which previously had financial intermediation without a flexible currency, now has flexibility without financial intermediation. Hence the central challenge for Argentina is how to reconstruct sustainable links between money and financial intermediation. It is the same challenge that haunts many weak currency countries regardless of their ostensible exchange rate arrangements.

What is specific to Argentina is the daunting difficulty in tackling that challenge. During the fifty years that preceded convertibility, Argentine citizens were subject to a history of intermittent debasement of the national currency. Convertibility soothed those nightmares away with a heavy legal armor designed to make people believe that the ultimate store of value for their savings was the dollar—a hard currency that national mischief could not debase. Then the currency board imploded via the forcible pesofication of financial contracts, which debased something even more fundamental than a national currency, namely, the contractual environment itself.

If major price instability is avoided, pesofied Argentina should be able to maintain and enhance the function of the peso as a means of payment. That is the relatively easy part. As long as inflation is not out of control, the transactions demand for pesos is likely to be resiliently stable. The difficult part would of course be the establishment of the peso as a reliable store of value that can underpin sound financial intermediation. In effect, the reestablishment of the peso as a means of payment, even if sustained through a viable fiscal process, is not of itself an automatic guarantee that the peso would become a trusted receptacle for saving, particularly considering that the bad memory of the forcible pesofication of their savings is likely to torment the Argentines for a long time.

If the goal in Argentina is to promote the peso as the currency for financial intermediation through limits or outright prohibition of dollar deposits and credit, then one might expect many years of a relatively narrow banking system (focused mainly on payments) while credible institutions are built and proven. Alternatively, a bimonetary scheme (peso transactions and dollar savings) may be considered to try to restore a degree of financial intermediation earlier in the game, although the prospects for the restoration of dollar-based financial intermediation appear also bleak, given the severe damage to the contractual environment inflicted by stock pesofication.[62] In either case, there is no substitute to the hard work of institution building to underpin sustainable linkages between money and banking.

---

[62] The prudential lessons drawn from the Argentine case should come in handy to better internalize and manage the attendant risks if financial redollarization is the option of choice.

REFERENCES

Baliño, T. and Enoch, C. (1997). "Currency Board Arrangements Issues and Experiences." *Occasional Paper 151*, International Monetary Fund, August.

Broda, C. and Levy Yeyati, E. (2003). "Dollarization and the Lender of Last Resort." In E. Levy Yeyati and F. Sturzenegger (eds.), *Dollarization*. Cambridge, MA: MIT Press, pp. 101–32.

Calomiris, C. and Powell, A. (2001). "Can Emerging Country Bank Regulators Establish Credible Discipline? The Case of Argentina, 1992–1999." In F. S. Mishkin (ed.), *Prudential Supervision*. University of Chicago Press, pp. 147–98.

Calvo, G. (2002). "The Case for Hard Pegs." Mimeo, University of Maryland.

Chang, R. and Velasco, A. (2000). "Liquidity Crises in Emerging Markets: Theory and Policy." In B. Bernanke and J. Rotemberg (eds.), *NBER Macroeconomics Annual 1999*. Cambridge, MA: MIT Press, pp. 11–78.

de la Torre, A. (2000). "Resolving Bank Failures in Argentina." Policy Research Working Paper 2295, Washington, DC: World Bank. http://econ.worldbank.org/docs/1049.pdf.

——, García-Saltos, R., and Mascaró, Y. (2002a). "Banking, Currency, and Debt Meltdown: Ecuador Crisis in the Late 1990s." Washington, DC: World Bank, in process.

——, Levy Yeyati, E., and Schmukler, S. (2002b). "Financial Globalization: Unequal Blessings." *International Finance*, 5 (3): 335–57.

Dornbusch, R. (2001). Argentina at the End of the Rope, MIT, unpublished. http://web.mit.edu/rudi/www/media/PDFs/argentinaend.pdf.

Eichengreen, B. and Hausmann, R. (1999). "Exchange Rates and Financial Fragility." *NBER Working Paper* No. 7418, November.

Feldstein, M. (2002). "Argentina's Fall: Lessons from the Latest Financial Crisis." *Foreign Affairs*, 81 (2): 8–14.

Frankel, J., Fajnzylber, E., Schmukler, S., and Servén, L. (2001). "Verifying Exchange Rate Regimes." *Journal of Development Economics*, 66 (2): 351–86.

Gavin, M. and Perotti, R. (1997). "Fiscal Policy in Latin America." In B. Bernanke and J. Rotemberg (eds.), *NBER Macroeconomics Annual 1997*, 12. Cambridge, MA: MIT Press, pp. 11–71.

Goldfajn, I. and Olivares, G. (2001). "On Full Dollarization: The Case of Panama." *Economía*, 1 (2): 101–40.

Hausmann, R. (2001). "A Way out for Argentina: The Currency Board Cannot Survive Much Longer." *Financial Times*, October 30: 23.

—— and Velasco, A. (2003). "Hard Money's Soft Underbelly: Understanding the Argentine Crisis." In S. M. Collins and D. Rodrik (eds.), *Brookings Trade Forum 2002*. Washington, DC: The Brookings Institution, pp. 59–104.

Ize, A. and Levy Yeyati, E. (2003). "Financial dollarization." *Journal of International Economics*, 59 (2): 323–47.

Krugman, P. (2001). "Notes on Depreciation, the Yen, and the Argentino." *New York Times*, December 28, www.wws.princeton.edu/~pkrugman/argentino.html.

Levy Yeyati, E. (2001). "10 años de convertibilidad: la experiencia Argentina." *Revista de Análisis Económico*, 16 (2): 3–42.

Martinez Peria, M. S. and Schmukler, S. (2001). "Do Depositors Punish Banks for 'Bad' Behavior? Market Discipline, Deposit Insurance, and Banking Crises." *Journal of Finance*, 56 (3): 1029–51.

Mussa, M. (2002). *Argentina and the Fund: From Triumph to Tragedy*. Policy Analyses in International Economics 67, Washington, DC: Institute for International Economics.

Powell, A. (2003). "Argentina's Avoidable Crisis: Bad Luck, Bad Economics, Bad Politics, Bad advice." In S. M. Collins and D. Rodrik (eds.), *Brookings Trade Forum 2002*. Washington, DC: The Brookings Institution, pp. 1–58.

Razin, A. and Sadka, E. (2001). "Country Risk and Capital Flow Reversals." *Economic Letters*, 72 (1): 73–7.

Roubini, N. (2001). *Should Argentina Dollarize or Float? The Pros and Cons of Alternative Exchange Rate Regimes and their Implications for Domestic and Foreign Debt Restructuring/Reduction*, New York University, unpublished. www.stern.nyu.edu/ %7Enroubini/asia/argentinadollarization.doc.

Schmukler, S. and Servén, L. (2002). "Pricing Currency Risk Under Currency Boards." *Journal of Development Economics*, 69 (December): 2, 367–91.

Tornell, A. and Velasco, A. (2000). "Fixed Versus Flexible Exchange Rates: Which Provides more Fiscal Discipline?" *Journal of Monetary Economics*, 45 (2): 399–436.

World Bank (1998). *Argentina: Financial Sector Review*. Report No. 17864-AR, September.

— (1999). *Argentina: Implementation Completion Report*. Provincial Bank Privatization Loan and Bank Reform Loan, Report No. 19467, June.

Appendix 11.A1   Post-1994 Banking System Strengthening

Effective and ambitious financial sector reforms vigorously adopted in the second half of the 1990s were translated in a major consolidation and internationalization of the banking system (Table 11.1). The number of banks shrunk from 166 in 1994 to eighty-nine in 2000. Banks exited not just through mergers and acquisitions but also through bank closures. The number of public banks decreased from thirty-two in 1994 to fifteen in 2000, reflecting an aggressive privatization process of provincial banks. The number of branches of foreign-owned banks increased from 391 in 1994 to 1863 in 2000, while the share of these banks in the system's assets rose from 15 to 73 percent.

This process was accompanied and underpinned by an acceleration in the pace of legal, regulatory, and supervisory innovations. The main improvements in the regulatory and contractual environment for the banking system are briefly described below.

1. A quantum leap forward in a market-friendly approach to prudential oversight.   Much of this process was organized around the innovative BASIC program (in Spanish: B = bonos; A = auditoría; S = supervisión consolidada; I = información; and C = calificadoras de riesgo). BASIC was an Argentine-bred approach, superimposed on internationally recognized CAMELS-based supervisory methodology, to enhance the complementarity between official and market monitoring. The "B" in BASIC emphasized the requirement on banks to issue subordinated debt so as to generate better price signals of bank risk. The "A" stood for a program to improve internal and external audits. The "S" referred to the implementation of consolidated supervision of financial conglomerates. The "I" reflected a major program to enhance the quality, depth, coverage, and dissemination of information—through higher reporting standards for financial statements, broader and easily accessible information on debtors, and more stringent information requirements on financial group structure and ownership. And the "C" referred to the requirement on larger banks to have annual ratings by international rating firms. Partly as a result of the implementation of the BASIC program, it was broadly believed that Argentina in the late 1990s was near full compliance with the Basle Core Principles for Effective Banking Supervision.

Particularly noteworthy in the Argentine regulatory reform was the introduction of rigorous system of capital requirements, defined to absorb both credit and market risks, and significantly more stringent than the Basle minimum standard. The system featured various components. One component was minimum capital requirement for credit risk of 11.5 percent of risk-weighted loan exposures to the private sector, with variable weights within each loan class depending on the risk of individual loans, as measured by the interest rate charged on the loan. This ratio, moreover, was augmented by a factor for banks receiving lower CAMEL ratings. In addition, during 2000, positive risk weights were introduced for loans to the government and mark to market requirements were introduced for holdings of government bonds. Finally, capital requirements were set separately to absorb unexpected fluctuations in interest rates and in the prices of private sector securities.

Also noteworthy were the stringent liquidity requirements, high by international standards, and intended to work counter-cyclically—that is, to be tightened during buoyant times and relaxed during times of systemic liquidity squeeze. By 1998, most deposits (those with maturities of less than ninety days) required a 20 percent (remunerated) reserve.

2. A "best practice" scheme for troubled bank resolution. After the Tequila, Argentina introduced key institutional innovations to enhance the bank exit framework, including Article 35bis of the banking law—which created an efficient system for bank closure and resolution—and a privately managed limited deposit insurance scheme (SEDESA). This framework greatly contributed the consolidation of the banking system through the exit of unviable banks. Argentina became a salient case in the region where unviable banks (and not just small ones) were actually closed—between 1995 and 2000 about twenty banks were closed using the powers of Article 35bis.

3. Privatization of provincial banks. Between 1994 and 1998, sixteen provincial banks were privatized within a process that, though not perfect, was among the most aggressive and successful in the region.

4. Contingent repo facility. This was an over-collateralized facility, structured in order to compensate partially for the virtual lack of a domestic lender of last resort and to strengthen the banking system's capacity to weather a liquidity crisis. The facility gave the BCRA the option to sell dollar-denominated Argentine government bonds to a consortium of reputable international banks, subject to a buyback clause (with an embedded implicit interest rate). In 1999, the World Bank reinforced this facility by committing contingent funds to help meet margin calls in the event it was activated. By the end of the 1990s, the contingent repo line ensured the liquidity of about 10 percent of the system's deposits, in addition to the equivalent of nearly 20 percent of deposits already held in the form of liquid and safe FX assets (dollar cash and near-cash in the central bank and commercial banks).

5. Improvements in the framework for creditor rights and corporate insolvency. In 1995, Argentina enacted a new modern insolvency law that fostered a substantially improved system of corporate liquidation and rehabilitation. Similarly important reforms were implemented to improve the enforcement of secured and unsecured creditor rights. The World Bank assessment of Argentina's degree of compliance with international standards on insolvency and creditor rights found that, if one ignores the changes introduced most recently (in March 2002), the "permanent" framework for corporate insolvency and creditors rights is "largely consistent with the Principles."

12

The Anatomy of a Multiple Crisis: Why was Argentina Special and What Can We Learn from It?

GUILLERMO PERRY AND LUIS SERVÉN

The Argentine crisis has been variously blamed on fiscal imbalances, real overvaluation, and self-fulfilling investor pessimism triggering a capital flow reversal. This chapter provides an encompassing assessment of the role of these and other ingredients in the collapse. The chapter shows that in the final years of Convertibility Argentina was not hit harder than other emerging markets in Latin America and elsewhere by global terms-of-trade and financial disturbances. Hence, the crisis reflects primarily the high vulnerability to disturbances built into Argentina's policy framework. Three key sources of vulnerability are examined: (a) the hard peg adopted against Optimal Currency Area (OCA) considerations in a context of wage and price inflexibility; (b) the fragile fiscal position resulting from an expansionary stance in the boom; and (c) the pervasive currency mismatches in the portfolios of private corporations and the government. While there were important vulnerabilities in each of these areas, none of them was by itself higher than those affecting other countries in the region, and thus there is not *one* obvious suspect. However, the three reinforced each other in such a perverse way that taken jointly they led to a much larger vulnerability to adverse external shocks than in any other country in the region. Underlying these vulnerabilities was a deep structural problem of the Argentine economy that led to harsh policy dilemmas before and after the crisis erupted. The Argentine trade structure made a peg

This chapter is the output of a collective effort led by the authors, and based on background work on (a) fiscal issues, by Norbert Fiess, Rodrigo de Jesús Suescun, and Guillermo Perry; (b) exchange rate issues, by Humberto López and Luis Servén; (c) financial sector issues, by Augusto de la Torre and Sergio Schmukler and (d) capital flows and spreads, by Norbert Fiess and Luis Servén. We are grateful to these colleagues for their respective contributions. Though we borrow freely from them, the interpretations and conclusions offered in this chapter are our exclusive responsibility. We also thank Christian Broda for his kind collaboration on exchange rate issues, José Luis Machinea for helpful discussions, and Myrna Alexander, Jerry Caprio, Bill Cline, Daniel Lederman, Paul Levy, Ernesto May, Pedro Pou, Andrew Powell, David Rosenblatt, Nick Stern, Adolfo Sturzenegger, and Federico Sturzenegger for very useful comments. Ana María Menéndez and Patricia Macchi provided valuable assistance.

to the dollar highly inconvenient from the point of view of the real economy. However, the strong preference of Argentineans for the dollar as a store of value led to a highly dollarized economy in which a hard peg or even full dollarization seemed reasonable alternatives, at least from a financial point of view.

12.1 Introduction and Summary

The severity and high cost of the Argentine crisis have come as a surprise to most observers, even to those that had been predicting a crisis since the Brazilian devaluation of 1999. There were very few who predicted one before 1999. Indeed, the Argentine economy appeared to be in relatively good shape at least until before the Russian crisis. Even then the attention of the markets and the International Financial Institutions was focused on Brazil. That country had more apparent macroeconomic imbalances and suffered severe speculative attacks in October 1997 and again after the Russian crisis, leading to the demise of the exchange rate band and a sharp devaluation of the real in January 1999.

In a relatively benign external environment, Argentina outperformed most other economies in the region until 1997 in terms of growth per capita though income distribution did not improve and unemployment stayed at high levels. This growth was only temporarily interrupted in 1995 when Argentina suffered severely from the Tequila crisis. After the 1999 slowdown in growth that affected the whole region, other countries began a modest recovery. Argentina instead plunged into a protracted recession that reversed most of her previous gains at poverty reduction. We explore in Section 12.2 if this difference in performance can be attributed to Argentina receiving more severe external shocks than other economies in the region. We find that Argentina was hit no harder than other Latin American countries either by the terms of trade decline after the Asian crisis or by the U.S. and worldwide slowdown in 2001 or the capital flows reversal and the rise in spreads after the Russian crisis. The fact that Argentina did worse than other countries after 1999 must be attributed to her higher vulnerabilities to shocks, weaker policy responses, or a combination of both. Indeed, we find in Section 12.2 that the capital flow reversal of 2001 was largely driven by Argentina-specific factors. We view this as evidence that "sudden stops" of capital flows acted more as an amplifier than as a primary cause of the crisis.[1]

The bulk of this chapter is devoted to examining to what extent and why the Argentine economy was more vulnerable to adverse external shocks than other Latin American economies, and to what extent policy mistakes, particularly during the de la Rúa administration, were the main culprit, as has been often claimed.[2] We examine the vulnerabilities associated with deflationary

---

[1] This view is in contrast with the interpretation put forward in Calvo et al. (this part), though in most other aspects our conclusions agree with those in Chapter 10.

[2] There is by now an extensive literature analyzing the causes of the Argentina crisis. See, for example, the papers by Hausmann and Velasco (2002), Mussa (2002), Powell (2003), and Teijeiro (2001).

adjustments to shocks under a hard peg in Section 12.3; those associated with a large public debt and a fragile fiscal position in Section 12.4; and those hidden under a façade of strength in the banking sector in Section 12.5. We conclude that vulnerabilities in each of these areas reinforced each other in such a perverse way that taken jointly they led to a much larger vulnerability to adverse shocks than in any other country in the region.

The hard peg and inflexible domestic nominal wages and prices imposed a protracted deflationary adjustment in response to the depreciation of the euro and the real, the terms of trade shocks and the capital market shock of 1998. This led to a major overvaluation of the currency and a rapidly deteriorating net foreign asset position. Such imbalances were aggravated by weak fiscal policies during the decade, especially after 1995. In Section 12.3 we estimate that all these factors led from 1997 to an increasing overvaluation of the currency that peaked in 2001 at over 50 percent. Given the large debt, the weak primary fiscal balance and low growth, the need to address the rising concern with solvency led to tax hikes and budget cuts in 2000 and 2001 that deepened the economic contraction. The endogenous capital flow reversal and a steep rise in the risk premium in 2001 amplified these problems by requiring a large external current account adjustment. To aggravate matters, such an adjustment under the hard peg had to take place mostly through demand reduction and aggregate deflation—a lengthy, costly, and uncertain process.

The hard peg actually hid from public view the serious deterioration in fiscal solvency and the mounting financial stress. Indeed, the protracted deflationary adjustment required to realign the real exchange rate (RER) under the hard peg would have unavoidably eroded the debt repayment capacity of the government, households, and firms in non-tradable sectors—the debtors whose incomes would be more adversely affected as a direct result of the deflation.[3] The full force of these latent problems was revealed by the collapse of the peg in 2002. They were made worse by the exchange rate overshooting and the disruption of the payments system derived from the deposit freeze (the so-called "corralito"), which might partially have been avoided by better policy responses. Financial stress was amplified by the large exposure of banks and Pension Funds to increasing government risk. A vicious circle of economic contraction, fiscal hardship, and financial stress ensued.

The authorities and the Argentine polity were faced with very harsh dilemmas after 1998 (as discussed in Section 12.6). One option was to accept a painful and protracted deflationary adjustment while keeping the Currency Board. This, while attempting to retain market confidence, would have entailed a severe test of the fragile Argentine political and fiscal institutions.

---

[3] While some debtors from the tradable sector might be affected by an economy-wide deflation as well, the increase in the real value of the debt relative to real income due to the recession and price deflation would have impacted most strongly on the non-tradable sector. On this see also the discussion in Roubini (2001).

An early adoption of full dollarization might have reduced the pains and duration of the deflationary adjustment, thereby increasing the likelihood of success of such an option. But it would have left the Argentine economy exposed to a repetition of these problems in the future.

The other option was to allow a nominal devaluation and adopt a float, in an attempt to shortcut the protracted deflationary adjustment. However, this would have precipitated a latent corporate, banking, and fiscal crisis, given the open currency exposures in the balance sheets of both the public and the private sectors and the large degree of overvaluation of the currency. In order to avoid such a scenario, financial contracts would have had to be *pesofied* before floating. This, in turn, posed the serious danger of a deposit run, which would have forced a deposit freeze and/or some kind of Bonex plan,[4] fatally eroding the public's confidence in money as a store of value.

The authorities did not use their limited margin of maneuver well. When they finally engaged in fiscal adjustment—something that should have been done in the boom years before 1999—it was too little, too late. They also hesitated on the ultimate choice of exchange rate regime, and postponed too long the needed public debt restructuring. Finally, they precipitated a major financial and payments crisis, first by reducing the liquidity buffers of the banking system and overexposing it (along with the Pension Funds[5]) to government risk, and later by adopting an arbitrary asymmetric *pesofication* of assets and liabilities and a particularly disruptive deposit freeze, which was kept in place for an excessively long period of time without resolution. Such actions and omissions deepened the crisis.

These hard choices were a reflection of a deep structural problem. The Argentine trade structure made a peg to the dollar highly inadequate—from a real-economy point of view. However, the strong preference of Argentineans for the dollar as a store of value (after the hyperinflation and confiscation experiences of the 1980s) had led to a highly dollarized economy in which a hard peg or even full dollarization seemed a reasonable alternative. This made sense from a financial point of view, not only to avoid massive capital gains and losses resulting from exchange rate changes, but also as an expeditious shortcut to nominal stability and monetary credibility. It is not surprising that informed analysts favored, and continue to favor, opposite exchange regime choices depending on the relative weight they assign to real-economy or financial considerations.

With the benefit of hindsight, the boom years up to mid-1998 have to be seen as a major lost opportunity. Staying with the hard peg, but minimizing the risks associated with adverse external shocks would have required four supporting ingredients: First and foremost, significant fiscal strengthening, not just to protect solvency but with the broader objective of providing some room for

---

[4] The Bonex Plan implemented in 1989 involved a forced swap of frozen bank deposits for long-term public debt.

[5] After the Social Security reform of 1994, the Pension Funds (AFJPs) became major holders of Argentine public debt.

countercyclical fiscal policy. This contrasts with the expansionary procyclical stance actually followed during most of the decade, and especially during the boom from end-1995 up to mid-1998 once the implicit pension debt (as well as other implicit liabilities) had been brought into the open by pension reform (as documented in Section 12.4). Second, considerable flexibilization of labor and other domestic markets (including utility prices). Third, a significant unilateral opening to trade. None of this was done in the 1990s. And fourth, there should have been even stricter prudential regulations for banks than actually adopted (in spite of the significant progress achieved in this field). These should have included harder provisioning and/or capital requirements for loans to households and firms in non-tradable sectors, a "firewall" between banks and the government, and some form of earmarking of liquidity to demand deposits in order to protect the payments system in the event of a systemic deposit run (as discussed in Section 12.5).

Alternatively, those years would have been the right time to engage in a more orderly change of the exchange rate regime. But the exit, whether towards a successful flexible exchange rate regime with a monetary anchor or to full dollarization, would have also required significant structural reforms and institution building. Instead, this was a period of inaction and laxity on many fronts with the seeds of crisis planted in good times by imprudent behavior or lack of precautionary action. A key lesson from Argentina is the need to adopt economic and political institutions that align incentives to face hard choices and facilitate timely reforms, and in particular that are less prone to amplify economic cycles.

The analysis of the Argentine crisis yields many useful lessons for other Latin American economies. After all, the exchange rate system dilemma faced by a highly dollarized economy that conducts only a fraction of its trade with the United States, in a world economy characterized by highly volatile currencies, is not exclusive to Argentina. But even economies with less stringent structural dilemmas often face a similar tension. On the one hand, a flexible exchange rate regime with a monetary anchor offers flexibility in responding to shocks. On the other hand, major RER adjustments can wreak havoc in balance sheets made vulnerable by unhedged foreign-currency debt of firms in non-tradable sectors and of governments themselves.[6] Even those economies could draw useful policy lessons from the Argentine debacle.

12.2 Economic Performance and External Shocks in the 1990s

During the period 1990–97, Argentina outperformed most other economies in the region in terms of growth (Table 12.1). The external environment (terms of trade, capital inflows, sovereign spreads, and world growth) was relatively benign in those years, apart from the short-lived but abrupt Tequila crisis of 1995 from

---

[6] What Calvo and Reinhart (2002) have described as "liability dollarization" that leads to "fear of floating" and Hausmann et al. (2000) have attributed to the inability to issue long-term debt in local currency.

Table 12.1. *Real GDP growth rate (percent per year)*

	1981–90	1991–97	1998	1999	2000–01
Argentina	−1.3	6.7	3.9	−3.4	−2.6
Bolivia	−0.4	4.3	5.0	0.4	1.8
Brazil	2.3	3.1	0.1	0.8	3.0
Chile	4.0	8.3	3.9	−1.1	3.6
Colombia	3.4	4.0	0.6	−4.1	2.0
Costa Rica	2.4	4.8	8.4	8.2	1.6
Ecuador	2.1	3.2	0.4	−7.3	4.0
Mexico	1.5	2.9	5.0	3.6	3.2
Peru	0.0	5.3	−0.5	0.9	1.7
Venezuela	0.3	3.4	0.2	−6.1	3.0
Average	1.4	4.6	2.7	−0.8	2.1

Source: World Bank, World Development Indicators (WDI) Database and the Unified Survey.

which Argentina suffered a severe contagion. The growth performance remained fairly satisfactory even in 1998. But after the region-wide growth slowdown of 1999—largely a consequence of capital flow retrenchment following the Russian crisis—other Latin American countries began a modest recovery, while Argentina plunged into a protracted recession.

Unemployment showed a slightly increasing trend up to the Tequila crisis, when it jumped sharply (Figure 12.1). The fact that unemployment was rising even when the economy was growing at full steam reflects a combination of rising participation rates (likely stemming from an "encouragement effect" due to the growth upturn), declining labor-intensity of production techniques (encouraged by the real appreciation of the peso), productive restructuring towards less labor-intensive activities, and probably also the poor operation of the labor market.[7] The unemployment rate declined in the boom years 1996–98, and then rose again during the ensuing recession.

Poverty indicators display a similar trajectory (Figure 12.1). Poverty declined sharply until 1994, but rose with the Tequila crisis and then continued on an upward trend during the recession of 1999–2001. By 2001 the gains at poverty reduction achieved in the early part of the decade had been wiped out. Even more striking is the trajectory of inequality, which appears to have risen without interruption from 1993 on, after an initial decline in 1990–92.

Was Argentina's poor growth performance from 1999 onward a reflection of more adverse external shocks than those affecting other Latin American and Caribbean (henceforth LAC) countries? To answer this question, we first consider real shocks stemming from terms of trade changes and global growth and then look at capital flow disturbances.

[7] See Galiani (2001) for a recent assessment of the state of Argentina's labor market.

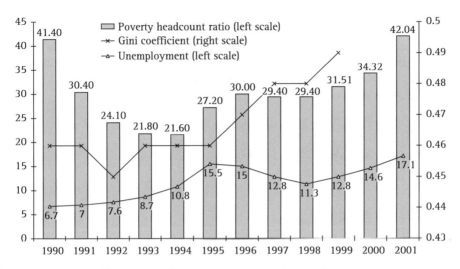

Figure 12.1. *Poverty, inequality, and unemployment*

Note: Data for urban areas.

Sources: Unemployment from INDEC, Gini Coefficient, and Poverty Head Count ratio from World Bank Poverty Assessment Report (2000) except for the 1999–2002 ratios which are estimated using the trend observed for the Greater Buenos Aires headcount ratios from INDEC.

Argentina's terms of trade declined by over 10 percent in 1998–99, but recovered fairly quickly in 2000–01. This temporary drop followed a rise that had occurred in 1996–97. Relative to other countries, Argentina's terms of trade decline in 1998–99 was less severe than that suffered by oil exporting countries like Venezuela and Ecuador (Figure 12.2a). Likewise, the cumulative decline in Argentina's terms of trade from 1997 through 2001 was smaller for Argentina than for Chile, and much smaller than for Peru.

The economic impact of these gyrations in the terms of trade was much less significant for Argentina than for other countries. The reason is that Argentina is a fairly closed economy, thus terms of trade movements entail only modest changes in real income. This is highlighted in Figure 12.2(b), which portrays the terms of trade *shocks* suffered by various LAC economies, calculated multiplying the changes in import and export prices by the respective magnitudes of imports and exports relative to GDP. It is immediately apparent that Argentina's terms of trade shocks over the second half of the 1990s were smaller in magnitude than those of any other country in the graphs, perhaps with the only exception of Brazil (which is also fairly closed). Indeed, Argentina's real income loss from the terms of trade fall in 1998–99 amounted to less than 0.5 percent of GDP.

The other source of adverse real shocks was the global growth slowdown that started in 2000. Relative to that year, 2001 real GDP growth declined by 3 percentage points both in the United States and the industrialized world as a whole. Like with the terms of trade decline, however, Argentina was much less affected than other countries in the region, again because of its lower degree of openness. As a result, the growth deceleration and the ensuing slowdown in export markets translated into a fairly modest aggregate demand decline for Argentina—the smallest among the countries shown in Table 12.2.[8]

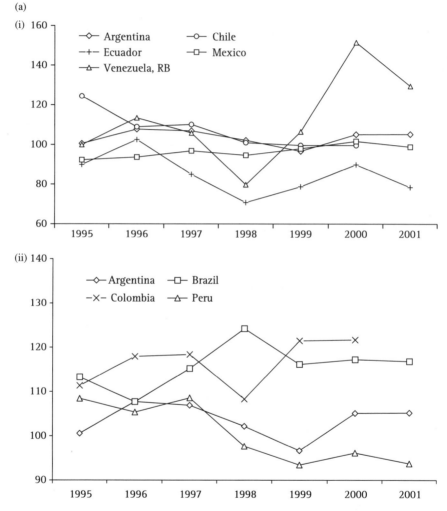

Figure 12.2. *(a) Terms of trade 1992 = 100 and (b) Terms of trade shocks (percent of GDP)*

Source: For (a) WDI 1995–2000 and domestic sources 2001 and for (b) WDI.

[8] The impact on export demand shown in the table is calculated using an income elasticity of 2.2 for both U.S. and OECD imports.

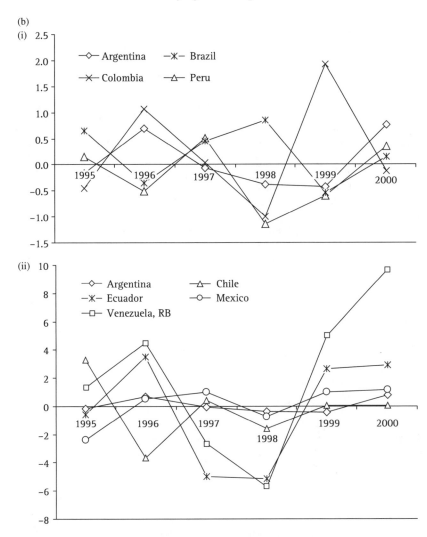

Figure 12.2. (*Continued*)

Next, we turn to the disturbances stemming from world financial markets.[9] Following the Russian crisis, Latin American countries, like other emerging economies, had to face a generalized increase in the cost of market borrowing. Figure 12.3, which allows a comparison of sovereign spreads faced by different

[9] The role of external financial shocks in the Argentine crisis has been underscored in particular by Calvo et al. elsewhere in this volume (this part).

Table 12.2. *Impact of the global slowdown 2001: The income effect via trade volume*

	Exports/GDP (%) (a)	Exports of goods to U.S./Total exports (%) (b)	Exports of goods to OECD/Total exports (%) (c)	Impact of the decline in U.S. growth (% of GDP) (c) = −[(a)∗ (b)∗2.2]∗0.03	Impact of the decline in OECD growth (% of GDP) (d) = −[(a)∗ (c)∗ 2.2]∗0.03
Argentina	10.81	10.90	33.09	−0.08	−0.24
Bolivia	17.55	13.86	25.27	−0.16	−0.29
Brazil	10.81	24.70	57.11	−0.18	−0.41
Chile	31.85	18.48	62.44	−0.39	−1.31
Colombia	21.34	43.45	60.22	−0.61	−0.85
Costa Rica	48.09	41.38	72.01	−1.31	−2.29
Dominican Rep.	29.93	86.47	94.37	−1.71	−1.86
Ecuador	42.43	38.55	67.05	−1.08	−1.88
Guatemala	19.93	56.40	70.80	−0.74	−0.93
Jamaica	42.94	30.86	85.80	−0.87	−2.43
Mexico	31.06	88.55	94.31	−1.82	−1.93
Peru	15.98	25.39	63.55	−0.27	−0.67
Venezuela, RB	28.45	53.81	64.14	−1.01	−1.20

Notes:
(a) Exports of Goods and Services and GDP of 2000, *source*: WDI.
(b) Exports of goods in 2001, *source*: IMF Direction of Trade.
(c) 2.2 is the U.S. expenditure elasticity (Clarida 1994), and 3% is the decline in the U.S. economic growth between 2000 and 2001.
(d) 3% is the decline in the OECD economic growth between 2000 and 2001.

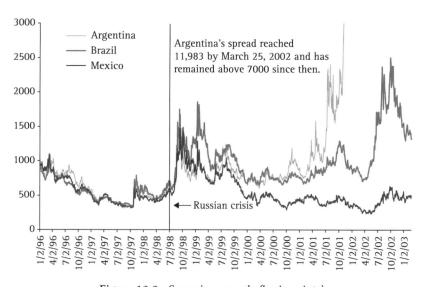

Figure 12.3. *Sovereign spreads (basis points)*
Source: JPMorgan Chase.

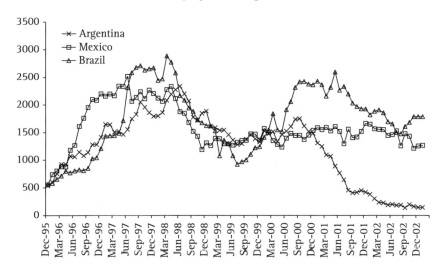

Figure 12.4. *Gross capital flows (twelve-month moving average, million US$)*
Source: HAVER.

countries, shows that Argentina did not fare worse than the rest of the region in this regard. As a matter of fact, Brazil's spreads rose above Argentina's in 1997–99, with speculative attacks on the real taking place in October 1997 and October 1998. It was only in late 2000 that the Argentine spread began to drift above Brazil's. And the same happened with Venezuela and Ecuador, whose spreads (not shown) increased more than Argentina's in 1998 and remained higher until 2001.

The comparative evolution of the current and capital accounts across LAC countries tells the same story (Figure 12.4). Until late 2000, Argentina's capital account surplus (as percentage of GDP) remained above the regional average (Figure 12.5a). Its current account deficit likewise exceeded the region's norm (Figure 12.5b). Indeed, the current account adjustment that Argentina undertook in 1999, due to the capital flow decline that followed the Russian crisis, was fairly modest by regional standards. Among the larger countries, it exceeded only Mexico's, and was dwarfed by the current account correction undertaken by Chile, Colombia, and Peru—not to mention the dramatic adjustments of oil-exporting Ecuador and Venezuela (Table 12.3).

In summary, while the global contraction in capital flows that occurred in 1999 reached virtually all Latin American economies, Argentina was not affected as severely as (and certainly not more severely than) other countries in the region. Thus, Argentina was able, at first, to continue running large current account deficits, as it had done in the previous years. After 1999, however, capital flows to most LAC countries recovered somewhat, except for Argentina (and Venezuela), where they continued to fall, most sharply in 2001. The tentative

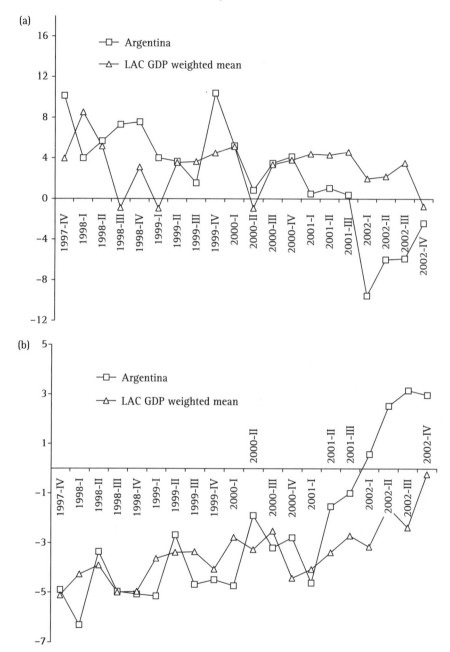

Figure 12.5. *(a) Capital account and (b) current account (percentage of GDP)*

Source: Balance of payments from domestic sources via HAVER. Latin America average includes
Arg, Bra, Chi, Col, Mex, and Perú.

Table 12.3. *Current account adjustment*

	As share of GDP		As share of imports	
	1998/99	2000/01	1998/99	2000/01
Argentina	0.77	1.29	7.16	14.51
Bolivia	1.44	1.54	4.96	7.83
Brazil	1.11	−0.55	13.83	−7.33
Chile	5.56	−0.86	22.38	−3.64
Colombia	5.20	−3.14	34.37	−22.55
Costa Rica	−0.91	−0.34	−2.07	−0.83
Ecuador	15.84	−12.20	56.03	−41.16
Mexico	0.37	0.31	1.13	0.92
Peru	3.19	0.50	20.75	3.37
Venezuela, RB	7.24	−5.56	42.99	−41.67
Average	3.98	−1.90	20.15	−9.06

Note: Current account adjustment is defined as the year on year difference in the Current account surplus as share of GDP or imports.

Sources: Imports (US$) from Direction of Trade (IMF); GDP and Current Account Balance (US$) from WDI (World Bank).

conclusion is that the deterioration of capital flows to Argentina at the end of the decade reflected mostly Argentina-specific factors rather than global forces.

We can more formally assess the relative role of global and country-specific factors in the observed pattern of capital flows to Argentina and other countries using a suitable statistical decomposition separating the common component of sovereign spreads from their country-specific component. Loosely speaking, the common component reflects global conditions (both interdependence and "contagion"), and hence captures global risk. The country-specific component reflects each country's economic fundamentals (or, more precisely, investors' perceptions about them), and thus provides a measure of its pure-risk premium.[10]

This procedure yields a synthetic "global factor," whose role in the observed evolution of emerging-market spreads is depicted in the top panel of Figure 12.6.

[10] The full details are spelled out in Fiess (2002). In a nutshell, we use principal component analysis to construct an indicator of global co-movement of spreads using end-of-the-month JP Morgan EMBI data for Argentina, Brazil, Mexico, Venezuela, and the non-Latin EMBI index over the period from January 1991 to March 2002. The indicator is the percentage of the total variance of the (normalized) spreads explained by their first principal component, constructed using a rolling window of forty-eight months. We smooth the resulting series by averaging the values obtained for each data point over the forty-eight windows in which it appears. As a robustness check, we redo the exercise using a broader set of countries: Argentina, Bulgaria, Brazil, Ecuador, Mexico, Nigeria, Panama, Peru, Poland, Russia, and Venezuela. However, not all of them possess observations over the entire sample period. We also construct alternative global indicators incorporating the effects of U.S. interest rates on country spreads. Finally, we redo these experiments with alternative window lengths. All these specification changes have only minor effects on the qualitative results. See Fiess (2002) for details.

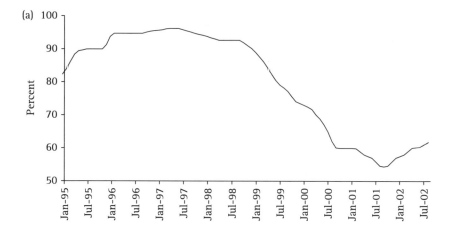

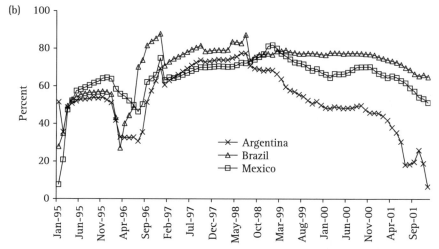

Figure 12.6. *Sovereign spreads: The role of global factors (a) Contribution of first principal component to overall variation of spreads and (b) variation in individual country spreads (percent)*

Source: Fiess (2002).

The figure plots the degree of co-movement of the spreads, as measured by the fraction of their total variation (computed over moving forty-eight-month windows) attributable to the global factor. The graph shows that the global factor accounts for the vast majority of the variation in spreads up to 1998. After that date, there is a steady decline in the degree of co-movement of spreads, reversed only in part in September 2001.

The bottom panel of Figure 12.6 performs the same exercise for Argentina, Brazil, and Mexico. For each of these countries, the figure shows the fraction of the total variation in its spread attributable to the global factor just described. In all three countries analyzed, sovereign spreads reflect both global and country-specific risk. However, the roles of these two factors are not the same across countries and time periods. In accordance with the previous figure, the global factor plays the main role up to 1998. Indeed, in 1997–98 it accounts for the bulk of the variation in spreads in all three countries. After the Russian crisis in 1998, though, the contribution of the global factor declines for the three countries. Importantly, the extent of the decline differs across countries. In the case of Argentina, it is more marked, and accelerates noticeably at the end of 2000. In fact, after that moment, global factors account for less than half of the observed variation in Argentina's spreads. The conclusion is that such variation increasingly reflects country-specific factors after 1998, and especially so from late 2000 onward.

The above analysis of country spreads can be extended to capital flows with the aid of a suitable econometric model of their determinants, a task undertaken in Fiess (2002). In brief, the model describes the simultaneous determination of flows and spreads making use of the decomposition of the latter into their global and local components shown above. Empirical implementation of this framework shows that capital flows are negatively affected by both global and local risk. In turn, local risk rises with the total volume of debt and the primary fiscal deficit, both expressed as ratios to GDP.

Using this framework, we can assess the roles of local and global factors in the observed time path of capital flows to Argentina. This is done in Figure 12.7,

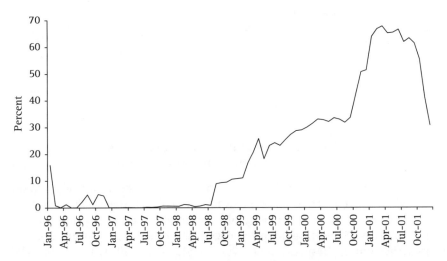

Figure 12.7. *Capital inflows to Argentina: Contribution of local factors (percent of total variance explained)*

Source: Fiess (2002).

which plots the variation in flows to Argentina attributable to local factors, as a fraction of the total variation explained by the model.[11] The figure shows that Argentina-specific factors played a negligible role until 1998, but became increasingly important following the Russian crisis, and especially after October 2000. Indeed, from the latter date up to September 2001, local factors account for two-thirds of the total variation in capital flows to Argentina explained by the model.

These model-based results reinforce the more informal evidence shown earlier that Argentina was not affected as severely as other countries by the global slowdown in capital flows after the Russian crisis. To the contrary, the econometric models confirm that the sharp reversal of flows to Argentina in late 2000 and 2001 was driven mainly by country-specific factors. By then, the fragility of the Argentine macroeconomy had already become evident. This strongly suggests that the "sudden stop" of capital flows in 2000/2001 acted as an amplifier of the effects of domestic factors, rather than being the primary, exogenous cause behind the crisis.

We summarize this section by noting that Argentina was not hit harder than other LAC countries either by the terms of trade decline after the Asian crisis, or by the global capital flow reversals and spread increases that followed the Russian crisis, nor was it hit harder by the U.S. and worldwide slowdown that started in 2001. On the contrary, the sharp capital flow reversal from 2000 onwards was primarily an Argentina-specific phenomenon driven mostly by Argentina-specific factors.

Since these "standard" external shocks were no worse in Argentina than in the rest of the region, the fact that after 1998 Argentina's performance fell short compared to other LAC countries must reflect either higher vulnerabilities or weaker policy responses, or both. It is true that Argentina was particularly affected by other external events, such as the appreciation of the dollar and the depreciation of major trading partner currencies. But such differential effects were a consequence of policy decisions—specifically, the peg to the dollar under the Currency Board arrangement—and the handicaps that they created. Most important among the latter were the significant balance sheet vulnerabilities that plagued the Argentine economy.

12.3 Overvaluation and Deflationary Adjustment Under the Hard Peg

We now assess the role of the dollar peg in Argentina's malaise: How it added to the economy's external vulnerability and how it hampered adjustment to real shocks.

The pros and cons of hard pegging, as was adopted by Argentina under Convertibility, have been traditionally assessed in the framework of OCA theory. In brief, the latter suggests that an irrevocable peg is more likely to be beneficial

---

[11] As in the previous figures, we use a forty-eight-month moving window for these exercises. Alternative window lengths result in qualitatively similar results.

Table 12.4. *Argentina's trade structure (2001)*

	Geographical composition of imports plus exports (percentage of the total)
Brazil	25
Main LAC w/o Brazil*	17
U.S.A.	14
Europe**	20
Rest of the world	24

* Bolivia, Chile, Colombia, Ecuador, Guatemala, México, Perú, Paraguay, Uruguay, and Venezuela.
** Austria, Belgium, Switzerland, Czech Republic, Germany, Spain, Finland, France, United Kingdom, Greece, Italy, Netherlands, Norway, Poland, Portugal, Sweden, and Switzerland.

Source: International Monetary Fund, *Direction of Trade Statistics*.

for the client country if much of its trade is with the anchor country, and if client and anchor are not exposed to significant asymmetric shocks which would demand monetary policy responses of opposite sign in the two countries. If the scope for asymmetric shocks is substantial, the peg might still make sense if the client country can easily adjust to real shocks through nominal price and wage flexibility, or through other mechanisms such as a system of fiscal transfers and/or unrestricted labor mobility with the anchor.

Argentina did not meet any of these conditions for an OCA with the U.S. dollar. The United States accounted for less than 15 percent of the country's total trade, equivalent to less than 3 percent of its GDP, leaving a very large scope for asymmetric shocks (Table 12.4).[12] Wage and price flexibility were limited, making adjustment to real shocks difficult.

Indeed, the adoption of Convertibility was not guided by OCA arguments, but by the credibility-enhancing effect that renouncing monetary discretion was expected to have after many years of acute monetary instability, as well as by Argentinean investors' stated preference for dollar-denominated assets. As we shall see below, however, this purported shortcut to credibility left the economy highly exposed to adverse disturbances.

12.3.1 Was there an overvaluation? Where did it come from?

Argentina's real (effective, i.e. trade weighted) exchange rate (henceforth RER) experienced a considerable appreciation during the 1990s.[13] Between 1990 and

---

[12] In fact, on these grounds a peg to the euro would have made more sense than a peg to the U.S. dollar. See Alesina et al. (2002).

[13] Trade weights are taken from the IMF's *Direction of Trade Statistics* and correspond to 1995. They refer to total goods trade (imports plus exports).

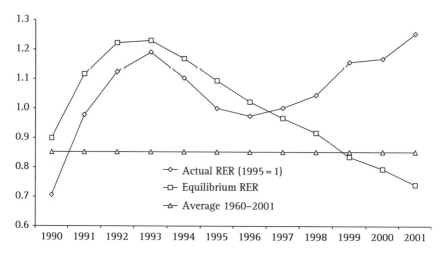

Figure 12.8. *Actual and equilibrium RER*

Source: Alberola et al. (2003).

2001, the RER rose[14] by over 75 percent (Figure 12.8). The bulk of the appreciation developed before 1994. In fact, the RER depreciated after that date and until 1996, but then appreciated again to reach its peak in 2001.

This evolution of the RER was duly reflected in Argentina's export performance. While real exports did show positive growth over the decade, they grew less than in comparable countries, and their rate of expansion was closely associated to the evolution of the RER. During the initial real appreciation at the time when the currency board was established, Argentina's exports stagnated. As the RER depreciated after 1993, exports expanded vigorously, at rates similar to, or higher than, those experienced by other countries. When the RER started appreciating again in 1997, export performance fell significantly behind that of comparable countries (Table 12.5).

Real appreciation is not necessarily a symptom of imbalance in need of correction. Indeed, during the 1990s, especially in the early part of the decade, a number of reasons were offered by different observers in order to explain the persistent real appreciation of the peso as an equilibrium phenomenon. Most importantly, it was argued that the efficiency-enhancing reforms of the early 1990s had led to a permanent productivity increase in the tradable sector of the Argentine economy, which would have justified a permanent RER appreciation. Nevertheless, over the final two or three years of Convertibility, an increasing number of independent observers and financial market actors expressed the view that the peso was overvalued, although the precise extent of the overvaluation

---

[14] Throughout we define the RER so that an increase represents a real appreciation.

Table 12.5. *Average annual growth of real exports (goods and non-factor services, percentages)*

	1992–93	1994–97	1998–2001	1992–2001
Argentina	1.8	14.4	3.6	7.6
Seven major LAC countries w/o Argentina*	7.7	11.1	7.8	9.1
Upper middle-income LDCs**	7.8	11.9	8.9	9.8
World	3.8	8.4	6.6	6.8
Memo item				
Argentina's RER growth (appreciation +)	10.4	−4.1	5.8	2.8

* Bolivia, Brazil, Chile, Colombia, Mexico, Peru, and Venezuela.
** World Bank classification: American Samoa, Antigua and Barbuda, Argentina, Barbados, Botswana, Brazil, Chile, Costa Rica, Croatia, Czech Republic, Dominica, Estonia, Gabon, Grenada, Hungary, Isle of Man, Latvia, Lebanon, Libya, Lithuania, Malaysia, Malta, Mauritius, Mayotte, Mexico, Oman, Palau, Panama, Poland, Puerto Rico, Saudi Arabia, Seychelles, Slovak Republic, St. Kitts and Nevis, St. Lucia, Trinidad and Tobago, Uruguay, and Venezuela.

Source: WDI.

was disputed, depending on the measure of the equilibrium RER used as benchmark of comparison.[15]

Such views were most often based on simple comparisons of the prevailing RER with its historical value, under the view that the equilibrium RER is constant—the so-called *purchasing power parity* (PPP) view. Figure 12.8 illustrates the use of this approach to assess the misalignment of the Argentine RER over the 1990s, taking as equilibrium value the RER average over the last four decades (1960–2001). The latter is depicted by the horizontal line in the figure. Comparison with the actual RER suggests that the peso was initially undervalued in 1990, but became increasingly overvalued after the introduction of the Convertibility Law in 1991. The overvaluation peaked initially in 1993, declined later through 1996, and rose again to nearly 50 percent in 2001.

However, this approach neglects two important factors that may cause the equilibrium RER to change over time. The first one is the relative level of productivity across countries. Other things equal, an increase in productivity in traded goods sectors relative to non-traded goods sectors in a given country above that experienced by its trading partners should lead to a RER appreciation—precisely the argument advanced by some observers to justify the rapid real appreciation of the Argentine peso in the early 1990s.[16] The second

[15] For example, Deutsche Bank perceived the peso to be some 20 percent overvalued in real terms in mid-2000. See also Sachs (2002) and Hausmann and Velasco (2003) for assessments of the degree of overvaluation of the peso.   [16] This is the so-called Balassa–Samuelson effect.

ingredient is the adequacy of the current account to sustain equilibrium capital flows. The RER must be consistent with a balance of payments position that does not lead to explosive accumulation of external assets or liabilities. In this framework, the equilibrium RER is that which allows the economy to achieve a sustainable long-run net foreign asset position.[17] Below we offer an assessment of Argentina's equilibrium real exchange based on an analytical model encompassing these two ingredients. We take into account simultaneously the internal (productivity) and external (asset position) equilibrium of the economy to draw inferences about the overall equilibrium or disequilibrium position of the RER.[18]

Empirical application of this analytical framework to Argentina using data for 1960–2001 yields the estimated equilibrium RER shown in Figure 12.8. The figure suggests that the trajectory of the equilibrium RER consists of two stages: (a) an initial real appreciation in 1991–93 that was particularly sharp in the first two years and (b) a steady depreciation from 1994 on.

The equilibrium and actual RER are compared in Figure 12.9, which presents the percentage deviation of the actual RER from its equilibrium value, along with the 95 percent confidence bands derived from econometric estimation of the model. In the figure, a positive value indicates overvaluation, and a negative one means undervaluation. The graph reveals two stages of real misalignment. Between 1990 and 1996, the RER was undervalued, although after 1991 the degree of undervaluation was fairly small. From 1997 on, however, the RER exceeded its equilibrium counterpart by a widening margin, resulting in an increasing overvaluation. By 2001, the RER exceeded its equilibrium value by 53 percent.[19]

Notice the contrast between the degree of misalignment derived from the equilibrium model and that arising from the simple PPP calculations mentioned earlier. By both yardsticks the peso was overvalued by roughly 50 percent in 2001. However, the PPP calculations imply that much of the overvaluation of the peso had already developed between 1991 and 1993, while the model-based calculations suggest that the overvaluation arose only in the last few years of Convertibility. What lies behind these contrasting assessments? As discussed earlier, the analytical model used here encompasses two key determinants of the time path of the equilibrium RER: (a) the relative productivity differential across sectors between Argentina and her trading partners, and (b) Argentina's net foreign asset position.

---

[17] While this stock-based asset view of RER determination has become mainstream, an alternative *flow*-based view assigns to exogenous capital flow fluctuations a dominant role in the determination of the equilibrium RER. According to this approach, the equilibrium level of the RER is that which makes the current account balance equal to the (exogenously given) supply of net foreign financing.

[18] The details are spelled out in Alberola et al. (1999) and Alberola et al. (2003).

[19] To be specific, this figure is the difference between the logarithms of the actual and equilibrium RER.

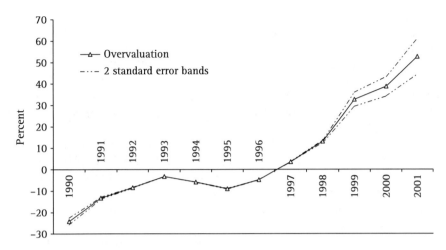

Figure 12.9. *Argentina: Real overvaluation of the peso*

Source: Alberola et al. (2003).

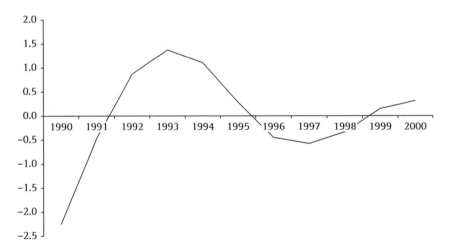

Figure 12.10. *Argentina's relative productivity level*

Source: Alberola et al. (2003).

Figure 12.10 portrays the time path of a measure of the productivity differential, based on the (log) ratio of non-tradable to tradable prices of Argentina relative to its trading partners.[20] An increase represents an improvement in Argentina's productivity differential, and calls for an appreciation of the equilibrium RER.

---

[20] This measure was proposed by Kakkar and Ogaki (1999); see Alberola et al. (2003) for more details on its construction. An alternative measure based on ratios of aggregate labor productivity yields broadly similar qualitative results.

The figure suggests a clear rise in relative productivity in the early 1990s and hence, given other things, an appreciation of the equilibrium RER between 1990 and 1993. Much of this gain in productivity is likely to reflect efficiency gains derived from the end of hyperinflation achieved in 1991. After 1993, however, there were no additional gains in relative productivity, and in fact a partial reversal appears to have taken place after 1994. This absence of further productivity gains appears consistent with a stalling of Argentina's structural reform process in the second half of the decade.

If the initial productivity gains are largely responsible for the appreciation of the equilibrium RER in the early 1990s, its depreciation in the late 1990s is mainly driven by the changes in Argentina's net foreign asset position, shown in Figure 12.11. In the figure, an increase represents a rise in Argentina's NFA position (relative to GDP) and hence calls for an appreciation of the equilibrium RER, given other things.

The figure displays an initial rise of NFA in 1991, followed by a steady decline between 1993 and 2001, during which the NFA/GDP ratio falls by over 20 percentage points. The decline proceeds at a particularly fast pace after 1997. In the face of a stagnant productivity differential, as shown above, this deterioration in the NFA position is the driving force behind the steady depreciation of the equilibrium RER in the late 1990s.

Argentina's falling NFA/GDP position over the late 1990s results from the combination of current account deficits, which were particularly large in 1997–99, and, a persistent decline in growth in the final years of the decade. It is true that by 1999–2000 Argentina's current account imbalance, while large, was not far above the region's norm, at least if the large surpluses of the oil-importing

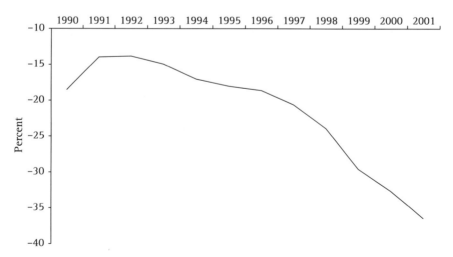

Figure 12.11. *Net foreign assets (percent of GDP)*

Source: Alberola et al. (2003).

countries are excluded from the comparison. But Argentina's deficits were being incurred in the midst of a severe recession with escalating unemployment. This suggests that the full-employment current account deficit would have been much bigger than that actually observed.[21] In the next section we examine how these persistent current account imbalances relate to the fiscal gaps that developed over the decade.

This empirical framework also allows us to reassess the role of external shocks in the misalignment of the Argentine peso. In particular, we can gauge the impact of changes in the RERs of third currencies. It has been argued that much of the overvaluation of the peso can be attributed to the appreciation of the U.S. dollar in the late 1990s relative to the currencies of major trading partners of Argentina, especially the euro, and also to the Brazilian devaluation of 1999, which abruptly reduced Argentina's competitiveness *vis-à-vis* its top trading partner.[22] As already noted, these are not "external shocks" in the strict sense of the term, but self-inflicted ones resulting from Argentina's choice of currency regime—they are a result of pegging to the wrong currency.

We can assess the contribution of these factors to the overvaluation of the peso by decomposing the latter into three parts. The first one is due to the divergence in fundamentals between Argentina and the United States, which causes the equilibrium RERs of the dollar and the peso to diverge. This reflects primarily the pursuit of policies inconsistent with the dollar peg which must eventually lead to misalignment even if the peg is otherwise "right" for the Argentinean economy. The other two components reflect the inadequacy of the dollar peg itself. One is just the overvaluation of the dollar, which is translated to the peso through the dollar peg. The other problem results from differential exposure to changes in the RER of the peso with third currencies, particularly the Brazilian real.[23] In the former case, misalignment results from pegging to a misaligned anchor currency, while in the latter it results from asymmetries in the trade structure of the client and anchor countries.

The decomposition is presented in Figure 12.12, which shows the contribution of each of the three ingredients to the cumulative change in the misalignment of the peso between 1997 and 2001. As shown earlier, the empirical model suggests that peso overvaluation rose by 50 percent between those dates.[24] The figure suggests that both the wrong choice of peg and inconsistent fundamentals were behind the mounting overvaluation of the peso in the final years of Convertibility. Indeed, the former accounts for 27 of the 50 percentage points of

---

[21] This point is underscored by Roubini (2001).

[22] In contrast, adverse terms of trade shocks had presumably a very modest impact on the extent of misalignment of the peso. As already discussed, in 1998–99 Argentina's terms of trade declined by 11 percent. However, the shock was only temporary, and was reversed in 2000. In addition, the decline followed a terms-of-trade windfall in 1995–96.

[23] See Alberola et al. (2003) for further details on this decomposition.

[24] As before, this figure and the ones that follow refer to logarithmic deviations.

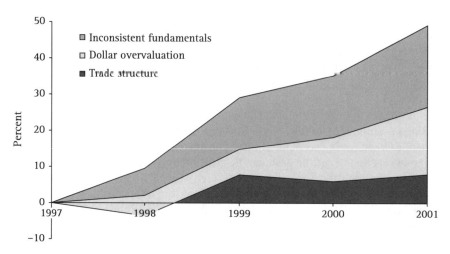

Figure 12.12. *Sources of cumulative peso overvaluation, 1997–2001 (percentages)*
Source: Alberola et al. (2003).

overvaluation accumulated between 1997 and 2001, while the latter contributed the remaining 23 percentage points.

The graph also shows that most of the misalignment due to inadequacy of the peg can be traced to the overvaluation of the U.S. dollar in the late 1990s. In contrast, trade structure asymmetries worked *against* overvaluation prior to 1999, because the Brazilian real was itself appreciating in those years. The figure clearly shows that Brazil's abrupt devaluation in 1999 added significantly to the misalignment of the peso. In fact, Figure 12.9 before showed that the overvaluation of the peso increased by almost 20 percent in 1999. Numerical calculations suggest that the depreciation of the real was directly responsible for about half of this amount (11 percent).[25]

Finally, it is important to note that these calculations may understate the true contribution of the dollar overvaluation and the depreciation of the real to the misalignment of the peso. To the extent that the overvaluation due to these two factors led to larger current account deficits over time, and hence declining net foreign assets and a falling equilibrium RER, such factors would be indirectly responsible for additional peso overvaluation. It seems safe to conclude that the choice of a "wrong peg" accounts for the majority of the observed overvaluation of the peso.

We conclude that the peso had become substantially overvalued after 1997, in the face of stagnant productivity and mounting net foreign liabilities relative to GDP. We find that the appreciating U.S. dollar and the depreciating Brazilian real

[25] See Alberola et al. (2003). This figure is, in fact, very similar to those reported at the time by financial market analysts.

accounted directly for over half of the overvaluation. The rest can be attributed to the divergence in fundamentals between Argentina and the United States. Such divergence largely reflects the external imbalances that Argentina incurred throughout the decade, which, as we shall see later, were mainly the result of persistent public deficits.

We reach these conclusions in a framework in which exogenous capital flow fluctuations play no role in the determination of the equilibrium RER. This is consistent with the analysis in the preceding section, which found that factors governing global capital flows became relatively less important in explaining the observed pattern of flows to Argentina in the late 1990s.

12.3.2 Misalignments and deflationary adjustment under hard pegs

Real misalignments can and do occur under both fixed and flexible exchange rate regimes. But the key difference is that under a floating regime a real misalignment can be eliminated quickly through a nominal exchange rate adjustment. Thus, if a temporary spending boom, say, causes the RER to appreciate above its equilibrium value, as the spending boom unwinds the nominal exchange rate will typically depreciate, helping eliminate the real overvaluation.[26]

In a pegged regime, in contrast, the RER adjustment has to occur through changes in the domestic price level *vis-à-vis* foreign prices. Disturbances requiring a real depreciation, such as the Brazil devaluation or the U.S. dollar appreciation just reviewed, call for a decline in the inflation differential *vis-à-vis* trading partners in order to restore RER equilibrium. If trading partner inflation is low, this means that domestic prices need to fall in *absolute* terms. Under nominal inertia of wages and other prices, deflation in turn requires a recession, making the adjustment process slow and costly in terms of output and employment. This generates a second difference with floating regimes: In the presence of a large overvaluation, the fact that the required adjustment process may entail large (and politically unpalatable) output losses can in turn undermine confidence in the sustainability of the peg itself, especially when fiscal institutions are weak, as was the case in Argentina (see Section 12.4 below).

The cost of adjustment under a hard peg can be illustrated on the basis of empirical evidence on the adjustment to real disturbances from a large sample of industrial and developing countries under different exchange rate regimes. Figures 12.13 and 12.14 portray the adjustment of countries with floating regimes and hard pegs (such as Argentina's currency board) to a trajectory of the terms of trade similar to that experienced by Argentina in 1998–99—a cumulative drop of 11 percent.[27] The figures show the time path of output and the RER, in percentage deviation from the initial (pre-shock) level.

---

[26] Because of this, large and persistent overvaluations are less frequently observed under floating than under fixed regimes. See Goldfajn and Valdés (1999).

[27] This is based on an extension of earlier work by C. Broda (2001).

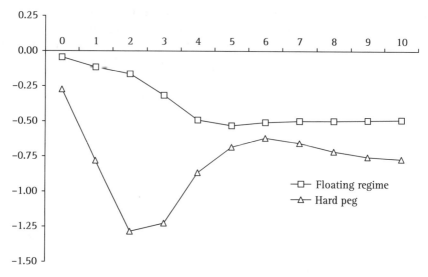

Figure 12.13. *GDP response to a terms of trade deterioration (percent of GDP)*

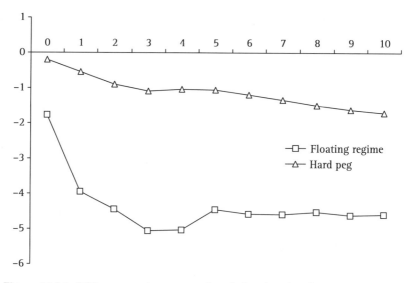

Figure 12.14. *RER response to a terms of trade deterioration (percentage deviation from pre-shock level)*

Figure 12.13 shows the adjustment of real GDP. In floating regimes the output loss is small—it never exceeds 0.5 percent of initial GDP. In hard pegs, in contrast, the terms of trade deterioration leads to a sizable output contraction in the short-run—up to 2.5 percent by the second year. The initial contraction is followed by a partial recovery of GDP, which approaches the level of the floating regime by the fifth year.

The other side of the coin is shown in Figure 12.14, which presents the time path of the RER, again distinguishing between floating regimes and hard pegs. In floating regimes, the terms of trade loss causes an immediate real depreciation. The RER depreciates by over 1.5 percent on impact, and continues to depreciate over the following periods—by up to 5 percent by the third year. In contrast, under hard pegs the real depreciation is gradual and of very modest magnitude— less than 2 percent after ten periods—in spite of the sharp output contraction. Moreover, it is possible to show that the adjustment patterns under both regimes are significantly different in the statistical sense.

These empirical results conform with the experience of Argentina. As noted earlier, Argentina's RER overvaluation was partly a reflection of specific disturbances to which the currency board was vulnerable such as the appreciation of the U.S. dollar and the Brazilian real devaluation. In the adjustment to these disturbances, prices did fall, but by a very modest magnitude: A total around 3 percent over 1998–2001. This price deflation was wholly insufficient to offset the impact of the shocks on the misalignment of the RER; even though nominal deflation was the only way to achieve RER adjustment under the hard peg. However, a faster deflation would have been politically very difficult, as it would have required an even deeper recession and higher unemployment than actually witnessed in 1999–2001.

12.3.3 Summing up

We can highlight four facts that emerge from the discussion. (*a*) Regardless of the approach taken to assess the equilibrium RER—simple PPP calculations or a model-based approach—we find that the peso had become grossly overvalued by 1999–2001. We reach this conclusion in a framework in which exogenous shifts in capital flows play no independent role for exchange rate misalignment. (*b*) A considerable portion of the overvaluation of the peso by 2001 can be traced to the U.S. dollar appreciation against the euro, as well as the Brazilian real depreciation. This shows the dangers of a hard peg adopted in violation of standard OCA criteria, which in the case of Argentina pointed clearly against the U.S. dollar as anchor currency, even though finance-based arguments may have pointed in the opposite direction. (*c*) The experience of Argentina provides a striking illustration of the rigidities imposed by a hard peg. The observed degree of downward price flexibility proved wholly insufficient to absorb the adverse real economic shocks of the late 1990s.[28] While deflation provided the only

---

[28] This is also in accordance with the international evidence reported by Goldfajn and Valdés (1999). They show that once a real overvaluation exceeds some threshold (around 30 percent), it becomes very difficult to reverse via nominal deflation, and a collapse of the nominal exchange rate is virtually assured to occur.

mechanism for RER adjustment under the peg, the deflation required to adjust to the shocks would have been politically hard or impossible to achieve.[29] In this regard, the hard peg provided for a persistent and large RER misalignment to go unchecked. As we shall see below, it also hid from public view a rapidly mounting fiscal solvency problem. (d) Finally, a key ingredient behind the mounting overvaluation of the peso after 1996 was the persistent decline in Argentina's equilibrium NFA position. This, in turn, can be traced to the large external imbalances that developed over the 1990s which led to an escalation in external liabilities relative to GDP, especially in the context of slow or negative growth at the end of the decade. As we shall discuss below, public sector imbalances were a major element in this process.

12.4 Fiscal Vulnerabilities

Many observers have blamed the Argentine crisis on the lack of fiscal discipline, which was essential to preserving the Currency Board.[30] Others have argued that even until mid-2001 conventional debt and fiscal indicators appeared no worse in Argentina than in other emerging markets (Table 12.6), and that the fiscal deterioration was due mainly to the recession. The contribution of Social Security reform to the fiscal imbalances of the 1990s has also attracted attention.[31] In this section we assess those claims.

12.4.1 Fiscal policy during boom and bust

We begin our inquiry by examining how and when fiscal vulnerabilities developed during the 1990s. Most analysts have pointed to the deterioration of fiscal balances (both at the Federal and provincial levels) and the corresponding increase in debt indicators since 1995 and, especially, since 1999, which are shown in Figures 12.15 and 12.16, respectively.[32]

However, it is true that the observed deterioration in Argentina's fiscal balance in the final years of the decade reflects in part the effects of declining growth on tax collection and those of rising interest rates on debt service. To assess the fiscal stance adopted by the authorities, we need to gauge the effects of these factors beyond their immediate control.

---

[29] This view is also shared by Rodrik (2003) and Sachs (2002).

[30] See in particular Teijeiro (2001) and Mussa (2002).

[31] See Teijeiro (2001) and Hausmann and Velasco (2002).

[32] Argentina's fiscal balances during the first part of the nineties look better than they actually were, as they include some privatization receipts above the line and hide important fiscal liabilities (in both Federal and Provincial pension systems and other items) that were later partially recognized, especially from 1994 onwards. Public debt decreased up to 1993 thanks to large privatization receipts and the Brady deal, while from 1994 onward the debt path reflects the recognition of some of the previously hidden liabilities (see Teijeiro 2001). Also, from 1995 on the Federal Government absorbed cash flow deficits previously included in the Provincial pension system. This latter change does not affect the consolidated (Federal + Provinces) deficit but only its composition.

Table 12.6. *Debt indicators in emerging markets*

	Public debt	Public debt interest payments		
	Percentage of GDP	Percentage of GDP	Percentage of tax revenue	Percentage of debt
Argentina	62.2	5.4	30.8	8.7
Brazil	65.0	9.5	33.8	15.5
Colombia	50.8	5.0	25.3	9.8
Mexico	27.7	2.6	25.7	9.4
Venezuela	35.3	3.3	18.7	9.3
Poland	39.1	2.9	11.0	7.4
Russia	52.3	3.0	7.9	5.7
Turkey	85.1	23.7	133.1	27.8

Note: Data are for 2000 except for Argentina (2001).

Source: Goldman Sachs and IMF.

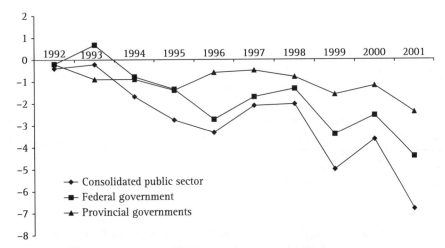

Figure 12.15. *Overall budget balance excluding privatization revenues (percentage of GDP)*

Source: Ministerio de Economía de la República Argentina and World Bank.

Consider, first, the effects of cyclical variation in output on the fiscal balance. Unfortunately, we do not have sufficient data to correct for this factor at the level of the consolidated public sector, but only for the Federal government. Nevertheless, Figure 12.15 shows that the time profile of the Federal and consolidated deficits is roughly similar, so the cyclically adjusted fiscal stance should also be fairly similar for both definitions of the deficit.

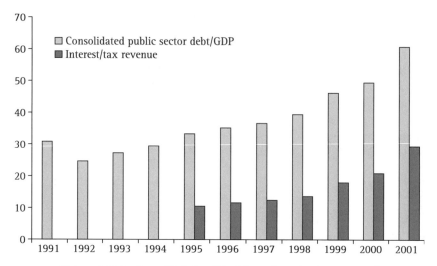

Figure 12.16. *Consolidated public debt and service (percentages)*
Source: International Monetary Fund.

Construction of cyclically adjusted fiscal figures typically requires estimates of potential output. Their calculation near sample endpoints is subject to considerable inaccuracy, due to the difficulty in distinguishing between temporary output movements and changes in trend at the beginning and end of the sample period.[33] To remedy this problem partially, we construct two potential output estimates—one through a Hodrick–Prescott (HP) filter, and another using linear extrapolation. Figure 12.17 shows that the HP method appears to underestimate potential output at the end of the period—as it projects zero or even negative potential growth—while the linear extrapolation probably overestimates it. Thus, we opt for a middle-of-the-way estimate (shown in the figure) between these two.

Using this estimate, we can correct the Federal primary balance for cyclical revenue effects.[34] This yields the structural primary balance of the Federal government, shown in Figure 12.18. It deteriorated markedly (by nearly 1.5 percent of GDP) during the boom period from the end of 1995 to mid-1998, and improved significantly thereafter. The improvement was punctuated by brief periods of relaxation, mostly during the run up to the election at the end of 1999.[35]

Indeed, estimates of the fiscal impulse, defined as the change in the structural primary deficit relative to GDP, also reveal a significant expansionary change

---

[33] See Orphanides and van Norden (2002) for a discussion.

[34] To do this, we use a cyclical revenue-elasticity to GDP of 1.14, which is obtained from a regression of current revenues on trend and cyclical GDP.

[35] In private communications, Andrew Powell has suggested to us that inclusion of the Provinces in the analysis would reveal an even larger relaxation in that year.

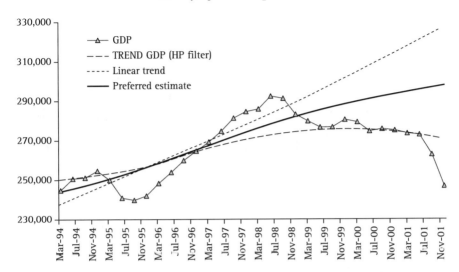

Figure 12.17. *GDP and Potential GDP (Hodrick–Prescott trend and linear trend)*
Source: Ministerio de Economía de la República Argentina and Ministerio de Obras y Servicios Públicos.

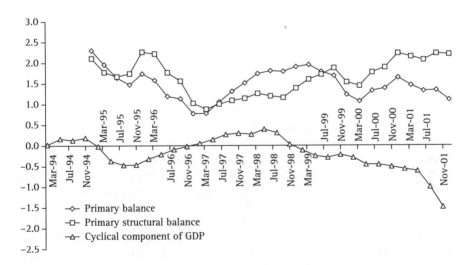

Figure 12.18. *Current and structural primary budget balance of federal government*
(percentage of potential output and percentage deviation from potential output)
Source: Ministerio de Economía de la República Argentina and Ministerio de Obras y Servicios Públicos.

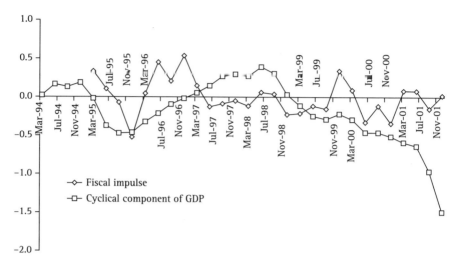

Figure 12.19. *Fiscal impulse of federal government (percentage change and deviation from potential output)*

Source: Ministerio de Economía de la República Argentina and Ministerio de Obras y Servicios Públicos.

in the stance of the Federal government during the boom period, followed by progressive adjustment after mid-1998 except for a few months in the run up to the 1999 election (Figure 12.19).

The above analysis is based on the cyclically adjusted primary deficit estimates described earlier. To assess its robustness, we can examine an alternative measure of the change in the fiscal stance, due to Blanchard (1993), which avoids taking a stand on the nature of business fluctuations or on trend-cycle decomposition techniques. It compares actual revenue and expenditure with those that would have happened if the "economic environment" (as described by unemployment and trend output) had been the same as in the previous year. Such a calculation is reported in Figure 12.20. The qualitative pattern is very similar to that shown earlier in Figure 12.19: A major expansionary change in fiscal policy from mid-1996 to 1998, reversed after that date (with brief interruptions in 2000 and 2001).

However, the adjustment in the structural primary balance after 1998 was not enough to compensate for growing interest rate payments. Figure 12.21 shows how the Federal government's structural overall balance, calculated as the structural primary balance plus actual interest payments, remained negative (around 1 percent of GDP) from the end of 1996 through 2001. Interest payments rose from around 2 percent of GDP in 1995/96 to 4.1 percent in 2000 and 5.4 percent in 2001. Interest rates on public debt were on the rise, especially after the Russian crisis and even more in 1999–2001, due to the perceived weakening of Argentine fundamentals. As Table 12.7 shows, however, less than half of the

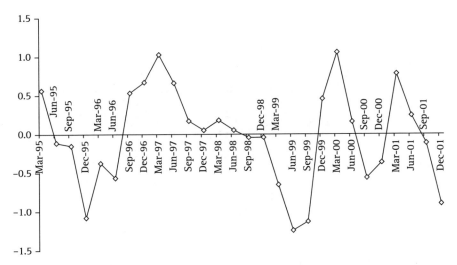

Figure 12.20. *Blanchard's indicator of fiscal impulse (percentage of GDP)*
Source: Our elaboration using data from Ministerio de Economía de la República Argentina.

Table 12.7. *Interest payments on public debt*

	Interest payments on debt (percent of GDP)	Change in interest burden (percent of GDP)	Contribution to change in interest burden	
			Debt volume effect	Interest rate effect
1991	2.8			
1992	1.6	−1.1	−0.4	−0.8
1993	1.4	−0.2	0.1	−0.3
1994	1.6	0.1	0.1	0.0
1995	1.9	0.3	0.2	0.1
1996	2.1	0.2	0.1	0.1
1997	2.3	0.3	0.1	0.2
1998	2.6	0.3	0.2	0.1
1999	3.4	0.8	0.5	0.3
2000	4.1	0.7	0.3	0.4
2001	5.4	1.3	1.0	0.3
Total				
1991–2001		2.6	2.2	0.5
1993–2001		3.9	2.4	1.5

Source: Ministerio de Economía de la República Argentina and International Monetary Fund.

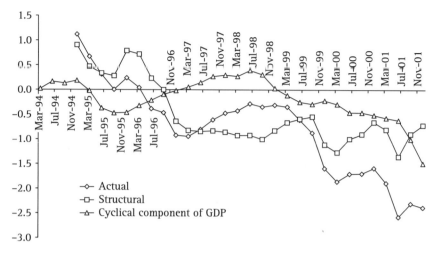

Figure 12.21. *Current and structural overall federal budget balance (percentage of potential GDP)*

Source: Ministerio de Economía de la República Argentina y Ministerio de Obras y Servicios Públicos.

increase in the interest bill between 1995 and 2001 can be attributed to the rise in interest rates. The rest of the increase in the interest burden was due to the steady growth in the stock of outstanding debt. The additional deterioration in the Federal government's overall balance, beyond that due to the changing fiscal stance and interest charges, can be attributed to the effect of the slowdown, which is captured by the gap between the actual and structural budget deficit measures in Figure 12.21.

More often than not Latin American fiscal problems have originated in booms, when weak fiscal institutions and policy complacency do not facilitate the achievement of surpluses. As a consequence, fiscal policy has to be pro-cyclical also in bad times, contributing to a deepening of recessions and social tensions, and occasionally ending up in a severe fiscal crisis. Argentina in the 1990s was no exception to this unfortunate Latin American policy tradition.[36]

12.4.2　Fiscal solvency assessments

We next explore debt sustainability. First, we attempt to estimate debt sustainability on the basis of growth expectations formed using the information available each year. These estimates, reported in Table 12.8, reveal that declining

---

[36] The procyclicality of fiscal policy in LAC has been examined in Gavin et al. (1996), Gavin and Perotti (1997), and Perry (2002).

Table 12.8. *Indicators of fiscal sustainability*

	Average growth rate (three preceding year average) (percentage)	Implicit interest rate on gov. debt (percentage)	Consolidated gov. primary balance (percentage of GDP)	Sustainable balance (av. growth rate based on last three year observations, percentage of GDP) (a)	Sustainable balance (av. growth rate based on last five year observations, percentage of GDP) (b)
1991	0.7	8.6	-0.4	2.7	2.8
1992	5.7	6.2	1.4	0.1	1.4
1993	7.3	5.0	1.2	n.s.p.	0.5
1994	6.5	5.1	-0.1	n.s.p.	n.s.p.
1995	2.6	5.4	-1.0	0.8	0.1
1996	2.8	5.6	-1.3	0.9	0.4
1997	3.6	6.1	0.2	0.9	0.6
1998	5.8	6.4	0.6	0.2	0.9
1999	2.9	7.1	-1.6	1.7	2.0
2000	-0.1	8.0	0.3	3.9	2.5
2001	-2.9	8.7	-1.4	6.0	4.0

Note: n.s.p. means "no sustainability problem."

Source: Estimates based on IMF and Ministerio de Economía de la República Argentina data.

future growth projections (influenced by the deflationary adjustment under the hard peg) may have been even more important than public debt interest rate increases in shaping perceptions about fiscal sustainability. Indeed, assuming that markets assessed long-term growth potential based on a (three and five year) moving average of past growth, the simulations indicate that by the year 2000, and certainly by 2001, debt sustainability was clearly open to question, in the sense that the required primary balance of the consolidated government approached or even exceeded 4 percent of GDP, a figure that looked unlikely given Argentine fiscal history and institutions. In practice, although fiscal discipline had been a concern for years, it is fair to say that most analysts in investment banks and elsewhere began to seriously question fiscal solvency in these years and not before. However, Argentine economists focused already in the election year 1999 on the need for further fiscal adjustment, and the Fiscal Responsibility Law was enacted in mid-1999 as a means to guarantee fiscal solvency. Non-compliance with its goals in the run-up to the election and afterwards contributed to undermining confidence in solvency.

The protracted deflationary adjustment to the external shocks imposed by the hard peg to the dollar (as discussed above) thus had a major effect on debt sustainability perceptions, through two channels. On the one hand, it reduced future growth expectations, and on the other it made further fiscal adjustment more difficult and painful as the ratio of revenues to GDP collapsed. In this context, further tax hikes (like the "impuestazo" in 2000) or expenditure cuts (like those undertaken during the second half of 2001) aggravated the recession and the ensuing social and political tensions.

Even more, the observed adjustment in the structural primary balance was clearly insufficient if we take into account both the direct and indirect effects of exchange rate overvaluation since 1997 on the balance sheet of the government. The overvaluation implied that measures of sustainability based on the observed ratio of public debt to GDP understated the public sector's difficulties by a considerable margin. Most public debt was denominated in dollars, while government assets (in particular its capacity to tax) were not. Thus, a real depreciation restoring RER equilibrium would have raised public debt ratios by a large amount—up to 20–30 percentage points of GDP in 2000–01, as shown in Table 12.9. It is important to note that this would have occurred irrespective of whether the real depreciation was achieved under Convertibility through nominal deflation or through a nominal devaluation, and thus a collapse of the Currency Board.[37] In either case, the real depreciation eventually would have revealed the reduced capacity of the government to pay back its debt. Table 12.9 shows that once this is factored into the analysis, by 2001 government solvency would have required an additional primary surplus of about 2 percent of GDP annually. The peg actually hid from public view the increasing precariousness of

---

[37] This is underscored by Roubini (2001).

Table 12.9. *Fiscal sustainability and the exchange rate*

	Debt output ratio (%)	Debt output ratio adjusted for RER misalignment (%)	Consolidated gov. primary balance (percentage of GDP)	Sustainable balance (av. growth rate based on last three year observations, percentage of GDP)	Sustainable balance adjusted for RER misalignment (percentage of GDP)
1991	32.3	28.0	−0.4	2.7	2.1
1992	26.1	23.9	1.4	0.1	0.1
1993	28.7	27.7	1.2	n.s.p.	n.s.p.
1994	30.9	29.1	−0.1	n.s.p.	n.s.p.
1995	34.8	31.6	−1.0	0.8	0.8
1996	36.6	34.9	−1.3	0.9	0.9
1997	38.1	39.4	0.2	0.9	0.9
1998	40.9	46.2	0.6	0.2	0.2
1999	47.6	63.2	−1.6	1.7	1.9
2000	50.9	70.6	0.3	3.9	5.1
2001	62.2	95.0	−1.4	6.0	8.4

Note: n.s.p. means "no sustainability problem."

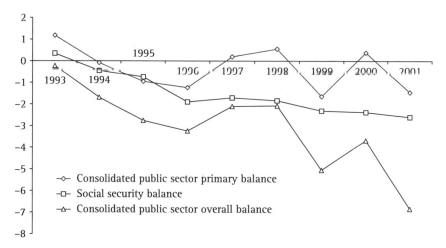

Figure 12.22. *The social security deficit in perspective (percentage of GDP)*
Source: Ministerio de Economía de la República Argentina and International Monetary Fund.

the fiscal situation, and thus made it more difficult to elicit political support for an adjustment while there was still time for an orderly correction.

In the same vein, even if the Currency Board had not collapsed, households and firms in non-tradable sectors would have suffered severe financial stress through the required RER adjustment, as their capacity to repay dollar and peso debts would have been eroded through the deflationary process. This would have had a major impact on the quality of bank portfolios, and the government would have been faced with large fiscal contingencies; though not as large as it incurred after the nominal devaluation as will be discussed below in Section 12.5.

12.4.3 The role of social security reform

Much of the observed deterioration in Argentina's fiscal accounts reflects the widening deficit of the Social Security system following its reform in 1994.[38] As a consequence of the reform, workers' Social Security contributions were diverted from the public sector towards the new private pension funds. Figure 12.22 plots the Social Security surplus along with the primary and overall balances of the consolidated public sector. It is apparent from the figure that from 1995 on (and especially in 1997–98) the deficit of the Social Security system accounted for a large portion of the overall public sector deficit. Further, comparison of the public sector primary deficit with the deficit of the Social Security system reveals

[38] See Hausmann and Velasco (2002). The economic, as opposed to accounting, merit of this view is disputed by Teijeiro (2001).

that from 1993 on the non-Social Security component of the public sector ran a primary surplus every year except 1995.

However, not all of the observed deterioration in the Social Security balance is attributable to the reform. Specifically, between 1994 and 2000–01 the Social Security deficit increased by roughly 2 percent of GDP. About half of this total, around 1 percent of GDP, was due to the reform. The rest resulted from a reduction in employers' contributions and other factors.[39] An amount equal to 1 percent of GDP is small relative to the extent of the fiscal correction that would have been required to address the fiscal sustainability problem identified in the previous tables. Thus, the fact that public finances were headed for insolvency after 1999 is not just a consequence of the reform-induced increase in the Social Security deficit.

Nevertheless, it is true that this growing deficit added to the conventionally measured fiscal imbalance in the post-reform years. In this regard, it is important to emphasize that the reform aimed at improving the long-term structural fiscal position of the country in the first place. Just as nominal devaluation in 2002 revealed the true volume of explicit public debt, pension reform revealed a hidden public sector debt, which had been kept out of sight by the former Pay-as-You-Go System (just like the hard peg did after 1997 with conventional debt).[40] The implication is that the Argentine fiscal situation up to 1994 had been worse than shown by the published figures.[41] In this sense, it must be concluded that fiscal imbalances (both explicit and implicit) were prevalent during the whole decade.

Yet, the fact that the reform led to a higher measured fiscal deficit still carries a lesson. From the economic, as opposed to accounting, perspective, the higher deficit had existed all along, and the "lifting of the veil" just put it in the open. The conversion of the implicit into explicit debt had two effects: (*a*) Public sector financing needs were raised by the amortization of the newly recognized debt that was measured by the present value of the benefits that the public sector had to keep on paying. This entailed additional demands on domestic and/or foreign financial markets. (*b*) Perceptions of Argentina's fiscal position may have been affected as well, to the extent that markets did not see fully through the veil separating explicit from implicit government debt.

The lesson is that extra care is needed regarding the consequences for financial markets of revealing and floating hidden pension liabilities. Even if doing so improves the long-term fiscal position, it must be accompanied by further fiscal adjustment in the short term (to absorb at least part of the increased medium-term cash deficit) and the issuance of appropriate long-term domestic debt instruments. With the benefit of hindsight, the boom years from the end of 1995 to mid-1998 appear as a major lost opportunity to tackle the fiscal Figure imbalances revealed by the pension reform.

---

[39] On this point, see Teijeiro (2001) and Cetrángolo and Jiménez (2003).

[40] As mentioned before, in Argentina the hidden liabilities also refer to Provincial pension systems, which were absorbed after 1995 by the Federal Government.

[41] Strictly speaking, the same is true for any other country with unfunded pension liabilities.

12.4.4   Public deficits, external debt, and the current account

Finally, we explore to what extent fiscal imbalances contributed to the persistent current account deficits of the 1990s. The latter posed two risks: They increased vulnerability to capital flow reversals, and also added to the overvaluation of the currency since, as we found above, much of the peso overvaluation can be traced to a steady deterioration of the net foreign asset position of the country.

What were the contributions of the private and public sectors to Argentina's external imbalance? Figure 12.23 depicts the overall fiscal balance of the consolidated government (exclusive of privatization revenues) and the private sector overall surplus—with the latter defined as the difference between the current account and the fiscal balance; thus, the sum of the private and public deficits equals the current account deficit by construction.

The figure reveals a contrast between the private and public sectors. While the public sector exhibited a deficit every year since 1993, the private sector alternated between deficit and surplus. In particular, after 1994 the private sector contributed to the current account deficit only in the boom years of 1997–98. By 1999 it had moved to a position of surplus, while the public sector continued to show large deficits.

Likewise, we can also examine the roles of the private and public sectors in Argentina's foreign debt build-up process. Table 12.10 shows that the economy's total external debt increased from 27.7 to 52.5 percent of GDP between 1993 and 2001. About half of this change reflects higher public indebtedness, while the other half seemingly reflects aggressive private sector borrowing abroad. Indeed, private external debt increased from 5.6 percent of GDP to 17 percent

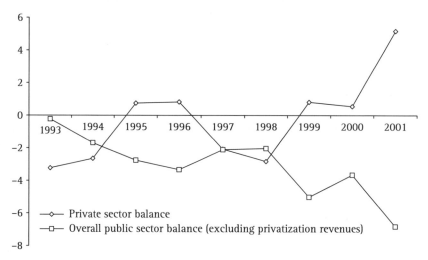

Figure 12.23. *Private and public current account balances (percentage of GDP)*
Source: Ministerio de Economía de la República Argentina and World Bank.

Table 12.10. *Debt stocks (percentage of GDP)*

	Total external	Consolidated government debt			Nonfinancial private and financial external debt (II)	Private external debt net of gov. bond holdings (III) = (II) − (I)
		Total	External	Domestic (I)		
1993	27.7	28.7	22.1	6.6	5.6	−1.0
1994	29.6	30.9	23.5	7.4	6.2	−1.3
1995	39.0	34.8	26.8	7.9	12.2	4.2
1996	41.8	36.6	27.4	9.3	14.4	5.1
1997	44.8	38.1	28.2	9.9	16.6	6.7
1998	48.6	40.9	30.2	10.6	18.3	7.7
1999	52.6	47.6	33.4	14.3	19.2	5.0
2000	52.7	50.9	33.8	17.1	18.9	1.8
2001	52.5	62.2	35.4	26.8	17.0	−9.7

Source: WDI.

during the period. One could view this as evidence that the private sector, as much as the public sector, was behind the accumulation of foreign liabilities.

However, Table 12.10 also shows that at the same time the public sector was borrowing massively from the private sector in the domestic capital market Indeed, between 1993 and 2001 domestic public borrowing rose by over 20 percentage points of GDP. This effectively means that the private sector was borrowing abroad on behalf of the government.

In summary, Argentina's large external imbalances and its deteriorating net foreign asset position reflected the action of both the private and public sectors at different times. During the boom of 1997–98, the private sector was the one showing the larger imbalance. However, the public sector failed to put its finances on a firm footing during those years, and especially after the pension reform made explicit part of the liabilities accumulated in the pension system. In turn, after 1998 the expanding saving–investment gap of the public sector was the main force at work behind the rising foreign liabilities of the Argentine economy.

12.5   The Banking System[42]

12.5.1   Strengths

Hyperinflation and deposit confiscation at the end of the eighties[43] wiped out confidence in the peso and domestic financial intermediation. After Convertibility was enacted, a major effort was launched to recreate a solid financial sector mostly based in dollar-denominated deposits and loans. In 1995 Tequila contagion led to a run on 18 percent of total deposits and to systemic illiquidity which, in the absence of a domestic lender of last resort, required prompt support from the IFIs to avoid a collapse of the banking and payments systems. The authorities responded by "building" a large liquidity buffer and through other ambitious reforms in order to consolidate a highly resilient financial system. Results were impressive. By 1998 Argentina ranked second (after Singapore, tied with Hong Kong, and ahead of Chile) in terms of the quality of its regulatory environment, according to the CAMELOT rating system developed by the World Bank[44] (Table 12.11).

The banking system was apparently in a very solid position not only by 1998, before the Brazilian devaluation of January 1999, but also afterwards and

---

[42] This section, and part of the next, is based on a technical note prepared for the first version of this chapter by Augusto de la Torre and Sergio Schmukler. The paper by de la Torre, Levy Yeyati, and Schmukler (this part) develops the summary analysis presented here in much greater detail.

[43] The 1989 Bonex plan already mentioned before.

[44] The CAMELOT index combined separate rankings for capital requirements (C); loan loss provisioning requirements and definition of past-due loans (A); management (M), defined by the extent of high-quality foreign bank presence; liquidity requirements (L); operating environment (O) as measured by rankings with respect to property rights, creditor rights, and enforcement; and transparency (T), as measured by whether banks are rated by international risk rating agencies and by an index on corruption. Argentina ranked 1 for C (tied with Singapore), 4 for A, 3 for M, 4 for L, 7 for O, and 2 for T. For further discussion see World Bank (1998: 39–61; and Appendix 12.A1).

Table 12.11. *CAMELOT ratings for banking system regulation*

Country	Total score[a]
Singapore	16
Argentina	21
Hong Kong	21
Chile	25
Brazil	30
Peru	35
Malaysia	41
Colombia	44
Korea	45
Philippines	47
Thailand	52
Indonesia	52

[a] Lower numbers indicate better ranking.

Source: World Bank, Argentina Financial Sector Review (1998).

through the end of 2000, despite the post-1998 continued economic contraction. In effect, through the year 2000 conventional indicators of financial health depicted a well-capitalized, strongly provisioned, and highly liquid banking system, although it was experiencing losses and increasingly burdened by bad loans after 1998 (Table 12.12).[45] The banking system's prudential buffers were sufficient to enable it to withstand sizable liquidity and solvency shocks—including a flight of more than one-third of the system's deposits as well as a sudden and complete default in up to 10 percent of the loan portfolio—without endangering the convertibility system.[46] The important presence of reputable foreign banks in the domestic system (they accounted for over 70 percent of total banking assets in 2000) was broadly perceived to implicitly augment these liquidity and solvency cushions (Table 12.13). These banks were expected to stand behind the capital and liquidity of their affiliates in Argentina, at least in the context of bad states of the world associated with bad luck (few were thinking then of bad states of the world caused directly by confiscatory government policy).

[45] Profits had turned negative already in 1998, and became deeply negative during 1999–2000 mainly because of the need to constitute provisions in the face of rising bad loans. Non-performing loans spiked to 10.2 percent of total loans in 2000, from 7.1 percent the year earlier, and the increase in provisions started to lag behind (Table 12.12).

[46] Table 12.12 puts systemic core liquidity (disposable international reserves of the central bank plus foreign exchange in cash or near-cash held abroad by banks) at above 35 percent of banking system deposits. However, there was a significant variance in the distribution of such liquidity across banks. This may explain why the "corralito" was imposed at the end of 2001 before deposits had fallen by 30 percent.

Table 12.12. *Selected banking system indicators (percentages at end-year)*

	1997	1998	1999	2000
Net worth/assets	12.11	11.44	10.72	10.52
Capital/Risk-weighted assets	18.13	17.64	18.56	21.18
Non-performing loans/Total loans (a)	8.23	5.98	7.14	10.21
Provisions/Total loans	7.70	7.10	7.82	8.65
Provisions/Non-performing loans (a)	108.64	140.40	122.25	77.13
Systemic core liquidity (b)	42.98	39.58	40.89	38.69
Return on equity before provisions	22.59	10.61	8.43	7.76
Return on equity after provisions	7.41	−2.24	−6.71	−9.42
Return on assets after provisions	1.04	−0.27	−0.77	−1.01
Leverage ratio (not in percent)	6.11	7.26	7.74	8.33

Notes:
(a) Non-performing loans is defined as the sum of loans with problems (category 3), loans with high risk (category 4) and non-recoverable loans (categories 5 and 6).
(b) Defined as the ratio of international reserves of the Central Bank in foreign currency and other liquidity requirements held abroad to total deposits.

Source: Central Bank of Argentina.

Table 12.13. *Consolidation and internationalization of the banking system*

	Dec. 1994	Dec. 1998	Dec. 2000
Number of total banks	166	104	89
Foreign banks			
Number of banks	31	39	39
Number of branches	391	1,535	1,863
Share of total assets (%)	15	55	73
Number of public banks	32	16	15

Source: Central Bank of Argentina.

12.5.2 Vulnerabilities

As the policy intent was to reinforce the viability of convertibility, it made no sense for the authorities to issue prudential norms that would discourage the use of the dollar in financial contracts *per se*. To be sure, the markets did not take the permanence of the Currency Board completely to heart—the peso problem continued throughout the 1990s, as evidenced by the always positive "currency risk" implicit in forward contracts, which showed spikes during turbulent times (Figure 12.24). But the authorities could not signal the possibility of a *nominal* devaluation through prudential norms without undermining their own quest to raise the credibility of Convertibility above all doubts. The hard peg and prudential regulation, thus, contributed to the high and increasing share of dollar deposits and dollar loans in the domestic financial system (Figure 12.25). The share of dollar deposits

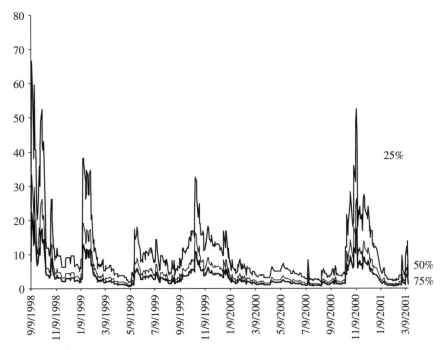

Figure 12.24. *Anticipated devaluation implied by the thirty-day NDF discount—up to 3/15/01 (at different perceived probabilities, percentage)*

Source: Schmukler and Servén (2002).

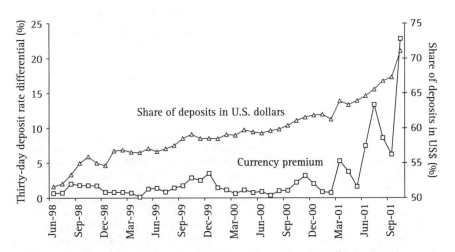

Figure 12.25. *Deposits in dollars and interest rate differential*

Source: Deposits from Ministerio de Economía (www.mecon.org); 30 day deposit interest rates in pesos and dollars from Bloomberg. Currency premia is defined as the difference of domestic interest rates in pesos and U.S. dollars.

increased after the Russian crisis and the Brazilian devaluation, and especially after mid-2001 when expectations of devaluation soared.

It was, thus, no secret that a disorderly breakdown of the rule of one-peso-one-dollar would wreck the banking system, and this was the main reason why many Argentine economists and external analysts preferred an exit from the Currency Board towards full dollarization over an exit towards a flexible exchange rate regime and a monetary anchor–and some still hold this view.

However, with the benefit of hindsight we can now identify at least three crucial vulnerabilities in the financial sector and weaknesses in the regulatory framework, even under the hypothesis that the Currency Board was to be permanent. The shortcomings relate to

(1) the link between debtor capacity-to-pay and the required deflationary adjustment to a more depreciated equilibrium RER;
(2) the growing exposure of the banking system to government default; and
(3) the insufficient realization that *general* liquidity buffers, even if high, do not adequately protect the payments system from a run.

The first vulnerability had to do with credit risk–the latent non-performing loans (NPLs) in the context of an overvaluation of the RER relative to its *equilibrium* level. As mentioned, it is estimated that, by the year 2001, the Argentine RER was overvalued by more than 50 percent. Under convertibility, the adjustment of the RER towards equilibrium was bound to imply a protracted and painful deflation and recession, which would have certainly eroded the capacity-to-pay of debtors whose earnings came from the non-tradable sector.[47] Hence, the first prudential shortcoming was the failure to recognize the special risk of loans to debtors in the non-tradable sector–a credit risk that would materialize in the event of significant adverse shocks that led to a deflationary adjustment.[48] Taking the one-peso-one-dollar rule as given, it would have been advisable for the authorities to require tougher loan classification criteria (higher loan-loss provisions and/or a higher weight for the purposes of measuring capital requirements) in the case of loans to the non-tradable sector, regardless of whether the loans were peso or dollar-denominated.[49]

---

[47] By contrast, in a country with a flexible exchange rate (i.e. where a fixed parity is *not* part of the social contract) and *without* a liability dollarization problem, the adjustment to a more depreciated equilibrium RER would come through a nominal depreciation, which would be associated with an *improvement* (through debt dilution) in the capacity-to-pay of debtors in the non-tradable sector.

[48] In a private communication to the authors, Andrew Powell noted the use of an "interest rate factor" in determining the required capital weight for individual loans, as an indirect way to take into account, among other things, such currency risks. However, as de la Torre et al. (this part) argue, such factors failed to capture the specific risk of loans to the non-tradable sector associated with eventual RER depreciations, and might have even encouraged further dollarization (as peso loans carried higher interest rates than dollar loans).

[49] These suggestions apply also to fully dollarized economies such as Ecuador. The same prescription should apply, *but only to dollar loans* to households and firms in the non-tradable sectors, in countries with a high degree of domestic financial dollarization that keep flexible exchange rate systems, such as Uruguay, Bolivia, and Peru, among others. See de la Torre et al. (this part).

The second vulnerability and prudential shortcoming also had to do with credit risk, but derived from exposure to Government risk. It consisted in the failure to isolate the solvency of the banking system from the solvency of the government. In countries with recurrent fiscal problems, like Argentina, it appears worthwhile to endeavor to delink financial system solvency from fiscal solvency, through the use of prudential norms. The authorities moved in this direction belatedly, in 2000, when they introduced mark-to-market requirements for government bond holdings and established a positive weight for loans to the government for the purposes of determining capital requirements. It would have been advisable to complement this prudential approach by not allowing government securities to count as part of the assets eligible to meet liquidity requirements. In this manner, the stability of the banking system and the viability of convertibility would have been better insulated from the vagaries of the fiscal process, including an event of government debt default. Direct exposure of banks to Government risk was not high until 2000—less than 20 percent of total assets. However, in 2001 the Government began to fund itself using available liquidity in the banking system in response to increasing external borrowing constraints (see Figure 12.26 and Section 12.6). Other components of the financial system, most notably private pension funds, had even higher exposure to Government risk.

The third vulnerability and prudential regulation shortcoming relates to the insufficient realization that *general* liquidity safeguards, even if high, do not adequately protect the payments system from a run. To be sure, high liquidity requirements, like those in effect in Argentina during the second-half of the 1990s, enhance the resiliency of the banking system: They cushion the system *vis-à-vis* liquidity shocks and deter runs, thereby reducing the scope for multiple

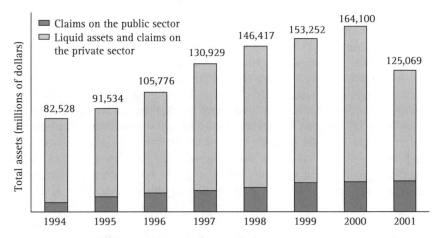

Figure 12.26. *Financial system: Exposure to public sector*

Source: Central Bank of Argentina.

equilibria. Thanks to its liquidity requirements, the Argentine banking system withstood a prolonged and severe process of deposit withdrawal during 2001. At the same time, however, the Argentine experience illustrates that once a run is under way, relaxing liquid reserve requirements can have adverse signaling effects that exacerbate the run on the peso (instead of spurring credit growth as Minister Cavallo had wrongly hoped[50]), further weakening confidence.

Moreover, Argentina illustrates that, as confidence collapses, a *general* liquidity requirement (available to all deposits) fails in its most basic intended function—it does not protect the payments system. The lesson is sobering. In the absence of a credible lender of last resort, the payments system is vulnerable and can collapse under a run even where liquidity is high, but still a fraction of deposits, and equally available to finance *any* deposit withdrawal. Thus, under a currency board and formal dollarization, protection of the payments system from bank runs may actually require a structure where there is full liquidity backing for transactions balances. This may amount to a sort of narrow banking for demand deposits, or to liquidity earmarking for those balances (under specified conditions) to allow the payments system to continue functioning, without deposit freezes and payments interruptions, even when banks are unable to honor withdrawals of time deposits.[51]

12.6   Policy Options Before and After 1999

12.6.1   Argentina's *via crucis*

Right from the beginning, the de la Rúa administration (which assumed power in December 1999) was caught in a trap of low growth, high and increasing debt rollover requirements, and an overvalued and inflexible exchange rate. The government's strategy to break free from this trap focused on reviving growth while reducing fiscal imbalances, although the means to achieve this objective changed dramatically after April 2001, when Cavallo took the post of Minister of Economy (see Appendix 12.A1 for a complete chronology). During 2000, growth resumption was sought indirectly, trying to regain investor confidence through fiscal adjustment. It was hoped that improved confidence would eventually lead to lower interest rates, more capital inflows and growth, making the debt and current account sustainable. To be sure, the authorities also tried to address the problem of currency overvaluation directly, through the flexibilization of labor markets. But the passage of labor reform through Congress was linked to a bribery scandal that led to the resignation of the Vice-President, further exacerbating confidence problems and weakening governance. In addition, as confidence was not restored and growth failed to pick up, the authorities shifted

---

[50] Many analysts actually cautioned about the potential negative effects of this move, and the extent of the reduction was a major cause of dispute between the Central Bank and the Government.
[51] de la Torre et al. (this part).

their attention towards calming fears of a possible debt default. The December 2000 IMF package (US$40 billion) was negotiated with this latter objective prominently in mind. However, none of these actions achieved the expected results and hopes of reviving growth faded away.

Minister Cavallo lent his prestige to the rescue effort. He also focused on rekindling growth, but this time more directly, through heterodox measures (in addition to enacting a revenue enhancing financial transactions tax). These included imposing a tax on imports and subsidizing exports (a fiscal devaluation for trade flows), lowering reserve requirements, and announcing the eventual peg of the peso to the dollar *and* the euro (with equal weights), once these two currencies reached parity (the "Convergence factor"). With hindsight, it is clear that this growth-focused strategy, particularly in Cavallo's heterodox version, was naïve. Not only did it fail to yield growth, it also increased uncertainty about the two other components of the trap, namely the debt rollover and the currency arrangement. The trap thus tightened.

Doubts about convertibility soared—the one-peso-to-one dollar rule had already been broken through the back door for trade transactions and could be easily broken also for financial transactions. Perhaps more importantly, the government procrastinated in taking a decision on the debt front. Instead of recognizing that debt restructuring was becoming a necessity following the failed attempts to restore confidence and growth, the government averted debt service arrears by draining the financial system's liquidity, as shown in Figure 12.26 above. This increased the financial system's exposure to a government default and heightened concerns about a potential abandonment of the currency board. As choices to finance the deficit through debt shrank rapidly, the specter of money printing loomed larger.

In the process, the fates of public finances, the banking system, and the dollar peg became tightly linked. This link foreshadowed the catastrophe, namely the disorderly abandonment of the one-peso-one-dollar rule in an economy with widespread public and private sector balance sheet vulnerabilities (i.e. dollar debts without dollar earnings). As a result, what little confidence remained soon was lost, and the crisis exploded as investors and depositors ran for the exit, forcing a deposit freeze (the "corralito"[52]) and a change in government.[53]

---

[52] The fact that the crisis had been widely anticipated for several months made it worse because depositors (mostly large and informed ones) had time to withdraw around 18 percent of total deposits, leaving only small depositors in the system.

[53] It has been argued that actions taken during Cavallo's tenure were instrumental in raising doubts about the permanence of the Currency Board and hence perceptions of fiscal unsustainability (given the large contingencies associated with a nominal devaluation), thus precipitating the final collapse. Careful inspection of the time path of currency and country premia shows that some of those actions—the announcement of changes in the peg, adoption of the "Convergence factor," the ousting of the Central Bank president, the changes in banks' liquidity requirements—did raise currency risk, followed by increases in country risk. However, these effects were only transitory: Both currency and country premia returned to their previous levels after a while. Irreversible effects began to appear only by July 2001, although it is difficult to identify any single event as the trigger.

12.6.2   Policy dilemmas and options

We now return to the discussion of the harsh policy dilemmas that Argentine authorities confronted after 1998. A large overvaluation developed as a consequence of adverse real shocks and insufficient price flexibility, as well as the deterioration of the economy's net foreign asset position. Keeping the hard peg, that had served so well until then, required a protracted deflationary adjustment to bring back the RER to equilibrium. This deflationary adjustment would have reduced the debt repayment capacity of households and firms—especially those in the non-tradable sectors—and, together with the long recession, led to a deterioration of the loan portfolio of banks. It would have also reduced the debt repayment capacity of the Government, raising increasing doubts about debt sustainability, and requiring large expenditure cuts in the face of declining revenues. The harsh fiscal adjustment that had to be unavoidably imposed to restore solvency would add further to the recession, complicating the adjustment for households, firms, banks, and the government. Argentina's fragile institutions, both economic and political, were to be put to a major test.

To achieve the required RER depreciation quickly, rather than by a protracted and painful deflationary adjustment, would have required a large nominal devaluation. This, however, would have brought immediate bankruptcy to a large number of households and firms in the non-tradable sector with dollar-denominated debts, thereby abruptly lowering the quality of banks' loan portfolios. The ratio of public debt to GDP would have ballooned and the government might have found itself suddenly cut off from credit. Although all these effects would have happened gradually anyhow under the hard peg, the abruptness of the balance-sheet effects might have precipitated an even larger wave of bankruptcies than in the alternative scenario and, as a consequence, the insolvency of the banking system and a major deposit flight. A plain devaluation in an economy with such large balance-sheet mismatches in both the public and private sectors would in all probability have led to an immediate banking and fiscal crisis—as many analysts predicted at the time.

What were the alternatives? The authorities might have attempted an earlier forced *pesofication* of all domestic contracts before devaluing. This would have contained the adverse balance-sheet effects of the devaluation on the government and on dollar-indebted firms in non-tradable sectors, helping to protect the financial sector.[54] However, forcefully breaking dollar deposit contracts would in all probability have led to a major deposit flight and would have required a deposit freeze in order to protect the payments system. In addition, this option would have demanded significant efforts to restore confidence in the peso as a store of value and to gain credibility for the new monetary authorities, as well as the creation of an alternative anchor to the hard peg. In reality, the

---

[54] This was publicly proposed by Ricardo Hausmann in Montevideo, at the October 2001 LACEA Annual Conference.

process was conducted in a highly disorderly way. Financial sector exposure to government debt had been on the rise. The arbitrary asymmetric *pesofication*, and its discriminatory implementation, resulted in a widespread violation of property rights. The deposit freeze was maintained too long and with changing rules, creating high uncertainty about the prospects for deposit recovery. The weakest banks received almost unlimited lender-of-last-resort support, instead of confronting the need for their resolution through equity injections or liquidation. All these unfortunate actions and omissions contributed to magnify the unavoidable cost of the exit from Convertibility.

The authorities might have accepted instead the need of a protracted deflationary adjustment and gone the opposite route, establishing full dollarization. This would have eliminated currency risk and perhaps achieved a reduction in interest rates, thus limiting somewhat the duration of the recession and alleviating the required fiscal adjustment. It might have been the option with lower short-term costs, if it had succeeded in avoiding a deposit run[55] and if it had been politically viable. However, debtors would have had to cope eventually with the adverse, although delayed, impact of the deflation on their repayment capacity. Most importantly, Argentina would have remained liable to similar episodes in the future, in which large adverse external shocks would have required slow and painful deflationary adjustments. To minimize these potential future costs, the authorities would have had to engage in significant fiscal strengthening, not just to protect solvency, but more broadly also to provide some room for countercyclical fiscal policy. They would have needed to adopt stricter prudential regulations on banks, including harder provisioning or capital requirements on loans to households and firms in non-tradable sectors, a "firewall" between banks and the Government, and liquidity earmarking to protect the payments system in the event of a systemic run. Considerable flexibilization of labor and other domestic markets (including the pricing of utilities) would have been required as well. Those actions would have had salutary effects also under an eventual floating exchange rate regime, but were sorely needed under a hard peg or dollarized system.

One variant[56] that could have reaped the short-term benefits of full dollarization while avoiding its long-run inflexibility costs, would have been to follow the full dollarization of financial stocks with "pesofication at the margin" through the introduction of a new domestic currency, initially limited to transactions uses.[57] In principle, this might have been the best exit option at the time the crisis erupted.[58] But forging the necessary consensus and implementing it smoothly would have been no easy matter under the circumstances.

---

[55] Such an outcome, of course, was far from assured, as de la Torre et al. (this part) recognize.

[56] This option was first proposed by Levy Yeyati and Schmukler (2001), and its adoption was indeed announced by President Rodriguez Saa during his short tenure.

[57] In fact, the new currency could have pre-empted the disorderly issuance of quasi-monies by cash-strapped provinces and the Federal Government.

[58] This option is discussed in detail by de la Torre et al. (this part).

Aside of political–economy considerations, implementation of any of these alternative courses would have been easier and less costly before solvency doubts had arisen. The boom years of 1996–97 were the "best" period for an orderly exit into either *pesofication* and floating or full dollarization. Any of these courses of action should have been accompanied by fiscal tightening, instead of the expansionary fiscal policy followed at the time. Considerable institutional strengthening would also have been required to permit a credible monetary policy under the options of *pesofication* (whether in full or at the margin, as just explained) and to reduce the deflationary consequences of future adverse external shocks under the option of full dollarization. However, this was precisely the time when everything was going fine, nobody was asking for a change and it might have been difficult to get political support for a major shift of policy and institution building. This is by no means a new finding: We have always known that the exit from an exchange rate regime should be undertaken in good times, precisely when nobody sees the need for it. Still, it would have been convenient at least to strengthen the fiscal position, instead of the structural weakening that was taking place (even after the pension reform and the recognition of other hidden liabilities had revealed the true extent of the fiscal problems), and to adopt stricter prudential regulations in the boom period.

The authorities now face a familiar dilemma. If they succeed in restoring confidence in the peso as a store of value, a floating exchange rate regime with a new monetary anchor can have a fair chance to succeed. Otherwise, they will have to opt for full dollarization. In that case they will have to achieve enough market flexibility and adopt a sufficiently robust fiscal stance together with strict prudential regulation to allow the economy to adjust in less painful ways to adverse external shocks in the future. In either case, the authorities will have to build stronger and more resilient institutions. After the recent confiscation of deposits and forced breach of contracts, restoring confidence in institutions, in the peso and the financial system—under whatever exchange rate regime and monetary arrangements emerge—will be a major challenge. Most likely Argentina will have to move forward for a while with a domestic banking system basically limited to current transactions. Such situation will give an extra premium to the development of a sound capital market and to restoring prompt access to external credit. Deep crises, however, offer the opportunity for bold changes. It is now imperative for Argentine society to seize the chance to construct stronger institutions than those of the past so as to build a more resilient economy.

REFERENCES

Alberola, E., Cervero, S., López, H., and Ubide, A. (1999). "Global Equilibrium Exchange Rates—Euro, Dollar, 'Ins,' 'Outs,' and Other Major Currencies in a Panel Cointegration Framework." *IMF Working Paper* No. 99/175.

—— López, H., and Servén, L. (2003). "Tango with the Gringo: The Hard Peg and Real Misalignment in Argentina." Unpublished paper, World Bank.

Alesina, A., Barro, R., and Tenreyro, S. (2002). "Optimal Currency Areas." *Harvard University Institute of Economic Research Discussion Paper* No. 1958.

Blanchard, O. (1993). "Suggestions for a New Set of Fiscal Indicators." In H. Verbon and F. van Winden (eds.), *The Political Economy of Government Debt*. Amsterdam: North Holland, pp. 307–24.

Broda, C. (2001). "Coping with Terms-of-Trade Shocks: Pegs Versus Floats." *American Economic Review*, 91(2): 76–80.

Calvo, G. and Reinhart, C. (2002). "Fear of Floating." *Quarterly Journal of Economics*, 117(2): 379–408.

Cetrángolo, O. and Jiménez, J. (2003). "La Sustentabilidad Fiscal." Unpublished paper filed in Estudios Macroeconómicos 1.EG.33.2, CEPAL.

Clarida, R. (1994). Cointegration, Aggregate Consumption, and the Demand for Imports: A Structural Econometric Investigation. *American Economic Review*, 84(1): 298–308.

Fiess, N. (2002). "Capital Flows, Country Risk and Contagion." World Bank, http://econ.worldbank.org/view.php?type=5&tid=22969.

Galiani, S. (2001). "Labor Market Reform in Argentina: Where Do We Stand?" Center for Research on Economic Development and Policy Reform Working Paper, Stanford University.

Gavin, M. and Perotti, R. (1997). "Fiscal Policy in Latin America: Volatility, Cyclicality and Modes of Adjustment." *NBER Macroeconomics Annual 1997*, 12: 11–71.

— Hausmann, R., Perotti, R., and Talvi, E. (1996). "Managing Fiscal Policy in Latin America and the Caribbean: Volatility, Procyclicality, and Limited Creditworthiness." *IADB Working Paper* No. 326.

Goldfajn, I. and Valdés, R. (1999). "The Aftermath of Appreciations." *Quarterly Journal of Economics*, 114(1): 229–62.

Hausmann, R., Panizza, U., and Stein, E. (2000). "Why Do Countries Float the Way they Float?" www.iadb.org/res/publications/pubfiles/pubWP-418.pdf, *IADB Working Paper* No. 418.

— and Velasco, A. (2003). "The Argentine Collapse: Hard Money's Soft Underbelly, Understanding the Argentinean." In S. M. Collins and D. Rodrick (eds.), *Brookings Trade Forum 2002*. Washington, DC: The Brookings Institution, pp. 59–104.

Kakkar, V. and Ogaki, M. (1999). "Real Exchange Rates and Non-tradables: A Relative-Price Approach." *Journal of Empirical Finance*, 6(2): 193–215.

Levy Yeyati, E. and Schmukler, S. (2001). "Dollarization and Floating of a New Currency: A Way Out of the Currency Board." Unpublished paper, World Bank.

Mussa, M. (2002). *Argentina and the Fund: From Triumph to Tragedy*. Washington, DC: Institute for International Economics.

Orphanides, A. and van Norden, S. (2002). "The Unreliability of Output Gap Estimates in Real Time." *Review of Economics and Statistics*, 84(4): 569–83.

Perry, G. (2002). "Can Fiscal Rules Help Reduce Macroeconomic Volatility in LAC?" World Bank, http://wbln0018.worldbank.org/LAC/lacinfoclient.nsf.

Powell, A. (2003). "Argentina's Avoidable Crisis: Bad Luck, Bad Economics, Bad Politics, Bad Advice." In S. M. Collins and D. Rodrick (eds.), *Brookings Trade Forum 2002*. Washington, DC: The Brookings Institution, pp. 1–58.

Rodrik, D. (2003). "Argentina: A Case of Globalization Gone Too Far or Not Far Enough." In J. J. Teunissen and A. Akkerman (eds.), *The Crisis that Was Not Prevented: Lessons for Argentina, the IMF, and Globalization*. The Hague, NL: Forum on Debt and Development (FONDAD), pp. 15–21.

Roubini, N. (2001). "Should Argentina Dollarize or Float? The Pros and Cons of Alternative Exchange Rate Regimes and their Implications for Domestic and Foreign Debt Restructuring/Reduction." Stern School of Business, New York University, www.stern.nyu.edu/globalmacro.

Sachs, J. (2002). "Understanding and Responding to Argentina's Economic Crisis." Unpublished paper, Center for International Development–Harvard University.

Schmukler, S. and Servén, L. (2002). "Pricing Currency Risk under Currency Boards." *Journal of Development Economics*, 69(2): 367–91.

Teijeiro, M. (2001). Una Vez Más, La Política Fiscal..., Centro de Estudios Públicos, www.cep.org.ar/format.inc?body=trabajos_investigacion.inc.

World Bank (1998). *Argentina: Financial Sector Review*, Report No. 17864-AR.

Appendix 12.A1.   Argentina's *via crucis*

December 1999   President de la Rúa assumes power when the country is already in recession and public debt has reached high levels. The government tries to gain confidence, and thus restore growth, through fiscal adjustment.

January 2000   The "impuestazo" is implemented. The new tax scheme includes, among other things, an increase in the taxation on consumer goods, an extension of VAT to health insurance and transportation, and an expansion of the income tax base. The fiscal adjustment does not bring growth. Rather, the recession deepens and doubts about debt sustainability increase dramatically.

October 2000   The political weakness of the de la Rúa's administration becomes evident when vice-president Carlos Alvarez resigns.

December 2000   Minister Machinea negotiates a US$40 billion package with international financial institutions and domestic financial institutions to extend the public debt maturity and try to ease fears of default. The deal implied a much lower amount of fresh funds, around US$12 billion.

March 2001   The government's bet is that once these fears were eased, growth would resume, but growth does not pick up and Mr. Machinea resigns.

March 16, 2001   The newly appointed economy minister López Murphy resigns after two weeks in office, upon strong opposition to the new fiscal austerity package he sent to Congress.

April 16, 2001   Domingo Cavallo becomes Economy Minister once more. He is empowered by Congress with special powers and tries different, more direct, measures to revive growth. He proposes to congress an amendment to the convertibility law, according to which the peso would be pegged to a basket consisting of U.S. dollars and euros with equal weights when the dollar–euro exchange rate reaches 1:1. Congress approves the amendment in mid-June 2001. This change aims at better aligning the peso with Argentina's trading partners.

April 25, 2001   The president of the central bank, Pedro Pou, resigns amid disagreements with Cavallo and other members of the government. Roque Maccarone replaces Pou.

July 10, 2001   The government, after being forced to pay 1410 basis points over U.S. Treasuries to place a short-term bond, announces a "zero-deficit" rule. It thus becomes obvious that the government cannot tap capital markets without the debt exploding. To implement the zero-deficit rule, the government pushes hard for an IMF-supported program. But to obtain it, an agreement with the provinces on tax revenue sharing is needed. John Taylor, Under Secretary of the U.S. Treasury, declares that there will not be any external help for Argentina until it can comply with its objective of a zero deficit.

October 26, 2001   Negotiations toward an agreement with the provinces on the distribution of tax revenues fail (again).

October 28, 2001   Minister Cavallo starts negotiations to obtain resources from the IMF and the U.S. Treasury to purchase collateral for new bonds to be issued in an exchange for the nearly US$100 billion of local and external debt.

November 19, 2001   The IMF announces that it will not make any new disbursements to Argentina without being satisfied that the country has secured the goals previously defined.

December 2, 2001   The government announces measures restricting deposit withdrawals (the corralito). Withdrawals are limited to 250 pesos (dollars) per week per account.

December 19, 2001   Cavallo and all other ministers resign.

December 20, 2001   President de la Rúa resigns and Ramon Puerta becomes interim president.

December 23, 2001   Rodriguez Saa, governor of one of the provinces, becomes interim president. His tenure is supposed to last sixty days, until elections are called on March 3, 2002. He declares the suspension of external debt payments for at least sixty days.

December 24, 2001   The government announces that a new fiat currency (i.e. without foreign-currency backing) would be created, the "argentino."

December 30, 2001   President Saa resigns. The legislative assembly chooses Eduardo Duhalde as new president on January 1, 2002. To garner support for his administration, Duhalde promises to leave office in December 2003 and not to run for re-election.

January 3, 2002   Jorge Remes Lenicov becomes new minister of economy. The government prepares a plan of controlled devaluation of the peso.

January 6, 2002   The peso is officially devalued to 1.40 per dollar.

January 7, 2002   The government enforces an asymmetric pesofication program that worsens the imbalances of commercial bank balance sheets. President Duhalde vetoes the pesofication of debts over US$100,000.

January 18, 2002   Maccarone resigns from his post as Central Bank president due to differences of opinion with the government. He is replaced by the vice-president, Mario Blejer.

February 3, 2002   The authorities decide to abandon the hard peg and let the peso float.

April 23, 2002   The financial crisis deepens and Lenicov resigns after Congress rejects an executive-sponsored bill for the compulsory exchange of frozen deposits for government bonds. A banking holiday is decreed from April 22 through 25.

April 27, 2002   President Duhalde designates Roberto Lavagna as new Economy Minister.

June 25, 2002   The peso closes at its lowest level of 3.86 per dollar.

June 26, 2002   The Central Bank accepts the resignation of Blejer. Aldo Pignarelli takes his place.

July 3, 2002   President Duhalde brings forward the presidential elections by six months to March 2003 and schedules the handover to the new government for May 2003. Open internal primaries are announced for November 2002.

November 23, 2002   Lavagna announces the end of the "Corralito" and the non-payment of debt service due to the World Bank.

December 11, 2002   Pignatelli resigns as Central Bank president and Alfonso Prat Gay replaces him.

January 2003   The Congress sanctions the Ley de Lemas, which allows each political party to field more than one presidential candidate.

April 8, 2003   The authorities lift restrictions on withdrawals of time deposits (the "corralón").

April 27, 2003   Two Peronist candidates, Carlos Menem and Néstor Kirchner, win the first round of the presidential election.

May 14, 2003   Menem withdraws from the second round of the presidential election.

May 25, 2003   Kirchner is inaugurated as Argentina's new president.

PART IV

Common Monies, Political Interests, and Infrastructure

13

America's Interest in Dollarization

BENJAMIN J. COHEN

What is the U.S. interest in dollarization? Formal adoption of the dollar by other governments creates both opportunities and risks for the United States, political as well as economic. But few benefits or costs can be estimated in advance, leaving much room for debate and disagreement. The argument here is that no presumption can be established either way, whether for or against dollarization, from a strictly U.S. point of view. Unless directly challenged by efforts elsewhere to establish formal currency blocs, the United States has no interest in promoting a wider role for the greenback.

13.1 Introduction

What is America's interest in dollarization? As more countries contemplate following the examples of Ecuador and El Salvador, which have dollarized unilaterally, it is natural to ask whether the United States can expect to gain or lose in the process. The central focus is on Latin America, considered the most natural home for an incipient dollar zone. Other chapters in this volume consider the pros and cons of dollarization from the point of view of the Latins themselves. This chapter, by contrast, evaluates the possibility from a U.S. perspective.

Formal adoption of the dollar by neighboring governments creates both opportunities and risks for the United States, political as well as economic. But few benefits or costs can be estimated in advance with any degree of precision, leaving much room for debate and disagreement. The argument of this chapter is that no presumption can be established either way, whether for or against dollarization, from a strictly U.S. point of view. Unless directly challenged by efforts elsewhere to establish formal currency blocs, the United States has no interest in promoting a wider role for the greenback.

13.2 The Status Quo

We start with the status quo. Much of Latin America is already extensively dollarized on a de facto basis, as a result of currency substitution—a spontaneous, market-driven process now distinguished as *informal* (unofficial) dollarization. America's interest in *formal* (official) dollarization must be compared with this reality, from which, it may be argued, the United States already derives significant economic and political advantages.

13.2.1 The dollar's market leadership

Broadly speaking, currencies may be employed outside their country of origin for either of two purposes—for transactions either between nations or within foreign states. The former is conventionally referred to as international currency use or currency internationalization; the latter goes under the label currency substitution and can be referred to as foreign–domestic use. For both purposes, the U.S. dollar is used today on a very broad basis. Indeed, the greenback is indisputably the market leader among world currencies, its only serious rivals being Europe's new euro (succeeding the deutschmark) and the Japanese yen.

The clearest signal of the greenback's leadership in international currency use is sent by the global foreign-exchange market where, according to the Bank for International Settlements (2002), the dollar is the most favored vehicle for currency trading worldwide, appearing on one side or the other of some 90 percent of all transactions in 2001 (the latest year for which data are available). The euro, in distant second place, appeared in just 38 percent of transactions—higher than the share of its popular predecessor, the deutschmark, which had appeared in 30 percent of transactions in 1998, but lower than that of all euro's constituent currencies taken together that same year (53 percent). The yen was even further behind with only 23 percent. The greenback is also the most favored vehicle for the invoicing of international trade, where it has been estimated to account for nearly half of all world exports (Hartmann 1998), more than double America's share of world exports. The DM's share of invoicing in its last years, prior to its replacement by the euro, was 15 percent, roughly equivalent to Germany's proportion of world exports; preliminary evidence from the European Central Bank (2001: 18) suggests that this share was maintained by the euro after its introduction as a "virtual" currency in 1999. The yen's share was just 5 percent, significantly less than Japan's proportion of world exports.

A parallel story is evident in international markets for financial claims, including bank deposits and loans as well as bonds and stocks. Using data from a variety of sources, Thygesen et al. (1995) calculated what they call "global financial wealth," the world's total portfolio of private international investments, estimated at more than $4.5 trillion in 1993. Again the dollar dominated, accounting for nearly three-fifths of foreign-currency deposits and close to two-fifths of international bonds. The DM accounted for 14 percent of deposits and 10 percent of bonds; the yen, 4 percent of deposits and 14 percent of bonds.

The clearest signal of the greenback's leadership in foreign–domestic use is sent by the swift increase in the currency's physical circulation outside the borders of the United States, mostly in the form of $100 bills. Authoritative studies by the Federal Reserve (Porter and Judson 1996) and U.S. Treasury (2000), consistent with estimates suggested by Feige and Dean (this volume, Part III), put the value of all Federal Reserve notes in circulation abroad at between 50 and 70 percent of the total outstanding stock—equivalent in 2000 to roughly $275–375 billion in all. Estimates also suggest that as much as three-quarters of the annual increase of U.S. notes now goes directly abroad, up from less than one-half in the 1980s and under one-third in the 1970s. By the end of the 1990s, as much as 90 percent of all $100 notes issued by the Federal Reserve were going directly abroad to satisfy foreign demand (Lambert and Stanton 2001). Appetite for informal dollarization appears to be not only strong but growing.

By contrast, estimates by the Deutsche Bundesbank (1995) put circulation of the DM outside Germany in recent years, mainly in East–Central Europe and the Balkans, at no more than 30–40 percent of total stock, equivalent at end-1994 to some DM 65–90 billion ($45–65 billion). And even that total may have been reduced somewhat after 1999, when Europe's monetary union first got under way, owing to uncertainties about the conversion of DM notes into euros that finally took place in early 2002 (Sinn and Westermann 2001; Stix 2001). It remains unclear to what extent euro notes may surpass the level of popularity previously enjoyed by the DM. On the other side of the world, Bank of Japan officials have been privately reported to believe that of the total supply of yen bank notes, amounting to some $370 billion in 1993, no more than 10 percent was located in neighboring countries (Hale 1995).

13.2.2 Advantages for the United States

Not surprisingly, all this foreign use of the dollar appears to translate into considerable advantages for the United States, both economic and political. Though minimized by some (e.g. Wyplosz 1999: 97–100), the benefits of market leadership in currency affairs can in fact be quite substantial. Four distinct gains may be cited.

Most familiar is the potential for seignorage. Expanded cross-border circulation of a country's money generates the equivalent of a subsidized or interest-free loan from abroad—an implicit transfer that represents a real-resource gain for the economy as a whole. Consider just the circulation of Federal Reserve notes abroad. Updating earlier estimates by Jeffrey A. Frankel (1995) and Alan S. Blinder (1996), current interest savings may be conservatively calculated at some $16–22 billion a year. To this may be added a saving of interest payments on U.S. government securities, which are uniquely attractive to foreign holders because of their greater liquidity. Richard Portes and Hélène Rey (1998: 309) call this an "often neglected source of seignorage to the issuer of the international currency." In their words (1998: 309): "This international currency effect reduces the real yields that the United States government has to pay"—a "liquidity discount" that they suggest could amount to at least $5–10 billion a year. Put these numbers together and, paraphrasing former Republican Senator Everett Dirksen's celebrated remark about the Federal budget, we are beginning to talk about real money.

A second gain is the increased flexibility of macroeconomic policy that is afforded by the privilege of being able to rely on one's own money to help finance foreign deficits. As in any form of monetary union, expanded cross-border circulation reduces the real cost of adjustment to unanticipated payments shocks by internalizing through credit what otherwise would be external transactions requiring scarce foreign exchange. In effect, it reduces the need to worry about the balance of payments in formulating and implementing domestic policy. Who can remember the last time Washington decision-makers actively incorporated concern for our large current deficits or our exchange rate in debating the course of monetary and fiscal policy?

Third, more psychological in nature, is the gain of status and prestige that goes with market dominance. Money, as I have written elsewhere (Cohen 1998), has long played a key symbolic role for governments, useful—like flags, anthems, and postage stamps—as a means to cultivate a unique sense of national identity. But that critical role is eroded to the extent that a local currency is displaced by a more popular foreign money, especially a money, such as the greenback, that is so widely used on a daily basis. Foreign publics are constantly reminded of America's elevated rank in the community of nations. "Great powers have great currencies," Robert Mundell once wrote (1993: 10). In effect, the dollar has become a potent symbol of American primacy—an example of what political scientist Joseph S. Nye (1990) has called "soft power," the ability to exercise influence by shaping beliefs and perceptions. Though obviously difficult to quantify, the role of reputation in international affairs should not be underestimated.

Finally, there is the gain of political power that derives from the monetary dependence of others. On the one hand, an issuing country is better insulated from outside influence in the domestic arena. On the other hand, it is also better positioned to pursue foreign objectives without constraint or even to exercise a degree of influence internationally. As political scientist Jonathan Kirshner reminds us: "Monetary power is a remarkably efficient component of state power . . . the most potent instrument of economic coercion available to states in a position to exercise it" (1995: 29, 31). Money, after all, is simply command over real resources. If another country can be denied access to the means needed to purchase vital goods and services, it is clearly vulnerable in political terms. Kirshner lists four ways in which currency dependence can be exploited: (*a*) enforcement—manipulation of standing rules or threats of sanctions; (*b*) expulsion—suspension or termination of privileges; (*c*) extraction—use of the relationship to extract real resources; and (*d*) entrapment—transformation of a dependent state's interests. The dollar's widespread use puts all of these possibilities in the hands of Washington policymakers.

Admittedly there are limits to these benefits, which are likely to be greatest in the early stages of cross-border use when confidence in a money is at a peak. Later, as external liabilities accumulate increasing supply relative to demand, gains may be eroded, particularly if an attractive alternative comes on the

market. Foreign holders may legitimately worry about the risk of future depreciation or even restrictions on the usability of their holdings. Thus, the currency
leader's autonomy may eventually be constrained, to a degree, by a need to discourage sudden or substantial conversions through the exchange market. Both
seignorage income, on a net basis, and macroeconomic flexibility will be reduced
if a sustained increase of interest rates is required to preserve market share.
Likewise, overt exploitation of political power will be inhibited if foreigners can
switch allegiance easily to another currency. But even admitting such limits, there
seems little doubt that on balance these are advantages of considerable significance, as numerous sources acknowledge (e.g. Portes and Rey 1998: 308–10). The
question is: Given the already widespread foreign use of the dollar, what would
be added by formal dollarization in one or more countries?

13.3 Economic Impacts

As compared with the status quo, three economic benefits are generally expected
to accrue to the United States from formal dollarization: An increase of seignorage, a decrease of transaction costs, and an improved environment for foreign
trade and investment. Conversely, there could also be a cost in terms of possible
constraints on the conduct of U.S. monetary policy. Though none of these effects
need be trivial, their magnitudes can be easily exaggerated. In fact, none is apt
to be of more than marginal significance to an economy as large as that of the
United States.

13.3.1 Seignorage

Formal dollarization, when undertaken unilaterally, means that a government
must give up interest-bearing dollar reserves in order to acquire the greenback notes and coins needed to replace local cash in circulation. The interest
payments thus forgone represent an additional flow of seignorage to the United
States—a material gain that comes at the direct expense of the dollarizing country.
For Latin American economies, many of which are quite small, these costs would
not be inconsiderable—in comparative terms, a potentially "very high financial
tribute to the United States," as George von Furstenberg (2000: 109) asserts. But
for the United States, with its 10-trillion dollar GDP, gains would be barely visible,
especially given the sizable amount of seignorage that Washington already
accrues from the circulation of dollars in the Western Hemisphere and elsewhere.
According to economists at the International Monetary Fund (Baliño et al. 1999),
the greenback even now accounts for a substantial portion of the broad money
supply of many Latin American economies—more than half in Nicaragua and Peru
and as much as 80 percent in Bolivia and Uruguay. The greater the degree of prior
informal dollarization in a country, the smaller will be the additional transfer
generated by formal dollarization.

13.3.2   Transaction costs

By eliminating any possibility of exchange-rate change, formal dollarization also reduces transactions costs. This is the standard economic benefit expected from monetary integration, an efficiency gain that is shared by both sides, the United States as well as the country that dollarizes. Once a local money is replaced by the dollar, there is no longer a need to incur the expenses of currency conversion or hedging in transactions between the United States and its partner economy. The usefulness of money is enhanced for all its basic functions: Medium of exchange, unit of account, and store of value. Again, however, benefits for the United States are unlikely to be considerable, since most U.S. trade with Latin America, as well as a good part of the nation's portfolio investment, is already contracted in dollars. Certain specific sectors will profit, of course. Earnings could be increased at U.S. banks, for example, which are naturally advantaged relative to their rivals in dollarized countries by their privileged access to the resources of the Federal Reserve. Economists have long recognized that international use of a currency generates "denomination rents" for financial intermediaries based in the country of issue. Gains should also accrue to other market actors who currently may still be exposed to exchange risk in the Hemisphere. These would include export and import interests and portfolio investors. They would also include American tourists who are fond of travel south of the border. But, overall, additional gains for the U.S. economy will be slight.

13.3.3   Environment for trade and investment

Finally, formal dollarization is widely predicted to benefit the United States by bringing greater stability to the countries of the Hemisphere, creating an improved environment for regional trade and investment. Latin American central banks, with their histories of high inflation and debauched currencies, do not enjoy a great deal of credibility. Adoption of the dollar, by contrast, would mean that loose monetary policy could no longer threaten renewed financial crisis. In the words of investment banker Michael Gavin (2000), monetary regimes would now be "accident-proof," ostensibly removing a key impediment to economic development. Faster and steadier growth, in turn, would mean healthier markets for U.S. exports and direct investments.

But would monetary regimes really be accident-proof? Dollarization addresses only one among many of the causes of economic instability in Latin America—exchange-rate risk—but offers no direct corrective for other critical deficiencies, such as undisciplined fiscal policy, poor banking supervision, or labor-market rigidities. The hope is that by strait-jacketing monetary policy, additional structural reforms will fall into place. But as Walter Molano (2000: 52) has warned, this could be "just wishful thinking." Molano continues (2000: 60): "Dollarization is a one-sided look at the problem ... Dollarization is not a solution to the institutional flaws that led to the crisis in the first place. It does nothing to shape the political will needed to sustain the exchange rate regime." A case in point is Argentina, where the discipline of the dollar-based currency board instituted in 1991 sadly failed to bring about any significant reform of fiscal policy. As a result, once foreign creditors lost faith in the government's debt-service capacity, the economy was plunged into deep recession and ultimately, in late 2001, into default and financial chaos. Too much faith, in short, should not be invested in a single institutional innovation such as dollarization. In reality, the market environment for U.S. business could turn out to be considerably less stable than suggested.

13.3.4 Economic disadvantages

On the negative side, the key economic risks concern possible disadvantages for the conduct of U.S. monetary policy. Most salient is the possibility that by placing a large share of greenbacks in circulation abroad, formal dollarization could impose an awkward constraint on Federal Reserve decision-makers. If money demand in dollarizing countries is subject to sudden or frequent shifts, net flows would be generated that might increase the short-term volatility of U.S. monetary aggregates. Such liquidity shocks could make it tougher for the Fed to maintain a steady course over time.

But here, too, it is easy to exaggerate, since a large share of the outstanding stock of U.S. bank notes, as noted, is already in circulation outside U.S. borders, with little or no evident impact on policy. The Fed recognizes the phenomenon of informal dollarization and, as part of its daily open-market operations targeting the federal-funds rate, already factors overseas circulation into its behavior. In any event the additional sums involved, even if many governments were to dollarize, are unlikely to be great enough to make much practical difference in America's still relatively closed economy.

More remote is the possibility that at some point one or more dollarized countries might suddenly decide to reintroduce currencies of their own—to *de*-dollarize—precipitating a mass dumping of greenbacks in global exchange markets. The result for the dollar could be a serious depreciation, generating increased inflationary pressures in the United States. The probability of major defections, however, is undoubtedly low, given the high exit costs that would have to be borne by seceding governments; and in this event too, unless the number of states involved was large, the sums are unlikely to be great enough to make a real difference for U.S. policy.

13.4 Political Impacts

What, then, about possible political impacts? Politically, two main benefits are expected to accrue to the United States, summarized by the words "power and prestige," along with one possible cost in terms of added responsibility for the fate of client states. All of these potential effects are undeniably real.

Sincere people, however, may sincerely disagree over how important they may turn out to be in actual practice.

13.4.1 Power

In geopolitical terms, preservation of a national currency is useful to governments wary of external dependence or threat. Control over the issue and circulation of money within their own borders enables policymakers to avoid dependence on some other source for this most critical of economic resources, in effect providing a kind of insurance policy against risk. Money creation can serve as an emergency source of revenue—a way of finding needed purchasing power quickly when confronted with unexpected contingencies, up to and including war. Conversely, that same measure of autonomy is lost when a foreign money is formally adopted. The relationship with a dollarized country is clearly hierarchical—a link of dominance and dependence—and hierarchy unavoidably implies vulnerability.

An apt illustration is provided by Panama, which since its independence in 1903 has always used the greenback as its main legal tender. Although a national currency, the balboa, notionally exists, only a negligible amount of balboa coins actually circulates in practice. The bulk of local money supply, including all paper notes and most bank deposits, is accounted for by the dollar. In economic terms, observers rightly have mostly praise for Panama's currency dependence (e.g. Goldfajn and Olivares 2001). Though reliance on the dollar has by no means induced a high degree of fiscal discipline, it has succeeded in creating an environment of monetary stability, helping both to suppress inflation—a bane of most of Panama's hemispheric neighbors—and to establish the country as an important offshore financial center. In political terms, however, Panama has been especially vulnerable in its relations with Washington, as Panamanians learned in 1988 when the Reagan administration initiated a campaign to force Manuel Noriega, the country's de facto leader, from power. Panamanian assets in U.S. banks were frozen, and all payments and dollar transfers to Panama were prohibited, effectively demonetizing the economy. The effect on the economy was devastating despite rushed efforts by the Panamanian authorities to create a substitute currency, mainly by issuing checks in standardized denominations that they hoped recipients would then treat as cash. Over the course of the year, domestic output fell by a fifth, undoubtedly hastening Noriega's eventual downfall in 1989.

Such vulnerability clearly enhances Washington's political authority: Its capacity to exercise influence or threaten coercion. But again, it is crucial not to exaggerate. For many, Panama was a special case, unlikely to be repeated anywhere else in the hemisphere. In any event, what may work with an economy as small and defenseless as Panama's might be less effective when attempted against a larger and more developed country. Moreover, the United States has worked long and hard to erase unpleasant memories of dollar diplomacy in Latin America. One may legitimately wonder whether any administration in Washington, Democrat or

Republican, would wish to do anything that might revive past resentments of *Yanqui* imperialism. The power derived from dollarization is tangible but, like nuclear arms, may be something of a doomsday weapon—in practice, more or less unusable except *in extremis.*

13.4.2 Prestige

Somewhat less tangibly, the United States could also gain yet greater status and prestige from formal dollarization. Symbols, however, can prove to be a two-edged sword, depending on circumstances. What in prosperous times may be accepted as benign, even natural, might become a focal point for hostility in the event of recession or crisis. Formal dollarization creates a convenient target for protest. When the greenback was adopted in Ecuador, demonstrators marched in the streets denouncing what they feared would be the "dollarization of poverty." It is easy to imagine similar manifestations in the future, in Ecuador or elsewhere, blaming the dollar—and thus the United States—for any failures of economic management at home. It is even possible to imagine politicians deliberately fomenting popular protests as a way of diverting attention from their own policy errors. Prestige could come at a very high price, creating an easy target for grievances.

13.4.3 Political disadvantages

Nor is that exposure the only political price that might be exacted from the United States. By adopting the greenback, a government voluntarily surrenders control over its own money supply and exchange rate. All authority is ceded to the Federal Reserve, making the country a monetary dependency, a client of the United States. Formally, there need be no promises of any kind: No assurance that the dollarizing economy's circumstances will be taken into account when monetary decisions are made, nor access to the Fed's lender of last resort facilities should the country's banks get into difficulty. Indeed, Washington officials have gone out of their way to deny that U.S. policy or institutions would be adjusted in any way. In reality, however, as frequently noted (e.g. Samuelson 1999), it might be very difficult for the American government to ignore adverse developments in the periphery of its own currency bloc. Even in the absence of any explicit commitment, dollarization could create an implicit expectation of future monetary bailouts – a kind of contingent claim on U.S. resources. Such an expectation is the flip side of America's enhanced political authority. With primacy comes not only greater influence but also, potentially, greater responsibility.

Therefore, like it or not, policymakers could find themselves periodically under pressure to accommodate specific needs or fragilities. The Fed might be lobbied to take explicit account of the priorities of dollarized economies in setting its policy goals—especially in the event of asymmetric payments shocks—or to open its discount window to local financial institutions. In time, governments might even begin to campaign for indirect or even direct representation on the Federal Reserve Board or Federal Open-Market Committee. Likewise, the Treasury might be importuned to come to some country's rescue in the event of financial crisis. Once again, however, it is crucial not to exaggerate. Though the risk is evident, the probabilities involved are unknowable. No one can forecast with assurance how dollarized countries will behave in actual practice. As with all the effects of dollarization, there is no strong presumption one way or the other. The national interest is uncertain.

13.5 Options for U.S. Policy

What, then, should the United States do? Until now, as I note elsewhere (Cohen 2002), U.S. policy has remained cautiously neutral—a strategy of "benign neglect," to borrow a phrase from an earlier era. Governments considering dollarization may be given moral support, and perhaps some technical assistance, but otherwise are left more or less on their own. No formal commitments are offered. Adoption of the greenback must be entirely unilateral, as has already occurred in Ecuador and El Salvador. The question is: Should Washington do more?

The answer follows directly from the analysis. No change of policy appears warranted unless present gains are threatened. Benign neglect makes sense in current circumstances, where the U.S. already derives considerable advantage from the dollar's market leadership. Why do more if there is so little promise of additional net benefit? Only if the dollar's leadership is directly challenged, jeopardizing present gains, would a more proactive policy be called for. Washington has little interest in augmenting the greenback's global dominance but much interest in defending it.

This means that a good deal will depend on what actions are taken on behalf of the greenback's principal rivals, the euro and yen. Europe and Japan too enjoy critical advantages as a result of the international use of their respective moneys and both Europeans and Japanese have spoken of aspirations for currency leadership of their own. In this connection, however, it is useful to draw a distinction between two different kinds of leadership in monetary affairs: *Informal* and *formal*. The implications of each are quite different.

That Europe and Japan will do all they can to sustain the underlying competitiveness of their respective moneys, relative to the dollar, is a foregone conclusion. The multiple benefits of extensive cross-border use are well understood, providing more than enough incentive to motivate policymakers to promote widespread adoption of the euro or yen by *market* actors. Above all, this means enforcing structural reforms of financial markets to reduce the cost of doing business in either currency. Aggressive challenge at this level has long been accepted by Washington as an inevitable by-product of open markets. Commercial rivalry for market share—what we may call informal leadership—is natural in a setting that can be accurately described as analogous to an oligopoly (Cohen 2000) and would be unlikely to trigger a defensive response from U.S. authorities.

But what if Europe or Japan were to go a step further, seeking actively to promote adoption of their moneys by *state* actors—formal leadership? Inducements of various kinds could be offered to persuade foreign governments to "euroize" or "yenize," in effect sponsoring formation of organized currency blocs. Challenge at this level, by generating potentially attractive alternatives to the dollar, could seriously compromise the gains presently enjoyed by the United States. Such a development, therefore, could hardly be ignored by Washington. In effect, any move by Europe or Japan to promote formal leadership would transform the low politics of market competition, by definition, into the high politics of international diplomacy. The risk of policy tensions would be great, particularly if euroization or yenization were perceived as encroaching on America's established regional relationships.

Is the risk serious? A challenge from Europe is certainly possible—but improbable. The Europeans will no doubt make every effort to promote the use of their new euro at the market level. It is also evident that they will not discourage some form of official linkage to the euro by nearby governments, particularly in East–Central Europe and the Balkans. But none of this is likely to provoke a more proactive policy in Washington unless the aspirations of the European Union (EU) spread beyond its immediate neighborhood—what the European Central Bank (2001) calls the "Euro time zone"—to regions more traditionally aligned with the United States, such as Latin America. The chances of a more aggressive scenario along those lines, however, are slim at best. In fact, European authorities are generally agreed that they already have more than enough on their plate coping with the EU's impending enlargement. A confrontation with America over formal currency leadership is the last thing they are looking for.

From Japan, by contrast, the chances of a challenge are higher. The reason is simple: The Japanese have more to lose. The euro, clearly, is a currency on the rise. Even if European authorities do nothing, a euro bloc will continue to coalesce as a natural result of EU enlargement. The yen, *per contra*, is a money in retreat. Over the last decade international use of the yen, in relative terms, has actually decreased rather than increased, mirroring Japan's economic troubles at home (Cohen 2000). If Tokyo does nothing the currency's slide could become irreversible, even in East Asia, a region that the Japanese prefer to think of as their own privileged backyard. It is difficult to imagine that Tokyo will accept such a loss of status without a struggle. Indeed, Japanese officials have made no secret of the fact that their aspirations now extend beyond mere informal currency leadership. But it is also difficult to imagine that any Japanese challenge would be carried to the point of open confrontation with the United States, which has its own established relationships in East Asia. Given the broader geopolitics of the region, there is good reason to believe that tensions between the two governments on currency matters, though almost certainly unavoidable, will not prove unmanageable.

13.6 Conclusion

The conclusion is evident. America has every interest in preserving and defending the advantages it presently derives from the market leadership of the dollar. But unless directly challenged by Europe or Japan, America has no clear interest in going any further, to promote or underwrite formal adoption of the greenback by other governments. Benign neglect remains the logical policy choice.

REFERENCES

Baliño, T. J. T. and Enoch, C. (1997). *Currency Board Arrangements: Issues and Experiences*. Washington, DC: International Monetary Fund.

Bank for International Settlements (2002). *Central Bank Survey of Foreign Exchange and Derivatives Market Activity 2001*. Basle.

Blinder, A. S. (1996). "The Role of the Dollar as an International Currency." *Eastern Economic Journal*, 22 (Spring): 127-36.

Cohen, B. J. (1998). *The Geography of Money*. Ithaca, NY: Cornell University Press.

—— (2000). *Life at the Top: International Currencies in the Twenty-First Century*, Essay in International Economics No. 221, Princeton, NJ: International Economics Section.

—— (2002). "U.S. Policy on Dollarization: A Political Analysis." *Geopolitics*, 7 (Summer): 5-26.

Deutsche Bundesbank (1995). "The Circulation of Deutsche Mark Abroad." *Monthly Report*, 47 (July): 65-71.

European Central Bank (2001). *Review of the International Role of the Euro* Frankfurt.

Frankel, J. A. (1995). "Still the Lingua Franca: The Exaggerated Death of the Dollar." *Foreign Affairs*, 74 (July): 9-16.

Gavin, M. (2000). "Official Dollarization in Latin America." *Monetary Stability in Latin America: Is Dollarization the Answer?* Hearings before the Subcommittee on Domestic and International Monetary Policy, Committee on Banking and Financial Services, U.S. House of Representatives, June 22: 45-50.

Goldfajn, I. and Olivares, G. (2001). "Full Dollarization: The Case of Panama." *Economía*, 1 (Spring): 101-55.

Hale, D. D. (1995). "Is it a Yen or a Dollar Crisis in the Currency Market?" *Washington Quarterly*, 18 (Autumn): 145-71.

Hartmann, P. (1998). *Currency Competition and Foreign Exchange Markets: The Dollar, the Yen and the Euro*. Cambridge: Cambridge University Press.

Kirshner, J. (1995). *Currency and Coercion: The Political Economy of International Monetary Power*. Princeton, NJ: Princeton University Press.

Lambert, M. J. and Stanton, K. D. (2001). "Opportunities and Challenges of the U.S. Dollar as an Increasingly Global Currency: A Federal Reserve Perspective." *Federal Reserve Bulletin*, 87 (September): 567-75.

Molano, W. T. (2000). "Addressing the Symptoms and Ignoring the Causes: A View From Wall Street on Dollarization." *Monetary Stability in Latin America: Is Dollarization the Answer?* Hearings before the Subcommittee on Domestic and International Monetary Policy, Committee on Banking and Financial Services, U.S. House of Representatives. June 22: 51-60.

Mundell, R. A. (1993). "EMU and the International Monetary System: A Transatlantic Perspective." *Working Paper No. 13*, Vienna, Austrian National Bank.

Nye, J. S., Jr. (1990). "Soft Power." *Foreign Policy*, 80 (Fall): 153–71.

Porter, R. D. and Judson, R. A. (1996). "The Location of U.S. Currency: How Much is Abroad?" *Federal Reserve Bulletin*, 82 (October): 883–903.

Portes, R. and Rey, H. (1998). "The Emergence of the Euro as an International Currency." In D. Begg, J. von Hagen, C. Wyplosz, and K. F. Zimmermann (eds.), *EMU: Prospects and Challenges for the Euro*. Oxford: Blackwell, 307–43.

Samuelson, R. J. (1999). "Dollarization—a Black Hole." *Washington Post*, May 12, A27.

Sinn, H.-W. and Westermann, F. (2001). "The Deutschmark in Eastern Europe, Black Money and the Euro: On the Size of the Effect." *CESifo Forum*, 2 (Autumn): 35–40.

Stix, H. (2001). "Survey Results about Foreign Currency Holdings in Five Central and Eastern European Countries." *CESifo Forum*, 2 (Autumn): 41–8.

Thygesen, N. et al. (1995). *International Currency Competition and the Future Role of the Single European Currency*, Final Report of a Working Group on European Monetary Union-International Monetary System. London: Kluwer Law International.

United States Treasury (2000). *The Use and Counterfeiting of United States Currency Abroad*, Washington, DC.

von Furstenberg, G. M. (2000). "A Case Against U.S. Dollarization." *Challenge*, 43 (July/August): 108–20.

Wyplosz, C. (1999). "An International Role for the Euro?" In J. Dermine and P. Hillion (eds.), *European Capital Markets with a Single Currency*. Oxford: Oxford University Press, pp. 76–104.

14

Dollarization and Euroization in Transition Countries: Currency Substitution, Asset Substitution, Network Externalities, and Irreversibility

EDGAR L. FEIGE AND JAMES W. DEAN

We examine the extent, causes and consequences of transition countries' use of foreign currency as a cocirculating medium of exchange and store of value. Using new estimates of foreign cash in circulation, we obtain unique measures of currency substitution, asset substitution, and dollarization, and examine the consequences of network externalities for hysteresis and irreversibility. Finally, we examine factors leading some transition countries to euroize officially and bilaterally, and others to euroize unilaterally—that is, without prior sanction by the European Monetary Union (EMU).

14.1 Introduction

Introduction of the euro on January 1, 2002 has implications far beyond the present borders of the European Union. A crucial aspect of Central and Eastern European Countries' (CEECs') transition from planned to market economies is their transition toward new exchange rate regimes. At issue is first, whether and when certain CEECs will officially euroize, that is adopt the euro *de jure* as their sole legal tender. Official euroization could be bilateral, by joining the EMU. Alternatively it could be unilateral, without joining EMU and without explicit prior sanction by the authorities in Brussels and Frankfurt who control EMU membership.[1] An important element in determining this choice is the extent to which these countries are already unofficially euroized or dollarized. Unofficial (de facto) euroization or dollarization results from individuals and firms voluntarily

---

[1] A similar discussion is underway in several Latin American countries about possible adoption of the U.S. dollar as official currency: Indeed, Ecuador, El Salvador, and Guatemala have all recently done so.

choosing to use foreign currency as either a transaction substitute (currency substitution) or a store of value substitute (asset substitution) for the monetary services of domestic currency.

Advocates of dollarization or euroization suggest that adopting a strong foreign currency enables countries to eliminate the temptation of inflationary finance, and thereby avoid currency and balance of payment crises, reduce the level and volatility of interest rates, and ultimately stimulate growth. Opponents cite loss of seignorage and loss of an independent monetary policy.[2]

Often overlooked in this normative debate are positive issues surrounding the extent to which these countries are already de facto euroized or dollarized. The major limitation of any analysis of unofficial foreign currency use is that the amount of foreign cash in circulation (FCC) is typically unknown. There is virtually no reliable empirical information concerning the actual extent of dollarization or euroization in transition countries.

Asset and currency substitution is induced by past inflations, devaluations, and currency confiscations. When de facto dollarization or euroization is widespread, the effective money supply is much larger than the domestic money supply and is, moreover, less easily controlled by the monetary authority because of the public's propensity to substitute foreign for domestic currency. For example, de facto use of FCC will thwart government efforts to employ inflationary finance to impose implicit taxes on domestic monetary assets. Extensive currency substitution not only makes domestic monetary policy less effective, it also makes active exchange rate intervention more dangerous.

Currency substitution also has fiscal consequences that are particularly salient for transition countries. Foreign cash transactions reduce the costs of tax evasion and facilitate participation in the "underground" economy. This weakens the government's ability to command real resources from the private sector and deepens fiscal deficits. The shifting of economic activity toward the unreported economy distorts macroeconomic information systems (Feige 1990, 1997), thereby adding to the difficulty of formulating macroeconomic policy. By obscuring financial transactions, currency substitution reduces the cost of enterprise theft and facilitates corruption and rent seeking.

There is now a growing body of evidence (Feige 1994, 1997; Porter and Judson 1996) suggesting that 40–60 percent of U.S. cash is held abroad. The "official" estimate now published by the Bureau of Economic Analysis and the Federal Reserve Board is based on an adjusted version of the proxy measure proposed by Feige (1994). The official estimate suggests that in 2001, 50 percent of the $580 billion of U.S. currency in circulation was held abroad. Studies by Seitz (1995) and Doyle (2000) find that 35–70 percent of D-Marks (DM) were held outside of Germany. In this paper we present newly collected data on the location of U.S. dollars abroad as well as the location of certain former European national currencies held in transition countries. These data enable us finally to

---

[2] For a wide range of views on the pros and cons of dollarization, see Dean et al. (2003).

circumvent the problem of "unobservability" that has plagued the currency substitution literature since its inception, permitting a refinement of definitions and measures of currency substitution, asset substitution and unofficial foreign currency use.

Once unofficial foreign currency use is measurable, it becomes possible to examine its causes, as well as the circumstances under which it is likely to become persistent, if not irreversible.[3] Oomes (2001) and Feige (2002, 2003) find that hysteresis and irreversibility are induced by network externalities associated with the use of foreign currency. When network externalities become sufficiently large, countries may decide to dollarize or euroize their economies, forgoing the flexibility of domestic monetary management in exchange for greater financial stability and an enhanced ability to attract foreign investment.

In Section 14.2 we briefly review earlier International Monetary Fund (IMF) efforts to measure dollarization by employing foreign currency deposits (FCD) as a proxy for the degree of dollarization. We then define several new measures of dollarization, currency substitution, and asset substitution that take explicit account of newly available information on holdings of U.S. cash in various transition countries. In principle, currency substitution occurs when a foreign currency substitutes as a medium of exchange for the domestic currency, whereas asset substitution refers to the holding of foreign rather than domestic money as a store of value. In practice, we will define currency substitution in terms of U.S. dollar *cash* holdings, and asset substitution in terms of U.S.-dollar-denominated *bank deposits*.

In Section 14.3 we present estimates of per capita holdings of U.S. dollars in various transition countries, and also review several indirect means of estimating FCC that have been employed in Croatia (Feige 2002). We also present new survey estimates by the Austrian National Bank (ONB) of both the amount and composition of FCC holdings in several CEECs. FCC estimates are then employed to obtain new dollarization indices. In Section 14.4 we compare these new indices to earlier proxy measures of dollarization employed by the IMF. We find that IMF dollarization measures are highly correlated with our measure of asset substitution but appear to be imprecise measures of currency substitution. Section 14.5 employs, *inter alia*, our estimates of unofficial foreign currency holdings to analyze the likelihood that various CEECs will choose to euroize officially, and if so whether they are likely to do so bilaterally or unilaterally.

14.2 Definitions

In an economy with unofficial dollarization, the *effective* broad money supply (EBM) consists of local cash in circulation outside the banking system (LCC), FCC outside the banking system, local checkable deposits (LCD), FCD held with

---

[3] For an elaboration of the irreversibility problem see Guidotti and Rodriguez (1992) and Balino et al. (1999).

domestic banks, and local currency time and savings deposits (LTD). Quasi money (QM) consists of FCD and LTD.[4] The typical definition of broad money (BM) falls short of the EBM by the unknown amount of FCC. The narrow money supply (NM) is typically defined to include only LCC and LCD. In a dollarized economy, the effective narrow money supply (ENM) also includes FCC.[5]
Thus

$$EBM \equiv LCC + FCC + LCD + QM \equiv BM + FCC, \tag{1}$$

where

$$QM \equiv FCD + LTD, \tag{2}$$

$$BM \equiv LCC + LCD + QM, \tag{3}$$

$$NM \equiv LCC + LCD, \tag{4}$$

$$ENM \equiv NM + FCC. \tag{5}$$

In a regime with de facto dollarization, the recorded money supply falls short of the effective money supply due to the omission FCC, which is typically unknown and not directly controllable by the local central bank. Due to lack of data on FCC, research on the currency substitution process has been forced to accept the observable amount of FCD as a proxy for dollarization. Studies of currency substitution, often associated with the IMF, employ the ratio of FCD to broad money to establish the extent to which countries are dollarized.[6] We denote this common dollarization index:

$$(DI_{IMF}) \equiv FCD/BM. \tag{6}$$

De facto dollarization is often a response to hyperinflation or a history of bank confiscations. Under such circumstances, a foreign currency may first serve as a unit of account and store of value and only later as a circulating medium of exchange. Currency substitution suggests that the foreign currency largely displaces the domestic currency as the medium of exchange. When a foreign nation's currency has substituted for local currency primarily as the medium of exchange, it is useful to define an explicit *currency substitution index*

---

[4] This conceptual framework is adopted from Feige (2002).

[5] We ignore those rare institutional circumstances in which transfers between foreign currency deposits are employed for transaction purposes.

[6] Balino et al. (1999) choose to define highly dollarized countries as those whose ratio of FCD/broad money exceeds 30 percent. The major shortcoming of this definition is that it takes no account of foreign cash in circulation. Further study is required to determine whether there exists a unique threshold value of the dollarization index at which dollarization is likely to become irreversible because of network externalities.

(CSI), which shows the fraction of a nation's total currency supply held in the form of foreign currency.[7] Thus,

$$CSI \equiv FCC/(FCC + LCC).\qquad(7)$$

Since domestic transactions are typically settled by debiting and crediting LCD accounts, it may also be useful to modify the CSI and use instead, (CSI_n) defined as the fraction of the effective narrow money supply made up of foreign currency.

$$CSI_n \equiv FCC/(ENM).\qquad(8)$$

When dollarization primarily involves the use of foreign denominated monetary assets as substitutes for domestic ones in their capacity as stores of value, it is useful to define an *asset substitution index* (ASI) as the ratio of foreign denominated monetary assets to domestic denominated monetary assets excluding cash outside banks[8]

$$ASI \equiv FCD/(LCD + QM).\qquad(9)$$

When both asset substitution and currency substitution take place, or when FCDs are used by firms to make transactions with international partners, we define a broader *unofficial dollarization index* (UDI) that represents the fraction of a nation's broad effective money supply composed of foreign monetary assets. Thus

$$UDI \equiv (FCC + FCD)/EBM.\qquad(10)$$

Each of the forgoing indices depends upon a number of incentives to hold the different assets described in the denominator and numerator. These incentives include relative rates of return as reflected in interest rate differentials, inflation differentials, and exchange rate depreciation, as well as the relative benefits and costs associated with network externalities and switching costs.

The conventional IMF dollarization index (DI_{IMF}) will be an adequate proxy of de facto dollarization when foreign currency holdings are of marginal importance, or when FCC and FCD are highly complementary. If, however, significant amounts of foreign currency circulate for transaction purposes, or if FCC and FCD are in fact substitutes, the IMF dollarization measure is likely to perform poorly as an indicator of de facto dollarization. Typically, the IMF dollarization index will understate the true extent of dollarization due to its omission of FCC holdings. Moreover, DI_{IMF} does not permit one to distinguish between the

---

[7] In some countries foreign banknotes may simply be hoarded and treated purely as a store of value. When this part of FCC can be estimated, it should be treated as a store of value and included in the asset substitution index.

[8] The quality of ASI as a definition of asset substitution also depends upon the particular institutions of a nation. Its quality is high when the amount of FCD and LTD used for transactions purposes is low in comparison to the amount of those deposits used as income earning assets.

dynamic currency substitution and asset substitution processes that our more refined indicators attempt to capture. In order to examine the adequacy of the IMF index, we turn first to a discussion of our efforts to obtain direct estimates of U.S. currency holdings in transition countries.

14.3   Measurement

14.3.1   Direct measurement of FCC

Empirical studies suggest that roughly 50 percent of U.S. currency circulates abroad. U.S. currency (cash) has many desirable properties. It has a reputation as a stable currency, and is therefore a reliable store of value. It is available in many countries, is widely accepted as a medium of exchange, and protects foreign users against the threat of bank failures, devaluation, and inflation. Cash usage preserves anonymity because it leaves no paper trail of the transaction for which it serves as the means of payment. Indeed the very characteristics that make the U.S. dollar a popular medium of exchange also makes it difficult to determine the exact amount and location of U.S. notes circulating abroad. Nevertheless, there is a direct source of information that can be used to determine the approximate amounts of U.S. cash in circulation in different countries.

Over the past two decades, the United States Customs Service has been mandated to collect systematic information on cross border flows of U.S. currency. The Currency and Foreign Transactions Reporting Act (also known as the "Bank Secrecy Act") requires persons or institutions importing or exporting currency or other monetary instruments in amounts exceeding $10,000 to file a Report of International Transportation of Currency or Monetary Instruments (CMIR).[9] The information contained in the millions of confidential individual CMIR forms has been aggregated in order fully to preserve the confidentiality of individual filers' information. The aggregated data yield time series observations on the gross inflows and outflows of U.S. currency to different destinations. By cumulating the CMIR recorded net outflows of U.S. dollars to each destination, we are able to obtain estimates of the amount of U.S. currency held abroad as well as the location of U.S. currency in various transition countries. The 1999 CMIR estimates of per capita FCC holdings in U.S. dollars in various transition countries are presented in Column (1) of Table 14.1.

A second source of data on per capita holdings of U.S. currency is obtained from informal interviews and surveys (U.S. Treasury Department 2000) conducted by Federal Reserve and Treasury officials. These estimates are presented in Column (2) of Table 14.1. Although the CMIR estimates and informal interview estimates for some countries are quite different, both sources confirm the belief that per capita holdings of U.S. currency are highest in Russia, Latvia, Kazakhstan, Turkey, and Bulgaria.

---

[9] See Feige (1996, 1997) for greater detail concerning CMIR data.

Table 14.1. *Alternative estimates of per capita FCC holdings in various transition countries, 1997–2001*

| Country | CMIR estimates (1999) (dollars only) (1)[a] | Treasury informal survey (dollars only) (2)[b] | Per Capita $FCC | | | |
			ONB survey (all currencies) (3)	ONB survey blowup (all currencies) (4)	Denomination displacement (all currencies) (5)[c]	Money demand (all currencies) (6)[c]
Armenia	10.6	n.a.				
Azerbaijan	21.1	n.a.				
Belarus	0.8	288				
Bulgaria	63.1	120				
Croatia	n.a.	n.a.	166	831	273	1,386
Czech Republic	n.a.	n.a.	220	1,098		
Estonia	34.7	n.a.				
Hungary	2.2	n.a.	29	145		
Kazakhstan	288	n.a.				
Kyrgyzstan	7.1	n.a.				
Latvia	432	208				
Lithuania	24	139				
Poland	90	26				
Romania	10.3	52				
Russia	448	407				
Slovak Republic	n.a.	n.a.	148	742		
Slovenia	n.a.	n.a.	246	1,231		
Turkey	74.7	157				
Ukraine	23.9	n.a.				

[a] Author's calculations
[b] United States Treasury Department (2000)
[c] Feige (2002).

There is considerable anecdotal evidence that many of the CEECs employed national currencies of European nations, in addition to dollars, as cocirculating currencies. Unfortunately CMIR type data are not available for European currencies. Residents of several transition countries are however known to hold various amounts of DM and other European currencies such as the Austrian schilling (AST) and the Swiss Franc (SF). In anticipation of the euro conversion, the ONB commissioned Gallup to conduct a series of surveys in five CEECs in order to determine the extent of FCC holdings of various non-local currencies. Each of the ten surveys conducted between June 1997 and November 2001 involved approximately 1,000 persons above the age of 14.[10] Column (3) of Table 14.1 presents the average estimate of total per capita FCC holdings expressed in terms of U.S. dollars over the period 1997–2001.

Survey results concerning self-admitted currency holdings are best considered as lower bound estimates of actual currency holdings since such surveys are known to suffer from underreporting bias. For example, Federal Reserve Survey of Currency Usage reveals that U.S. households admit to holding less than 10 percent of the nation's total currency supply in circulation outside of banks. Official estimates of U.S. dollar holdings abroad suggest that roughly 50 percent of U.S. currency is presently held overseas. Since firms hold a negligible amount of cash, it appears that the Federal Reserve currency survey results require a blowup factor of five in order to obtain a true estimate of actual domestic currency holdings. Assuming that the ONB survey estimates are subject to the same types of underreporting bias observed in similar Federal Reserve studies, we present in Column (4) of Table 14.1, upper bound ONB estimates employing the same blowup factor required for the Federal Reserve survey estimates.[11]

14.3.2   Indirect measures of FCC

14.3.2.1   *Denomination displacement method*
Feige (2002) developed indirect methods for estimating the amount of unobservable FCC in Croatia. The first of these, known as the denomination displacement method, derives from the observation that in dollarized countries using U.S.

---

[10] We are indebted to the ONB for providing us with the underlying survey data that permitted computation of the estimates presented in the accompanying tables and figures.

[11] One important contribution of the ONB surveys is that they provide insight not only into the total amount of FCC held in the five survey countries, but also into the currency composition of these FCC holdings. In each of the five countries, the DM is the largest component of FCC holdings, followed by the U.S. dollar. The consensus estimate of DM held outside of Germany is roughly the equivalent of $50 billion. Using the ONB survey blowup estimates of total DM held in the five countries implies that these countries collectively account for roughly 23 percent of the DM believed held outside of Germany. The Czech Republic appears to hold almost 10 percent of estimated DM abroad, followed by Croatia with 6 percent.

currency as a means of exchange, most transactions are effected with the largest denomination bills available: that is, with $100 U.S. bills. Similarly, it is suspected that in Croatia, the bulk of transactions involving cocirculating currency are carried out with larger denomination foreign currency notes, particularly 500 and 1,000 DM bills. The denomination displacement method is based on the hypothesis that countries that are heavily dollarized, with large denomination foreign bills, will have domestic currency (LCC) denomination structures that are unusually skewed away from the higher denomination domestic bills. Denomination displacement occurs as higher denomination FCC bills substitute for high denomination LCC bills. It is however recognized that as network externalities lead to the more pervasive use of foreign currency, lower denominations may also be employed for various transactions. It is, therefore, appropriate to view this indirect method as yielding a lower bound estimate.

In order to employ the denomination displacement method to estimate FCC holdings in Croatia, Feige (2002) employed CMIRs to obtain estimates of FCC in both highly and only partially dollarized countries. The denomination structure of local currency was then examined in order to determine the extent to which denomination displacement took place. The denomination structure of the Croatian kuna was then compared to the denomination structures of currencies from other transition countries. By examining the denomination structures for currencies in both dollarized and non-dollarized countries, Feige (2002) was able to estimate the extent of denomination displacement in dollarized regimes. The dollarization displacement was estimated by regression analysis and the displacement parameters were then applied to Croatia in order to obtain an estimate of the amount of FCC in circulation. The resulting estimates are presented in column (5) of Table 14.1.

14.3.2.2 *Money demand method*

The second indirect approach to estimating the unknown amount of FCC in circulation in Croatia was to investigate the demand for money in a highly dollarized country for which data were available on the actual amount of currency substitution that had taken place. Argentina was chosen as the country whose dollarization process could be directly modeled. Since the Argentina hyperinflation experience and subsequent stabilization program was similar in many respects to that of Croatia, Feige (2002) estimated an empirical demand function for FCC in Argentina that depended upon independent variables that are readily measured in Croatia. The parameters derived from the estimated FCC demand function for Argentina were then used to simulate the unobserved demand for FCC in Croatia. The resulting estimates of FCC holdings in Croatia are reported in column (6) of Table 14.1. The table reveals that the blown up ONB survey estimate of FCC holdings in Croatia falls within the range bounded by the two indirect methods of estimation.

14.4   Comparison of Alternative Dollarization Indices

14.4.1   Overall dollarization indices

Given the estimates of FCC holdings displayed in Table 14.1 it is now possible to examine the consequences of employing the new unofficial dollarization index (UDI) as compared to the conventional IMF dollarization index (DI_{IMF}). Feige (2002) examined these ratios for a sample of twenty-four countries for which data were available and found that the widely used IMF dollarization index is highly correlated with the asset substitution index but is an imprecise measure of currency substitution.

Figure 14.1 displays a country-by-country comparison of the conventional IMF dollarization proxy (DI_{IMF}) as well as our broader UDI that takes explicit account of the estimated amount of FCC in circulation in each nation in 1999.[12] By definition, the IMF dollarization index understates the true extent of unofficial dollarization due to its omission of FCC. The corrected UDI index reveals that of the transition countries in our sample, Croatia and Russia exhibit the highest degree of de facto dollarization, that is, the highest fraction of the effective broad money supply in the form of foreign-denominated assets. Armenia, Belarus, Bulgaria, Kyrgyzstan, Latvia, Turkey, and the Ukraine score above 40 percent in the de facto dollarization ranking.

14.4.2   Currency substitution and asset substitution indices

Feige (2002) examined the relationship between the (DI_{IMF}) index of unofficial dollarization and found that the widely used IMF dollarization index is highly correlated with the asset substitution index but appears to be an imprecise measure of currency substitution.

Figure 14.2, therefore, presents the more refined CSI and ASI indices that respectively measure the degrees of currency and asset substitution for each of the transition countries in 1999.[13] The figure reveals that the fraction of the total currency supply made up of foreign cash (CSI) exceeds 75 percent for Russia, Kazakhstan, Croatia, and Belarus. These are countries in which the extensive use of foreign currency has likely surpassed the threshold level making it highly unlikely that it can be reversed. These are also countries that earn relatively little seignorage from their own currencies since FCC has largely displaced them. Conversely, Poland, Estonia, and Hungary are nations whose total currency supply consists of more than 80 percent local currency. These countries would bear highest seignorage costs by unilaterally euroizing; *bilateral* adoption of the euro, by contrast, would be compensated by seignorage sharing with the rest of the EMU.

---

[12] The calculations for both indices employ the average values of FCC obtained by the various methods in each of the transition countries.

[13] These indices are based on the average estimated FCC holdings over all methods of estimation.

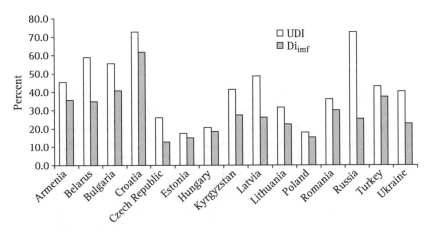

Figure 14.1. *Comparison of alternative dollarization indices—1999*

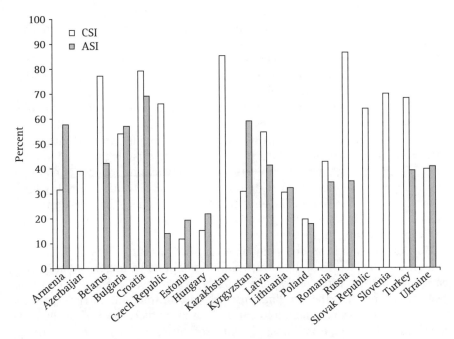

Figure 14.2. *Measures of currency and asset substitution—1999*

Figure 14.2 also reveals that patterns of currency substitution and asset substitution are in fact quite different among the countries observed. Armenia and Kyrgyzstan exhibit a pattern in which asset substitution dominates currency substitution by a wide margin. The converse is true for Belarus, Croatia, Czech Republic, Latvia, Romania, Russia, and Turkey. The reasons for these differences may be quite complex, but the data indicate that asset substitution and currency substitution need not go hand in hand.

14.5 The Future

What can we infer from our data and indicators on nineteen transition economies about the direction of dollarization and euroization in CEECs in future: Say over the next five to ten years? Of course the data themselves carry limited information, but in the context of probable accession to the EU, and accounting for the so-called "network externalities," they are certainly suggestive.

Politically, it is likely that five of the countries on our list—a group that was "first tier" until this ranking system was replaced by an informal queue after the November 1999 Helsinki summit—will join the EU on or about January 2005. At least another five—the original "second tier" group—is likely to join before, say, 2010. Once these countries join the EU, they will be expected—indeed, required—to adopt the euro officially and bilaterally as soon as they meet the five "Maastricht" criteria for accession to EMU. Of the remaining nine countries on our list, two or three may also join the EU within the next decade, and will then be expected to euroize officially. Finally, the remaining seven or eight countries are likely to become increasingly dollarized or euroized de facto, and some may be tempted to withdraw their domestic currencies from circulation altogether and adopt foreign currency exclusively and unilaterally.

Now consider network externalities. Feige (2003) derives plausible conditions under which dollarization becomes "irreversible," essentially because the benefit/cost ratio attached to the external currency rises rapidly with the number of users relative to users of the domestic currency. The same logic would suggest that euroization might become irreversible as an increasing number of contiguous and nearby countries euroize. In other words, the network externality logic suggests that even in those CEECs not presently in the queue for accession to the EU—countries like Croatia—the potential benefits from unilateral euroization are likely to rise rapidly in the near future.

Most of our data is on dollar holdings, not DMs or euros. It is misleading to extrapolate the latter from the former, since ratios of dollar to non-dollar foreign currency holdings vary widely from country to country. Nevertheless, it seems realistic to infer that the marginal costs of shifting from one foreign currency into another (i.e. from dollars into euros) are substantially lower than the marginal costs of shifting from foreign to domestic currencies. Hence, countries that have partially dollarized are more likely to move toward euros than back to local currencies. In addition, we can infer that the relative benefits attached to euros as opposed to dollars—at least for transactions purposes—will rise as contiguous and nearby countries euroize. These two inferences together—both of them consistent with network externality models—suggest that as official euroization spreads eastward, the incentive will rise for CEECs to move unilaterally from unofficial, partial dollarization or euroization to official, exclusive euroization.

The network externality logic can be elaborated by considering certain conventional measures of criteria for optimal currency areas (OCAs). Most of these criteria are not strictly separable from network effects: For example, the extent to which a country trades with the so-called "Euroland" interacts with and enhances network benefits from using the euro domestically, as does the extent to which labor and capital are mobile to and from Euroland.

A final factor that is likely to influence a CEEC's decision to euroize unilaterally is the Maastricht criteria. Two of these criteria in particular are likely to prove problematic for countries in early stages of transition: The inflation criterion, and the exchange rate criterion. The former requires a country aspiring to adopt the euro officially to run an average inflation rate of no more than 1.5 percentage points above the best three "member states": that is, countries already in EMU. The latter requires that its nominal exchange rate remain within "normal fluctuation margins" (plus or minus 15 percent) for at least two years prior to adoption of the euro.

The potential problem with meeting these criteria results from the likelihood that productivity growth in the tradables sectors of CEECs will increase faster than in the EU. It then follows from the Balassa–Samuelson condition that the real exchange rate (in terms of euros per unit of CEEC currency) will rise.[14] Now, of course, the real exchange rate can rise in one, or a combination, of two ways: The domestic price level can rise relative to EU levels, or the nominal exchange rate can rise. The upshot is that the first is likely to violate the EMU's inflation criterion, and the second is likely to violate its exchange rate stability criterion.

Countries aspiring to join the EMU are likely to be put through a wringer of sorts in order to meet the inflation criterion. With prices of non-tradables rising faster than in the EU, they may be forced to impose a recession, and/or limit wage increases in controllable sectors like government, education, and health. This, in turn, would increase incentives for labor to emigrate to Western Europe, and exacerbate tensions between CEECs and the EU. An easier out would be to allow nominal exchange rate appreciation (which would lower inflation in tradables), but large short-term exchange rate changes are similarly proscribed by the Maastricht conditions. Substantial nominal exchange rate appreciation would also obviate the post-accession inflationary pressure that could come from joining the EMU at an undervalued rate, as happened with the Irish punt after March 1998.

However, countries *not* aspiring to EMU in the near future—in practice, countries currently ineligible to join the EU—might well be tempted to euroize unilaterally, so as to sidestep the Masstricht criteria. More precisely, in the post-euro era, the likelihood that non-accession CEEC countries will unilaterally euroize

---

[14] More precisely, this result follows from a higher excess productivity growth differential between traded and non-traded goods sectors in CEECs than in the EU. In recent years a lively literature has debated the relevance of Balassa–Samuelson for CEECs. See for example Buiter and Grafe (2001).

depends on three factors: The extent to which they are already euroized *or* dollarized; the extent to which they meet OCA criteria, particularly those that involve trade, capital and labor flows with the EMU countries; and finally the length of time they are likely to have to wait before they become eligible for accession to the EU. In the next section we ask what light our new dollarization data can cast on the first of these three factors.

14.5.1 Partial dollarization as an incentive for full euroization

Consider first what we will call Group A: The five countries likely to enter the EU by 2005: Czech Republic, Estonia, Hungary, Poland, and Slovenia. Figure 14.2 reveals that the Czech Republic and Slovenia have CSIs of sixty-five or more: that is, at least 65 percent of their total currency supply is held in the form of foreign currency. Poland has 20 percent, with Hungary and Estonia at less than 15 percent. However, the ONB surveys suggest that Hungary has long been a heavy user of the DM and the Austrian Schilling. What we will call Group B consists of Bulgaria, Latvia, Lithuania, Romania, and the Slovak Republic. Three of the five have CSIs of fifty-four or more; Romania is also high, at forty-three, and Lithuania is at 30 percent. Now consider Group C, the remaining countries on our list: Belarus, Croatia, Kazakhstan, Russia, Turkey, Armenia, Azerbaijan, Kyrgyzstan, and Ukraine. The first five of these nine countries have CSIs ranging from sixty-eight to eighty-six, with the other four between thirty-one and forty. Moreover, in all cases the ASI is thirty-five or above.

Overall, the CSI average for Group A is 36 percent, for Group B, 49 percent, and for Group C, 60 percent. What this admittedly casual comparison suggests is that the degree of currency substitution increases as the country's remoteness from EU membership increases. While it may be that some Group A and B countries' CSI indices would exceed Group C's if all DM holdings were included, these figures nevertheless suggest that at least five Group C countries may already be irreversibly addicted to foreign currency. Indeed, a network externality analysis of Argentina (Feige 2003) suggests that countries with more than 60 percent of their currency in the form of external currency are likely to be irreversibly dollarized.

Moreover the high ASI scores of Group C countries reinforce their incentives to lock into external currency, since the costs of continuing with local currency rise with asset substitution. Dean (2001) discusses three phenomena, all related to asset and liability substitution, that add to a country's incentives to exclusively adopt foreign currency. The three phenomena are liability dollarization, risk premia on interest rates, and exchange rate impotence. They are related to asset substitution in the sense that lenders, including domestic lenders, would much rather hold dollar claims than local currency claims; hence developing and transition country borrowers must either issue dollar-denominated liabilities (in fact that is in practice their only option for external borrowing), or pay currency-risk premia on local-currency liabilities. Moreover, even dollar liabilities carry a *default* risk premium that derives from the risk of currency depreciation and consequent increase in the local-currency debt burden. The upshot is that countries are afraid to permit exchange rate depreciation: hence the exchange rate's "impotence" as a policy tool.

In short, most of the non-EU-accession CEECs on our list (Group C) are: (*a*) more highly currency- (i.e. cash-) dollarized than most EU-accession countries; and (*b*) more highly bank-deposit-dollarized as well. We infer from this that (*a*) for network externality reasons the use of foreign currency (be it in dollars or euros) for transactions purpose is unlikely to be reversible in these countries, even if they pursue moderate macroeconomic policies and hence reduce inflation risk, and (*b*) for currency and default risk reasons the net benefits from full dollarization or euroization are likely to be high. Such benefits rise in proportion to their foreign-currency-denominated asset holdings and debt liabilities.

According to CSI criteria, the Group C countries where foreign currency use is least likely to be reversible (with CSIs above 60 percent) are Belarus, Croatia, Kazakhstan, Russia, and Turkey. According to ASI criteria, those that would benefit most from full dollarization or euroization are Armenia, Croatia, and Kyrgysztan. Moreover, Kazakhstan probably has an ASI over fifty, but data are unavailable.

If some of these countries do withdraw their domestic currencies, are they likely to dollarize, or will they euroize? Here, once again, we distinguish between the network benefits that are related to currency substitution, and the liability dangers that are related to asset substitution. The latter, we would argue, are likely to be decisive. Belarus and Russia, each with manageable foreign currency debt, are likely to choose to live without the additional transactions benefits that could come from full dollarization. In addition, much of their extraordinarily high cash relative to bank deposit holding derives from asset rather than transactions motives: Their relative reluctance to hold dollars as bank deposits reflects both distrust of banks, and a desire to avoid taxes. In any case, nationalism and hubris will prevail against full dollarization in Russia for the foreseeable future.

Croatia, Kazakhstan and Turkey are different: There, network externality motives are much more likely to prevail. In Croatia and Turkey this will be reinforced by their strong trade (and tourism) links to Western Europe; the euro, not the dollar, is likely to be the foreign currency of choice. Kazakhstan may be different because of its oil industry, which dominates both external trade and much internal commerce.

Ukraine is a case in point. The dollar is not commonly used (in fact is technically illegal) for transactions purposes, although most foreign firms, aid agencies and non-government organizations pay their employees in dollars, which are then converted into domestic currency for transactions. Moreover Ukraine's dollarized debt is relatively small and it runs a fiscal surplus; therefore putative currency depreciation does not jeopardize either the private or public sectors. (In fact, the Ukrainian Hryvnia has recently begun to appreciate, a la Balassa–Samuelson.) Finally, inflation has been well under control for the past six years. In fact introduction of the Hryvnia in 1995 coincided with the end of hyperinflation, which has helped to establish the currency as an important icon of Ukraine's independence. In short, Ukrainians do not hold dollars primarily for either transactions purposes or as a hedge against inflation or devaluation. And since they still receive considerable FDI from, and trade substantially with, Russia (though their investment and trade with Euroland is growing),[15] they have less immediate reason on OCA grounds than do CEECs to adopt the euro.

14.6 Summary and Conclusions

In an effort to overcome the "unobservability" problem that has plagued the currency substitution literature, we present direct estimates of the amounts of U.S. dollar foreign currency in circulation in various transition countries. We also review other evidence on the use of European national moneys, particularly the DM, as cocirculating currencies. Finally, we present estimates of FCC based on two indirect methods.

Traditional measures of dollarization largely relied on foreign currency deposits as an indicator of currency substitution because actual measures of foreign currency in circulation were unavailable. Employing aggregated data derived from CMIRs on dollar inflows and outflows to and from the United States, as well as estimates of other European currencies that cocirculate with local currencies, we estimate the total amounts of FCC in various transition countries. These new estimates permit a refinement of definitions and indices of currency and asset substitution, as well as broader indices of the extent of de facto dollarization. Traditional measures of dollarization tend to be indicative of asset substitution but perform poorly as measures of currency substitution.

Our measures of currency and asset substitution help us to infer how countries that will not qualify for EU or EMU membership in the near future are, nevertheless, motivated to abandon their domestic currencies and adopt the euro unilaterally. Although our CSI and ASI indices suggest that the incentives to do so are particularly high in Armenia, Belarus, Croatia, Kazakhstan, Kyrgyzstan, Russia, and Turkey—that is, all have strong transactions, asset or bank-credibility motives for euroization—other considerations make it unlikely that Belarus, Russia, and Ukraine will do so for the foreseeable future.

REFERENCES

Baliño, T., Bennett, A., and Borensztein, E. (1999). "Monetary Policy in Dollarized Economies." *Occasional Paper 171*, Washington, DC: International Monetary Fund.
Buiter, W. H. and Grafe, C. (2001). "Central Banking and the Choice of Currency Regime in Accession Countries." *Revue D'Économie Financière*, Special Issue: Ten Years of Transition in Eastern European Countries, Achievements and Challenges, 287–318.

[15] For a recent study of Ukraine's evolving trade and investment patterns with Western Europe *vis-à-vis* the former Soviet Union see Dean and Mankovska (2002).

Dean, J. W. (2001). "Should Latin America's Common Law Marriages to the U.S. Dollar be Legalized? Should Canada's?" *Journal of Policy Modeling*, April 23: 291–300, reprinted in Dean, Salvatore, and Willett (eds.) (2003).

— and Mankovska, N. (2002). "Foreign Direct Investment and Trade Flows in a Transition Economy: The Case of the Ukraine." In S. von Cramon-Taubadel and I. Akimova (eds.), *Fostering Sustainable Growth in Ukraine*. Heidelberg and New York: Physica-Verlag, pp. 252–63.

— Salvatore, D., and Willett, T. D. (eds.) (2003). *The Dollarization Debate*. New York: Oxford University Press.

Doyle, B. M. (2000). "Here, Dollars, Dollars ..." Estimating Currency Demand and Worldwide Currency Substitution." *International Finance Discussion Paper* No. 657, Washington, DC: Board of Governors of the Federal Reserve System.

Feige, E. L. (1990). "Defining and Estimating Underground and Informal Economies: The New Institutional Economics Approach." *World Development*, 18(July): 989–99.

— (1994). "The Underground Economy and the Currency Enigma." *Supplement to Public Finance / Finances Publiques*, 49: 119–36. Reprinted in G. Fiorentini and S. Zamagni (eds.) (1999). *The Economics of Corruption and Illegal Markets*. International Library of Critical Writings in Economics, Cheltenham, UK: Edward Elgar, pp. 23–40.

— (1997). "Revised Estimates of the Size of the U.S. Underground Economy: The Implications of U.S. Currency held Abroad." In O. Lippert and M. Walker (eds.), *The Underground Economy: Global Evidence of its Size and Impact*. Vancouver, BC: Fraser Institute, pp. 151–208.

— (2002). "Currency Substitution, Unofficial Dollarization and Estimates of Foreign Currency Held Abroad: The Case of Croatia." In M. Blejer and M. Skreb (eds.), *Financial Policies in Emerging Markets*. Cambridge, MA: MIT Press, pp. 217–49.

— (2003). "Unofficial Dollarization in Latin America: Currency Substitution, Network Externalities and Irreversibility." In J. W. Dean, D. Salvatore, and T. D. Willett (eds.), *The Dollarization Debate*. New York: Oxford University Press.

Guidotti, P. E. and Rodriguez, C. A. (1992). "Dollarization in Latin America: Gresham's Law in Reverse?" *International Monetary Fund Staff Papers*, 39 (September): 518–44.

Hausmann, R., Gavin, M., Pages-Serra, C., and Stein, E. (2000). "Financial Turmoil and the Choice of Exchange Rate Regime." In Eduardo Fernández-Arias and R. Hausmann (eds.), *Wanted: World Financial Stability*. Washington, DC: Inter-American Development Bank, pp. 131–64.

Oomes, N. A. (2001). "Essays on Network Externalities and Aggregate Persistence." University of Wisconsin, Ph.D. Dissertation.

Porter, R. and Judson, R. (1996). "The Location of U.S. Currency: How Much is Abroad?" *Federal Reserve Bulletin*, 82 (October): 883–903.

Seitz, F. (1995). "The Circulation of Deutsche Mark Abroad." Economic Research Group of the Deutsche Bundesbank, *Discussion Paper 1/95*, Frankfurt a.M.

United States Treasury Department (2000). "The Use and Counterfeiting of United States Currency Abroad." A Report to the Congress by the Secretary of the Treasury, in consultation with the Advanced Counterfeit Deterrence Steering Committee, pursuant to section 807 of PL 104–132, January.

15

Electronic Money and the Optimal Size of Monetary Unions

CLÁUDIA COSTA STORTI AND PAUL DE GRAUWE

We analyze the question of how the advent of electronic money affects the size of optimal currency areas. In particular, we study whether currencies of small countries will tend to disappear as a result of electronic money. We distinguish three different forces that will be set in motion during the transition to a cashless society with different implications for the question at hand. These forces are (*a*) the potential for financial instability during the transition, (*b*) new network externalities that affect the costs and benefits of national media of exchange, and (*c*) the emergence of new stores of value.

15.1 Introduction

The new information technologies (ITs) promise to change the monetary landscape, creating new and more efficient payment systems. These new ITs affect the monetary landscape in three ways. First, they lead to increasing international mobility of capital reducing the capacity of nation-states to insulate themselves from the rest of the world, and making it possible for individuals to quickly switch from the use of one national money to another. Put differently, the new IT is likely to increase the substitutability between existing national moneys. Second, the new ITs create new substitutes for traditional forms of money (cash). In particular, electronic money (e-money) may further reduce the importance of cash in the payments mechanism. Whether this will lead us to a "Cashless Society" in the foreseeable future is difficult to say. There is no doubt, however, that payments systems will move in the direction of a progressive reduction of the importance of cash. Third, the new IT create the possibility of the emergence of entirely new private payment systems that are parallel to the existing ones. It is not inconceivable that these new electronic payment systems may drive out the existing publicly supported ones. These movements are likely to affect the boundaries of the existing national monetary areas.

Paper prepared for the Fordham/CEPR conference on the euro and dollarization, New York, April 5–6, 2002. We are grateful to Jerry Cohen and George von Furstenberg for many useful comments.

The question we analyze in this chapter is how the new IT are likely to affect the optimal size of monetary areas.

15.2   Money and Network Economics

One of the essential qualities of money is that it generates network externalities, that is, the utility of money for any individual increases with the number of users. In this sense money is like a telephone network: Expanding the size of the network increases the value of using the telephone to the original subscribers.[1]

One of the major issues in network economics is how to internalize these network benefits so that these are fully exploited and so that the optimal size of the network is reached. In general it is accepted now that a competitive market system will not necessarily lead to the optimal size of the network (see Economides 1996).[2] We will return to this issue because it constitutes the core of the theory of optimal currency areas. The issue we will want to analyze is whether the new IT can facilitate this process of internalization of network benefits.

In Figure 15.1 we represent the network involved in the use of money. Each transaction necessitates the use of money. The service of money is provided by an issuer, B, (central bank, commercial banks, or any other kind of company which decides to provide money). The users of the network are N_1, N_2, ... A transaction between N_i and N_j can be represented by N_iBN_j. The money network in Figure 15.1 is a two-way network and is formally equivalent to a telephone network.

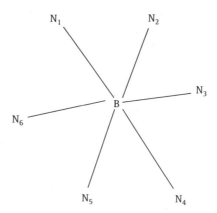

Figure 15.1. *The monetary network*

---

[1] There is, sometimes, confusion between network externalities proper and pecuniary externalities. The latter can easily be internalized by the market by price changes. The network externalities that are considered here cannot easily be internalized by competitive market forces. See Liebowitz and Margolis (1994) on this issue.

[2] Although there is wide consensus about this, there is also dissent. The dissent is based on the analysis of Hayek (1978). See also Klein (1974).

Adding another user to this monetary network increases the value of the network to the six original users.

Each issuer can be represented by a similar network as in Figure 15.1. Clearly there are gains to be made by the users of these different networks from merging these networks into one, a larger currency area. This however rarely happens; the exceptions being Belgium and Luxembourg during the second half of the twentieth century and the recent merger of the monetary networks in the European Union. We analyze in the next sections under what conditions such outright mergers are likely to occur.

What has happened much more frequently in monetary history is a partial merger of these different national networks. This has been achieved by making currencies convertible into one another. This was first done during the international gold standard when national currencies were convertible into gold at a fixed rate. In the language of network economics we can describe this process as follows. In the absence of convertibility, the different monetary networks are not compatible with each other. It is therefore impossible for a user of one network to make a monetary transaction with users of another network. This was the case in Europe during the 1950s. Convertibility of the national currencies has the effect of introducing compatibility between different networks (see Matutes and Regibeau 1992). We show this in Figure 15.2.

There are now two issuers, B_1 and B_2. These provide monetary services to the members of their own networks. In addition, with convertibility, B_1 and B_2 are willing to convert their currency against the other (at a price charged to the user of this service). This is represented by the link between B_1 and B_2. It is now possible for N_i to make a transaction with M_j. This transaction is represented by $N_i B_1 B_2 M_j$.

This link-up of the two networks creates potentially large benefits for their users. These benefits, however, are smaller than those generated by an outright merger (a monetary union). The first reason is that the two moneys use a different numeraire making the valuation of the transaction more complicated. In

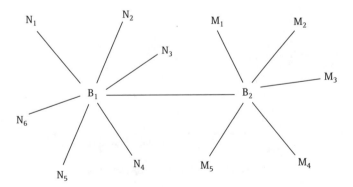

Figure 15.2. *Partial merger of two monetary networks*

addition the relative value of these numeraires (the exchange rate) can change and is thus inherently uncertain. Finally, the cost of the transactions between members of the two different networks is larger than the cost of the transactions between the members of the same network. Thus, the link-up of the two monetary networks represented in Figure 15.2 falls short of fully exploiting the network externalities. This can only be achieved by a monetary union (a full merger). The issue, however, is whether a full merger adds sufficient additional benefits compared to those achieved already through convertibility.

Figure 15.2 represents the situation of developed countries that have made their currencies convertible. The issue we want to analyze is whether the new IT has the capacity to strengthen networks of the type of Figure 15.2, so that outright mergers become less attractive.

15.3   The Optimal Size of a Monetary Network

It is useful to start from an analysis in which *individuals* in a closed economy face the problem of setting up a monetary network. Thus, we focus on the question of how e-money can emerge and provide for a new monetary network. We disregard the international context. This will be the focus of Sections 15.4 and 15.5.

Consider N individuals. Each of them would benefit from being able to use the same payments network. We represent the willingness to pay for such a network as a function of the number of members in the network in Figure 15.3.

More precisely the curve in Figure 15.3 represents the price, P, consecutive new subscribers to the network are willing to pay.[3] The existence of network externalities ensures that there is an upward sloping part to the willingness-to-pay curve, that is, as the number of members increases, the value of the payments service increases so that consecutive new subscribers are willing to

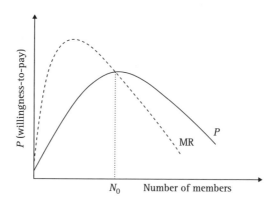

Figure 15.3. *Willingness-to-pay curve*

---

[3] Note that the nth subscriber expects the network to be of the size n (see Economides 1996).

pay increasingly more for the network service. However the willingness to pay does not increase monotonically. In N_0 it reaches a maximum. As N becomes very large, consumers with increasingly lower willingness to pay must be attracted, offsetting the positive network effect.[4] Beyond N_0 we face the normal downward sloping demand curve. (Note that we have also drawn the corresponding marginal revenue curve, MR.)

It should be stressed that the exact shape of the willingness-to-pay curve will also be influenced by the quality of the services provided in the network. This quality depends to a large degree on the capacity of the provider of the network to maintain monetary stability. We return to some aspects of this problem in Section 15.6.

The cost structure in the supply of a monetary network is represented in Figure 15.4. We show the average and the marginal cost curves that are typical in the supply of monetary networks.

Fixed costs are high and marginal costs are approximately constant. As a result, the economies of scale in the supply of a payments system are very large. Thus, economies of scale in the provision of payments systems occur both at the level of demand (due to network externalities) and supply. It should be stressed that we assume implicitly that monetary networks lack compatibility. We will come back to the issue of compatibility and we will argue that when monetary networks are compatible economies of scale in the supply can potentially be reduced.

The combination of network externalities in the demand and economies of scale in the supply has important implications for the market structure of monetary networks. We analyze these in Figure 15.5 where we combine the willingness-to-pay curve with the marginal cost curve.

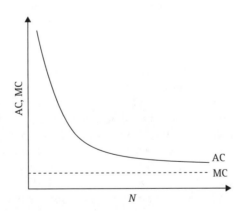

Figure 15.4. *Average and marginal costs of network*

---

[4] See Economides (1996) for a derivation of this willingness-to-pay line.

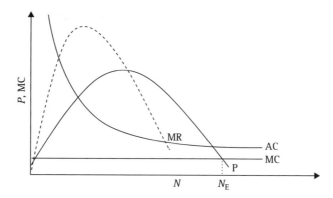

Figure 15.5. *Optimal size of network*

The Pareto optimal point is obtained in N_E where the price equals marginal cost. There is a coordination problem, though. Perfect competition is unlikely to sustain this optimal point. The reason is that the scale economies leave room for only a few profitable suppliers. Thus in the process towards N_E, few of the initial suppliers survive. The dynamics towards N_E will be characterized by frequent failures and collapses of payment networks. Since these are of crucial importance in economic activity, the process towards the optimum will be accompanied by great monetary and macroeconomic instability with great losses.[5] This is the fundamental reason why governments at some point got involved in the supply of a monetary network, either by taking it over and/or by regulating it.

All this should be kept in mind when thinking about the potential for new monetary networks to emerge from e-money. In short, there is no doubt that the private sector can supply new monetary networks. In fact, it could be argued that the new IT makes it easier for these to emerge. The reason is that it lowers the marginal cost of supplying the service. In addition, the ease of use for the subscriber to the network shifts the willingness-to-pay curve upwards. As a result, e-money increases the optimal size of the monetary network. The issue, however, is whether this can be done in an orderly way, avoiding collapses and crises with severe implications for the stability of the economy at large.

The previous analysis suggests that the emergence of new IT-based monetary networks will not be more successful than the private monetary networks of the past in providing these networks in a stable manner, because the basic *economic* structure of supply and demand of monetary networks has not changed by the introduction of new information technologies.

---

[5] The classic reference on the inherent fragility of a banking system is Diamond and Dybvig (1983).

15.4   Compatibility and Monetary Networks

In the previous analysis we have left out one important aspect, that is, the possibility that suppliers of network services emerge who promise to make the use of their network compatible with other networks. This feature of compatibility can be achieved by promising to make the liabilities of the network provider convertible into another monetary network. This possibility transforms the network into one with the structure of Figure 15.2. It also has the important implication that each individual supplier, even if relatively small, can capture a part of the network externalities. In other words, convertibility removes the need for individual suppliers to achieve a large scale in order to capture the benefits of the network externalities. We illustrate this in Figure 15.6.

Assume that one or several monetary networks are in existence. A new supplier now emerges to sell network services, which include compatibility with the existing network services. As a result, the willingness-to-pay schedule faced by this new provider (P') has shifted to the left (relative to the willingness-to-pay curve, P, for the existing monetary network), that is, the first subscribers enjoy large network benefits, and are therefore willing to pay more than if they subscribed to a network without this compatibility feature. Thus, the network provider is able to achieve profitability at a lower scale of operation. It also follows that with compatibility the market can, in principle reach an equilibrium with many profitable suppliers of monetary networks.

In the previous discussion we did not specify whether the convertibility is to be guaranteed at a fixed or at a flexible price (exchange rate). It is important to make this distinction. If convertibility is guaranteed at a variable price (exchange rate) the benefits gained from linking the networks will be lower than if convertibility is guaranteed at a fixed and credible price (exchange rate). In the latter case, the link to another network generates more value to the subscriber, because the future value of "joining the club" is known in advance. (There is no risk that the value of linking the networks declines with time.) As a result, he will be willing to pay more

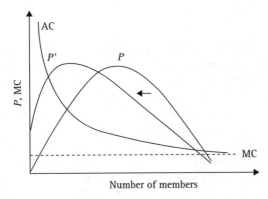

Figure 15.6. *Willingness-to-pay schedule for new providers*

for the network service, than if the link with another network occurs at a variable exchange rate. Graphically, when conversion occurs at a fixed exchange rate, the shift in the willingness-to-pay curve to the left is more pronounced than in the case of conversion at a variable exchange rate. As a result, fixed-price convertibility in principle allows for a larger number of small producers of networks.

The problem with the fixed-price convertibility, however, is the credibility of such a commitment. Economic theory and history have shown that these commitments have a low credibility. Sooner or later, they lead to crises and collapses of the fixed exchange rate regime. Much of the benefit of the monetary network is lost.

Within the nation-state this problem has typically been solved by state regulation of individual banks, vastly increasing the credibility of the fixed price conversion of each individual bank. The issue can be raised whether state regulation was really necessary, and whether self-regulation could not have been used. The fact is that in practically all countries state regulation has been the main instrument. This can be used as prima facie evidence of the difficulties for markets to apply self-regulation.

15.5   E-Money, Compatibility, and Monetary Networks

How does e-money affect the picture drawn in the previous sections? There are essentially two ways e-money can affect the existing monetary networks. First, the new ITs should facilitate compatibility. For example, an Internet firm could create its IOUs to be used for payments. If it does this, using the dollar as a unit of account and promising to convert these IOUs in "real" dollars at par, its IOUs can easily gain acceptance in payments with very small conversion costs. The elimination of distance and other sources of transaction costs will make it easy for individuals to access this new money wherever it is created. In this sense the new technologies can create new payments instruments, "piggybacking" on the existing traditional payments systems.

If the new e-money takes the form just described, a proliferation of new monetary instruments becomes possible. However, the credibility problem will still loom large. The fact that compatibility is made easier technically has no bearing for the credibility of these commitments.

A second possibility is that the new ITs lead to the creation of new payments systems bypassing the existing national monetary networks. Thus, the IOUs created by our Internet firm are expressed in a new unit of account without a promise attached to it of conversion at a fixed price. Such a development is inherently more difficult to lead to success because of the nature of network economics. As argued earlier, the combination of economies of scale and of network externalities necessitates the development of a network with sufficient size. The existence of national payments systems will at least initially work as an obstacle for the development of alternative networks with sufficient size. Such a development, however, is not to be excluded in the long run. Further technological improvements in ITs may make these alternative payments systems so cheap that they become serious competitors to the existing national payments systems.

The success of the development of alternative monetary networks critically depends on credibility. Thus, if electronic money provided by, say, Internet firms, is to make inroads into the existing monetary networks, the credibility of these firms must be established. This will only be possible with time (each firm builds its own credibility history) or if issuing firms are subjected to the same kind of supervision and regulation as the traditional providers of monetary services (the traditional banks).[6]

From the previous discussion we conclude that the development of electronic money could affect the future trends in payments systems in two very different ways. In a first scenario it could lead to completely new payments systems that bypass the national payments systems, and that may even lead to the latter's disappearance. In this scenario the nation-states lose their grip over the monetary networks. The national payment systems disappear and are supplanted by private payments systems because of the latter's superior technological efficiency. This scenario could be characterized by turbulence and monetary instability for the reasons described earlier. It is quite likely that after the turbulence only a few private monetary networks are left over. There will be no national impediments preventing the private networks to expand so as to use fully the benefits of network externalities. In the end, it is quite likely in this scenario the monetary networks will be much larger than the national networks in existence today. The question that remains to be analyzed is how the movement towards private payments systems that supplant the national ones can be realized without endangering price stability. We return to this issue in the next section.

The second scenario looks very different. In this scenario, the new ITs lead to e-moneys that piggyback on the existing national payments systems. In this case, the increased ease of compatibility is the driving force. As a result, the national moneys remain in place and form the basis for the expansion of substitute moneys. This leads to the question of whether the new ITs may not lead to political incentives for countries to look for more (or less) monetary cooperation. We analyze this issue in Section 15.6 where we ask the question of whether the emergence of e-money will change the optimal dimension of national currency areas.

15.6 Monetary Stability and the Private Supply of Payment Systems

As argued earlier, the new IT has the potential of leading to the emergence of private monetary networks that supplant the existing national ones. This is also a movement into a cashless society. We analyze how the new IT and the ensuing movement towards a cashless society will affect monetary stability.[7]

---

[6] There is an important issue here of how supervision and regulation should be organized. Some aspects of supervision can be performed by private institutions, for example, rating agencies. We do not go into the issue here what the role is of public and private institutions in supervision and regulation.

[7] Much of the discussion in this section is based on Costa and De Grauwe (2001).

The new IT has the potential of creating new monetary networks that are not based on cash and which are not under the control of national monetary authorities. Let us for the sake of the argument assume that new privately supplied monetary networks emerge as a result of the new IT. The problem with privately supplied money is well-known. It lacks a mechanism that ties down nominal variables like the money stock and the price level. This problem has been analyzed in great detail by economists (see Patinkin 1965; Fama 1980; Woodford 1999). It can be formulated as follows. The value of the assets of the banks depends on the present and expected future price levels. When the price level is expected to increase the nominal rate of return on these assets increases, thereby increasing their nominal value. The present and future price levels, in turn, depend on the supply of money. The latter consists of the liabilities of the banks. This leads to a potential self-fulfilling price bubble in a system lacking an outside nominal anchor. An expectation of high nominal returns increases the value of the bank's assets, which raises the liabilities of the bank. Since the liabilities of the banks represent money, the higher money stock validates the expectation of a higher price level in the future. Thus, without an outside nominal anchor there is no mechanism that prevents the price level from drifting upwards.[8]

The issue now is to what extent the central banks will be able to perform their function of providing a nominal anchor in a world where an increasing amount of money is privately supplied and not based on cash. It can be argued that in such a "cashless society" the central banks will find it increasingly difficult to control the nominal money stock and the nominal interest rate (see Friedman 1999; Costa and De Grauwe 2001).[9] As a result, the price indeterminacy problem may become more acute, leading to greater monetary instability.

This is likely to lead to the following scenario. Some issuers will be more successful than others in maintaining monetary stability (for instance, designing outside institutions capable of dealing with the new IT-induced monetary developments). These issuers are likely to act as magnets on other less successful private issuers. New monetary unions may then arise around these successful firms.

Whether these developments will increase the optimal size of monetary unions is difficult to say. Much will depend on the capacity of the international community to create new institutions capable of dealing with the potential instability generated by the emergence of privately supplied and cashless monetary networks.

15.7   Optimal Currency Areas

The second scenario looks quite different. As we argued earlier in this second scenario the publicly supported national monetary networks remain firmly in place and provide the basic collective support for new forms of money, like

---

[8] Nominal anchoring can be done by targeting the money stock. Alternatively an "aggressive" Taylor rule performs the same trick (see Woodford 1999 on this).

[9] For a dissenting view, see Goodhart (2000) and Woodford (2000). These views are discussed in Costa and De Grauwe (2001).

e-money. The issue that arises now is whether the new IT will give incentives to national governments to move into larger (or smaller) monetary unions.

In order to analyze this issue, we apply our model of network externalities to a different environment. Instead of being individuals, our basic units are now countries. Within each country a unified monetary network exists. Thus, in each country the coordination problem inherent in setting up a monetary network has been solved by giving the state a prominent role in it. The question at hand is whether it is profitable to merge these national networks into a bigger supranational network, and how this can be done. Again we will ask the question whether the emergence of the new IT changes the nature of the problem.

We use a model that is very similar to the previous one. Let's start by assuming that countries are of equal size. (When countries are of different size the analysis gets complicated because the benefits from joining a network then depend not only on the number of members but also on the size of these members.)

In Figure 15.7 we draw the willingness-to-pay curve, which looks very similar to the one used in the previous section. It is assumed that the issuers involved (which are countries) have already achieved a partial merger of their monetary networks through the device of convertibility (see our discussion related to Figure 15.2). Thus, the willingness-to-pay curve expresses the willingness to pay for a full merger, given the existence of a partial merger of national monetary networks.

The cost analysis is quite different from the analysis of individual agents. The reason is that each of the countries involved uses its own national monetary network as the basis to conduct monetary policies. These are aimed at stabilizing the economy in the face of shocks. To the extent that these shocks are idiosyncratic, the merger into a larger union reduces the capacity of each individual issuer to control the "monetary policy" of the aggregate. This should be seen as

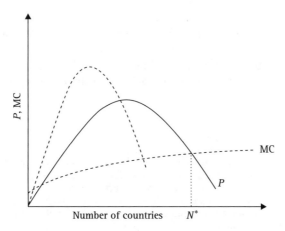

Figure 15.7. *Optimal size of monetary union*

a cost of belonging to a supranational monetary network. This cost is assumed to increase with the size of the supranational monetary network. We show this feature in Figure 15.7 by an upward sloping marginal cost curve, that is, each addition of a new member increases the risk of adopting a non-stabilizing monetary policy.

Put differently, when another issuer joins while the network is small, it can have some influence on the monetary policy of the network, so that the loss of the individual monetary policy is less costly than for an issuer joining the network that is already large. Note that asymptotically the MC curve stabilizes at some fixed number, that is, when the network becomes very large the difference in the MC with successive additions of members becomes very small. Note also that the MC curve starts at point B on the y-axis. This reflects the fixed cost of operating the supranational monetary network, over and above the fixed cost of operating the national networks.[10]

The Pareto optimal size[11] of the monetary union is given by N_1 in Figure 15.8. We now turn to the question of how the new IT is likely to affect this optimum. We analyze first how the new IT affects the willingness-to-pay curve, and second how it affects the MC curve.

Our claim is that the new IT shifts the willingness-to-pay curve downwards, as shown in Figure 15.8, so that the optimum size of the monetary union declines from N_1 to N_2. This may seem paradoxical. It can be explained as follows. We have stressed that we analyze issuers that have achieved a partial merger of their monetary networks, in the way shown in Figure 15.2. The new IT is likely to affect the way this partial merger functions. In particular it is likely to facilitate the conversion (increase the compatibility) of currencies that are linked up. To give an example, the new IT makes the use of e-money much easier in international transactions. Whereas in the past, consumers traveling abroad had to exchange currency or carry travelers' checks, which were costly operations, now they can pay directly using their computer. In addition, the capacity of individuals to order goods and services through the Internet and pay with cards, is a technological innovation that has increased the compatibility of the national currencies, thereby making the link-up of different national monetary networks less costly. The result is that the additional network benefits to be obtained from a full merger of these networks declines. The willingness to pay for a fully merged network declines, and the optimal size of the monetary union declines.

---

[10] There are many complications underlying the marginal cost curves. For example, some countries peg their exchange rate; others allow the exchange rate to float. The latter lose more when joining a monetary union than the former. This affects the shape of the MC curve. Note that the fixers also experience a cost when joining a monetary union for the simple reason that they lose their ability to change the exchange rate in the face of an asymmetric shock.

[11] We call this the Pareto optimal size of the monetary union because it is the point where the price the last member is willing to pay equals the marginal cost. It is also the point that maximizes the net benefit of the monetary union.

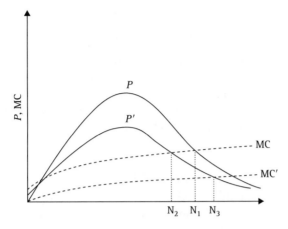

Figure 15.8. *Effect of IT on optimal size of monetary union*

The question that arises here is how important this decline in the willingness to pay for a full merger is likely to be. The main difference between the full merger of two monetary networks and the partial one depicted in Figure 15.2 is that in the latter case it is difficult to make a credible commitment of convertibility at a *fixed* price. In the case of a full merger this commitment is fully credible. Technical innovations in information technologies do not affect this difference. As a result, even if technically improved, the partial merger will not fully exploit the benefits of network externalities. Put differently, as long as there exists uncertainty about the exchange rate at which the two moneys in the partial merger can be converted, the move to a full union is a significant one. The technical improvements in compatibility may be of second order. It also follows that the downward movement of the willingness-to-pay curve may also be of relatively little importance.

How does the new IT affect the MC curve in Figure 15.8? One aspect of the new IT is that it increases the size and the speed of capital movements. This has the effect of reducing the capacity of issuers to stabilize their supply. This holds both for fixed exchange and floating exchange rate systems. In the former case increased capital mobility makes the fixed exchange rate more exposed to self-fulfilling speculative attacks (see Obstfeld 1986), leaving the fixed exchange rate regime more fragile.

In a floating exchange rate regime the volatility of the exchange rate reduces the capacity of the national monetary authorities to maintain domestic monetary stability. This is likely to be the case, especially in small regions (see von Furstenberg 2002 on this issue).

We conclude that, whether the pre-union situation was characterized by fixed or flexible exchange rates, the new IT is likely to reduce the cost of a monetary union, thereby shifting the MC-curve downwards. This effect then increases the optimal size of the monetary union.

Thus, the new IT has opposite effects on the optimal size of monetary unions. There is a presumption that the downward shift of the MC-curve may be the most important effect. As we argued earlier, the downward shift of the willingness-to-pay curve may be rather small, because of the weak credibility of the fixed exchange rate systems. Thus, we arrive at the conclusion that the new IT is likely to increase the optimal size of a monetary union.[12]

15.8   Conclusion

Is the new IT going to affect the optimal size of monetary unions? The answer, not surprisingly is: It depends. We distinguished two possible future scenarios. In the first one, the new IT leads to new and privately supplied payment systems that supplant the existing publicly supported ones. If this scenario materializes, it is likely to lead to monetary areas that are significantly larger than the present ones. We argued, however, that this scenario is bound to lead to much monetary turbulence. The political issue here is how national authorities will react to these developments. Within the nation-state this problem was solved by letting the national law do the coordination. The same problem exists at the international level. The movement towards the larger monetary areas cannot easily be organized in the absence of government action, for the same reasons as those that apply within the nation-state. In order to move towards larger monetary zones, governments may have to solve the coordination problem. This remains true even in a world of Internet and electronic money.

In the second scenario, the new IT "piggyback" on the existing national monetary networks. We analyzed how, in this scenario, the new IT creates incentives for nations to join in monetary unions. By increasing the technical efficiency of the payments systems, the new IT makes the conversion of one money into the other easier. As a result, the existing monetary networks are made more compatible with each other and the attractiveness of full monetary unions declines. The optimal size of monetary unions declines.

However, we argued that this effect is likely to be small relative to two other effects of IT. First, the new IT is likely to reduce the capacity of individual countries (especially the small ones) to build credibility about its stabilization purposes. As a result, relinquishing these instruments by joining a monetary union becomes less costly. Second, we argued that the new IT has the potential of weakening the credibility of fixed exchange rate regimes. If that is the case, the desire to move to larger monetary areas could actually increase. Thus, on the whole the new IT may very well increase the optimal size of monetary unions.

---

[12] A similar conclusion is reached by von Furstenberg (2002). See also Cohen (2000).

REFERENCES

Bank for International Settlements (cited as BIS) (1996). Implications for Central Banks of the Development of Electronic Money, October.

Boeschoten, W. C. and Hebbink, G. E. (1996). "Electronic Money, Currency Demand and Seignorage Loss in G-10 Countries." *De Netherlandsche Bank Staff Report*, No. 1, May.

Cohen, B. (2000). "Life at the Top: International Currencies in the Twenty-First Century." *Essays in International Economics*, No. 221, International Economics Section, Princeton University, December.

Costa, C. and De Grauwe, P. (2001). "Monetary Policy in a Cashless Society." *CEPR Discussion Paper* No. 2696.

Diamond, D. and Dybvig, P. (1983). "Bank Runs, Deposit Insurance and Liquidity." *Journal of Political Economy*, 91 (August): 401–19.

Economides, N. (1996). "The Economics of Networks." *International Journal of Industrial Organization*, 14 (March): 673–99.

Fama, E. (1980). "Banking in the Theory of Finance." *Journal of Monetary Economics*, 6 (May): 39–57.

Friedman, B. (1999). "The Future of Monetary Policy: The Central Bank as an Army with only a Signal Corps." *International Finance*, 2 (November): 321–38.

Goodhart, C. (2000). "Can Central Banking Survive the IT Revolution?" Paper presented at the conference *The Future of Monetary Policy*. Washington, DC: World Bank, July 11.

Hayek, F. (1978). *Denationalising Money: The Argument Refined*. London: Institute of Economic Affairs.

Klein, B. (1974). "The Competitive Supply of Money." *Journal of Money Credit and Banking*, 6 (November): 423–53.

Liebowitz, S. J. and Margolis, S. E. (1994). "Are Network Externalities an New Source of Market Failures." Draft, Management School, University of Texas at Dallas.

Matutes, C. and Regibeau, P. (1992). "Compatibility and Bundling of Complementary Goods in a Duopoly." *Journal of Industrial Economics*, 40 (January): 37–54.

Obstfeld, M. (1986). "Rational and Self-Fulfilling Balance of Payments Crises," *American Economics Review*, 76 (March): 72–81.

Patinkin, D. (1965). *Money, Interest and Prices*, 2nd ed. New York: Harper and Row.

von Furstenberg, G. M. (2002). "One Region, One Money: Implications of Regional Currency Consolidation for Financial Services." *Geneva Papers on Risk and Insurance*, 27 (January): 5–28.

Woodford, M. (1999). "Price Level Determination Under Interest Rate Rules." Draft, Department of Economics, Princeton University.

— (2000). "Monetary Policy in a World without Money." Paper presented at the conference *The Future of Monetary Policy*, Washington, DC: World Bank, July 11.

16

Currency Substitution in Anticipation of EU Accession

HANS GENBERG

Countries in Eastern and Central Europe that are likely to join the European Union will eventually also join the European Monetary Union (EMU). The process of accession will entail a transition period at the end of which it is certain that the domestic currency will be replaced by the euro. This chapter argues that this programmed demise of the domestic currency may bring about significant spontaneous euroization already during the transition period. If the euro is adopted by the private sector in anticipation of the official changeover, the country incurs a resource cost in the form of lost seignorage. Compared to the initial members of the EMU that could print euros equal to the outstanding monetary base, a country where euroization takes place before the entry into the EMU will use real resources to obtain the euros. I propose ways to deal with this difference in treatment.

16.1 Introduction

For countries in Eastern and Central Europe that hope to join the European Union, the process of eventually being accepted into the EMU will take some time if one is to believe official descriptions of the steps that need to be followed. It is virtually a foregone conclusion, however, that the national monies will be replaced by the euro at the end of this transition period. Since euros are already circulating in the economies of the twelve current members, citizens of the accession countries will already start to use them when they travel and when they engage in trade with the EMU members. In view of the impending phasing out of the domestic currency, they may also start using euros as a store of value or in certain domestic transaction before the official changeover.

This chapter analyzes the extent and consequences of spontaneous adoption of the euro in anticipation of membership in the EMU. In the next section I discuss the likelihood that spontaneous adoption of euros will actually come about.

The author is grateful to Thomas Courchene and George von Furstenberg for insightful comments on an earlier draft of this chapter, and to participants at the Fordham University conference on "Euro and Dollarization: Forms of Monetary Union in Integrating Regions" for useful suggestions.

I argue that the drawn-out accession period will provide the opportunity to euroize before the quasi-certain end point involving official adoption of the euro. The official changeover may even constitute a coordinating mechanism that will lead to a larger domestic use of the euro than is frequently thought.

Section 16.3 investigates some consequences of spontaneous adoption of the euro in the accession countries. In particular, I discuss the loss of seignorage for the new members. The argument is that spontaneous euroization leads to a reduction in the local currency monetary base, and therefore in the amount of euros that the accession countries can print upon entry into the euro area. Spontaneous euroization in other words implies that new members will have to spend real resources to obtain euros, whereas the original members could simply print them. I discuss whether this is something to be concerned about, and if it is, what could be done to limit its extent. A final section of the chapter considers the applicability of the analysis to other countries in the world that may consider unilateral euroization or dollarization.

16.2 Incentives For Spontaneous Dollarization

In the popular debate about the effects of staying outside the European Monetary Union, it has sometimes been suggested that economic agents will spontaneously adopt the euro because of the advantages associated with using a common currency. Often the arguments start with the proposition that a firm, which is heavily dependent on exports to EMU countries, and therefore invoices in euros would avoid currency risk if it could also contract wages and other costs in this currency. Applied to the tourist industry, or other export services that have to be consumed in the selling country, the argument would go further and claim that prices of hotel and similar services will be set in euros in those non-member countries that earn a large part of their revenues from EMU residents.

Although physical euros have not been in existence for more than a few months, it seems that the claims that they would be adopted in domestic transactions in *advanced* European non-EMU countries are quite off the mark.[1] There are very few signs of any noteworthy currency substitution in these countries as yet. This is also consistent with what is known about spontaneous dollarization in general; it occurs principally when the inflation rate in the domestic currency is very high and unstable, and/or when the domestic central bank has lost all credibility. Hence, there seems to be little reason to expect the euro establishing itself in non-EMU countries where monetary policy is stable even if they are close to Euroland both geographically and economically.

But what would happen if a country has taken a formal decision to adopt the euro, but for administrative or practical reasons, the changeover will not take place for some substantial period of time (a year or two, say)? When it is known

[1] The euro has been adopted in Kosovo and Macedonia. This is due to the virtual non-existence of a stable alternative currency arrangement.

that the domestic money will be phased out and replaced by the euro, will that not introduce additional incentives for the private sector to anticipate the official changeover?

In this section I will investigate these questions by analyzing the incentives that may exist for increased currency substitution in the run-up to joining a monetary union as well as the obstacles that prevent it. Not surprisingly the net effect of these two forces is ambiguous. It would certainly be beneficial for some segments of the economy to be able to switch rapidly to the new currency. However, unless a critical mass of economic agents adopts the euro simultaneously, it may not be profitable for anyone to do so. This externality gives the incumbent currency a natural advantage. A trigger that makes many agents switch their currency use in a coordinated fashion could be the announcement of the upcoming official changeover.

16.2.1 Search-theoretic models of currency use

Theoretical models where the choice of currency for transactions is determined endogenously typically imply multiple equilibria. Applied to an international context, this means that it is possible to generate equilibria where no, one or several currencies become accepted for transactions, and are therefore held, in a country.[2] Factors, such as the openness of the economy and its integration with other economies will play a role in determining which outcomes are possible. But these models also predict that the equilibria may not be unique. For a given set of characteristics an equilibrium with no foreign currency holdings and another equilibrium with positive foreign currency holdings are both possible. Which of the two possibilities prevails will depend on the expectations of economic agents as to the outcome. The one that is expected to prevail will actually emerge as the self-fulfilling equilibrium.

The reason for the multiplicity of equilibria is that the choice of currency is basically viewed as a coordination problem in the presence of externalities. The externality emerges because the more frequently a currency is used and accepted by others, the more useful will it be for any given individual. The coordination problem is due to the fact that any one of several currencies could potentially serve as a transactions vehicle provided that a sufficiently large number of economic agents happen to decide on it. The importance of expectations is now easily understood. If a sufficiently large number of agents expect currency A to be adopted as the transactions currency, then they will hold that currency and use it. By so doing they provide the incentives for others to use it as well, and the currency emerges as money. If expectations instead had focused on currency B, it would have been chosen as the currency in the region.

An incumbent money will have a natural advantage in this situation. It is already used and will, therefore, be resilient to challenges from potential alternatives.

---

[2] See Trejos and Wright (1996) for an accessible illustration of how these search-theoretic models are constructed, and what kinds of conclusions they yield.

A coordinated switch by many economic agents to another currency would come about if the costs of maintaining the incumbent became very high. Alternatively, if some factor would lead to a significant change in expectations, it may be possible that a shift in currency use will take place even if the direct costs of keeping the incumbent money are not large. An official announcement that a country is on schedule to join a monetary union could generate such expectations. Contracts that extend beyond the entry into the monetary union are likely to be denominated in the new currency. Long-term savings decisions can likewise be expected to emphasize the currency of the union. To be sure, legal tender considerations will still give the existing money an advantage, but this advantage will surely be eroded over time as the date of the official changeover approaches.

16.2.2   Informal arguments for currency substitution

For the current EMU members the timetable for the introduction of euro notes and coins included a three-year period during which the old national monies continued to circulate. This was to permit institutions in the public sector and firms and households in the private sector to carry out the necessary preparations for the adoption of the new money. National changeover plans were drawn up enumerating the required preparations, and these were usually calculated to take two to three years.[3]

The reasons for the relatively long preparation period seem to originate mainly in the public sector and are mostly related to changes in administrative routines and laws.[4] In the private sector it is usually argued that a changeover can be carried out more quickly. Firms that are internationally active already have the ability to conduct business in other currencies than the local one, and smaller purely local firms usually have less complicated systems to alter. It is, therefore, likely that a large part of the private sector would be able to adopt a new currency relatively quickly after a decision to dollarize has been taken. But will they in fact engage in spontaneous dollarization?

To answer that question, consider briefly the arguments why the demand for domestic money might fall in the transition period.

16.2.2.1   *Money as a store of value*
Faced with a programmed official dollarization, an investor knows that any asset denominated in the local currency will have to be changed into the new currency at the conversion date. If the investment horizon is beyond this conversion date, he or she might decide to complete the changeover earlier so as to match the currency composition of his or her assets with the currency

---

[3] See Genberg (2000) for a discussion of these issues in the Swedish context.

[4] For the first wave of EMU members, the logistics of printing euro notes and minting euro coins was a significant contributing factor for the relatively long transition period. This need not be a bottleneck for new members who can use the facilities that have already been developed for the production of additional notes and coins.

composition of the planned future expenditures. To be sure, arguments of this type probably apply principally to the demand for broad measures of money, but indirectly this will change the demand for base money on the part of financial intermediaries.

16.2.2.2 *Money as a unit of account*

Firms that trade significantly with the rest of the world are routinely managing invoices, price lists, etc. in both domestic and foreign currencies. One of the cost savings associated with dollarization is presumably that there will be one less currency to deal with. To the extent possible, a firm may therefore anticipate the changeover, and phase out the domestic currency when the occasion presents itself during the transition period. While this will increase the familiarity with the new currency, it does not by itself change the demand for monetary base denominated in the domestic currency.

16.2.2.3 *Money as a means of transaction*

As described by the search-theoretic models of money, the usefulness of money for transactions purposes involves an externality. The more agents that use a money, the more useful it is for an individual. Hence, to switch from the domestic money for transactions purposes requires some degree of coordination. This is why there is a presumption that the incumbent money will continue to be used heavily until the official changeover date. In some contexts, especially in border regions and in sectors dealing with tourism, there will be strong incentives to accept the new currency, and this may be a trigger that induces greater generalized use of this currency for transactions.

In the context it is important to note that a significant amount of currency substitution has already taken place in several Eastern and Central European countries. This process started as a reaction to the instability and uncertain purchasing power of the existing currencies, but it persists even though a certain measure of confidence has now been restored. It is therefore to be expected that the extent of currency substitution will increase once a time schedule of accession to the European Union (EU) has been established.

16.3 Consequences of Spontaneous Adoption of the Euro in Accession Countries

16.3.1 Loss of seignorage

New members in the euro area will be able to print an amount of euros that corresponds to the monetary base at the time of entry into the euro system. If there is no spontaneous euroization in the run-up, the conversion will look exactly like that of the first wave of members that replaced their national monies with the euro starting in January 2002. No real resources other than printing and distribution costs had to be incurred at the changeover.

If there is some spontaneous adoption of the euro before the official introduction, the situation is different. To illustrate what might happen suppose realistically that the country has decided to maintain a fixed exchange rate *vis-à-vis* the euro during the transition period. If there is no currency substitution during this period, the local coins and notes will simply be replaced by the corresponding amounts in euros when the conversion day comes. The euros will either be printed directly by the country in question, or the Eurosystem will provide them.

Before the decision to euroize the domestic money supply is backed by domestic and foreign assets in the balance sheet of the central bank. As there is no currency substitution during the transition, the demand for money can be assumed not to change, so at the time of the official euroization the balance sheet is fundamentally the same as before. The stock of domestic money will simply have been replaced by the stock of euros as the monetary assets of the private sector and the corresponding liability of the central bank. There has been no change in the net financial position of the country as a whole.

Consider, now, what happens if there will actually be a significant amount of spontaneous currency substitution during the transition period. Currency substitution implies a reduction in the demand for the local currency in favor of the euros. To obtain the euros, residents will sell the home currency in the foreign exchange market, putting pressure on the exchange rate. To prevent depreciation, the central bank intervenes resulting in a loss of foreign exchange reserves. When these reserves are exhausted, the central bank may borrow abroad in order to continue the interventions. In the balance sheet of the central bank there will be an increase in external liabilities that corresponds to the increasing domestic demand for euros for monetary purposes. When the time comes to replace the domestic currency officially with the euro, the remaining money supply will be replaced by euros as before, but because of the currency substitution during the transition, the central bank's balance sheet has now been altered, in particular its net foreign asset position has deteriorated.

To prevent the deterioration of the balance sheet at the time of the changeover, the central bank would have to receive (or be able to print) euros equal to the money in circulation at the beginning of the transition period, and not at the end. If that were done, the euros that would not be needed to replace the domestic money in circulation could be used to restore the net foreign asset position to its level at the beginning of the transition period.

While this solution is relatively straightforward if it is the central bank that borrows abroad during the transition, the situation will be more complicated if the central bank has induced the private sector to do so. In this case the end result will be that private sector financial intermediaries will have a negative net foreign asset position corresponding to the international borrowing it was induced to do on behalf of the central bank. At the time of the changeover to euros, the central bank could, of course, exchange these liabilities for newly minted euros, but it will not be obvious how to distinguish foreign asset positions contracted on behalf of the central bank from regular transactions that these intermediaries might have engaged in.

Table 16.1. *Reserve money as a percentage of GDP in EU accession countries*

1998 Accession group Country	Czech Republic	Estonia	Hungary	Poland	Slovenia
Average 1995–99 (%)	23.2	13.1	10.8	9.2	4.7
2000 Accession group Country	Bulgaria	Latvia	Lithuania	Romania	Slovak Republic
Average 1995–99 (%)	15.7	12.7	9.5	7.9	12.9

Source: IMF International Financial Statistics CD-ROM, and own calculations.

The solution to this problem might be that the Eurosystem provides a conversion facility in euros to the central bank in the euroizing country for the entire amount of the monetary base at the beginning of the transition period. This conversion facility can be drawn on to stabilize the exchange rate and would be sufficient to deal with any amount of currency substitution that might occur.

16.3.2 Is the loss of seignorage quantitatively important?

The maximum size of the potential loss of seignorage is indicated in Table 16.1 for the ten potential accession countries. They range from 4.7 percent of GDP in Slovenia to 23.2 percent in the Czech Republic. These figures represent the upper limit of the potential loss because they would be realized only if spontaneous euroization before the official changeover was complete in the sense that the entire monetary base was transformed into euros.[5] However, even if only a fraction of this transformation were to take place, the loss to the country could be substantial.

16.3.3 Should we do anything about it?

On equity grounds, it seems unfair that new members in the EMU should have to spend real resources to obtain euros when the original members did not. Moreover, since GDP per capita of the potential new members is generally lower, one might question the fairness of the transfer to the richer existing members resulting from uncompensated spontaneous euroization.

Of course, since spontaneous euroization would be completely voluntary, the citizens are presumably better off compared to a situation where they would be prevented from using the euro during the transition. However, this does not

---

[5] Note that some additional loss of seignorage has already occurred since euros are already held in the accession countries.

change the fact that such euroization involves resource costs and transfers to the existing EMU members.

It might be argued that since the new accession countries did not have to incur any of the setup costs of the Eurosystem, the transfers simply reflect contributions to these costs, a bit like an entrance fee to an exclusive club to cover the costs of building of the clubhouse. While the principle that new members of the EMU should have to contribute to the initial setup costs does have some merit, there is no reason why the size of this contribution should be related to the amount of currency substitution that takes place in the transition.

Another argument might be that the transfer represents a penalty that countries have to incur for not preventing the premature adoption of the euro in the private sector. It is well known that the official view in the Eurosystem is quite negative regarding euroization in accession countries. It seems that they are expected to follow a path towards EMU membership that involves maintaining their own currencies and staying in an ERM2 arrangement for two years before they are considered eligible to enter the monetary union. Whatever the merit of the view that transition to EMU membership should not involve *official* euroization, it is not clear that a government in an accession country can do much to prevent spontaneous adoption of the euro in the private sector. Attempts to discourage it may in fact have the opposite impact if the private sector interprets this as a sign that the domestic authorities want to preserve the demand for domestic base money in order to extract additional seignorage through inflation.

I conclude from this discussion that the transfers from accession countries to EMU members associated with spontaneous euroization is both inequitable and inefficient. It is, hence, important to search for ways of minimizing their size. This is the topic of the next section.

16.4   Limiting the Size of the Resource Transfer Due to Euroization

Assuming that we cannot or do not want to limit by decree the extent to which the private sector ends up using the euro during the accession period, what can be done to limit the size of the implied resource transfer?

As already noted, one approach involves allowing the domestic authorities to print or obtain an amount of euros equal to the size of the monetary base outstanding at the beginning of the transition period rather than at the end. This can be accomplished in several ways. One would be activated at the time of joining the monetary union and would allow the Central Bank to print an amount of euros equal to the value of domestic-currency monetary base at the time the country joins the EU. This would ensure that all spontaneous euroization during the transition would not result in any resource loss. A similar effect could be obtained by creating a conversion facility during the transition period whereby a new EU member would be able to obtain euros from the Eurosystem in exchange for domestic currency at a fixed conversion rate. Such a facility would make it possible to stabilize the exchange rate without losing foreign exchange reserves.

Another approach to limit the loss of seignorage would be to reduce the volume of euroization in the private sector by shortening the transition period from EU to EMU membership. When one of the accession countries enters the EU it will also commit itself to joining the EMU once it has met the convergence criteria. One of these requires membership in an ERM2 arrangement for a period of at least two years. After being admitted into the EMU but before replacing the national money with euros it might be necessary to allow for an additional transition period in order to make the necessary technical preparations. Since newcomers have the experiences of the current members to draw on, the latter period can be made relatively short, provided some preparations are already started when the country enters the ERM2.

We see that the real bottleneck is the two-year period spent in the ERM2 arrangement. In order to limit the potential for spontaneous euroization and the resulting transfers, it would be necessary to reduce its length substantially. As the economic arguments for maintaining such a long transition period are in any case suspect, the argument advanced here suggest that it should be modified.

16.5   Final Remarks

I have argued that the prospect of joining a currency union can constitute a triggering mechanism that induces spontaneous currency substitution in anticipation of the official changeover. The logic applies particularly to the case of those Central and Eastern European countries that aspire to become members of the European Union. Is it also relevant elsewhere?

I think the answer is yes. Consider the basic underlying logic. The extent to which the private sector uses a foreign currency (the dollar, say) in parallel with the domestic currency depends on a number of factors, among them the probability that the government will dollarize officially. In turn, the incentives for the government to do so depend in part on how dollarized the private sector already is. It is possible that these two processes interact so as to bring the country gradually closer and closer towards full dollarization both in the private sector and inescapably therefore by the government.[6]

The argument that dollarization involves a real transfer from the dollarizing country is also of course generally valid. In the context of the new members of the European Union I have argued on equity grounds that the relatively poor accession countries should be compensated for this real transfer. Alternatively steps should be taken to reduce the transition period during which spontaneous euroization is likely to take place.

It is less clear that the compensation argument applies to countries that dollarize unilaterally. Although it would be almost costless for the United States to provide the dollars in exchange for the local currency, the equity motive for

---

[6] The dynamics involved is studied in Genberg (2003).

Hans Genberg

doing so does not apply with the same force exactly because the decision to dollarize is unilateral. However, on strategic grounds it may be profitable for the United States to provide a country with the initial stock of dollars in order to collect the continuous flow of seignorage thereafter. This is particularly the case if the country has the alternative of giving up the domestic currency for the euro. Analyzing the intriguing possibility that the "dollarizing" country can extract a portion or even all the present and future seignorage gains from competing suppliers of an international money is however beyond the scope of the present chapter.

REFERENCES

Genberg, H. (2000). "Managing Sweden's Transition to EMU." SNS (Studieförbundet Näringsliv och Samhälle) *Occasional Paper* No. 83, February.

—— (2003). "Endogenous Dollarization," Unpublished paper, Institute of International Studies, Geneva, Switzerland.

Trejos, A. and Wright, R. (1996). "Search-Theoretic Models of International Currency." *Federal Reserve Bank of St. Louis Review*, 78 (May/June): 117–32.

17

Allocating Lending of Last Resort and Supervision in the Euro Area

CHARLES M. KAHN AND JOÃO A. C. SANTOS

The Maastricht Treaty created the European System of Central Banks (ESCB) and the European Central Bank (ECB) to head this system. The Treaty entrusts the ECB with the responsibility for monetary policy, but national authorities remain responsible for financial stability. In this chapter, we focus on potential efficiency implications and consequences of the allocation of the lender of last resort (LLR) and supervisory functions for the degree of forbearance in closing distressed banks and for the level of diligence in bank supervision. We conclude that the integration of banking markets without the integration of regulatory functions increases forbearance and decreases supervision. Centralizing regulatory functions will tend to reverse this decline. If only one of the two functions is centralized, then it will be more effective to centralize the supervisory function.

17.1 Introduction

Historically, the European Union (EU) has been building its bank regulatory framework through a process that fully harmonizes some components of this framework while leaving others at the national discretion. Over time, as more of these components are harmonized, questions of regulatory competition and of maintaining a level playing field with the remaining components have become more acute. With monetary policy moved from national levels to the ECB, the decision to leave supervision and lending of last resort with national authorities has generated concern about financial stability in the EU area. We contribute to this debate by focusing on the efficiency implications of the institutional allocation of regulation and by studying the relative importance of centralizing different functions such as bank supervision and LLR in the euro area.

The authors thank George von Furstenberg, Charles Goodhart and seminar participants at the Fordham University conference, The Euro and Dollarization: Forms of Monetary Union in Integrating Regions, for useful comments. The views stated herein are those of the authors and are not necessarily those of the Federal Reserve Bank of New York or the Federal Reserve System.

Throughout the chapter we use the term bank regulation in a broad sense, to include not only formal rules and standards but also LLR, supervision, and deposit insurance.

The goal of creating a single financial market in Europe dates back to the 1957 Treaty of Rome that established the European Economic Community. The Treaty set out provisions to meet this goal, but the financial services industry remained a national business because obstacles to free entry remained in place. The 1977 First Banking Directive's requirement that entry rules in a member state had to be those applicable to the host country's domestic institutions reduced these obstacles. However, entry standards remained different across countries.

In time, it became evident that market forces alone were not capable of dismantling existing barriers to the single market in the short term. It also became increasingly clear that it would be difficult to implement the single market through the harmonization of all national standards because these were very different, and reaching agreement would be an extremely long process.

This motivated the adoption of a harmonization approach based on three principles: Harmonization of minimum standards, home-country control, and mutual recognition. Minimum standards would prevent regulatory standards from reaching an undesirably low level as a result of market forces. Home-country control, in turn, would guarantee that all financial institutions were supervised. Finally, mutual recognition of national authorities' supervision would avoid the duplication of supervision.

This new approach has facilitated the introduction of key legislation defining the regulatory framework that supports the single financial market. This framework, however, increasingly had standards that were harmonized or centralized at the European level while others, closely related to the former, were different across countries because they had been left under national control.

This dichotomy is evident in the 1988 Second Banking Directive which introduced the single banking license. This allowed a bank to offer anywhere in the EU all of the services it was allowed to offer at home. It also harmonized the set of activities that a bank could offer. Other accompanying directives harmonized the solvency standards they had to meet. National authorities, however, were not required to allow their home banks to offer these activities. In addition, all of the other elements of the bank regulatory framework were left at national discretion. It was only in 1994 that deposit insurance was harmonized, however, as with previous regulations, only partially.

The 1994 Deposit Insurance Directive required all banks to enroll in a guarantee scheme that insures depositors up to a given minimum amount. Left at the country's discretion were the choice of a level of coverage above this minimum, and the design and administration of the scheme.

The Maastricht Treaty, the most recent example of the partial harmonization approach, established the conditions for the introduction of the euro on January 1, 1999. The treaty harmonized monetary policy by transferring it from national central banks to the ECB.[1] However, it left the responsibility for the stability of the financial system, including supervision and LLR, with national authorities.

This institutional allocation of bank regulation has generated an intense debate over its implications for financial stability and a level playing field in the euro area. We focus instead on its efficiency implications, particularly, the consequences of the existing institutional allocation of LLR and supervision on the degree of forbearance in closing distressed firms and the level of diligence in bank supervision. The integration of banking markets without the integration of these regulatory functions increases forbearance and decreases supervision. Centralizing regulatory functions will tend to reverse this decline. If only one of the two functions is centralized, it will be more effective to centralize the supervisory function.

Section 17.2 briefly characterizes the current institutional allocation of bank regulation in the euro area. Section 17.3 reviews the literature on the institutional allocation of regulation in the euro area. Section 17.4 presents our model, and Section 17.5 discusses the implications of centralizing supervision ahead of LLR or vice versa. Section 17.6 offers some final remarks.

17.2 The Institutional Allocation of Bank Regulation in the Euro Area

The approach adopted by the EU to implement a single financial market has given rise to a bank regulatory arrangement where some components are fully harmonized and others left at countries' discretion within some limits. As we will show, the restrictions imposed by these limits vary considerably across the three main components of a bank regulatory arrangement: Deposit insurance, supervision, and LLR.

17.2.1 Deposit insurance

The 1994 Directive on deposit guarantee schemes was made mandatory in all member states and set a uniform minimum coverage of ECU 20,000 per depositor.[2] The Directive, however, left at the discretion of national authorities the design of national schemes, including funding and administration, and it allowed national authorities to offer higher levels of protection. As a result of this partial harmonization, nominal deposit insurance coverage varies considerably across the EU. The differences in coverage across countries remain quite large even when we adjust their nominal coverage by the country's GDP per capita (see Table 17.1).

---

[1] The eleven founding members were Austria, Belgium, Germany, Finland, France, Ireland, Italy, Luxembourg, the Netherlands, Portugal, and Spain. Greece became the twelfth member of the currency union in January 2001.

[2] The Directive required each scheme to cover the depositors of a state's credit institutions and the depositors of these institutions' branches in other member states.

Table 17.1. *Deposit protection schemes of euro area countries*

	Coverage per depositor		Funding[c]	Administration[d]
	In U.S. dollars[a]	Coverage ratio relative to GDP per capita[b]		
Austria	24,057	1	No	Private
Belgium	16,439	1	Yes	Joint
Finland	29,435	1	Yes	Private
France	65,387	3	No	Private
Germany	21,918	1	Yes	Private
Greece	21,918	2	Yes	Joint
Ireland	16,439	1	Yes	Official
Italy	125,000	6	No	Joint
Luxembourg	16,439	0	No	Private
Portugal	16,439	1	Yes	Official
Netherlands	21,918	1	No	Official
Spain	16,439	1	Yes	Joint

[a] Based on coverage limits that were in effect during the second half of 1999 and exchange rates at the end of June 1998.
[b] Ratios computed based on the 1998 GDP per capita.
[c] "Yes" indicates the system is funded *ex ante*. "No" indicates the system is unfunded.
[d] Systems administered by the central bank are also classified as official.

Source: Demirgüç and Sobaci (2000).

Table 17.1 illustrates several other differences between national schemes. For example, while most schemes are funded *ex ante* through premiums paid by the banks, there are schemes funded *ex post*, that is, where banks commit to contribute to the scheme in case funds are needed to reimburse depositors of a failed bank. In addition, while the majority of schemes are publicly administered, several countries use private arrangements.[3]

17.2.2   Supervision

The Maastricht Treaty entrusted the ESCB with the full responsibility for formulating monetary policy and transferred to the ESCB the responsibility to promote the smooth functioning of the payment system.[4] The Treaty, however, restricted the role of the ESCB with respect to safeguarding of financial stability, 'to the smooth

---

[3] See Demirgüç-Kunt and Sobaci (2000) for further details on the deposit insurance arrangements of the EU members.
[4] Art 105(2) of the Treaty stipulates that one of the basic tasks of the ESCB "shall be to promote the smooth functioning of the payment system" and Article 22 stipulates that "the ECB and National Central Banks may provide facilities, and the ECB may issue regulations to ensure efficient and sound clearing and payment systems within the Community and with other countries."

conduct of policies pursued by competent authorities relating to the prudential supervision of credit institutions and the stability of the financial system' (Art. 105 (5)), and to an advisory function in the regulatory process (Art. 105 (4)).[5]

The ambiguous role of the ECB in the maintenance of the stability of the financial system contrasts with the clear definition of its responsibilities with respect to monetary policy. This is similar to the Bundesbank Act, which does not assign the task of preserving of the stability of the financial system to the central bank, but is in contrast with the objectives of other central banks, including the Federal Reserve.

A consequence of this institutional allocation of responsibilities is that the home-country control principle together with cross-border cooperation remains a cornerstone of the euro area bank regulatory arrangement. This principle assigns the responsibility for consolidated supervision of a bank's business both inside and outside the EU to the "competent authority" of the member state where the bank has its head office.

Host country supervisors are expected to provide all necessary information to the home country authorities. Cross-border cooperation is implemented at the bilateral level through memoranda of understanding and at the euro area level through the Banking Supervisory Committee of the ECB. This committee brings together the authorities responsible for monetary policy and payments systems oversight in the ESCB with national banking supervisors. Cooperation between banking supervisors also occurs at the EU level through the European Commission's Banking Advisory Committee and its working group, the "Groupe de Contact."[6]

Given the different institutional allocation of bank supervision across member states, including a substantial difference in central bank's involvement in this function (Table 17.2), the current regulatory arrangement in the euro area requires the cooperation of agencies with quite different mandates. In addition, it promotes the supervision of similar institutions by authorities with different mandates and responsibilities.[7]

17.2.3 Lending of last resort

The Maastricht Treaty gave the ECB the responsibility for managing monetary policy. However, it did not give that institution an explicit mandate to act as LLR,

---

[5] According to Art 105 (6), the ECB role in supervision can be increased without a revision of the Treaty.

[6] The Banking Advisory Committee advises the European Commission with regard to the formulation and implementation of EC legislation for the banking sector. The "Groupe de Contact," which consists only of banking supervisors, deals with practical issues, including cooperation with respect to issues related to individual institutions. See European Commission (2000) for further details on these committees.

[7] Besides the differences in both the central bank and the deposit insurance provider involvement in bank supervision, in some countries such as the United Kingdom there is a single supervisor for all financial services while in others such as Germany there are multiple supervisory authorities. See Goodhart and Schoenmaker (1998) for further details on the supervisory arrangements of EU members.

Table 17.2. *Bank supervisory agencies of euro area countries*

Country	Supervisory agencies[a]
Austria	Ministry of Finance
Belgium	Commission Bancaire et Financière (S)
Finland	Rahoitustarkastus (S) and Suomen Pankki (CB)
France	Commission Bancaire (S) and Banque de France (CB)
Germany	Bundesaufsichtsamt für das Kreditwesen (S) and Deutsche Bundesbank (CB)
Greece	Bank of Greece (CB)
Ireland	Bank Ceannais na hÉireann (CB)
Italy	Banca d'Italia (CB)
Luxembourg	Institut Monétaire Luxembourgeois (CB)
Netherlands	De Nederlandshe Bank (CB)
Portugal	Banco de Portugal (CB)
Spain	Banco de España (CB)

[a] Throughout this table (S) stands for supervisory agency and (CB) stands for central bank.

Source: Goodhart and Schoenmaker (1998) and National Central Banks.

that is, to provide discretionary liquidity support directly to individual financial institutions with liquidity needs they are unable to meet through other sources.

The ECB can manage overall liquidity in the euro area through monetary operations, but the arrangements put in place in the Eurosystem, namely the pre-specification of what the ECB can accept as collateral, make it impossible for the ECB to meet the liquidity needs of an illiquid financial institution that runs out of assets qualifying as collateral according to the established list.

In contrast, by assigning the responsibility for financial stability to member states, the Treaty implicitly assigns the LLR task to national central banks. This function in the euro area is usually performed by central banks, with the exception of Germany where it is managed by the Liquidity Consortium Bank (Liquiditäts-Konsortialbank GmbH), a private company jointly owned by banks and the central bank.[8] Therefore National Central Banks remain responsible for deciding on the provision and cost of liquidity assistance to the institutions operating in their jurisdiction.

The recognition that this allocation of responsibilities could require some coordination between the unrestrained LLR facility of National Central Banks and the monetary policy of the ECB led to an agreement under which the ECB's Governing Council is to be consulted on LLR operations that have EMU-wide implications.

---

[8] National authorities may choose to deal with liquidity problems with public funds. However, in principle they become subject to the EU rules on state aid as set out in Article 92 of the EU Treaty. Thus, if state financial support is provided to banks, the Commission must establish whether that law is being respected. Exceptions can be made if a serious disturbance threatens the economy (Art. 92.3b).

17.3 The Debate on the Institutional Allocation of Bank Regulation

The continued reliance on the hybrid harmonization approach, whereby some elements of the regulatory framework are harmonized or centralized while other elements are left under national control has increasingly raised concerns with the level of the playing field within the EU. The arrival of the euro by harmonizing additional elements of the regulatory framework in the euro area heightened these concerns. As more elements of that framework are harmonized, the competitive distortions that may arise from differences across countries in the complementary elements left under home-country control grow in relative importance.

The move of monetary policy powers to the ECB, accompanied by the decision to maintain the responsibility for financial stability with national authorities, stimulated an intense debate on the institutional allocation of bank regulation in the euro area. Participants in this debate (e.g. Aglietta (2000), Di Noia and Di Giorgio (1999), Prati and Schinasi (2000)), Bruni and Boissieu (2000), Vives (2001) and Lannoo (2000)), note that giving national authorities the responsibility to maintain financial stability resulted in the separation of supervision and LLR functions from monetary policy, and the fragmentation of the former functions.[9]

This institutional allocation, they argue, may be a source of potential problems to financial stability in the euro area. A reason is that under the current diffused arrangement, information may not be shared with all of the important parties in a timely fashion. Further, the absence of an authority at the EU level charged with the responsibility, and endowed with the necessary means, may complicate efforts to maintain financial stability. It is now agreed that the ECB's Governing Council should be consulted on LLR operations at the local level that may have EMU-wide implications, implying that the ECB will coordinate LLR of truly European banks. However, the ECB is only allowed to lend against good collateral and, unlike the National Central Banks, it has limited financial means and is not backed by a Ministry of Finance for an eventual bank rescue. On the other hand, as banks expand across state lines, the potential for inadequate internalization of the externalities resulting from a bank failure grows as the home country's willingness to incur the costs of an eventual bank rescue declines.

To preserve financial stability in the euro area, most of the above researchers suggest the establishment of a European LLR. They do so after taking into account the potential synergies and conflicts of interest between monetary policy and bank supervision and several other reasons identified in the literature in favor of the separation of powers, including regulators' career concerns and reputation, monitoring of multi-task organizations, and industry capture of regulators.[10]

---

[9] It is worth noting that the separation between monetary policy and banking supervision in the EMU is only partial because some central banks are the country's bank supervisors and participate in the definition of monetary policy (Table 17.2).

[10] See Vives (2001) for a review of these and other factors that may play a role in the optimal institutional allocation of bank regulation.

They argue that a European LLR is necessary to internalize the EMU area-wide externalities inherent in systemic risk and that lending of last resort should be performed by the ESCB.

With respect to bank supervision, some of these researchers (e.g. Aglietta 2000), propose that national supervisors work as part of a network headed by the Banking Supervision Commission of the ECB to apply common criteria elaborated by the European lender of last resort. Others (e.g. Vives 2001) argue instead for separating supervision from the ECB and housing it in an independent institution, perhaps like the Financial Services Authority in the United Kingdom.

As we can see from this brief summary, there are important concerns with the arrangements currently in place, and some agreement on certain changes is needed to address these concerns. However, this debate, and the proposed changes, have been almost exclusively dominated by concerns with the implications of the institutional allocation of regulation for the preservation of financial stability. The potential implications for the efficiency of banking appear to have been given, at best, only very minor consideration. For this reason, our analysis focuses on the efficiency implications of leaving the regulatory systems at the national level. We also study the implications of centralizing supervision ahead of the LLR function or vice versa.

Participants in the debate on the institutional allocation in the euro area have focused almost exclusively on the allocation of supervision and LLR functions, implicitly assuming a passive role for the authority in charge of administering deposit insurance.[11] We will proceed along the same lines.[12] However, by concentrating on the efficiency of the banking system, we will come to a different conclusion: Leaving the regulatory systems at the national level reduces their effectiveness, but if only one set of regulators is to be integrated, it will be more effective to integrate the supervisory function, and leave the LLR function at the national level. Our earlier paper (Kahn and Santos 2001), which provides other arguments in favor of allowing multiple competing LLR, and this chapter both argue for a different pattern of regulation than heretofore proposed.

17.4   A Model of the Institutional Allocation of LLR and Supervision

Consider the following model. There are three periods, labeled 0, 1, and 2. There are three agents: the bank b, a bank supervisor s, and a LLR l. In addition, we will want to consider payoffs to the rest of the public p.

---

[11] Vives (2001) also discuss at length the institutional allocation of competition policy, that is, authority to approve mergers and acquisitions in the financial sector.

[12] For studies of institutional allocation of bank regulation where the deposit insurance provider plays an active role see Repullo (2000) and Kahn and Santos (2001).

In period 0 the bank chooses a portfolio i. In period 1 a signal n in $\{0, 1, \ldots, N\}$ is generated. The signal provides information about the bank's profitability and its liquidity shock. The signal is stochastic, with distribution $\lambda(i,n)$. If the signal is *not* equal to 0, then the bank will suffer a liquidity shock requiring a loan from the lender of last resort in period 1. If the loan is needed but is not provided, then the bank is closed in period 1. If it receives the loan (or if it does not require the loan), then the portfolio matures in period 2. In this case, it has a probability $\pi(i,n)$ of not failing in period 2. Let $\pi(i)$ be the *ex ante* probability of not failing as of period zero and assume $\pi(i) < \pi(i, 0)$–that is, needing to resort to a LLR is bad news for the bank.

Let P_a denote the payoff to agent a from a successful bank, P_b the profit from a successful bank, and P_p the social value to the public of the successful bank. In general these payoffs are functions of i and n. However, for simplicity we assume that P_p is constant and positive. Let C_a be the cost to agent a of closing the bank in period 1, and F_a be the cost of a failed bank in period 2. Again for simplicity, F_a and C_a are taken to be independent of i and n (as noted before, the probability of a failure is dependent on these variables). Finally, we make the following assumptions regarding F_a, C_a, and P_a:

1. $F_b = C_b = 0 < P_b(i,n)$,
2. $F_p > C_p \geq 0 \leq P_p$,
3. $F_s = C_s > 0 = P_s$,
4. $F_l > C_l > 0 = P_l$, with $(F_p + P_p)/(C_p + P_p) > F_l/C_l$.

These assumptions are justified as follows: 1 is simply limited liability. 2 is the assumption that while both closures and bank failures are costly to the public, early closings are less disruptive than failures. 3 indicates that the costs to the supervisor of closure or failure of a bank are bureaucratic costs and essentially identical. Finally, 4 indicates that the costs to the LLR of a failure are, in addition to bureaucratic costs, the costs of the funds lent and lost. Nonetheless, a failure is still relatively speaking more costly for the non-bank public than it is for the LLR–that is, we build into bureaucratic preferences a tendency towards forbearance.

By spending an amount k in period zero the supervisor is able to monitor the choice of i by the bank. The supervisor is then able to close the bank before the realization of the liquidity shock. If the supervisor leaves the bank open, and the liquidity shock occurs, then the LLR observes n and decides whether to provide the needed liquidity to keep the bank open.

17.4.1 Efficiency

The issue is the choice of efficient investment. We take the social benefits to be the sum of public and bank benefits (in other words, we put a weight of zero on bureaucratic preferences in the social calculus). The planner's problem is to choose a portfolio i and a closure policy to maximize social benefits. The optimal closure policy is to close the bank in any state n in which the profits from closing the bank are larger than those from letting it continue, that is

$$-C_p' > \pi(i,n)\,(P_b(i,n) + P_p) - (1 - \pi(i,n))\,F_p,$$

and the socially optimal portfolio i solves

$$\max_i E_{n|i}\,(\max\,\{-C_p,\, \pi(i,n)\,(P_b(i,n) + P_p) - (1 - \pi(i,n))F_p\}).$$

17.4.2 Laissez Faire Laissez-faire Profit Maximization

A bank which worked in a world without regulators and without publicly provided LLR would choose I to solve

$$\max_i \lambda(i,0)\,\pi(i,0)\,P_b(i,0).$$

A bank which worked in a world in which LLR was always provided would choose i to solve

$$\max_i E_{n|i}\,(\pi(i,n)\,P_b(i,n)).$$

17.4.3 Regulation

A regulator's objective will be some convex combination of what is socially desirable and what would arise from an assumption of bureaucratic costs. We begin with an extreme assumption that both regulators only take into account bureaucratic costs. The proof of Theorem 1 is straightforward.

Theorem 1. *If both regulators only take into account bureaucratic costs, the supervisor does not monitor the bank's choice of investment and never shuts the bank. The lender of last resort shuts the bank if* $\pi(i,n) < (F_l - C_l)/F_l$.

Under these circumstances, the bank will choose an investment to maximize

$$\max_i E_{n|i}(\pi(i,n)\,\xi(i,n)\,P_b(i,n)),$$

where ξ is an indicator function equal to 0 if $\pi(i,n) < (F_p - C_p)/F_p$ and 1 otherwise. Thus, the bank's choice of investment opportunities will be biased against those opportunities which leave it dependent on a reluctant LLR. This has two consequences: Even socially beneficial outcomes will not be permitted if the risk of a failure is above the cut-off level, and outcomes with little social value will nonetheless be permitted if they have failure risks below the cut-off level.

We now consider the more realistic case that the regulators' objectives are instead a function (weighted average) of social objectives and bureaucratic costs. We will use μ_a in [0,1] to denote the weight placed on social objectives by regulator a. $\mu_a = 0$ denotes a regulator with purely bureaucratic objectives, and $\mu_a = 1$ denotes a regulator with purely social objectives. The above theorem generalizes when regulators' objectives weight social objectives equally.

Theorem 2. *Suppose* $\mu_s = \mu_1$ *and suppose the supervisor would prefer a bank which is not in need of a lender of last resort to remain open. Then the supervisor does not monitor the bank and never shuts the bank.*

Of course, as the weight placed by the regulators on social objectives increases, the choices made by banks generally become more efficient. A LLR becomes less forbearing in states with low social values and more forbearing in states with high social payoffs.

Nonetheless, even an efficient regulator (that is, one who places full weight on social objectives and none on bureaucratic objectives), given limited regulatory powers, will not be able to force a bank into the globally efficient choice. The supervisor is limited in its ability to make timely interventions. The LLR's interventions are more timely, but only permitted when the bank actually needs liquidity.

17.5 Centralizing LLR or Supervision First?

If the market is integrated but the regulator remains tied to its home country, then the primary effect of integration on a regulator's incentives is to reduce the weight of the social benefit on the regulator's decisions, since costs and benefits accrued outside the home country will be regarded as less important. Thus, it would be expected that, in general, the decision to integrate banks without integrating regulation should lead to a lower weight on the efficiency of banking decisions and more excessive forbearance than previously (of course this ignores the increases in efficiency that might result within the banking system itself). In particular, there will be examples where regulators cease to monitor effectively as integration takes place, and integration will also increase the costs of monitoring.

What is the effect on regulator incentives of changing from a home-based to a community-wide regulator? In general, the effects of international versus local regulation on the relative weight of bureaucratic versus public-welfare goals will be ambiguous: Regulators will be more remote from the regulated public, but also more remote from the political pressures encountered locally. In one respect, however, the effect is unambiguous: The constituency now again takes in the entirety of the public not just the public within the home country. Thus the baseline effect of moving to European-wide regulation would be to decrease the weight of bureaucratic preferences relative to social preferences in the behavior of regulators.

If it is feasible only to move one of the regulators to a European-wide integration, what are the merits of choosing one versus the other of the two? The model can be used to make a quick evaluation of the question; in general it supports the argument that integrating the supervisory role will be more effective than integrating the LLR. To see the issues involved, consider the following extreme case. Start with the situation where both regulators have purely bureaucratic objectives and consider the differences arising from changing one or the other to purely social objectives. When both have only bureaucratic incentives, the supervisor does nothing. When the incentives of the LLR change, the supervisor continues to do nothing. Thus, in this extreme case, if we want both regulators to contribute to the regulation of the banking system, we will put bank supervision on a European-wide basis.

In this model, changes in the objective of the supervisor do not change the behavior of the LLR. However, changes in the objective of the LLR can change the behavior of the supervisor. As the following example shows, it is not difficult to construct cases in which by improving the objectives of the LLR, we eliminate the incentives of the supervisor to engage in monitoring. Such examples reinforce the intuition that it is more effective to centralize the supervisory function than the LLR function.

Consider the following example. Assume the values of the parameters of our model are

1. $F_p = 9$, $C_p = P_p = 0$,
2. $F_s = C_s = 2$,
3. $F_l = 3$, $C_l = 2$.

The bank chooses between two investments, x and y. Investment x is completely safe: Its profits are small: $P_b(x,0) = 1/4$ but there is zero probability of either the bank needing liquidity assistance or failing as a result of this investment. Investment y is a risky investment, with two states 0, 1. Most of the time it will require liquidity provision by the LLR ($\lambda(y,1) = 0.9$). Only rarely ($\lambda(y,0) = 0.1$) will it not require such services. Whether or not it requires such services the probability of the bank's failure is 50 percent ($\pi(y,0) = \pi(y,1) = 0.5$). We also assume $P_b(y,1) = 1/4$ and $P_b(y,0) = 8$. In other words if the bank requires liquidity assistance, investment y is no more profitable than the safe investment. But if the bank avoids needing liquidity assistance, investment y is extremely profitable. Note that, given the high cost to the public of a bank failure, investment y is socially undesirable, even though it is preferred by the bank.

We assume the supervisor weights bureaucratic values and public values equally. We will consider the effect on the behavior of both regulators of a change of the LLR from bureaucratic values to public values.

A bureaucratic LLR will lend to the bank which has invested in the risky project: The additional cost of a failure is not too great, so it is worthwhile to gamble on the bank's survival rather than to shut it down and endure the certain cost of early closure. To the extent that the LLR takes social values into account, however, the potential cost of the failure increases, and the lender of last resort, when given the opportunity, chooses to shut down a risky bank.

Since the bank receives little profit from the risky investment in the event of a liquidity shortfall, the LLR's behavior has no effect on the bank's decision: The bank prefers the risky investment whether or not the LLR will bail it out.

However, the LLR's policy will affect the behavior of the supervisor.[13] The supervisor finds it costly to let a bank continue with a risky project. It therefore sees forbearance by the LLR as a threat, and prefers to shut down the project preemptively, rather than allow the LLR to keep the project going. But if the supervisor knows that the LLR will shut down risky projects, the supervisor has less incentive to close them down on its own. If there is a cost to investing in supervision, then the improvement in the behavior of the LLR reduces the supervisor's incentive to invest.

To conclude, it is worth noting that the model actually leaves no role for the lender of last resort: Abolishing it would improve the situation. This can easily be modified: Let there be a probability that the safe project is also in need of liquidity; since the safe project will not fail, it is socially desirable for a lender of last resort to exist to provide that liquidity. The rest of the model is unaffected.

17.6   Final Remarks

In the recent past, academics and policymakers alike have shown a growing interest in the institutional allocation of bank regulation. Though initially most of the attention was on issues related to the institutional allocation of bank supervision and in particular on whether this function should be housed in the central bank, more recently the interest has broadened to the other regulatory functions. The decision in the euro area to leave supervision and LLR functions with national authorities has raised a new set of important questions. Banks are supervised by different authorities, they have access to different LLRs, and they are protected by different deposit insurance schemes. Yet they are now competing in an increasingly integrated area with both a single currency and monetary policy.

In this chapter, and in contrast with the existing literature which has focused on the level playing field and financial stability in the euro area, we show that the expected integration of the banking markets will have different implications for the degree of forbearance in closing distressed banks and for the diligence in supervision depending on whether supervision and LLR functions stay with member states or are centralized.

Following the EU practice of harmonizing certain functions while leaving related functions under national control, we investigate the implications of centralizing first one or the other of these functions and show that the order of centralization has important welfare implications. We show that centralizing supervision and LLR functions will tend to reverse the increase in forbearance and reduction in supervision diligence that comes with an integration of

---

[13] Note that this incentive does not depend on assuming any financial responsibility of the supervisor for the behavior of LLR. The issue is whether, given the knowledge of how the LLR will behave, it becomes more or less worthwhile for the supervisor to do its own investing and monitoring.

banking markets without the integration of these regulatory functions. If only one of the two functions is centralized, it will be more efficient to centralize the supervisory function. The reason is that centralizing the LLR function reduces supervisors' incentives to invest in monitoring, allowing them to rely on the LLR to repair the damage when necessary. In contrast, centralizing the supervisory function does not have such an effect. It does not take investments for a LLR to learn that there is a problem: Instead the problem tends to appear at their front door. Nor is there the opportunity to pass the problem along to other regulators: When the crisis arises the LLR must deal with it immediately.

One of the many related issues that we did not address here is the role of the other key component of the banking regulatory framework in the euro area: Deposit insurance. We considered only the institutional allocation of supervision and LLR functions, but the strong interdependencies between these three functions suggest that the extension of our analysis to include deposit insurance is a fruitful area for future research.

REFERENCES

Aglietta, M. (2000). "A lender of last resort for Europe." In C. A. E. Goodhart (ed.), *Which Lender of Last Resort for Europe?* London: Central Banking Publications, pp. 31–68.

Bruni, F. and Boissieu, C. (2000). "Lending of Last Resort and Systemic Stability in the Eurozone." In C. A. E. Goodhart (ed.), *Which Lender of Last Resort for Europe?* London: Central Banking Publications, pp. 175–96.

Demirgüç-Kunt, A. and Sobaci, T. (2000). "Deposit Insurance Around the World: A Database." Draft, Washington DC: World Bank.

Di Noia, C. and Di Giorgio, G. (1999). "Should Banking Supervision and Monetary Policy Tasks be Given to Different Agencies?" *International Finance*, 2 (3): 361–78.

European Commission (2000). "Institutional Arrangements for the Regulation and Supervision of the Financial Sector." European Commission, Internal Market Directorate General, Brussels.

Goodhart, C. and Schoenmaker, D. (1998). "Institutional Separation between Supervisory and Monetary Agencies." In C. A. E. Goodhart (ed.), *The Emerging Framework of Financial Regulation*. London: Central Banking Publications, pp. 133–212.

Kahn, C. M. and Santos, J. A. C. (2001). "Allocating Bank Regulatory Powers: Lender of Last Resort, Deposit Insurance and Supervision." Bank for International Settlements *Working Paper* No. 102.

Lannoo, K. (2000). "Challenges to the Structure of Financial Supervision in the EU." Draft, *Centre for European Policy Studies*, Brussels.

Prati, A. and Schinasi, G. J. (2000). "Financial Stability in European Economic and Monetary Union." In C. A. E. Goodhart (ed.), *Which Lender of Last Resort for Europe?* London: Central Banking Publications, pp. 169–74.

Repullo, R. (2000). "Who Should Act as a Lender of Last Resort? An Incomplete Contracts Model." *Journal of Money Credit and Banking*, 32 (3): 580–605.

Vives, X. (2001). "Restructuring Financial Regulation in the European Monetary Union." *Journal of Financial Services Research*, 19 (1): 57–82.

Name Index

Subject Index